OUT OF WHITENESS

WITHDRAWN

OUT OF

WHITENESS

COLOR,

POLITICS,

AND CULTURE

Vron Ware and Les Back

The University of Chicago Press

Chicago and London

Vron Ware is a lecturer in sociology and in women's and gender studies at Yale University. She is the author of *Beyond the Pale: White Women, Racism and History* (Verso 1992).
Les Back teaches sociology and urban studies at Goldsmiths College, University of London. He is the author of *New Ethnicities and Urban Culture: Racisms and Multiculture in Young Lives* (UCL 1996).

The University of Chicago Press, Chicago 60637
The University of Chicago Press, Ltd., London
© 2002 by Vron Ware and Les Back
All rights reserved. Published 2002
Printed in the United States of America

11 10 09 08 07 06 05 04 03 02   1 2 3 4 5

ISBN: 0-226-87341-2 (cloth)
ISBN: 0-226-87342-0 (paper)

Chapter 6 was originally published as "Nazism and the Call of the Jitterbug," in *Dance in the City*, edited by Helen Thomas (London: Macmillan, 1997), pp. 175–97. It appears here in slightly altered form by permission of Macmillan Press, Ltd.

Library of Congress Cataloging-in-Publication Data

Ware, Vron.
    Out of whiteness : color, politics, and culture / Vron Ware and Les Back.
      p. cm.
    Includes bibliographical references and index.
    ISBN 0-226-87341-2 (cloth : alk. paper) — ISBN 0-226-87342-0 (pbk. : alk. paper)
      1. Race. 2. Whites—Race identity. 3. Racism—United States. 4. Racism—Great Britain. I. Back, Les, 1962– II. Title.

HT1523 .W37 2002
305.8′00973—dc21

                                                                2001048010

TO STUART AND GEORGINA LAWRENCE AND

THEIR PARENTS, DOREEN AND NEVILLE

—V. W.

TO BOB'S MEMORY. AMONG THE MANY THINGS

THAT A FATHER TEACHES A SON, HE TAUGHT

ME THAT IN THE END WE ARE JUDGED NOT BY

WHAT WE SAY, OR EVEN WRITE, BUT WHAT WE

DO AND HOW WE ACT.

—L. B.

Contents

Acknowledgments

I don't remember exactly when Les and I decided to write this book together. It became such an obvious thing to do when we began talking about our work that I don't think I ever doubted its feasibility. I want to thank him first for his unwavering determination to get this joint undertaking started and then completed and for his insight, flexibility, and friendship along the way. Ongoing conversations with Paul Gilroy helped to sharpen the arguments and sustain the focus of the book, and the Carnival against Capitalism was fun, too.

Particular thanks go to Homi Bhabha for his support and encouragement at a crucial stage. I'm not sure the result is anything like he will have imagined, but an early discussion with him helped to clarify some of the important aims of the book and to sharpen its focus. Alan Thomas was consistently patient throughout, and his commitment to the book has been much appreciated.

I am grateful to Paul Stigant, formerly head of the School of Humanities at the University of Greenwich, for his support and to Mick Ryan and John Williams for their help in organizing research leave. My colleagues in Cultural Geography initiated me into the art and craft of field trips and showed me new ways to understand the city. Bridget Leach, Terry Cannon, Noel Campbell, and Sue Golding were steadfast companions and fellow conspirators during my time there. I am particularly grateful to Alev Adil, Azra Khan, and Paul Goodwin, who came in at short notice and under difficult conditions to take over my teaching.

At times writing about whiteness from a U.K. standpoint seemed like a lonely business, and none of this would make sense without a strong sense of solidarity radiating across the Atlantic. David Roediger not only made helpful comments on one chapter, but also helped through his own work to frame this particular intervention. My friendship with Matt Wray began on the airwaves as we were both invited to speak about whiteness on a BBC late-night radio show. The nearest thing I have to an on-line pen-friend, I have come to rely on his good sense, generosity, and solidarity in these transatlantic collaborations to smash white supremacy, and I am particularly grateful to him for his critical reading of the final draft. Anthony Foy told me about Ray Sprigle and then found me a copy of his book, which made all the difference to chapter 3. Rip Lhamon's work on minstrelsy helped to egg us on, and the wit and courage that shine through his own work were always encouraging.

Versions of chapter 3 were presented at Rutgers University, the University of Minnesota, and the University of California–Santa Cruz. Thanks to Wendy Brown, Jim Clifford, Greta Slobin, Ruthie Gilmore, and Craig Gilmore for their encouraging comments and positive response. Back home, Sue Benson at Cambridge University and Steve Pile and Andy Morris at the Open University geography group gave me a chance to try out different chapters, which helped, too. I am grateful to David Goldberg and John Solomos for commissioning a piece from me that was eventually the basis for chapter 1.

Many thanks to Dienke Hondius and Jan-Erik Dubblemans, who not only provide warm hospitality in Amsterdam, but also continue to do exemplary work around the legacy of Anne Frank.

Thanks to historians Pat Barrow and John Buckingham for their help when I called them up out of the blue.

This book has been a long time in the thinking, if not the writing. Many passing conversations with friends helped to make sense of difficult passages. Though they might not always have been aware of it, Vikki Bell, Max Farrar, Louise Hashemi, Isaac Julien, Bridget Orr, Ingrid Pollard, Ann Phoenix, Flemming Røgilds, Lynne Tillman, and Lynne Walker all encouraged me to get on with it. Patrick Wright, whose writing has also inspired me beyond measure, read another chapter. Tricia Bohn, Hazel Carby, Beryl Gilroy, Cora Kaplan, Angela McRobbie, Mandy Rose, Mark Slobin, and Olivia Storey read drafts of the whole book while I held my breath, and their critical opinions and generous comments were gratefully received, as always.

On the home front, the wit and wisdom of Marcus and Cora Gilroy Ware continue to set me straight, and their enthusiasm at my attempts to learn the cello (thanks, too, to the optimism of my teacher, Ed Jefferies) helped the last period of writing go with a swing.

Vron Ware

There are many people that I'd like to thank for helping me in writing this book. First and foremost I'd like to thank Vron, who was patient through difficult times and with whom I've shared ideas and disagreements over many cups of tea and coffee in the heart of our great city. I certainly learned a lot along the way. So thank you, Vron, particularly for all those times that I won the argument over whose turn it was to pay.

This book includes material drawn from several pieces of research conducted over the past eight years. Many of these projects have been collaborations. I would like to thank the people with whom I've worked—particularly John Solomos, Michael Keith, Tim Crabbe, Anoop Nayak, and Roger Hewitt—for providing their comments and for letting me use in these pages the fruits of our joint ventures.

Part of the pleasure and challenge of writing this book is that I have turned some of my musical loves into its key concerns. In particular, I'd like to thank the devotees of northern soul niters for their time and insight, including Ady Croasdell, Julia Honeywell, Sue Henderson, Butch, Tim Ashibende, Keb Darge, Dean Anderson, Elaine Constantine, Marco Santucci, and Ione Tsakalis. I'd particularly like to thank my old friend, poet and sociological traveler Flemming Røgilds, for that incredible night at the Volksbühne on Rosa Luxembourg Platz in East Berlin.

The other musical journey recounted in this book is the pilgrimage I made with my dear friend Ron Warshow through the American South to where the music we both love was made. I'd like to thank Ron for his perspicacity and companionship on this and many other journeys. I forgive you, Ron, for all the times you emerged with the finest vinyl. Also, I'd like to thank the musicians, songwriters, engineers, and producers who shared their memories and wisdom. I hope this books adds—in a small way—to a recognition that is long overdue. In particular, I'd like to thank Roger Hawkins, David Hood, Jimmy Johnson, Barry Beckett, Dan Penn, Spooner Oldham, Reggie Young, Bobby Wood, Bobby Emmons, Gene Chrisman, Donald "Duck" Dunn, Steve Cropper, Booker T. Jones, Wayne Jackson, Andrew Love, George Jackson, David Johnson, Jerry Wexler, Marvell Thomas, John Hornyak, Nancy Gonce, and Sherman Wilmott.

A number of people read draft chapters and made helpful comments. I've tried to rectify the shortcomings you all so clearly identified, and I am sure my chapters are all the better for it. Many thanks to Paul Gilroy, Caspar Melville, Dave Hesmondhalgh, Steve Cross, Fran Tonkiss, Claire Hemmings, Avtar Brah, Ben Gidley, Keith Harris, Lez Henry, Vic Seidler, Vikki Bell, Angela McRobbie, Ove Sernhede, Mette Andersson, Andy Simons, Ben Carrington, Graham Smith, and Dick Cooper. I'd also like to thank again John Solomos, Michael Keith, Ron Warshow, and Tim Crabbe, but this time for being such astute readers.

Thanks also to photographers Elaine Constantine, Dick Cooper, Ron Warshow, and Tommy Wright for letting me use their pictures. I'd also like to say a special thank you to Mark Edmondson, who did a wonderful job preparing the images digitally for publication. I'll try not to hold Burnley's promotion against you, Mark. Judith Barrett gave invaluable editorial advice, and I know that my prose benefited from the keen and sympathetic eye she cast over these chapters.

The completion of this book coincided with the death of my father. In so many ways his life echoes throughout these pages in terms of both the things I felt compelled to write about and the way I've tried to understand them. He always had faith that I knew what I was doing, even when I didn't. Some of the alterations and amendments to this text were made at his bedside while I watched him sleep through long, restless nights. George Orwell once wrote that the true cruelty of a hospital death is that the terminally ill "die amongst strangers." Mercifully, he was spared this fate. I'd like to thank my mother, Joan Back, and my brother and sister, Ken and Lynne Back, for the tenderness that can't be expressed in words. Also, I'd like to thank my friends, many of whom I've already mentioned, and especially Pete Merchant, John Drewery, Pete Jones, Jacqui Timberlake, Paul Moody, Sue Greenwood, John Curran, John and Irene Welsh, and Doreen Norman. Lastly, my love and thanks go to Debbie and our children, Stevie, Sophie, and Charlie.

Les Back

Introduction

In recounting the saga of the long hunt for the great white whale Moby-Dick, Ishmael displays a formidable knowledge of cetology and whale lore gained from extensive reading, hearsay, and experience. In one passage he exclaims how overwhelming a task he has set himself, since the subject seems unending. He feels compelled to describe in detail the bumps, wrinkles, marks, and shapes of each variant of whale, noting the particular characteristics of each species. But he acknowledges that even this is not enough, and the time comes for him to "unbutton" the sperm whale further, to lay him out "in his unconditional skeleton."[1] How, he challenges himself, can he write about things he has not seen with his own eyes? Take care, he warns, not to abuse the "privilege of Jonah," who was the only human said to have entered into the body of the whale and to have escaped to tell the tale. As it turns out, Ishmael, too, has led an eventful life; he has seen enough to allow him to give an eyewitness account of the structural details of the sperm whale's interior: "the joints and beams; the rafters, ridge-poles, sleepers, and underpinnings, making up the frame-work of the leviathan: and belike of the tallow-vats, dairy rooms, batteries, and cheeseries in his bowels."[2]

The chapters in this book stem from our conviction that, in sympathy with Ishmael's compulsion to catalogue the intricate details of the whale's body, we need to go beyond the surface appearance of whiteness to investigate its complex and awesome internal structures. We, too, can claim Jonah's privileged point of view, not necessarily on the basis of our own experiences, but by relying on the testimony of witnesses as aids by which to peer inside its inner compartments with something of

Ishmael's anatomical precision. Throughout this journey we have been engaged in intense conversation, debating our tactics, comparing our techniques, and refining our long-term goals. Prompted by ethical reflexivity, this book is certainly concerned with the most effective means of tracking down, identifying, and exposing the machinations of white supremacism, but this is no recreational whale-watching expedition: our main aim in writing about whiteness is not to describe it, but to work for its abolition.

Melville's *Moby-Dick* in particular has been revisited by many contemporary writers looking back at American and European culture for evidence of the ways in which whiteness has figured historically in the literary imagination. The famous chapter on the "Whiteness of the Whale" is a brilliant essay on the contradictory qualities not just of whiteness as a color, or indeed as an absence of color, but also of the contexts and places in which the charged symbolic presence of whiteness is to be found. Melville's examples in which whiteness evokes terror as well as innocence, guile as well as purity, remain the most frequently quoted passages on "that elusive quality" that "strikes more of panic to the soul than that redness which affrights in blood."[3] A great deal of the historical and literary labor inspired by revisiting and reinterpreting earlier writers like Melville has been extraordinarily effective in demonstrating both the evolution of the leviathan of white supremacism and the impact of countless attempts to halt its seemingly inevitable momentum.

The new scholarship on whiteness that helps to make these rereadings possible and plausible has, within the past decade, accumulated valuable practical and theoretical resources in the process of developing arguments against white supremacism, bigotry, and other superficially more benign forms of race-thinking. The field has spread within a relatively short space of time to include almost every discipline, from legal studies to architecture, geography, anthropology, sociology, and psychology. This book begins with a recognition of the significance of that growing body of work, but registers an impatience with what we see as a diversion from its radical potential for bringing about an end of whiteness. If a critical focus on whiteness can inspire such diverse assaults on academic disciplines, we demand to know how it can also be put to use in democratic social movements against injustice. For us it is impossible to separate the act of writing about whiteness from a political project that involves not simply the fight against racism, but also an attack on the very notion of race and the obstinate resilience of racial identities—one of its most disastrous consequences.

The themes and arguments threaded through the chapters that follow have emerged as a result of our collaborative conversations during the past few years and our engagement with antiracist campaigns over a much longer period. As it happened, by the time we met in 1992 we had both arrived by very different routes at an analysis of racism that demanded a focus on the social construction of whiteness in relation to other hierarchies of power and inequality. Using different methodologies, our work explored articulations of whiteness understood primarily as a racial category, the political and cultural meanings of which were inevitably transformed by other factors of social division and antagonism, notably gender, class, and sexuality. Of course, these projects were not carried out in isolation, but were endlessly shaped and refined by the writings of other people too numerous to mention here, but whose work we have endeavored to cite throughout this book. In addition, our contacts with friends and allies in Europe, the United States, and beyond have often provided the inspiration for new ways of thinking about both theory and strategy, particularly in relation to an uncompromising deconstruction of whiteness and a shared desire for its demise. This international perspective seems to us to be a crucial element of what has now become known as the New Abolitionism project.

Navigational Aids

One of the key shortcomings of the work that has been done thus far on whiteness is the way the debate is framed almost exclusively within North American terms. Like Moby-Dick roaming the oceans, the idea of white supremacy is not confined by national, cultural, or political boundaries. The new lease on life given to neo-Nazi groups by the Internet is just one example of the fluidity with which fantasies of White Power can travel the world, invoking a sense of commonality among different ethnic groups, while at the same time allowing them to express their delusions of racial purity in regionally inflected ways. But the dynamics of white supremacism have operated on different scales and produced very specific local ecologies in their wake. Writing from London, which can often feel like an island in the heart of Saint George's Middle England, we have been constantly provoked and guided by the exigencies of regional and national concerns. Bearing in mind that the histories of opposition to racial slavery, colonialism, Jim Crow, anti-Semitism, and apartheid have demonstrated over and over again the potential effectiveness of international solidarity and coordinated political activism, this is where we start and where we return. Applying some of the ideas expressed in this collection to a very specific issue in a particular place can often prove as challenging as making a convincing analysis on a more abstract level. In both cases it is necessary to have an overview, while remaining focused on the underlying elements of injustice, especially its causes, effects, and means of protest and redress.

One of the most significant events in Britain's recent history was the Government Inquiry into the Metropolitan Police's handling of the racist murder of eighteen-year-old Stephen Lawrence in south London in 1993.[4] The police's failure to prosecute anyone for his death and, in particular, their blundering neglect in following up evidence in the days after the murder were exposed in great detail throughout the long investigation. The resulting MacPherson Report, published in February 1999, castigated the police for their inept behavior and paid tribute to members of the Lawrence family for their perseverance in trying to obtain justice in the face of this obstruction. For several days the media focused almost exclusively on the question of racism in Britain: where it was to be found, what was to be done about it. For the first time in the country's history there was the possibility that the victim of a racist murder could actually be British, black, and innocent. In the aftermath of the report, the public was left with the impression that, while violent racism was something that was perpetrated by unruly working-class white boys, at the same time there was another kind of racism diffused throughout British institutions—the police, legal justice, education, and health service systems. This latter phenomenon entailed forms of discrimination that were often "unwitting," not necessarily conscious or malevolent, and therefore much harder to pinpoint and eradicate.

Several weeks after this convulsive examination of the state of multicultural health in the country, three nail bombs exploded, three weeks running, in crowded streets populated by the city's most visible minority groups: blacks in Brixton, South Asians in Brick Lane, and gays in Soho. Within hours of the first blast competing fascist groups began to claim responsibility, confirming fears of a backlash against the MacPherson Report, and with the help of closed-circuit television cameras the first suspects began to emerge. One man was arrested hours after the third bomb succeeded in killing a pregnant white woman with other members of her wedding party. The likelihood that he was acting alone conflicted with talk of an organized network of extreme-right-wing terrorists intent on destroying the precious evidence of London's cosmopolitan reality, but nonetheless the events had succeeded in making such groups visible for the first time in a long while. Another effect of the bombing was briefly to puncture the complacency with which many British people view comparable acts of brutality and violence in the United States. The first bomb went off only days after the massacre of high school students in Colorado by members of the self-styled Trenchcoat Mafia.

The contrast between the vicious racism that drives predominantly young men to terrorize and kill and the supposedly unconscious variant that allows prejudice, ignorance, and subtle bigotry to undermine democratic procedures is certainly not a new distinction. While the latter does not inevitably lead to or promote the former, it is a fundamental error to imagine, first, that these are the only two options and, second, that they are not connected in significant ways. Here the new writing on whiteness is able to offer alternative theories of how to identify the links between the premeditated violence of the disempowered white supremacist and the "unwitting" solipsism of the individual unaccustomed to questioning the idea that she or he occupies a privileged political and cultural category. There are those, for example, who maintain that it is impossible to understand whiteness as anything other than white supremacism; a set of beliefs, ideologies, and power structures rooted in the notion of natural, inherited, God-given superiority; a discourse produced and maintained in historically and geopolitically specific forms. But it does not exist in isolation; whiteness must be comprehended and analyzed as a purely relational construct. The primacy of whiteness is meaningful only in contrast with the qualities of other colors—not only black—and like the garments washed in different detergents in television advertisements, whiteness can be rendered in different shades, whiter even than white. The work of many abolitionist scholars and antiracist activists aims to deconstruct and expose the alchemical processes by which diverse people have been able to define the parameters of, achieve, and internalize these forms of racial particularity. Though individual authors place different degrees of emphasis on the role of organized white supremacist activity, the main focus tends to be on the complex ways in which raciality, ethnicity, culture, and identity are negotiated in everyday life. The routine normativeness of whiteness and the often camouflaged structures of privilege extended to those categorized as white can be compared to the notion of "institutional racism," which serves to prevent those citizens outside this category from enjoying equal rights and opportunities in nominally democratic societies.

Inside the Whale

This definition of whiteness, like the "institutional racism" recently under scrutiny in Britain, is often hard to identify and difficult to eradicate. Part of the challenge of this new work is to question the basis of what counts as normal and to expose the historical and contemporary devices that are employed to maintain those "white-friendly" systems and structures. But what should be done with this new knowledge, if that is what it is? A wide spectrum of political possibilities awaits the new recruit to "whiteness studies," since there is no unity of purpose binding this field together. Finding a position on this spectrum depends on an analysis of all social divisions and a readiness to address the fundamental causes of injustice. In plainer terms it will depend on whether or not race is seen as something that can be not only deconstructed on paper, but also eventually rendered obsolete as a system of discriminating among humans. Although Ishmael protested melodramatic faintness at the prospect of completing the gargantuan task he had set himself in describing the whales of the world, he had no intention of abandoning his attempts. He comes to mind once more because so many writers on whiteness have balked at the notion of doing away with all racial categories and have instead settled for the deceptively easier job of trying to remove the undesirable elements from whiteness without rocking the boat of raciology that keeps the whole concept in motion. For some it is possible, even desirable, to retain whiteness as a descriptive term, a potentially innocent aspect of individual and collective identity—in particular, one that needs to function as an integral part of the jigsaw of multicultural discourse within the United States. This is not hard to understand. Many of the scholars engaged in this debate are concerned primarily with teaching students in situations already fraught with feelings of defensiveness, guilt, and resentment. The editors of *White Reign: Deploying Whiteness in America* are, for instance, quite clear about the goal of a critical pedagogy of whiteness: "creating a positive, proud, attractive, antiracist white identity that is empowered to travel in and out of various racial/ethnic circles with confidence and empathy."[5]

One of the problems with this type of approach is that it is in danger of reifying the idea of race as a reliable index of human difference, and therefore of breathing stale life into a belief system that ought to have been consigned to the twentieth century. Our sometimes fierce scrutiny of those we have come to call White People (meaning those engaged in analyzing whiteness) is motivated by a fear that the radical impulse to change the terms of the whole discourse around race, openly expressed by much of the earlier work in this field, may be overwhelmed by a rush for more pragmatic and altogether more timid proposals that do not actively seek to disrupt existing racial frameworks. In any event the range of options available to the student encountering "whiteness studies" for the first time—whether eager or recalcitrant—resembles the 1996 Ralph Lauren paint catalogue, which boasted thirty-five variations of white. It is hard to believe once it is up on the wall that the shade really makes very much difference as long as it is still recognizably white. Pushing the analogy further it is equally hard to see how the historical discourses of raciology have been fundamentally challenged if the white walls that protect them are left basically intact.

In this book we have tried to stare into the fault lines running between these different positions, following the trajectory of the abolitionist path in order to confront some of the obstacles that appear to block the way. The stories and testimonies that we dissect and discuss have been chosen precisely because they offer complicated, sometimes controversial, and often contradictory viewpoints on this business of traversing and transgressing deeply racialized territorial markers. Our aim has been to comprehend, record, and reexamine disparate situations where groups and individuals have engaged in ways of thinking and acting that are demonstrably effective in challenging the prevailing racisms of their time. But more than this, however, we wanted to explore what it might mean to go beyond a pragmatic and palliative understanding of antiracism to discover forms of solidarity premised not on identity and sameness, but on other definitions of commonality and connection.

This is an attempt not to deny or play down significant conflicts between people that are routinely produced by the many variants of racism, but rather to use them as further clues to be guided by. Unlike Jonah, who, as George Orwell has reminded us, was "a passive acceptor of evil," our informants have, for the most part, struggled to free themselves from the blubbery cocoon of whiteness that has threatened to envelop them.[6] Where they have willingly and actively chosen to remain in that "dark, cushioned space," working as agents of white supremacism rather than its "unwitting" beneficiaries, their testimonies have provided useful material for our ethnographic analysis, and our encounters with them important moments of methodological reflexiveness.

Our turn toward the anthropological techniques and their critiques was partly precipitated by some of our encounters with self-proclaimed racists in the course of our research. We wanted to address some of the theoretical issues that emerge when investigating the parameters of white supremacist subjectivity, but the academic paradigms of "ethnographer" and "informant" seemed to us particularly inappropriate in the context of investigating avowedly racist worldviews and patterns of behavior. This situation, in which a supposedly neutral, or at least liberal, individual sets up a conversation with someone to whom, in other circumstances, she or he would be absolutely opposed, epitomizes the difficulties of maintaining an appropriately "objective" or dispassionate perspective toward the material gathered during interviews. The encounter may raise any number of moral or ethical questions that cannot be addressed by simply applying the conventional etiquette of ethnographic research. Though there exist many admirable precedents for carrying out this type of work, which benefit from being synthesized and compared, we saw that the problem was wider than that. One area of research opened up by the recent focus on whiteness entails questioning "ordinary" people on a range of topics designed to draw out their perception of what it means to be "white" in different social and geographical locations. Sometimes this work is intended to raise the interviewees' awareness of their "unwitting" complicity in structures of racialized power; sometimes it can be an exercise in demonstrating the complex and often unconscious ways in which people negotiate discourses of race in everyday life. In our view this type of investigation raises important issues about the aims, motives, and techniques of the ethnographer of whiteness. Almost built into this situation is the danger of imposing an invidious anthropometry that casts the ethnographer and the informant in opposing roles. While the former is eligible for the self-righteous moral high ground by virtue of possessing antiracist insight, the latter may be patronizingly consigned to the backwoods of bad-sense whiteness. The proliferation of research into "white" self-perception, regardless of whether the informants are blissfully ignorant, self-critical, or paid-up terrorists, brings no guarantees that either the process or the results will hasten the end of racism, but the methodological problems brought to light by these encounters underline crucial ethical and political questions involved in analyzing whiteness.

This last point introduces another theme that runs through this book: the importance of political will in bringing about radical change. Often opponents of abolitionism will retort that it is simplistic to think that whiteness can be dismantled "just like that" or by "mere political will." Where the concept of antiracism can suggest a more reformist stance, it is true that the call to abolish whiteness can sometimes sound deceptively peremptory. This partly helps to account for the hostility that its rhetoric produces, but the goals of the New Abolitionism project are in reality as long-term and as far off as those of any other social movement for emancipation from oppression, injustice, and exploitation. There is nothing in the literature that we have read that ever implies that the destination of a nonracial and nonracist world can be reached other than by taking a tortuous, dangerous, and unpopular route in that direction. What we have tried to show is, first, that this route is well trodden and, second, that the project demands a readiness to travel in hope, constantly on the alert for creatively subversive opportunities. We look to the situation in South Africa for evidence of how difficult but how necessary this vision continues to be for progressives trying to rebuild that country. A commitment to do away with all manifestations of white supremacy requires an intolerance of the way things are and an oppositional consciousness that can counteract Jonah-style resignation in the face of overwhelming difficulties. It means moving inexorably toward a place that lies beyond the homelands of color and the ghastly strictures of "thinking white."

Sediments of Culture

Tracing the histories of radical opposition to race-thinking can offer many salutary lessons to the would-be "race traitor" today. We have tried to argue for the importance of compiling genealogies of thought and activism dedicated to challenging the power structures of white supremacism. This can act as a resource, not necessarily in terms of tactics, since these are designed to take effect in particular times and places, but in terms of the courage, insight, and vision of many of the participants of these struggles. Taking inspiration from antiapartheid activist Albie Sachs's description of nonracialism as not so much an absence of racism as a new and infinitely richer cultural phenomenon that included "a way of telling a story," we suggest that there are substantial traditions of resistance available that can help to contextualize our contemporary efforts against racism. Investigating histories of opposition to whiteness means sifting through a heavy sediment of amnesia. It also means finding new ways of thinking about the histories of racist division and its transcendence.

Defining what counts as antiracism in earlier historical periods can be difficult, even with the benefit of hindsight. Sometimes actions that were intended to challenge racial attitudes and practices of the day can now provoke embarrassment and ridicule rather than posthumous respect. One of the liveliest areas of the new research on whiteness has been the topic of minstrelsy, covering everything from early blackface performance to the authenticity of contemporary rap artists, such as Eminem. W. T. Lhamon, author of *Raising Cain: Blackface Performance from Jim Crow to Hip Hop*, sums up the politically awkward implications of what he calls "minstrelsy studies": "Scholars can make simplifying generalizations about minstrelsy primarily because they still know very little about it, really. And one reason we continue to know so little is because we approach it like mad scientists, wearing rubber gloves, with clothespins on our noses: and we write about it as if it were paraphrasable as a formula."[7] Although he is referring here to the "people's culture" of the nineteenth century, the same "analytical disdain" that Lhamon himself scorns is directed toward many foolhardy and curious folk disobeying racial orders in more recent times. The international best-seller *Black Like Me* by John Howard Griffin was greeted with enthusiasm by countless antiracists who read it when it was first published, but today a mere mention of Griffin's name in public can provoke most American audiences to reach for their clothespins. One of Griffin's assignments in a little-known lifetime of activism consisted of darkening his skin and pretending to be a black man in the South for six weeks in 1959. The book he wrote as a result was read by a whole generation of young activists in the sixties and seventies and is still found in school libraries all over the world. To date there have been no studies of the impact of *Black Like Me* on its scattered readerships, but it is quite unusual to find antiracists of a certain age who have not heard of the book, even if they have not read it. It is Griffin's reflection on his experiment rather than his documentation of southern racism that has provided grist to our mill here. His ability to describe his conflicting emotional reactions to his discoveries makes his work a remarkable insight into what Franz Fanon has called "the lived experience" of the White Man.[8] Throughout his adult life Griffin struggled to transcend racial boundaries, not by altering his appearance, but by changing the way he thought about humanity, suffering, oppression, and spirituality. His consistent attempts to identify the deeply entrenched syndrome of what he called "thinking white" were guided by an acute awareness of the psychological harm that racism does to all members of a segregated society. The state of whiteness, in his view, was not about appearance and genetics, but about a refusal (or inability) to recognize basic human connections between groups of people racialized as different (not just in the United States, but in different parts of the world as well). His work deserves a prominent place in the genealogies of philosophical antiracism.

Musical cultures have also provided fertile breeding grounds for anti-race dissidents, and we follow several genealogical trails to explore the potential of sound to undermine the predominantly visual regimes of whiteness and racism. Calling on the evocative insights of Joachim-Ernst Berendt, we suggest that accounts of multiculture need to be rendered through "a democracy of the senses."[9] This means that we need to think less with our eyes in order to resist the all-too-familiar maxims of cultural geneticism, which designate music and cultural expression along absolute racial lines.[10] Musician and writer Anthony Jackson has written, with particular reference to jazz, that the nineties exhibited in America

no less than a "cultural parallel to Germany in the 1930s, with a megalo-
maniacal 'arbiter of good taste' undertaking a redefinition and reclassi-
fication of a country's expressive potential, ostensibly to weed out con-
taminating influences."[11] Here we are concerned with investigating histories of dialogue and transculturalism in music in order to look again at
the colors and tones of jazz, blues, soul, and country music.

Members of each succeeding generation may rise to face challenges
that they encounter as unprecedented and formidable. But looking back
to the past often reveals surprisingly novel and imaginative tactics that
can be usefully adapted and updated to suit the urgent needs of the
present. The various stories that we set out to tell about the past are
chosen because they are still relevant today, whether they are in danger
of being ossified in the form of musical legend or whether, like the real
bones in Rapparee Cove, they have recently surfaced to jolt the public
imagination. Where the notion of heritage is often firmly linked to a
particular national, regional, or local culture, we have tried to show how
relatively easy it is to demonstrate the wider circuits of communication
and conflict that have produced these stories in the first place. Again,
these international dynamics underline our efforts to seek solidarity
across national borders and to acknowledge the rich diversity of the crew
alongside whom we find ourselves.

Protest to Survive

At this point we abandon the metaphor of the *Pequod* to its disastrous
conclusions, since the image of the whale-hunting vessel is no longer
adequate to convey the broader elements of this particular political project: the abolition of white supremacism. Throughout the writing of
these chapters we have each participated in and been influenced by
waves of political activity and debate, and inspiration has come from
many different sources: from the extraordinary resilience and courage
of the Lawrence family, fighting for justice; the bravery and outrageous
foolhardiness of the British road-protesters, who dug tunnels under construction sites as a delaying tactic; the energy and inventiveness of the
transnational Jubilee 2000 Coalition to end Third World debt; and the
creativity and commitment of the Exodus Collective in its efforts to establish a peaceful community in the face of relentless harassment from
the police.[12] The last three decades have seen a phenomenal shift in accepted definitions of what constitutes politics. Many would argue that
this change amounts to more than the emergence of new social movements or the rapid increase in the number of single-issue campaigns that

have produced new generations of activists and organizers.[13] Introducing *Storming the Millennium: The New Politics of Change,* a collection of essays devoted to exploring this development at the end of the nineties, Tim Jordan asserts:

> The times are always right for change: new radicalism, new hopes, new politics of change are with us now. Neither the nostalgia of the left, those old bearers of hope, for the times when it knew the correct line, nor the arrogant insecurity of a right that simultaneously declares the grass roots dead while fearing its demands, can alter the fact that new forces for change have coalesced into a new politics. This did not begin yesterday: our roots are in civil rights movements, anti-colonial movements, the new left and feminist movements. . . . We might tip our hats to ideas and organisations past but we know we are our own politics now.[14]

Jordan goes on to outline the scope of the book, asking what "ravers, bisexuals, the disabled, anti-roads campaigners, cyberactivists and anti-racists" have in common. What do any of these constituents of the new politics have to say about downsizing, flexible accumulation, world debt, and the struggles of women for equal resources in other parts of the world? His point in asking these questions is to advance the claim made by contributors to the book that we are faced with a new paradigm of radical politics, a new framework for working toward liberation. As ravers encounter the restrictive measures taken to control their activities and so begin to develop skills in self-organization, legal defense, and other forms of self-protection and social protest, they are provided with opportunities to understand how power works and how it can be resisted and at what cost. There are countless examples where protesters from different nationalities and class backgrounds come together to work against a particular issue. Each situation, each place of protest, each example of DIY (do it yourself) culture[15] has the potential to unite people on the basis of hope, anger, determination, empathy, and a desire for change. Participants may be divided on other matters outside the one at hand, but the political conversations, disagreements, and insights that can happen are important elements of the process of politicization, which can lead to new subjectivities, new identifications, and an increased sense of acting politically.

This detour is necessary to explain some of the fervor with which we proclaim our commitment to abolishing whiteness. This is a project that certainly demands all the traditional sources of motivation suggested by these new forms of activism, which constitute liberating politics. It stems from a comparable yearning for an end to oppression and exploitation based on any notion of innate, embodied superiority, and it has demonstrably produced conversations and solidarities among people from different backgrounds, often with productive results. But if we can accept that the politics of race is played out differently in postcolonial times, we cannot agree that the demands made by abolitionists of whiteness are intrinsically new or unprecedented. Where the opponents of New Abolitionism are sometimes unwilling to see how the project is connected to other kinds of politics, we would want to emphasize both the honorable genealogy of "race treason" and the congruence of hatred of white supremacism with a new "politics of change." More than this, it offers a form of politics that does not provide short-term gratification: it is definitely not a campaign to be won, or lost, and then forgotten. A new social movement that seeks to expose and dismantle the machinations of White Power requires more than emotional energy, an open mind, and a commitment to direct action; it also needs a constant flow of analysis and theoretical debate in order to comprehend the ways in which racism is intrinsically interconnected with other forms of social division.

Arterial Routes

As we stated at the beginning, this book has been inspired and guided by our many conversations revolving around these central and unavoidable themes. However, each of the chapters was written individually, each a product of our specific empirical and methodological preoccupations. They run alternately, frequently picking up ideas and momentum from each other in an almost unspoken exchange. In our view, they are best read in the order in which they appear, but they can also be read as freestanding essays. These chapters constitute a series of invitations to look inside the leviathan in order to confront and dissect the blood-stained sinews of racist culture. Each of them in turn follows a particular vein of inquiry, together telling stories that range widely over time and place. Without intending to represent all aspects of political culture against racism or to supply a narrow proscriptive agenda, we mean to cast a shadow over the emerging literature on whiteness.

In summary, there are four main themes that unite the essays in this book. The first is a rejection of the ontological status of racial categories in relation to designating human attributes. Instead we focus on the ways in which whiteness is brought into being as a normative structure, a discourse of power, and a form of identity. It follows from this that we are skeptical about some of the emergent themes in the literature of the past decade that want to divest whiteness from its implication in racial domination, and all of the chapters in this book share the aspiration to make whiteness visible without reifying and naturalizing it. The second theme is concerned with widening the comparative focus of the debate on whiteness. Until now the field might be more accurately described as "American whiteness studies." In this sense the book offers a comparative focus that is both alert to the transnational relationships within the cultures of racism and sensitive to the histories of specific local and national arenas in which racial power is forged. Third, the book is concerned with excavating and understanding the sources of nonracial wisdom. When do people in societies structured in racial dominance turn away from the privilege inherent in whiteness? What difference does it make where the antirace act is performed, by whom, and in whose company? We find some answers to these questions through examining and comparing particular moments of political engagement and cultural politics. Finally, the book is concerned with addressing the question of what people of good faith might do. We are proposing a vigilantly antiracist position, which resists any move to civilize the history of white supremacism in the mistaken belief that this is the only way that "white people" can take their rightful place at the table of multiculturalism. We argue against the desire to construct a safe and innocent notion of "white identity" or to reinvent "white culture" in favor of a critical reckoning with the forces that continue to make people "white." So we are committed to opening up identities and cultures in order to investigate, valorize, and celebrate their polyglot registers and cosmopolitan potential.

Vron Ware

1. OTHERWORLDLY KNOWLEDGE: TOWARD A "LANGUAGE OF PERSPICUOUS CONTRAST"

A man should, whatever happens, keep to his own caste, race and breed. Let the White go to the White and the Black to the Black. Then whatever falls is in the ordinary course of things—neither sudden, alien nor unexpected.

This is a story of a man who wilfully stepped beyond the safe limits of decent everyday society, and paid for it heavily.

He knew too much in the first instance; and he saw too much in the second. He took too deep an interest in native life; but he will never do so again.

—RUDYARD KIPLING

Within the rigid order of colonial society, narrated here by Rudyard Kipling,[1] "decent everyday society" is constructed in opposition to "native life." This is naturalized in the formulation of "White" and "Black," defined along the knife edge of caste, race, and breed—three words, in case one is not clear enough. Franz Fanon, writing from Algeria in the 1960s, provides another view of the Manichaean separation of worlds within colonial society: "The colonial world is a world cut in two. . . . This world divided into compartments, this world cut in two is inhabited by two different species."[2] The physical organization of space that Fanon describes, in which the settler and the native live on opposite sides of a frontier patrolled by the policeman and the soldier, was both a cause and a consequence of the underlying economic order of French colonial society in North Africa. According to Fanon, the destruction of this colonial world depended not on establishing lines of communication between the two zones or on cultivating understanding between them, but on abolishing the zone of the settlers completely.

In 1940 W. E. B. Du Bois used the analogy of different worlds to describe his experience of growing up in a society founded and organized on the principle of white supremacy: "Much as I knew of this class structure of the world, I should never have realized it so vividly and fully if I had not been born into its modern counterpart, racial segregation, first into a world composed of people with colored skins who remembered slavery and endured discrimination; and who had to a degree their own habits, customs, and ideals; but in addition to this I lived in an environment which I came to call the white world."[3] Du Bois's theory of double consciousness, which he developed through living in these two worlds simultaneously, is well known, but it is worth repeating his account of exactly how he was conditioned and constrained by "the white world" from early childhood: "I could not stir, I could not act, I could not live, without taking into careful daily account the reaction of the white environing world. How I traveled and where, what work I did, what income I received, where I ate, where I slept, with whom I talked, where I sought recreation, where I studied, what I wrote and what I could get published—all this depended primarily upon an overwhelming mass of my fellow citizens in the United States, from whose society I was largely excluded."

"Of course," continued Du Bois, ". . . there was no real wall between us." He knew since childhood that "in all things in general, white people were just the same as I." However, one big difference was that whites did not have to take "into careful daily account" the reactions of the people who lived across the color line. Whites did not automatically, out of necessity, develop an intimate sense of their black "prisoners" that was passed down from one generation to another. The way in which the two groups perceived each other was as asymmetrical as their relationship to power and privilege. Perhaps this was what Cornel West meant when he spoke of the distance that still separates Americans from each other: "It's fairly clear that the gulf is quite deep between Black and white worlds and Black and Jewish worlds. Blacks and whites, Blacks and Jews, live in such different worlds and look at the world through such different lenses. This poses a huge challenge. We have to cultivate a much deeper understanding of the various perceptions from the different worlds."[4]

This extract from West's discussion with Michael Lerner reiterates the widely held view that race is the central organizing feature of U.S. society. There are different worlds, three it would seem (although we are not clear what the relationship is between the Jewish and the white worlds), and there are gulfs between them, and each world has its own lens through which it perceives the others. Clearly this is partly a rhetorical device dramatizing West's perception of the crisis in U.S. race relations that he addresses in his work. My initial reaction is to question the use of this metaphor as a basis for making progressive political alliances—as a basis for a politics of antiracism. In a country deeply divided by social and economic inequalities the discourse of separate worlds might make sense when you encounter people who hold opinions vastly different from yours and who have limited experience with and interest in people and cultures that are different from those with which they are familiar. But even if one experienced the world only through television, this viewpoint would begin to look strained after sitting through just a few hours of talk shows. Here the spectacle of public opinion and private testimony indicates a much smaller universe than West describes, and one in which social relations of gender, class, sexuality, and age and emotions such as love, desire, hatred, and jealousy are just as likely to affect one's lens as the color of one's skin and racial identification. With the expansion of the global media and the rise of phenomenal mass markets in consumer products it could also be argued that the walls between worlds are more likely than ever to be built on money rather than a spurious notion of "race" or hierarchies based on skin color.

On second thought, however, it is also important to acknowledge the mechanisms of segregation that continue to operate both in and beyond the United States. It is one thing to reject a racialized language that confines us all in different worlds or indeed on different planets according to ethnic and cultural background, but another to deny the very real social geographies of "race" and class, which are instrumental in determining where people live, the patterns of their daily lives, and their subjective view of the "environing world" and their place within (or outside) it. But even so, on what grounds can we who live in the overindustrialized, postcolonial world continue to use such Manichaean terms to describe the chaos of racialized order that exists today?

The first three writers quoted above testify to the difficulty, even the impossibility, of breaking this dualism and crossing the line between black and white, but that was under colonialism and Jim Crow. West is talking about the situation as he sees it in the contemporary United States—his bleak formula might appear to many to be a symptom of the typical race-thinking that consolidates the notion of unbridgeable difference rather than challenging it. One of the problems with this rhetorical dualism is that it erases all those who are not yet fully racialized as either black or white, or at least marshals them into one category or the other in the manner of Kipling. Added to this, West implies that being black or white or Jewish confers on the individual a prepackaged view of the world, which suggests that how you look largely determines how you see.

There are important theoretical debates today about the relationship between knowledge and experience. For the sake of argument we will begin by temporarily accepting the hypothesis that there are two types of people, black and white, and that they see the world through very different lenses. The blacks know a great deal about the whites, as they have been warily studying their reactions for hundreds of years. The whites know little of the blacks and, as Du Bois and many others have observed, rarely stop to think about what life looks like for them. One way out of this impasse might be, as West suggests, for each side to learn how the other half lives and to become more understanding of the other. But Kipling's foolhardy protagonist, Trejago, learned the hard way that having a partial inside knowledge about the ways of black folk did not prevent him from misunderstanding: "He knew too much in the first instance, he saw too much in the second." Had he not been able to decipher the coded message sent to him by his forbidden love, Bisesa, he would not have known to visit her in the alley at night. But had he been more conversant with native customs, he would have known that this illicit meeting would invite violent reprisals for both of them. Perhaps he was prepared to risk this outcome, driven by infatuation for the veiled woman. In the end it was only the permanent limp that bore witness to his lack of understanding and his desire to know and to see too much. However, in Kipling's story the object of Trejago's knowledge and vision, the seen one, paid far more heavily for his transgression and her acts as an accomplice by having her hands severed at the wrists. What would Kipling think of the technological advances in our ways of seeing now, which mean that all manner of things concerning native life can be learned without leaving the armchair position of decent everyday society for a minute? There are plenty of opportunities to view other people's worlds on screens, if not through lenses, and yet there is no substantive evidence to prove that this alone has hastened the progress of democratic multiculturalism.

Another view might be to follow Fanon's advice and destroy the zone of the whites so that there ceases to be a justification for believing there are two species. How this hypothesis is resolved will depend on what one considers to be the basis on which the original differences are premised. But by reducing the scale of the problem faced by all societies founded on histories of white supremacy to this absurd caricature of a planet inhabited by two types of people, we perhaps run the risk of trivializing it. In the light of the theoretical debates referred to above—which deal with the complexity of identity politics, the perils of essentialism, and the impact of other kinds of social divisions—the differences between people can neither be organized so neatly nor be done away with so comprehensively. This brings us to what might appear to be a glaring contradiction in our thesis: that in order to investigate what we call whiteness, the main aim of this book, we are in danger of reproducing an unhealthy dualism that does little to challenge the fundamental principle of "race."

It is necessary to confront this problem before embarking on the critical study of whiteness as a strategy for subverting or abolishing white racism, white supremacism, White Power (sometimes we do have to use several words). There is a need to guard against the prospect of a field of study that constructs the people who fall into the category of white as separate and homogenous and that effectively reifies whiteness as being marked in or on the body. This tendency can legitimize an insidious division of labor that allocates both scholarly and activist roles on the basis of color: "Let the White go to the White and the Black to the Black." Such crude separatism lies at the heart of what we call race-thinking, undermining any pretensions to radicalism and subversion that might be intended. Yet these criticisms and caveats are not meant to obscure the potential benefits to be gained from analyzing and disaggregating whiteness as part of a more holistic political project against injustice, and against the notion of "race" in general. Developing the tools to demonstrate the contingency, the changeability, the inconsistency of all racial categories, over time and place, requires rigorous and concerted work across the demarcation lines drawn by race-thinking. Within this context the deconstruction of whiteness presents vital opportunities to smudge and blur these lines instead of rendering the distinctions even sharper.

David R. Roediger argues that "making whiteness rather than simply white racism, the focus of study has had the effect of throwing into sharp relief the impact that the dominant racial identity in the US has had not only on the treatment of racial 'others' but also on the way that whites think of themselves, of power, of pleasure, and of gender."[5] If that is the case, then several tricky questions immediately suggest themselves as to how that whiteness is defined, in the first place, and how this research is to be carried out, not just in the United States, but also in different specific and comparative locations. How does gender, or class (not just wealth or poverty, but inherited, shared values), or sexuality, for instance, enter into the way in which the discursive power of whiteness is perceived, experienced, encountered, and rejected? Moving away from the stark duotone imagery of the colonial world, this chapter will resort to a more muted, messy, and chaotic palate that does not allow for the purity of any one color. But this is no empty canvas: the critical analysis of whiteness as outlined by Roediger has been under way for well over a decade. Before beginning to investigate some of the problems and possibilities that flow from this endeavor it is necessary to assess the conceptual work that has informed, influenced, and enraged the perspectives outlined in this book.

Peering into the Dark

[W]alk around the silent swelling of *When I am Pregnant*. Trace the shape as it grows obliquely out of the wall and then suddenly when you stand in front of it, face to face, it is there no longer; only a luminous aureole remains to return you to the memory of stillness, as the wall turns transparent, from white to light.

— H O M I   B H A B H A

In the process of writing this chapter I happened to visit an exhibition of sculptor Anish Kapoor's work at the Hayward Gallery in London. The first installation looked from a distance like a large rectangular painting of the deepest blue imaginable. Close up, it invited the viewer to locate its surface on a two-dimensional plane that seemed to retreat into the distance the more one tried to fix it. The security guard had her work cut out to prevent people from leaning over the ropes to touch the blue surface, to feel with their hands what their eyes refused to tell them. In another room the installation described above by Homi Bhabha had a similar effect,[6] although this time it was white and the perceptual disturbance was produced by the surface protruding into the room rather than disappearing into the wall. It was a curiously exhilarating experience trying to fathom what had happened to the bulge as you looked straight at it, seeing only a dense white flat surface. Only when you moved to the side could you see the profile reemerge and make sense of the title of this piece. I encountered a similar sensation with Kapoor's White Dark series as I stared into his hollow, three-dimensional shapes without being able to see corners, sides, edges, and depths. The white space inside was uncannily vacant, but also powerfully empty. It was hardly surprising that many complained of dizziness once they left the building.

This experience of peering into the dark light, or the light dark, reminded me of the problems inherent in trying to speak about whiteness as a central feature of raciology—by which I mean the various discourses that bring and keep the idea of "race" alive. Richard Dyer, whose work on the representational power of whiteness has famously illustrated its all-or-nothing quality, was one of the first to draw attention to the way that whiteness can become invisible to those who are caught up in its glare.[7] From one angle whiteness appears as normality; in a white supremacist society those people and those ways of thinking, behaving, and talking that are deemed white are the norm by which all else is measured. From another angle, to those who are placed outside this category, whether through birth or through behavior, the parameters of whiteness are visible to a greater or lesser degree. Depending on experience and understanding, whiteness can be seen in many guises: as pure terror, as property, as "a desperate choice."[8]

Just as it is difficult to describe the kind of sensory disorientation produced by the sculptures of Anish Kapoor, so it is hard at this point to delineate this new phenomenon of "whiteness studies" or "white critique," as some call it, which continues to expand at an exponential rate. What was recently perceived to be a radical and potentially subversive turn toward new perspectives on raciology and its effects can be described as something of a bandwagon to be jumped on by a host of writers anxious to explore their particular disciplinary take on the idea of whiteness. Given the proliferation of this work and the increasing difficulty of tracking its every direction, we intend to take issue with the field as a whole, without claiming to do justice to the key players. Having said this, there are dangers in trying to generalize about the work separately from the disciplinary contexts that the individual authors address. In other words, although it is appropriate to name David R. Roediger's *The Wages of Whiteness* (1991) as an original, pathbreaking book that is the first to chart the development of the white working class in the United States, it is clear from reading the introduction, "On Autobiography and Theory," that Roediger had been following a trajectory that made sense of his own political instincts, informed by the work of other social historians and cultural theorists such as Alexander Saxton, Stuart Hall, and, above all, W. E. B. Du Bois.[9]

Similarly, one can point to the publication of Toni Morrison's important essay, *Playing in the Dark: Whiteness and the Literary Imagination,* as an inspiration for concerted rereadings of U.S. literary texts.[10] But as Shelley Fisher Fishkin argues in an extraordinary review article on the "remapping of American culture" (1995), much of the groundwork for this new development in literary studies was laid in the previous decade by writers such as Eric Sundquist, Robert Stepto, and Aldon Lynn Nielson; she claims that her own work was inspired by encouragement and support from Ralph Ellison, whose observations on "the true interrelatedness of blackness and whiteness" had intrigued her throughout her career.[11] Similar arguments about genealogy may be made in other academic disciplines without playing down the relative explosion in books of all kinds that have sought to address the subject of whiteness in the 1990s.

Looking beyond the realm of scholarly activity, however, it is also important to connect this latest work to more accessible traditions of examining and challenging the white racial attitudes and behavior that have accompanied black struggles for emancipation and justice. How new, radical, or subversive does this interrogation of whiteness look next to the hugely important work of earlier writers like Lillian Smith or John Howard Griffin, who based their powerful deconstructions of southern racism on their own experience as white southerners, or next to the attempts of subsequent men and women who turned their attention to the history and psychology of white racism during the 1960s and 1970s—writers such as Joel Kovel, Winthrop Jordan, and David Wellman?[12] And, of course, this list does not even try to encompass the work of African Americans and others whose experiences of slavery and the histories of European colonialism obliged them to develop an expertise about the ways of white folk by taking their reactions into "careful daily account." So far from being new, the documentation and interpretation of whiteness that come from the perspective of those who are not categorized as white have only just begun to be recognized as a valid contribution to the way those white folks see themselves. Who can claim to know about whiteness? Roediger's most recent book, *Black on White*, reminds us of the view from the auction block, demonstrating how intimate knowledges of whiteness have been integral to what it means to be outside this category.[13]

Kovel's important precursor to the current scholarship on whiteness, *White Racism: A Psychohistory,* warned that racism had long served as a stabilizing function in U.S. culture: "It defined a social universe, absorbed aggression, and facilitated a sense of virtue in white America—a trait which contributed to America's material success."[14] Recognizing the extent to which white supremacism was a belief system that provided a rhythm to the very heart of the culture required an acknowledgment that any radical, concerted attempt to rid the country of racism would inevitably bring instability and anxieties in its wake. Matthew Frye Jacobson's contribution to the project of exposing the historical origins of whiteness, *Whiteness of a Different Color: European Immigrants and the Alchemy of Race,* both updates and renders more visible the cultural and political processes involved in giving meaning to raciality in the United States.[15] Like Kovel, he asserts that racism appears to be not "anomalous" to the workings of American democracy, but "fundamental to it." Though not altogether optimistic about the implications of deconstructing race as a way of finally overcoming white supremacism, he is more concerned to address the mayhem that it causes than the insecurities produced by a radical, utopian program to make the whole notion of race irrelevant.

Jacobson's elegant prose encourages the reader to conceive of the history of whiteness almost as a journey. The destination is the mythical place that W. E. B. Du Bois called Transcaucasia, a political realm beyond racism.[16] Jacobson's formidable historiography, "recasting the saga of Europeans' immigration and assimilation" in the United States as primarily a *"racial* odyssey," is offered as a first step in that direction. This trope of movement entails a constant level of flux, of "glacial, nonlinear" change. Racial identities are rarely static, but are subject to continuous political pressures, which help to forge, mold, and melt down the fatal distinctions produced by the fluid vicissitudes of race-thinking. The word "alchemy" in the subtitle is both poetic and powerfully expressive; it renders the worn-out figure of the melting pot as a more magical and rewarding process of racial transformation—rewarding, that is, for those who can pride themselves on having acquired the ultimate substance of whiteness, though always at a cost to their own humanity.

Jacobson's focus differs from that of fellow historians Roediger and Theodore W. Allen in that he diverges from what he sees as their overly economic models of history to explore other areas of national subjectivity and national belonging, "as they both inflect and are inflected by racial conceptions of peoplehood, self-possession, fitness for self-government, and collective destiny."[17] The political history of whiteness in the United States can be divided into three great epochs. The first began with the naturalization law of 1790, which limited naturalized citizenship to "free white persons." This signaled the relatively uncomplicated correlation between fitness for citizenship and possession of a European heritage. The second was ushered in by the mass settlement of immigrants from that continent from the 1840s until 1924, when restrictive legislation came into force. Coinciding with the development of so-called scientific racism during this period, this monolithic whiteness fractured into a hierarchy of white "subraces," dominated by the notion of Anglo-Saxon purity, the authentically white supremacist reference point. The third epoch best illustrates the alchemical fusion of these plural and differentiated white "races"—Jews, Greeks, Irish, Italians, Slavs, Poles, Portuguese—into a more unified Caucasian entity, brought unevenly into being by the migration of African Americans to the cities of the North and West and the ensuing struggles for civil rights. Jacobson's penultimate chapter argues that the liberalism of the mid-twentieth century actually helped to consolidate a black/white dyad still held in place by the apparently unbreachable color line, which in turn obscures the "in-between peoples"—not quite black, yet not white enough to be white.[18]

This brief summary of the broad sweep of chronological change serves as a backdrop to the extraordinarily rich accounts of the cultural processes with which Jacobson has engaged. Examples from fictional, documentary, legislative, and academic writing and from film are employed to chart, illustrate, and tease out the tortuous narratives of becoming and belonging that are central to his thesis. This is an exemplary deconstruction of whiteness that does not offer blackness as its inevitable and only counterpart. By exposing the historical contingencies of whiteness and the sheer changeability of racial definitions over time, Jacobson demonstrates that "the fabrication of race" both produces and relies on vastly unequal relations of power. This book is further indisputable evidence that the route to Transcaucasia demands a consistently radical critique of what it means to be human, let alone American.

Ruth Frankenberg, author of one of the first feminist investigations into the way that "race" shaped white women's lives, has provided a useful overview of recent work on whiteness in her introduction to a collection of essays entitled *Displacing Whiteness*.[19] Her summary is particularly useful because it does not limit the horizon of this work to the United States. She identifies four main areas. The first, historical studies, she notes, is arguably the fullest and best developed of these: "This scholarship helps make it evident that the formation of specifically white subject positions has in fact been key, at times as cause and at times as effect, to the sociopolitical processes inherent in taking land and making nations."[20]

The second and related area is cultural studies, where scholars and practitioners have been interested "both in the making of subjects and in the formation of structures and institutions." Third, and connected to this, is the whole question of whiteness as performance, "whether in daily life, in film, in literature, or in the academic corpus": at times what is at stake in such research is the "revealing" of the unnamed—the exposure of whiteness masquerading as universal. But at other times the stake is rather in examining how white dominance is rationalized, legitimized, and made ostensibly normal and natural.

Finally, Frankenberg suggests that there is an important body of work that examines racism in movements for social change. She draws attention here to the contribution of feminist critics of whiteness as well as a more established tradition of investigation that monitors and analyzes the making of white supremacist identity and political movement ideology and practice. The collection of essays that follows this introduction is interdisciplinary, and the authors move among these four areas in their brief to show how "whiteness operates in particular locales and webs of social relations."[21] Above all, whiteness is understood as a process that can be contested as well as deconstructed. Culture marked by whiteness is seen "as practice rather than object, in relation to racial formation and historical process rather than isolable or static."

This last point is admirably illustrated by John Hartigan Jr.'s ethnography of three residential areas in a major U.S. city, entitled *Racial Situations: Class Predicaments of Whiteness in Detroit*.[22] Taking his theoretical cue from Michael Omi and Howard Winant's seminal *Racial Formations in the United States*,[23] Hartigan set out to complicate the historical and political processes involved in defining, contesting, and interpreting racial categories and their meanings in the context of a very particular place and among people of differing class identities. Detroit, in his view, provides a unique setting to investigate the social ecology of what he calls "racialness" since 76 percent of its population is black. His substantial fieldwork in predominantly white neighborhoods allowed him to explore the "interpretive repertoires" of race within the context of highly complex but well-documented dramas of urban life, sensitively conveying the intricacies and contradictions of individual and collective responses. Throughout his interviews and conversations with mainly white Detroiters living within the distinct spatial order of the city he is guided by two simple questions: what does "race" mean to these people, and how do they decide a situation is "racial"? He concludes: "Instead of drawing generalized assertions and summary judgments about race, I suggest that the economy of racial explanations and analysis needs to be oriented towards a greater dependence on and retention of the particular situations and settings where race is at work. That is, by considering the specific circumstances of racial situations, we can counter the allegorical tendencies that render peoples' lives as abstractions, such as 'white' and 'black.'"[24]

In contrast with this type of politically engaged analysis of the new subject area, the mainstream media in the United States have followed its emergence into the public sphere with skepticism: Margaret Talbot, a senior editor of the *New Republic*, writing in the *New York Times Magazine*, questions the whole idea of analyzing the social construction of whiteness. She asks whether it is "a symptom of the kind of agonized muddle that well-meaning Americans tend to find themselves in when it comes to racial politics. Wouldn't it be easier to retreat into transfixed contemplation of one's own racial identity than to try to breathe life onto the project of integration?"[25] This interpretation of the new field of study happens to be grossly unfair in that it collapses together the projects of different authors mentioned in her article who are widely and openly at variance with one other. The idea that a new angle of reflexivity on the structures and processes of white supremacy automatically amounts to a bout of ineffectual navel-gazing is absurd, but Talbot's caricature (published under the heading "Getting Credit for Being White") is made all the more convincing by her focus on an increasingly popular genre of writing that does indeed explore the concept of whiteness as "racial" identity from an autobiographical perspective. This, in my opinion, is an area fraught with contradictions, not least of which are, first, that it tends to reestablish the first person firmly at the center of attention to whiteness and, second, that it is in danger of reifying the whole notion of "race" as a system of human classification that can be understood outside the histories of its invention and brutal enforcement. This, of course, needs to be qualified because there are examples of insightful autobiography that illuminate this process just as there are narcissistic versions that obscure it. However, the difficult question of defining what whiteness is or is not is just one of the awkward theoretical issues that has been identified not only by those working outside the critical study of "race," but also by those firmly located within it. I want to move now to a more directed consideration of the conflicts and opportunities that have emerged from this focus on whiteness.

Nothing Personal

The discovery of personal whiteness among the world's people is a very modern thing,—a nineteenth and twentieth century matter indeed.

—W. E. B. DU BOIS

Is White a race? The answer is *yes* it is. . . . The benefit in addressing race as an aspect of identity is beyond calculation.

—ROBERT T. CARTER

It is time we used our imaginations to invent alternative forms of white racial identity which, without having known victimization at the hands of other whites, nevertheless understand the disasters which constitute all forms of racial domination.

—MATT WRAY AND ANNALEE NEWITZ

The key to solving the social problems of our age is to abolish the white race. Until that task is completed, even partial reform will prove elusive, because white influence permeates every issue in U.S. society, whether domestic or foreign.

—*RACE TRAITOR*

These four quotes, all of which are taken outrageously out of context, highlight the wide range of approaches to the analysis of whiteness. The first, by an African American historian and sociologist,[26] represents a black view of the historical development of white supremacy referred to earlier, and the phrase "personal whiteness" always makes me smile with its associations of bodily hygiene. It is tempting to update Du Bois's observation by saying that "the rediscovery of personal whiteness by some of the world's people is a very postmodern thing, a very-late-twentieth-century matter indeed." The second quote, taken from an essay by psychologist Robert Carter,[27] enrages me, since it illustrates the tendency mentioned above to give substance to the notion of "race" as a static and unchangeable fact of identity that marks groups of people for life regardless of their behavior and beliefs; in my view this undermines the whole project of demonstrating that whiteness is an exclusive social category produced through history. I feel more sympathy with the third quote, written by antiracist cultural theorists,[28] but it still has me shouting, "No, no, that's where you're wrong!" From where I stand there is no need to perpetuate nineteenth- and twentieth-century notions of racial anything. As Andre Gorz says in *Farewell to the Working Class,* "The transformation of society . . . requires a degree of consciousness, action and will. In other words it requires politics."[29] If the twenty-first century is to transcend the color line inherited from earlier social, economic, political, and cultural formations, a progressive, forward-looking politics of social justice should embrace the will to abandon "race" as any kind of useful category, alternative or otherwise. There are other positions, of course, that share this possibly utopian but strictly necessary vision: the fourth quote is representative of the beliefs of a group often called the New Abolitionists,[30] whose manifesto is the complete abolition of whiteness. Their motto—"Treason to Whiteness Is Loyalty to Humanity"—has a rhetorical flourish that conveys the will to transform the state of things even if the theoretical or methodological details are not immediately clear.

These four perspectives do not begin to encompass the entire range of difficult questions I referred to earlier, but they may suggest the divergent agendas of many writers who identify whiteness as a central factor in the study of "race." In particular, these quotes demonstrate the different way that whiteness might be conceived as an aspect of cultural identity: the writers here suggest that white identity can be discovered, embraced, retained, re-imagined, or, given that whiteness is "nothing but an expression of race privilege," completely abolished.[31] These fundamental disagreements are not surprising or unexpected, although it is distressing that the conservatism that argues that whiteness is still an integral aspect of a "nonracist" identity is in danger of diluting the radicalism that painstakingly provides evidence of the *making* of whiteness as a social category and the possibility of its unmaking. The scholars and activists who now address whiteness as a means to understand and analyze inequality, exploitation, and injustice are not automatically in dialogue with each other and are not guaranteed to speak the same language.

What is at issue here is the very meaning of "race" and its status in contemporary culture, whether local, national, or global. It is hard to reconcile Carter's suggestion that the way to move forward is to "develop a positive nonracist White racial identity ego status"[32] with the perspective of historian Roediger, who quotes James Baldwin as saying: "As long as you think you're white, there's no hope for you."[33] The scholarly tradition exemplified by Roediger, Saxton, Allen, and, more recently, Grace Elizabeth Hale, whose book is entitled simply *Making Whiteness: The Culture of Segregation in the South 1890–1940,* can also be contrasted with the autobiographical, confessional tone of books like Jane Lazarre's *Beyond the Whiteness of Whiteness: Memoir of a White Mother of Black Sons.*[34] Both genres can be read as avowedly antiracist, but is one more effective than another in attacking mechanisms of exclusionary power, or do they complement each other in theorizing the pervasive and insidious dynamics of racism in conjunction with localized social ecologies, gender relations, and sexualities?

This discrepancy in perception and understanding is familiar to anyone who has been involved in trying to develop effective and challenging ways of thinking about raciology. It would be dishonest to deny that many writers and activists try to muddle through in one way or another, possibly without realizing the dangers of falling between the cracks in their conceptual frameworks. In other words, many writers want to have their racial cake and eat it, too. While it may be relatively easy to conclude that "race" refers to an outdated system of classification based on imagined notions of biological divergence of the species, the salience of those visible markers of racial difference continues to act as a mnemonic to the idea of race, which still has to be reckoned with in everyday life— in some places more than others. What does it mean to propose the abolition of whiteness in a world in which, as George Lipsitz puts it, structures of power offer all racialized minorities, not simply black and white, a "possessive investment in whiteness"?[35] Or, to put it another way, how do we separate the simple, descriptive term "white" from the ideologically charged "White"? Perhaps those who argue for an alternative, nonracist version of white identity are the pragmatists after all, while those who believe that it is possible to distance oneself from the trappings of light-skin privilege are in cloud-cuckoo land.[36] My point is that these opposing positions form a useful dialectic that can illuminate (as well as complicate) contemporary thinking about "race" as a feature of postmodern life.

It is vital that the impulse to identify, mark, and analyze whiteness does not lead into a trap of reifying the very concept of "race" that it is intended to question. The growing interest in theoretical whiteness risks producing an indifferent cultural pluralism, which does little to engage with the changing formations of local and global racisms. Mike Hill faces this area of contradiction that lies at the heart of the study of whiteness in another useful overview of recent work. He identifies the scholarship that emerged in the early 1990s as a "first wave of white critique," stating that it established whiteness as a distinct and relatively recent historical fiction.[37] He views it as ironic that this work was quickly problematized, or rather compromised, by this "newfound attention to the quintessentially unremarkable." Putting his finger directly on the erratic pulse of "white writing," he continues: "the presence of whiteness alas within our critical reach creates a certain inevitable awkwardness of distance. Whiteness becomes something we both claim (single out for critique) and avoid (in claiming whiteness for critique, what else can we be, if we happen to be identifiably white?))."

Hill suggests that this conflict, characterized by "the epistemological stickiness and ontological wiggling immanent in whiteness," might be called a second wave of white critique.[38] By this satisfyingly graphic formulation I think he is trying to represent the problem that many designated "white" writers confess to in their own work: their motivation stems partly from a recognition that their "whiteness" ties them historically into a system of race privilege from which it is hard to escape, but by providing a critique of whiteness, they begin to situate themselves outside that system. Does this mean that they are in two places at once? This is the conflict that opens up questions of knowing and being, which cannot be answered definitively. In a reference to Audrey Lorde's exhortation to her readers to "reach down into that place of knowledge . . . and touch that terror and loathing of any difference that lives there," Hill writes that the limits of this conflict over whiteness are "to articulate critically the power and banality of race privilege and to discover deep down (and of course on the surface) a 'face of terror' not unlike what one sees all around." He suggests that it is fruitful to return to feminist writing from the 1970s and 1980s in order to understand how to theorize this fraught relationship between identity and politics, between knowledge and consciousness. He specifically cites feminism as the place where activists, writers, and thinkers came to terms with the discovery that "distinctions of oppression are both portable and prolific."[39] Citing African American feminists like bell hooks and Lorde, he writes that "[w]hite feminists heard the charge that there were margins other than (and marginal to) those on which white women were located. That is, marginality is relational (but not relative or arbitrary)."

Hill is particularly interested in the way that some feminists responded to these charges. Marilyn Frye, for example, faced what she saw as a double bind inherent in white critique—a kind of damned if you do, damned if you don't situation. Her solution, as he reads it, is to call for disaffiliation from the structures of white privilege without losing sight of the way that gender and class compound identity and complicate the idea that individuals can simply choose to opt out of a category that they consider problematic. "It might indeed be said as a feminist lesson that 'disaffiliation' from the white race, its categorical disintegration, is perhaps a form of gendered interrogation already in progress."[40]

This is a difficult argument to compress, but an important point to grasp because the "epistemological stickiness" and "ontological wiggling" are so frequently cited as a reason to doubt the efficacy of the whole project of white critique, throwing the baby out with the bathwater so to speak—or at least caricaturing it as narcissism in the manner of Margaret Talbot in the *New York Times*. Hill's optimism that many writers are becoming bold enough to face the "trouble spots" of identity politics by moving into a space that is "neither white nor its opposite" is welcome, but what does it suggest about the need for an explicit politics of location in order to carry it out? To put this bluntly, how do we—whether in the United States, Europe, Australia, or South Africa—study the discursive production of whiteness in all its locally and socially differentiated forms, and how much does it matter not who we are when we do this, but where we are, theoretically, when we do it. Where and how should critics and enemies of whiteness locate or reposition themselves, and what are the most effective strategies for forcing a separation between an imposed identity that is still based primarily on skin color, on the one hand, and the less visible signs of identification and political solidarity, on the other? Adrienne Rich's insightful arguments in "Notes towards the Politics of Location"[41] have helped feminists to formulate similar questions in relation to gender, and I have also found it useful to adapt what Charles Taylor has called "a language of perspicuous contrast" in relation to the scrutiny of whiteness.[42]

Although Taylor is writing strictly about the relationship between the social scientist and his anthropological subjects, his attempts to formulate an "interpretive view" of the structure of interaction between agent and subject are rather helpful in theorizing the position of the ethnographer of whiteness. Take this passage, for instance, which is worth quoting at length, with my additions in brackets, to illustrate his method of steering a course between two unwelcome opposites:

> The interpretive view, I want to argue, avoids the two equal and opposite mistakes: on one hand, of ignoring self-descriptions [of white identity, white culture, white experience] altogether, and attempting to operate in some neutral "scientific" language; on the other hand, of taking these descriptions with ultimate seriousness, so that they become incorrigible. Social theory in general, and political theory especially, is very much in the business of correcting common sense understanding. It is of very little use unless it goes beyond, unless it frequently challenges and negates what we think we are doing, saying, feeling, aiming at. But its criterion of success is that it makes us as agents more comprehensible, that it makes sense of what we feel, do, aim at. And this it cannot do without getting clear on what we think about our action and feeling. That is, after all, what offers the puzzle which theory tries to resolve. . . . For otherwise, we may have an interesting, speculative rational reconstruction . . . but no way of showing that it actually *explains* anything.[43]

Although it might actually be quite appropriate to take the view of the modern ethnographer investigating the primitive tribalism of whiteness, I make no apologies for borrowing Taylor's insights on ethnographic work made in another context, nor am I suggesting that the whole of his argument fits here. My point is simply that the study of whiteness offers to all those individuals caught up in racial discourse against their will potentially new opportunities to make sense of their own political location and to recognize a degree of agency in challenging (and therefore changing) the many ways in which the beneficiaries of racial hierarchy are complicit with injustice.

Early on I used Homi Bhabha's elegant description of Anish Kapoor's installation to suggest the importance of looking at the structures and tentacles of white supremacy from different angles. The analogy ends here, however, for though it may be intriguing to wander to and fro in front of *When I Am Pregnant,* enjoying the disorientation produced by the white bump disappearing before one's eyes, the student of whiteness requires a map of possibilities and a steady compass to make sense of the field. It is not easy to investigate whiteness, nor should it ever be. In societies structured so deeply by racial hierarchies that operate through and simultaneously with systems of gender, sexuality, and class, creating a politics for social justice must entail willfully stepping beyond safe limits and refusing to recognize the odious confines of caste, race, and breed, without losing a sense of direction in exposing and destroying the technologies of white power.

Les Back

2. GUESS WHO'S COMING TO DINNER? THE POLITICAL MORALITY OF INVESTIGATING WHITENESS IN THE GRAY ZONE

I arranged to meet Nick Griffin at 5:30 P.M. outside Charing Cross Station in the heart of London. It was a mild gray afternoon; the streets of the capital were covered in the shiny gossamer of rain. Griffin, a key figure in the National Front during the seventies, was currently active in the British National Party (BNP). I didn't know it at the time, but he was a figure of rising importance in the party and would ultimately become its next leader.[1] I had spoken to him on his cell phone earlier that day to confirm the interview. He was in East London canvassing for the forthcoming local elections in the area where, in 1994, fellow BNP member Derek Beakon had become the first member of an extreme-right-wing party to be elected. I had approached Griffin for an interview because he was awaiting trial for incitement to racial hatred for his involvement in the production of an extremist tract entitled *The Rune,* which included, among other things, articles on Holocaust "revisionism," race and criminality, and white nationalism. I wanted to interview him in connection with a research project I was carrying out on nationalist movements and their use of information technology.[2] Although Griffin himself lived in rural Wales, the magazine was produced in Croydon, south of London—the place where my family lived and where I had been raised. He was late and I was anxious. I looked up at Nelson's column and then down at my watch; I would give him another twenty minutes.

My anxiety was compounded by the hostile reaction that my work had received from racists and activists on the far right. I had attracted the ire of the BNP's magazine, *Spearhead,* which cast me as a "politically correct liberal" and "mischief maker."[3] From less sophisticated critics I had received a string of anonymous hate letters that classified me as a conspiring "Jew" or a "race traitor."[4] The harassment had changed me, not least with respect to the experiential shock engendered from being loathed by strangers as an object—a traitor, a Jew. I should make it clear that I am not Jewish, but it was telling that the authors of the abusive mail I received seemed compelled to read my identity through the cipher of anti-Semitism because it enabled them to make sense of my research and writing. Their logic seemed to be this: "If you are against racism, you must be a Jew." Part of the shock was that my family and young children might also become exposed to this bile, a fear that thankfully was never realized.[5]

I was not quite sure what to expect from the imminent encounter with an outspoken advocate of white nationalism. In those minutes, which seemed to last forever, it became so clear that the stakes change when one decides to look into the face of racial extremism. For Emmanuel Levinas the notion of the face captures precisely both the fact of human difference and the ethics of communication. For him the ethical challenge is how we coexist while leaving difference and otherness intact and without losing our own integrity. He writes in *Totality and Infinity:* "The relation between the Other and me, which dawns forth in his expression, issues neither in number nor in concept. The Other remains infinitely transcendent, infinitely foreign; his face in which his epiphany is produced and which appeals to me breaks with the world that can be common to us, whose virtualities are inscribed in our *nature* and developed in our existence. Speech proceeds from absolute difference."[6]

But encountering the face *and* the voice of racial nationalism brought into sharp focus the tension between a Levinasian concern to leave the integrity of the "Other" intact while meeting head-on the pernicious content of much of what was said.

I had no qualms in talking to nationalists and racists over the phone or via the Internet, but somehow having to be in firsthand, real-time dialogue posed a whole series of questions about the ethical terms of such a conversation and the politics of assimilating those who espoused racism into the realm of understanding. In the simulated setting of cyberspace these issues had not felt quite so urgent. I had invented several personae on the Internet in the context of newsgroups and Internet relay chat lines and passed variously as a "potential recruit" or an "antifascist opponent." Taking on new names and engaging in self-invention are entirely normal within this world. Activists often write under pseudonyms. I had also created my own phantom nom de plume and used it when contributing articles to antifascist periodicals. But in the context of this meeting, and others, I decided that it was important to own my name and to perform a particular kind of masquerade: that of the liberal academic, so much the target of vituperative outpourings in racist publications. A few weeks earlier I had seen Griffin during the initial hearings of his case at Harrow Crown Court, on the outskirts of London. On that occasion he arrived with a group of young male followers or protectors. If I am honest with myself, I was afraid that he would appear on this occasion with a similar group, and they would not only know my name, but also find out what I looked like. I waited.

As Nick Griffin entered the car park in front of the station, I identified him not from his face but from his walk. I had seen many pictures of him leading National Front marches, and he had a loping stride that was immediately recognizable. I moved toward him; he was alone and we greeted each other and shook hands. The thing that was immediately striking about Griffin was how ordinary he looked in the context of the ebb and flow of London life at rush hour. He was dressed in a blue jacket, a white open-necked shirt, and khaki trousers. He was unremarkable in most respects, except for the fact that he had lost the sight of one eye during an accident and he had a false eye. There was nothing to signal that this was a man on the margins of the political spectrum. Born in Barnet, north London, he had grown up in a political household of parents who were right-wing Tories. His family moved to rural Suffolk when he was nine, where he completed his schooling. He went to his first National Front meeting in Norwich in his early teenage years and went on to form a group in Ipswich.[7]

As we walked along the Strand, we exchanged pleasantries. He suggested that we conduct the interview in a nearby restaurant. I asked him about the court case and why he had elected to defend himself. He told me that the barrister assigned to his case had suggested that he plead guilty, which he found unacceptable. It happened that Griffin had some knowledge of the legal system. A graduate of Cambridge University, he had studied law during his final year and had been awarded a second-class honors degree. During his time there he had also earned a "blue" representing the university as a featherweight boxer. He told me later that one of his great sporting idols was Muhammad Ali. While at Cambridge he had also become politically involved with the National Front, gaining notoriety among the students as a vocal supporter of the extreme right.

These details were surprising in many respects, but the overwhelming impression was how familiar Griffin seemed. He had done his homework on me, but not in a way that I expected. As we walked, he told me: "I know about you; you're an expert in multiculturalism, aren't you? I did a search of your publications, very interesting." In the Information Age researchers are not the only ones with inquiring eyes. At that point I was not completely sure who was researching whom. In another ironic twist the restaurant Griffin suggested was a Mexican restaurant in Covent Garden called ChiChi's. It was just a short walk away. The restaurant's manager that night was a young black woman who greeted us warmly. It seemed so incongruous. Here I was in the company of a white nationalist—in the midst of his prosecution for incitement to racial hatred—in a Mexican restaurant of his choice, being shown to our table by a young black woman. As Griffin tucked into his tostados salad, the conversation ranged over a variety of topics from Holocaust denial to his defense of "white culture."

In the course of an interview that lasted close to two hours, the tone of the conversation ranged from the convivial discourse of "educated men" to exchanges in which our political incommensurabilities were laid bare. "If you take out the political road and ban any political expression of white feeling or racial nationalism—call it what you will—then there are several thousand people who are sufficiently dedicated in *my* language—fanatical in *your* language—[and] they will think—if there is no possibility of a political road then they will think 'we must use some other road.' Then there will be serious racial trouble," he warned. His defense of revolutionary racial nationalism was that it posed a "safer option" and an alternative to the threat of white terrorism. We might have been speaking different political languages, but this encounter was also about uncomfortable resemblances—what Levinas refers to as the "virtualities" of social life: we were approximately the same age, university graduates, loving fathers. These uncomfortable congruencies undercut any simple separation between anthropologist and ethnographic subject or between liberal and fascist.

I will return to this encounter throughout this chapter as a way of opening up issues relating to the ethical stakes and the political and methodological issues raised in researching and understanding whiteness. While, in both Europe and the United States, there has been a long-standing debate about the politics of "race relations" research,[8] little, if any, connection has been made between these controversies and the nascent "white studies literature." In a more worrisome development, it seems that, particularly within the United States, many researchers have embraced the opportunity to explore whiteness as if it is somehow a less ethically problematic form of investigation to enter into because it does not involve the mediation of racial or cultural difference. In a strange way the radical potential of the early interventions might be reduced by the field's status as a "white thing that we *can* understand." The institutionalization of "white studies" threatens to inaugurate an invidious intellectual division of labor that designates white scholars to the study of whiteness and people of color to the study of difference. As a result, "white studies" is relegated to a politically safe form of "race talk," which, rather than pushing understanding to its limits, erects a racial palisade around the pursuit of wisdom.

The aim of this chapter is to destabilize the false comforts of distributing the analysis of the politics of race in this manner. I want to argue for the necessity of connecting the investigation of whiteness to a broader commitment for achieving social justice and dismantling systems of white supremacy. I want to focus on two related questions: How are the ethics of investigating racial power implicated in these strange acquaintances—necessitated by the research act itself—and the desire to understand the advocates of intolerance and racism? How should the investigation of whiteness be placed within the moral history of modernity? These questions have been largely unexplored because of the emphasis in the field on historiography, textual critique, and media studies. It is precisely to the relationship between these ethical concerns and the ethnography of whiteness that I now want to turn.

Anthropological Episodes

To say that anthropology is facing a crisis of authority has become something of a cliché. Compromised by its imperial antecedents, the discipline has been trying to reinvent itself at least since the sixties.[9] As Eric Wolf commented, anthropology is somewhat in a permanent state of identity crisis.[10] In the scramble to find "substitute savages," to use Robin Fox's undignified phrase,[11] it is hardly surprising that the anthropological view turned to "all things white." Recently, the British anthropologist Roland Littlewood has written of his encounter with a member of the British National Party in an essay entitled "In Search of the White Tribe."[12] The title of the article speaks volumes. What is extraordinary about the piece is the way it reveals the naïveté of applying classical anthropological modes in this way. Renato Rosaldo has pointed out that conventional modes of ethnographic reporting seem farcical and parodic when applied to familiar social settings.[13] There is something of this syndrome in Littlewood's account, revealing the danger of applying modes of modernist ethnography to the examination of racist politics.

In time-honored ethnographic style Littlewood announces, "My informant was not keen to discuss the sensibilities of racist targets,"[14] as if this was an unexpected fieldwork finding. His biggest "surprise," however, was to discover that the political language of the far-right had assimilated the rhetoric of cultural diversity, albeit in the form of an appeal for the preservation of English culture. As if in the midst of some ethnographic revelation, Littlewood writes: "The language was familiar, conjuring the picture of a disappearing culture around fish-and-chips and old English pubs, unable to practice its arts. What was this English diversity? Cockney music hall; Morris dancers? 'Yes, all that,' [the BNP member] replied. I suddenly felt a sense of unease: racial supremacy has co-opted the language of diversity and cultural choice."[15] Such assertions in racist politics are hardly recent, but what comes through in Littlewood's discussion is an overwhelming sense that the anthropologist is in the midst of something that he cannot tame (or name).

Littlewood ends in the anthropological tradition of the barroom confessional by acknowledging epistemological defeat: "I had worked hard to reconcile the vision of happy white English folk singers in a church hall, sponsored by a local grant, with the real implications of his beliefs—broken families and forced repatriation to countries hit by war, the hunt for people of mixed origins, the drive for pristine social categories, drained of ambiguities, the horror of defining culture through the human body—and then tidying it up to square biology with politics. I failed."[16] There is no ethnographic reconciliation, only failure and incomprehension. What is defined here is the sharpness of the distinction between the anthropologist and the white tribesman. The anthropologist never once has to confront the uncomfortable similarities between himself and his object. As a result, the encounter is set within a binomial anthropometry, in which the distinction between self and other/anthropologist and "informant" is the prime calculation. There is something deeply wrong and ethically disingenuous about this move. The danger in such a process is that the structure of anthropological authority remains intact, while the emblems of alterity are substituted. Developing the point made in the previous chapter, how then do we investigate the "primitive tribalisms of whiteness" without replacing the "dark tribes" of old with the newfound ethnographic fetish for exotic extremism?

It should also be clear that I am not suggesting that anthropological modes are fundamentally unable to transcend this syndrome, as I will show later. There is, however, another dimension to the issue of anthropological distance. Namely, what forms of social life qualify within the anthropological imagination for ethnographic attention? This was brought home to me as a postgraduate student in anthropology at Goldsmiths College, University of London in the early nineties. I had just completed my Ph.D., and I agreed to give a paper to my peers and fellow postgrads beginning their research. The thesis focused on the ways in which popular racism featured in the lives of young south Londoners and the forms of transcultural dialogue being established across the color line. The research had been conducted in the working-class multiethnic neighborhoods immediately surrounding the college. I had previously been a youth worker in the area, and one of the recurrent issues for staff like myself was how to react to racist name-calling. This type of abuse often occurred in the context of ritual forms of play known colloquially as "wind-ups" or "cussing." The prohibition of racist and sexist name-calling and the political grammar of municipal antiracism did not sit well with the vernacular cultures of young people. In the aftermath of these exchanges more often than not the young perpetrators were merely ejected from the youth club. My plan was to attempt an "anthropological analysis" of a series of incidents using Erving Goffman's notion of dramaturgy[17] and Gregory Bateson's insights on the relationship between play and meaning.[18] Academically plausible, even practically useful, I thought.

I arrived at the session, chaired by one of the lecturers in the department. I passed the transcripts around the table as I explained the focus of the presentation. I settled myself, took out my glasses, and prepared to start. The chair cast his eye over the faithfully transcribed lines of idiomatic working-class dialect and piped up, "Are you going to do the voices?" "What?" I replied a little confused. "Are you going to do the voices?" he reiterated. "What do you mean?" I answered, smiling in embarrassment. "You know." He paused for a moment before simulating the voice of a ignorant male hooligan. "You know—'YOU FUCKING CUNT!!!'"

The mimetic performance of the "white thug" by this "radical anthropologist" wiped the smile off my face. An awkward silence filled the room as I looked around the table at my peers. Glancing down at the typescript I began presenting the paper in monotone standard English. And, no, I did not do the voices.

I include this story because it illustrates a double standard concerning that which deserves the full seriousness of ethnographic attention and that which can be dismissed, parodied, even ridiculed. When found in the Amazon rain forest or the interiors of Southeast Asia, arcane, strange, and openly violent cultural patterns are treated with utmost seriousness, often reverence, by anthropologists. This is because they emerge from an authentic hinterland of discovery. But it seemed that prosaic "white voices" from just down the street, or in the youth club, or at a bus stop simply did not qualify for the cachet bestowed on the exotic. So the full weight of class prejudice was unloaded. Had the anthropologist parodied "violent savages" in his preamble to an equivalent paper about Yanomami dueling rituals, there would have been an uproar and accusations of ethnocentrism. But, for him, working-class south Londoners simply did not deserve to be taken seriously, anthropologically speaking. This was all the more difficult precisely because I had conducted "fieldwork" in contexts that were familiar to me, and in some respects my own background was similar to that of the people I was studying. So the refusal to "do the voices" was also part of a wider ambivalence.[19]

I want to emphasize two general points from this discussion. First, the ethnography of whiteness needs to avoid the construction of simplified and hermetic distinctions between the empirical objects of research and the recondite position of the ethnographer. In both of the cases discussed above the whiteness of the anthropologist is concealed. Thus, racist subjectivity and "the problem" itself are projected into the representational vessel of the "fascist" and the "white thug," respectively. Second, I want to argue for the importance of examining the complexities, contradictions, and ambivalences within the demotic whitenesses registered in everyday life. The emphasis proposed here is to find a language of understanding that can engender critical insight—particularly for subaltern whitenesses—without reinforcing bourgeois caricatures. Paradoxically, I want to argue that anthropology itself has the potential to provide the intellectual tools to resolve these hermeneutic and ethical problems.

For Charles Taylor, the solution to such problems is a matter of developing a *reflexive interpretive view* that neither accepts the idea that human cultures are incorrigible nor falls foul of arrogant ethnocentrism. This was discussed in the previous chapter, but what I want to do here is develop an argument about applying such a perspective empirically. While the anthropological syndromes described above are beyond the scope of ethnocentrism in the conventional sense, they certainly speak to broader issues of interpretation, ethics, and reflexivity. The issues of reflexivity in anthropology have been most recently formulated in relation to the work of James Clifford and George Marcus in their critique of the poetics of ethnographic writing. Here the notion of poetics means the analysis of the conventions whereby ethnography, or any other form of research, is constructed and interpreted.

The publication in 1986 of *Writing Culture* by James Clifford and George Marcus marked an important moment in the *literary turn* in anthropology.[20] One of the features of this movement is the application of perspectives from literary criticism to ethnographic writing through an analysis of the textual nature of anthropological monographs. The book is a collection of essays produced from a discussion forum on the "making of ethnographic texts" held at the School of American Research in Santa Fe, New Mexico. The fundamental starting point of this collection is that ethnography possesses a rhetorical structure, modes of authority, and processes of elision and omission. Clifford argues that ethnographic truths are inherently partial, committed, and imperfect. Vincent Crapanzano, one of the book's contributors, argues that ethnographers are like tricksters who promise not to lie, but on the other hand never tell the whole truth.[21] His point is that their rhetoric of absolute truth both empowers and subverts the message.

The task of critical reading is then to read against the grain of the text, to identify the exclusions and the trickery of ethnographic writing and authority. From this perspective ethnographic writing is viewed at best as "part truth." Clifford comments: "'Cultures' do not hold still for their portraits. Attempts to make them do so always involve simplification and exclusion, selection of a temporal focus, the construction of a particular self-other relationship, and the imposition or negotiation of a power relationship."[22] The point here is that in order to evaluate ethnographic writing more accurately, its discursive nature needs to be specified. In simple terms this means posing a number of questions in relation to the text: Who speaks? Who writes? What modes of description are used? What is the relationship between the style of writing and the reality that is represented through these means?

This critique had obvious resonance in a situation where white Europeans had long spoken for the people of the South. The advocate mode is deeply ingrained in the discipline. I remember being baffled and uncomfortable in seminars when asked, "Well, what do they think about . . . ?" I didn't know what "they" thought, but only what people told me. This was doubly ironic, given that the inscrutable "they" in this case was just outside the seminar door. The relevance of the writing culture critique was brought home very powerfully one afternoon when I accompanied a group of local young people into the Anthropology Department for a group discussion and disrupted a seminar full of undergraduates in full discussion about Evans Pritchard's *The Nuer!* After I explained what was going on and the undergrads filed out, one of the young people asked me, "Will they be reading about us in books like that someday?" Somehow the collision with the Nuer in New Cross brought the tensions surrounding the genesis of anthropological knowledge into sharp focus.

George Marcus has argued that, in the aftermath of this critique of ethnography, the classic observational objective "eye" needs to be supplanted with the personal "I" of the ethnographer.[23] Beyond this he identifies the need to make a shift from analytical exegesis toward dialogue between the anthropologist and the research participants. But what would an ethnographic dialogue with people who espouse xenophobia and racism look like? Much of the debate around dialogic fieldwork in postmodern anthropology seems predicated upon a very particular imbalance across the horizon of investigation, namely, the European anthropological "I" and the "they" of postcolonial subjects of former empire. What difference would it make if we situated the debate around dialogic fieldwork in the context of an encounter with a member of a white-supremacist organization? Are the commitments of polyphony the same if one is sharing ethnographic authority with an outspoken advocate of Holocaust denial?

It is here that Taylor's notion of "perspicuous contrast" becomes useful, in that it offers the possibility of combining critique with dialogue. He writes:

> It will almost always be the case that the adequate language in which we can understand another society is not our language of understanding, or theirs, but rather what one could call a language of perspicuous contrast. This would be a language in which we could formulate both their way of life and ours as alternative possibilities in relation to some human constants in both. . . . Such a language of contrast might show their language of understanding to be distorted or inadequate in some respects, or it might show ours to be so. . . . [24]

As Levinas points out, "[T]o see is . . . always to see on the horizon,"[25] but the task of interpretation, following Hans-Georg Gadamer, is a matter of the "fusion of horizons."[26]

This point is picked up by Clifford Geertz in his extraordinary essay "The Uses of Diversity." Criticizing both the ethnocentrism displayed in Claude Levi-Strauss's later writings and Richard Rorty's cultural self-centeredness, Geertz argues for a model of cross-cultural understanding that focuses on the space between self and other. For him the question of understanding is about an ethics of

> Learning to grasp what we cannot understand. . . . Comprehending that which is, in some manner or form, alien to us and likely to remain so, without either smoothing it over with vacant murmurs of common humanity, disarming it with to-each-his-own in-

differentism, or dismissing it as charming, lovely even, but inconsequent, is a skill we have to arduously learn and having learnt it, always very imperfectly, to work continuously to keep alive; it is not a connatural capacity, like depth perception or the sense of balance, upon which we can complacently rely.[27]

Implicitly, for both Taylor and Geertz, their argument against ethnocentrism is laced with assumptions about the integrity of the ethnographic subject and an appeal to give voice to what appears alien to us. It is telling that Richard Rorty, in his answer to Geertz, points to the limits of "wet liberalism" and the dilemma posed when "the alien" is a racist, fascist or political fundamentalist: "When we bourgeois liberals find ourselves reacting to the Nazi and the fundamentalist with indignation and contempt—we have to think twice. For we are exemplifying the attitude we claim to despise. We would rather die than be ethnocentric, but ethnocentrism is precisely the conviction that one would rather die than share certain beliefs."[28]

These are thorny issues and push the ethics of understanding to its limit. The resolution proposed here is to insist on the possibility of simultaneous dialogue and critique, to attempt to grasp an "alien turn of mind" that disrupts the ethnographer's preconceptions, while at the same time critically evaluating the taken-for-granted predispositions of the communities under study. A mutual destabilization is thus produced on both sides of the ethnographic divide.[29] Geertz pushes this approach further to suggest that the understanding of sameness and difference operates *both* where people share the same culture or patterns of subjectification—in our cases those interpellated as "white"—and in the context of cross-cultural communication. He writes: "Foreignness does not start at the water's edge but at the skin's. The sort of idea that both anthropologists since Malinowski and philosophers since Wittgenstein are likely to entertain that, say, Shi'ias, being other, present a problem, but, say, soccer fans, being part of us, do not, or at least not the same sort, is merely wrong."[30] Geertz shows the importance of avoiding the syndrome of only seeing the problem of otherness in distance cultures. It is equally misguided to make the "soccer fan" into an incorrigible "other." Rather, we should insist on an ethics of interpretation that can identify what is alien and what is other—that is, the "soccer fan" or the "BNP member"—and yet at the same time hold onto the possibility of a semblance of a shared likeness.

Geertz's invocation of the soccer fan conveniently provides the link with the example I want to use to illustrate what an ethics of interpretation might look like following this approach. In 1996 I followed a trial of two white soccer fans. On being refused entry to a match the two young men had gone to a local pub with a group of other friends. They followed the fortunes of their team on the teletext and started to drink heavily. Their team lost 2–0, and, disgruntled, they left the pub, itself just a short walk from the stadium. They were looking for opposition fans to confront as a way of compensating for the collective loss of honor engendered by the humiliating defeat by a local rival team. After a few abortive skirmishes they came upon a young black man waiting for a bus. They attacked him. But the lone black man fought the group off, to the extent that the white group started to walk away. The black man picked up a brick and followed his assailants up the street, since he wanted to make sure that they were going to leave him be. The police arrived and arrested all the young men, including the black person who had been attacked.[31]

After a few days the police dropped their inquiries into the behavior of the black man and focused attention on the group of white men. Of a group of six to eight youths only two were prosecuted. I observed the trial at its various stages, and over a period of months I got to know the families of the assailants. The two young men—Paul and Ken[32]—were from different backgrounds. Paul had been involved in petty crime and had a series of convictions for violence. Ken, on the other hand, had no prior convictions. He was from a respectable working-class family, and at the time of his arrest he was employed full-time and had a girlfriend whom he planned to marry. Neither of the two men had been involved in organized racist politics or associated with racist youth cultures. Their racism was of the quotidian variety.

The role of racism in the attack took up a good deal of the trial. Ken's barrister made much of the fact that Ken's sister was black; his family had adopted her at a young age, and they had grown up together. Ken's sister appeared in court as a character witness and denied the accusation that Ken was a racist. The prosecuting lawyer produced a policewoman as a witness. She had sat in the back of the police van with Ken after his arrest and read out what he had said, a mixture of drunken rant and resentful racism. The black victim of the assault also came and gave evidence, describing the racist epithets and insults directed at him during the incident. In the aftermath of his testimony I sat in the court restaurant with Ken's mother and stepfather. "When that boy who'd been attacked gave his evidence he just sat there smiling, didn't he?" she said. There was no attempt to dismiss what Ken had done or explain it away. Ken's stepfather replied, "Well, there's no getting around it—what they did to that boy was wrong and Ken's going to have face that. There's nothing we can do about it, what's done is done."[33] This was not a family of committed racists. They displayed no more racism and no less tolerance than any other white working-class family in south London that I had encountered, including my own.

The jury found the two young men guilty. As they stood up for sentencing, Paul's face was expressionless, as if this was almost routine. Ken was visibly shaken. He stood with his hands clasped together in front of him; he looked at them and held his head down. The judge said that the seriousness of the offense meant that it would be a custodial sentence: "I will be taking the racial character of your crimes into consideration." He sentenced Paul first to two years' imprisonment. Then, turning to Ken, he told him that he would be sentenced to eighteen months in prison. As Ken heard the news, his bottom lip started to quiver. There was a terrible fear written on his face. Dazed, he looked back at his parents and his girlfriend for a brief moment. Then the court guard led him away to the cells to begin his sentence.

Ken's expression at that moment haunted me for days afterward. It was the face of complete dread. From that moment this very ordinary young man would have the distinction of a criminal record for violent racism. What does it mean to empathize with perpetrators in this way? I think that moment affected me so deeply because I could almost see myself in his situation, it almost felt like part of me was standing in the dock with him. My family background was almost identical to Ken's; I had been socialized into commensurable amounts of working-class racism and understood equally the ritual embodiment of such territorial masculinities. Yet, at the same time, the account of his rant against black people in the back of the police van was deeply disturbing. Although this group had not been looking to attack a black person out of blind hate, it was their racism that identified a young black man standing at a bus stop as a substitute target for violent attack in the absence of fans from the rival team. It was in this space, replete with ambivalent tensions, that I was forming my interpretation of whiteness and my analysis of this particular incident of racist violence. Thus, by building on the interpretive schema of Charles Taylor and Clifford Geertz, what I am arguing for is a reflexive interpretive reading of whiteness that arises within the space between what is familiar and what is alien.

White on White? Research, Politics, and the Spectrum of the Gray Zone

Is it the implication of this argument that "white people" are in the best position to conduct the ethnography of whiteness? Am I thus reinforcing the Manichaean intellectual division of labor that I set out to argue against at the beginning of this chapter? I want to make it clear that such a conclusion is *not* the logical consequence of this argument. Rather, I want to suggest that the dialectic of difference and similarity embodied in this interpretive view is appropriate regardless of the positionality of the researcher. What may vary are the experiential materials that the interpreter utilizes in each case.[34] Beyond the philosophical dimensions of this process it is all too easy to assume that people who are identified as white will not "confess" to racialized subjectivities, or their commitment to racism, if confronted by persons who are not included in the category. I have heard this line of argument deployed, but what is strange about this logic is the way it inverts the debate about the relationship between race and research. Part of the defense that "white" researchers have made against the charge that they cannot adequately relate to black or ethnic minority interviewees is the claim that dialogue in the research encounter is complex and demonstrates a variety of social features (i.e., gender, sexuality, class, age, etc.),[35] none of which can be adequately accounted for through a notion of "race matching." However, it is alarming that a similar logic is not necessarily articulated when it is the other way around. The presumption that "whites will not talk" to a black or minority researcher does not tally with the experience of writers who have conducted such an inquiry.[36]

Raphael S. Ezekiel interviewed followers and leaders in the militant racist movement in America in researching his book *The Racist Mind.* He did participant observation at rallies and at the movement's social gatherings. He reflected:

> I have dealt openly and honestly with these people, making it clear that I am Jewish, a leftist opposed to racism, a professor at the University of Michigan. I have told them, honestly, that I think people build lives that make sense to them, and that my goal is to understand the sense the person's life makes to that person. I tape-recorded conversations so that the person's own words can be used. I listen much more than I talk. I try to ask searching questions. I try to encourage the respondent to give me a full picture of his life. I show him, periodically, how our basic beliefs differ and explore with him the bases of those beliefs. Occasionally I explain myself with passion; if I already know the respondent, I learn a lot from confrontation. Communication rests on my candor, their interest in being heard, my deep interest in understanding the phenomenon, and my background in a particularly racist culture.[37]

The fact that Ezekiel identified himself as Jewish appeared to have little bearing on the willingness of the neo-Nazis to be involved in the research. Indeed, it is exactly the combination of human difference and likeness that informs his interpretive scheme. This can be summed up in the clash among (1) the white supremacists' desire to be heard, (2) Ezekiel's interest in what makes them alien, and (3) his experience of belonging to a social group for which the people he is trying to understand profess a hatred. It is precisely in the processing of such confrontations that he develops an understanding through the "language of perspicuous contrast."

This experience also resonates with the ethnographic work on a male skinhead gang that I conducted in 1994 with my colleague Anoop Nayak. Anoop grew up in a predominantly white district of Liverpool, although his parents were from India. We worked jointly with this group of boys on a video project that aimed to give them a space to express their views around race and other issues. Discussions with the groups took place in a local youth club. The gang of boys—which included two black members—claimed not to feel inhibited in any sense by Anoop's presence.[38] On several occasions members of the group went into tirades about "Pakis that stink" and Asians who "walk about with towels round their heads" despite the fact that Anoop was sitting in the room, contradicting all their assertions by his very presence. The group listened to and answered Anoop's questions, as they did mine. But it was interesting that the boys never turned their hostility toward Anoop and in many respects were much more antagonistic toward me. On one occasion Anoop could not be present at the video session because of a prior commitment. I went ahead and conducted the session anyway. There was much discussion about why Anoop was not at the session. "Did we scare 'im off?" one of the boys asked.[39]

The session was focused on showing the video footage we had shot with the group. We had hoped that this would have provided a context to open up some critical dialogue around what they had said in previous weeks. However, watching the video only provided another context in which to celebrate their racism. After the video had been shown, a member of the group called Robbie came back and asked if we could do another session. I said that we could, and then he said, "Yeah what you should do is bring some Pakis down and we can have a debate. We can listen to what they got to say and we'll tell 'em what we think." He paused for a moment and then said excitedly, "Bring some big, dirty smelly Paki down and we can have an argument!" What is telling about this incident in terms of the issue of research practice was that for Robbie this monstrous image of Asian otherness was necessary in order for him to inflate his own "white selfhood" to the level of an equal opposite.[40] This not only demonstrates the interlocked process whereby white identity is expressed through the construction of a contrasting racial otherness, but also shows that the articulation of whiteness and racism is perfectly congruent with a situation where the audience is seen to be "other." As I said good-bye to the group, I asked them, "Does it make a difference when Anoop is here? Would you have said the same things you said to me tonight if he had been here?" Without hesitation Robbie replied, "No, it wouldn't make any difference! You've asked us to tell you what we think and that is what we did!"

It follows that one should be skeptical about the degree to which "racial matching" automatically guarantees reliable accounts of white racial subjectification. Establishing a kind of "white on white" methodology, to use Ruth Frankenberg's characterization,[41] need not in itself guarantee that participants will identify and confide in the researcher. Having things "in common" is not necessarily the prerequisite for insightful dialogue on the social construction of whiteness. Frankenberg, in her innovative empirical study of race and racism in white women's personal histories, points to the tension between times when she declared her antiracist political position and other moments when she "colluded in keeping [racial consciousness] repressed."[42] Frankenberg makes a strong and compelling argument against the research persona as the "neutral observer." Rightly, she points to the fact that all positions, especially those that invoke "objectivity" and "science," are committed. However, she developed a model of dialogic research in which she revealed her disagreement at the same time as opening up opportunities for empathy and the possibility of accord. She writes: "Central to my dialogical method were the ways in which I offered information both about myself as inscribed within racism and about my analysis of racism as systematic as well as personal. In effect, I broke the silence of the blank-faced interviewer in order to facilitate the breaking of silence on race by a diverse range of white women."[43] Frankenberg's research illustrates the tension between a commitment to women's empowerment through research[44] and the possible collusion in a shared whiteness that both concealed and normalized white supremacy.

For "white people," class and gender disadvantage is thus complicated by the advantage that whiteness confers. Such ambivalences between adversity and supremacy make a vanguardist notion of empowerment through research difficult to sustain. More broadly, Judith Stacey has argued that there are endemic tensions between feminism and ethnography. Her experience of field research placed her in "situations of inauthenticity, dissimilitude, and potential, perhaps inevitable betrayal. . . . Perhaps even more than ethnographic process, the published ethnography represents an intervention into the lives and relationships of its subjects."[45] But equally, should we aspire to empowerment in research when the ethnographic subjects are privileged by their "race"? In this sense the empowerment of research participants in the investigation of whiteness is a contradiction in terms.

The research process itself can be the context in which lines of political difference are drawn between researcher and researched. Rather than empowerment, this is about confrontation, as was profoundly manifested in my encounter with Nick Griffin described at the beginning of this chapter. In the course of our meal I mentioned that it was "interesting" that he had developed links with black separatist organizations, particularly in America. "Why should that be interesting as opposed to inevitable?" he said abruptly. "As not just nationalists but racial nationalists you can respect and understand the same views. You know precisely how someone else feels, even if they are a different color. It doesn't make any difference, if they have these same views." With the tone of irritation growing in his voice, he concluded, "Ultimately, I've probably got more in common with *them* than I have with *you!* They don't want their kids or grandchildren growing up half-caste. It is anathema to them as it is to me."[46]

These claims were not merely rhetorical. During the 1980s the National Front established links with a number of American Black separatist organizations in the Nation of Islam and the Pan African International Movement (PAIN).[47] Indeed, at Griffin's trial, which followed in late April 1998, Osiris Akkebala of PAIN gave evidence as a defense witness, with his expenses allegedly paid by the British National Party. Akkebala made a spectacular entrance at the trial. Dressed in a colorful African dashiki he stood up in the court and said, to the delight of the public gallery packed with BNP supporters: "Well it is not offensive to me as a black man to hear a white man indicate his proudness about his race. I think that is just a natural state of mind to be in. I know it is an international conception that anyone who advocates race separation and race pride walks hand in hand with racism. That I deny vehemently. I am not a racist. I am a true advocate of racial separation and it is not possible at this moment for me nor [sic] you to be a racist if you really understand the true definition of the term itself."[48] In his final question Nick Griffin directed Akkebala's attention to the cover of the *Rune* tract:

> [Nick Griffin:] The combination of the noose on the front and words such as "White unity, final victory, capital work" in this

piece, the prosecution said is a coded call to hang black people like the KKK, the Ku Klux Klan. Can you comment on this?

[Osiris Akkebala:] Well, I read the White Survival Piece and the only thing I would change here is the word "white" and replace it with "black," and the noose, in its shape, the rope, it is not offensive to me at all. . . . [49]

After the day's proceedings Akkebala and Griffin posed for press pictures outside the court.[50] To assume that I—as a white researcher—would have privileged access to Griffin's confidence is to elide the political chasm that existed between us. Also, it is important to make visible the fraternity that exists between racial nationalists regardless of their shade. These strange alliances also disrupt the idea that antiracist virtue can be attributed in crude black-and-white terms.

A further question is, What status should be given to the accounts of white perpetrators of racism? The group with whom Anoop and I had worked was on the peripheries of violent racism. Its members often had their own self-exonerating accounts of their involvement in racist conflicts. Nick Griffin, equally, was keen to exculpate racial nationalists, whom he cast as innocent victims: "As a revolutionary I decided a long time ago not to take the easy road, it's not easy, you don't choose to be in nationalist politics for an easy life. It's grief, being harassed, being trapped, being prosecuted and running the risk of being put in prison for your political beliefs. So you don't do that if you want an easy life."[51] There is a strong current of victimology in far-right discourse. But beyond just describing their accounts, how do we develop an interpretive framework to evaluate and analyze them? As Judith Stacey points out: "As author an ethnographer cannot (and, I believe, should not) escape tasks of interpretation, evaluation and judgement."[52] So what kind of credence should we give the accounts of perpetrators in order to assess and weigh them and ultimately use them to subvert and dismantle the structures of white supremacy?

This issue of the status of perpetrator accounts has been particularly key in the historiography of Nazism and the Holocaust. Daniel Jonah Goldhagen, author of the controversial *Hitler's Willing Executioners,* argued that such accounts should always be ruled out of consideration. In the methodological appendix to his voluminous study of the complicity of ordinary Germans in the persecution and extermination of the Jews he writes: "Attempting to explain the Germans' actions, indeed just writing a history of this period, by relying on their self-exonerating testimony would be akin to writing a history of criminality in America by relying on the statements of criminals as given to police, prosecutors, and before courts. Most criminals assert that they have been wrongly accused of the crimes."[53] For him such accounts are always compromised by the perpetrators' guilt, so that to accept them without corroboration "will lead one down many false paths, paths that preclude one from ever finding one's way back to the truth."[54]

Goldhagen's book is in large measure a response to Christopher Browning's study of the same period entitled *Ordinary Men*,[55] from which Goldhagen attempts to distance himself on virtually every issue, even when there is actually clear agreement between the two historians. One of Goldhagen's lines of criticism is that Browning's study is flawed because he gives too much credence to the testimony of the perpetrators.[56] Browning's response, first published in the newspaper *Die Zeit* in the middle of the furor caused by Goldhagen's book in Germany, is interesting because it picks up on the issue of the status of perpetrator accounts. Browning argues that always to rule out on principle testimony that is deemed to be self-exculpatory impoverishes the interpretive range of any study of perpetration. For him it is a matter of explicating those perpetrator accounts that possess the "feel" of plausibility. He offers an example of the testimony of one of the reserve policemen interrogated in 1964. Initially, this person denied having any involvement in the "Jew hunts" and executions. Browning characterizes this as a classic case of perpetrator denial. Then, two days later, the same man reappeared uninvited and recounted in graphic details his involvement in executions. In his testimony he claims he abhorred the killing, which made him physically sick. Browning concludes: "He then went on to explain his unusual return to the office of the investigators. 'I showed up here again today, to be rid of what I just said. . . . The reason for my return was to unburden my conscience.' This is the kind of testimony that Goldhagen's methodology excludes, and the result is a kind of 'methodological determinism,' screening out much that could give some texture and differentiation to a portrayal of the German killers. . . ."[57]

This attention to plausibility in racial narratives, while at the same time remaining sensitive to self-exculpating elements, is an appropriate bearing to bring to the hermeneutics of whiteness.[58] Revisiting my encounter with Nick Griffin, it seems clear to me now that we were partners in a dance of deceit that was to some degree mutual, though tacitly agreed. I presented myself as an academic, but Griffin made it clear that he knew I had been a public advocate of multiculturalism and no "neutral observer." He, on the other hand, fashioned what he wanted me to hear, no doubt aiming to present an image of racial nationalism that would confound conventional wisdom. The task of a reflexive interpretive analysis is to establish the plausibility of each account, while remaining attentive to the discursive and rhetorical moves utilized to both enunciate and legitimate a particular view of the world. Critical insight was produced where common ground was established and equally in moments when our respective worldviews came into direct confrontation.

Finally, I want to end this section by reflecting on what is at stake when we, as researchers, expand our moral imagination to incorporate the racist into the realm of understanding. To reiterate the central question posed in this chapter, what are the ethics of analyzing embodied forms of whiteness in everyday life? I want to make a case for the role of ethnography in bearing witness to white supremacy that is a matter neither of asserting an antiracist moral high ground nor of disclosing collusion with the very thing we aim to abolish. The challenge is to think beyond such an either/or logic, refusing both a vanguardist position and the confessional narcissism of apologia.

It is here that the work and thought of Primo Levi offer a way out of such forms of ethical simplification. Levi, an Italian chemist and nonreligious Jew, was transported to a Nazi death camp at the end of 1943. His books combine personal testimony of the genocide[59] with allegorical and analytical reflection.[60] As Murray Baumgarten has commented, Levi's thought demonstrates a "special combination of accurate observation, rigorous analysis, clear reasoning, linguistic sensitivity, imaginative conception [and] *multicultural understanding*. . . ."[61] Levi's last book, *The Drowned and the Saved,* was written just before he committed suicide in 1987. In it he points to a series of issues relating to the ethics and politics of understanding terror. In keeping with the sagacity of Levi's method, I want to be clear that I am not suggesting that interrogating whiteness is somehow the same as bearing witness to the Nazi genocide.[62] Rather, my point is that there are lessons to be learned from this specific genocidal moment, in particular with regard to what it means to replicate the quest to understand the contemporary imitators of the Nazis.

Levi writes in *The Drowned and the Saved* that the true witnesses of the terror of the Holocaust are not the survivors. Rather, those in full possession of its appalling exactness are the drowned, those who died. The survivors—the saved—speak in their stead; they are witnesses by proxy. Levi describes how the Nazis, through the camp system, reduced the humanity of the victims so that the prisoners were assimilated into a system of brutality. This integration compromised the victims: "It is naïve, absurd, and historically false to believe that an infernal system such as National Socialism was, sanctifies its victims: on the contrary, it degrades them, it makes them similar to itself, and this all the more when they are available, blank, and lack a political or moral armature."[63] The Nazis established hierarchies among the prisoners that set apart the functionaries, the "Special Squads," and, most debased of all, the "crematoria ravens." Not only did the spectrum of complicity include the German perpetrators and those bystanders who said and did nothing; it also implicated the victims. The result was a "grey zone, with ill-defined outlines which both separate and join the two camps of masters and servants. It possesses an incredibly complicated internal structure, and contains within itself enough to confuse our need to judge."[64] It is within this context that Levi invites us to understand the phenomenon of survivor guilt and the high incidence of suicide among the "saved."

The functionaries were not all collaborators, and Levi talks about the "camouflaged opponents" who recorded the truth of what was going on in the Lagers (concentration camps). Their "privilege" gave them access to secret information.[65] The SS delegated responsibility for the implementation of the massacre to the prisoners themselves. The task of the Special Squads, who numbered between seven hundred and one thousand, was to do the dirty work of genocide. They were the bearers of the terrible truth, and they were regularly killed to hide it. But some members kept diaries, "feverishly written for future memory and buried with extreme care near the crematoria in Auschwitz."[66] Levi demonstrated that for a minority it was because of their location in the "grey zone" that they became record keepers, witnesses, and scribes and were privy to an accursed truth.

Fellow Auschwitz prisoner and philosopher Jean Améry writes: "Nowhere else in the world did reality have as much effective power as in the camp, nowhere else was reality so real."[67] Améry was born in Vienna in 1912 into a family that was mainly Jewish, although he was assimilated completely into the culture of the Austro-Hungarian empire. In the Lager everything he turned to in his mind for solace and strength belonged to the enemy—be it Beethoven, Dante, or Nietzsche. The problem for him, as a Jewish intellectual of German education and cultural sensibility, was that the brutal reality of the camp meant the end of metaphysics, philosophy, and aesthetics:

> In the camp the intellect in its totality declared itself to be incompetent. As a tool for solving the tasks put to us it admitted defeat. However, and this is a very essential point, it could be used for *its own abolishment,* and that in itself was something. For it was not

the case that the intellectual—if he had not already been destroyed physically—had now become unintellectual or incapable of thinking. On the contrary, only rarely did thinking grant itself a respite. But it nullified itself when at almost every step it ran into its uncrossable borders. The axes of its traditional frames of reference then shattered. Beauty: that was an illusion. Knowledge: that turned out to be a game with ideas. Death veiled itself in all its inscrutability.[68]

For Améry the Lager did not make people more mature ethically; rather, it erected an uncrossable border in understanding: "we were not even left with the feeling that we must regret its departure."[69]

Améry committed suicide in 1978. In *The Drowned and the Saved* Primo Levi dedicated a whole chapter to the issue of the position of intellectuals in concentration camps, a posthumous dialogue with Améry. "To argue with a dead man is embarrassing and not very loyal,"[70] he wrote. But this "obligatory step," as he referred to it, was necessary. Levi developed in this essay other ways of looking at intellectual activity under the heel of Nazi terror. The chemist in the Lager—unlike the philosopher—set about interpreting and analyzing:

[F]rom my trade I contracted the habit that can be variously judged and defined at will as human or inhuman—the habit of remaining indifferent to the individuals that chance brings before me. They are human beings, but also "samples", specimens in a sealed envelope to be identified, analysed and weighed. Now, the sample book that Auschwitz had placed open before me was rich, varied and strange; made up of friends, neutrals and enemies, yet in any case food for my curiosity which some people, then and later, have judged as detached . . . I know that this "naturalistic" attitude does not derive only or even necessarily from chemistry, but in my case it did come from chemistry.[71]

Levi is equivocal about whether he was or was not an intellectual in Auschwitz, but he is sure that experience made him so afterward. For him "the Lager was a university; it taught us to look around and to measure men."[72] In Levi's writing we find not the sensibilities of a metaphysician of the mind and its limits, but a proto-ethnographer of human frailty and brutality.

Levi writes in *The Drowned and the Saved* about his relationship with the German translator of his Auschwitz memoir, *If This Is a Man*. He recounts both his initial skepticism and the complete faith that he later developed in the man who would bring his book to a German-speaking audience. In one of its most revealing passages he describes a recurrent argument that developed over the nature of the translation. The barks of the German guards were imprinted on Levi's aural memory. Levi was not a fluent German speaker; like many other non-German prisoners he often just understood the violence in the feral shouts of the SS. He wanted these sounds to be faithfully reproduced in the German edition of the book. His translator maintained that the language Levi recollected was not good German and that postwar readers would not understand. Levi insisted: "I was driven by a scruple of super-realism."[73] In a situation where reality was more real, Levi reached for a realism with greater acoustic life and aural brilliance. All of these elements—naturalistic method and realism—are the hallmarks of a putative ethnographer, but this is an ethnography of witness, of survival. At the heart of Levi's writing there is a uneasiness.[74] He, too, is positioned in the spectrum of the gray zone. As Paul Gilroy has said, his suicide casts a shadow over his written work. For Gilroy, at the heart of Primo Levi's work is a tension between, on the one hand, his desire to understand the Nazi terror and its German perpetrators and, on the other, the personal consequences of this brutality for Levi as a Holocaust survivor. Levi gives us a wealth of evidence and insight, but this dialectic is left unresolved.[75]

There are two lessons that I want to take from this with regard to the encounter with whiteness and today's imitators of fascism. The first is that we need to commit to Primo Levi's model of garnering evidence and his acute interpretive view. The second is that there is a contemporary equivalent to Levi's "grey zone" and that the ethnographer of whiteness is, perhaps inevitably, drawn into its spectrum. This occurred to me very powerfully during Nick Griffin's trial, which took place in Harrow Crown Court just a few weeks after we had had dinner in Covent Garden. I sat in the public gallery, packed with BNP members and journalists, and watched the trial unfold. On the second day Griffin called notorious French Holocaust denier Robert Faurisson, a former professor of literature at the University of Lyon-2. He had also given evidence at both trials of notorious Holocaust denier Ernst Zundel, in Canada.[76] Griffin had told me during his interview that he had met Faurisson while on his honeymoon in France. Faurisson, on the surface a harmless old man, took the stand. An older male BNP supporter clapped loudly and cheered, "He's a courageous man!"[77]

Faurisson told the court he was a specialist in "the criticism of texts and documents and in the investigation of meaning and counter meaning." The judge tried to keep Faurisson from commenting on the status of the revisionist claims made in *The Rune*, the pamphlet for which Griffin was being prosecuted. However, Faurisson continued to tell of his "research" into the gas chambers. He asserted that he had found no hole for the Zyklon B gas to pass into the gas chamber. The judge seemed slightly bewildered, but Faurisson continued unabated. "It is quite simple," he said in his broken English laced with French accent, "no holes, no Holocaust!" There was a stunned silence as those words filled the room. It was punctured only by the murmurs of agreement from Griffin's supporters. After his testimony several people approached Faurisson and shook his hand. He then entered the public gallery and sat down next to me.

I took the opportunity to speak to him. I introduced myself as an English academic, and he was instantly willing to talk. We walked out into the foyer of the court, and I conducted an interview with him. He talked for about forty-five minutes, and I scribbled down what he said. At one point Faurisson showed me an album of photographs taken after being physically assaulted by opponents. He offered the picture of his face swollen by having acid thrown into it as a kind of talisman. About halfway through the old BNP supporter who had applauded when Faurisson took the stand came over and handed me a leaflet, assuming that I was a sympathizer. My heart sank. I felt like I'd crossed a line. The interview finished and Faurisson got up. I stayed behind to check and correct my notes while his words were still echoing in my mind. About fifteen minutes passed. I packed up my bag and left the empty court. As I passed through the exit doors, Griffin and his supporters were standing in front of the building talking. He saw me and approached, holding out his hand. I shook it. He was enthusiastic and clearly pleased with the day's proceedings. Faurisson had managed to air in open court his revisionist views on the Holocaust. The Frenchman approached, stood, and listened; then he took my notepad and scribbled something down. He handed it back to me; it read:

> A "Nazi"? No: a Palestinian.
> My writings are the stones of my Intifada.
> I am living in an occupied country
> With a special apartheid law: the Lex Faurissonia

I read it and Faurisson explained: "There is one thing that I didn't tell you. Revisionism can be fun." "Fun," Griffin repeated laughing, "you get beaten up for it." Faurisson continued, "It's not great fun, but it is fun." I felt an enormous sense of doubt as to what I was doing there. It is obvious that Griffin and the BNP crave publicity and I was giving him precisely what he wanted—attention. I felt exhausted and drained from watching the trial. I really did not want to have any more to do with these people. But here I was standing with a world-famous Holocaust denier and a prominent member of the British National Party. I had entered the "zone of grey consciences."[78]

On my way home that night I kept hearing Faurisson's words—"No holes, no Holocaust! No holes, no Holocaust!" It was the eve of the fiftieth anniversary of the state of Israel. That night Pete, an old school friend, phoned me unexpectedly. He was not Jewish, but had married a Jewish woman and was living in Israel with his two children. My friend's tone was poignant: "It's hard, mate, everyone here is enjoying the celebration but I am separated from everyone in England and I don't completely belong here either." We talked and laughed about old times. "It's weird," he said, "but I start to see what independence means through the eyes of my children." It was fantastic to speak to a dear friend, but I couldn't get out of my mind that just a few hours earlier I had been talking to a man who claimed the gas chambers never existed. Faurisson invoked the cause of the Palestinians as a way of claiming that he had minority status and asserting that he was a victim. This opportunistic gesture elided the conditions and injustices of the Palestinians in Israel. The political point of investigating and listening to Faurisson and Griffin is to identify and counter their anti-Semitism. It is also a matter of being opposed to any politics of blood and soil that would also deny social justice to the Palestinians.

Perhaps the study of whiteness necessitates a kind of ethical ambivalence. The fact that people like Griffin and Faurisson seem so ordinary and prosaic is what should be disturbing. To admit to this is risky. Such an admission does not sit well with the tendency in our political culture to define whites as either chaste "antiracist angels" or rotten-to-the-core "racist devils." But such a dualism conceals much of the complexity in the argument developed here. Finally, I want to suggest that the critical engagement with whiteness should not aspire to resolve the tension created across the desire to understand. Rather, if the interrogation of whiteness is to possess ethical integrity, it must accept this ambivalence.

Dialogue, Judgment, and the Hermeneutics of Whiteness

To present white racists as humans is not to approve their ideas or their actions. But to picture them only in stereotype is to foolishly deny ourselves knowledge. Effective action to combat racism requires honest inquiry.

—RAPHAEL EZEKIEL

Throughout this chapter it has been argued that there is limited utility in caricaturing racists as monsters. This is precisely the point that Raphael Ezekiel makes in the above quotation.[79] I have argued against the application of crude anthropomorphic contrasts and suggested a reflex-

ive interpretive view in which understanding is established through "a language of perspicuous contrast."[80] Such a mode of interpretation is potentially more disturbing, since it invites new insight precisely because it is not predicated on stereotypes or political demonology. Kathleen Blee writes of similar challenges in her extraordinary study of women's involvement in the Ku Klux Klan:

> I was prepared to hate and fear my informants. My own commitment to progressive politics prepared me to find these people strange, even repellent. I expected no rapport, no shared assumptions, and no commonality of thought or experience. What I found was more disturbing. Many of the people I interviewed were interesting, intelligent, and well informed. Despite my predictions that we would experience each other as completely foreign, in fact I shared the assumptions and opinions of my informants on a number of topics (excluding, of course, race, religion, and most political topics).[81]

It is this combination of difference and likeness that I want to propose in the hermeneutics of whiteness. Such a position seeks to avoid the perils of political credentialism and the rhetoric of empowerment, while at the same time escaping the pale solipsism of confessing collusion. Following Levinas, through communicating with the "other" we enter a relationship with him or her, but this does not necessarily lead to a dependence. In *The Periodic Table* Primo Levi makes it clear that there can be no absolution for those who perpetuate intolerance, only judgment. This is an adversary who "perseveres in his desire to inflict suffering, [and] it is certain that one must not forgive him: one can try to salvage him, one can (one must!) discuss with him, but it is our duty to judge him, not to forgive him."[82] The investigation of whiteness must be coupled with a commitment to achieving social justice through understanding how racism functions and therefore how it can be dismantled. This brings me back to my dinner with Nick Griffin in London's Covent Garden.

As we left the restaurant, Griffin asked me which way I was heading. I told him I was walking back to Charing Cross. "Where do you live, do you live near Goldsmiths?" he asked. I balked at the question. The hate mail and harassment I'd received had been sent to my office. I didn't want "them" to find out the location of my home. So I lied and told him that I lived outside London in the countryside of Kent. He immediately seized on this—"Oh, I bet there's a lot of multiculturalism out there!" He smiled, as if to say, "Yes, you liberals champion the cause of 'the ethnics' but don't want to live with them." I changed the subject: "What about your wife, isn't she worried that you might go to prison?" The charges against him meant that he could get a prison sentence of six months. Up until this point Griffin had just shrugged off this suggestion or made light of it. It was almost like a game, a form of public school rebelliousness in which he was breaking the housemaster's rules. But he sobered as he talked about his wife and family. "Yes, she is worried because we have four children to bring up. It will be no fun if I am not around. My wife is a nurse and while she works shifts I usually work from home with my publishing and writing and take care of the children."

When we arrived at Charing Cross, we said our good-byes, and I thanked him for his openness. He went down to the Underground, and I walked into the mainline station to catch a train to my home in south London. I found myself feeling a kind of depressed pointlessness. Griffin's martyrdom to a cause that has quite clearly no moral or pragmatic foundation seemed so futile. It was a strange feeling because in many ways it was not an unpleasant experience to meet and talk to Nick Griffin. I sat on a train full of people of all shades. The faces in the train were evidence of the fact of multiculture. Griffin demonstrated all of the standards and codes of civility of his class and his education. It was not as if he was spitting racist bile and threatening behavior; it was all very genteel, a kind of racial nationalism with an Oxbridge face and polite bourgeois manners. The experience of meeting him left me feeling a strange combination of disgust and ease.[83]

It is precisely this sense of disorientation that I want to propose as an interpretive position from which the ethnography of whiteness should be conducted. It was important to have met him and it was important to have looked into his eyes and heard him articulate his sickening views about the Holocaust, race and crime, and the incompatibility of the "white tribes" with "immigrants" and "colored people." This was not the rampant ugly face of fascism, although I am sure he could, in the right circumstances, lapse into the demotic racism of the gutter.[84] But that night in Covent Garden I encountered racism with a genteel, well-mannered, and articulate voice. The ethics of such an inquiry must confront the fact that bearing witness to whiteness also involves being placed on the spectrum of the gray zone. This can never and should never be resolved. It is the comfortless condition of looking into the face of racism and seeing a trace of oneself reflected in its eye. It is precisely the embrace of this discomfort and its difficulties that politically engaged intellectuals should aspire to in the investigation of whiteness.

Vron Ware

3. SEEING THROUGH SKIN/SEEING THROUGH EPIDERMALIZATION

The deepest shock I experienced as a black man was the realization that *everything* is utterly different when one is the victim of racial prejudice.

— JOHN HOWARD GRIFFIN

Even the best ethnographic texts—serious, true fictions—are systems, or economies, of truth. Power and history work through them, in ways their authors cannot control.

— JAMES CLIFFORD

The hate stare was everywhere practiced, especially by women of the older generation. On Sunday, I made the experiment of dressing well and walking past some of the white churches just as services were over. In each instance, as the women came through the church doors and saw me, the "spiritual bouquets" changed to hostility. The transformation was grotesque. In all of Montgomery only one woman refrained. She did not smile. She merely looked at me and did not change her expression. My gratitude to her was so great it astonished me.

— JOHN HOWARD GRIFFIN

We have established that the very slipperiness of the category of whiteness makes it important to consider it from different points of view. The description of the "hate stare" in this last quote is peculiar in that it is recounted by someone who had gone out of his way to place himself within in its range.[1] The writer's fascination that elderly churchgoing women were its most ardent practitioners compounds his even more sobering discovery that he had not been able to identify this racist way of looking until he chose to become a target of hatred himself. This chapter will step back a little to consider what we might call epistemologies of whiteness: the different kinds of knowledge relating to the patterns of thinking and acting that flow from a belief in white supremacy. The range of work that has contributed to this field in the last decade can be said to have offered many different ways of knowing, some clearly more valuable and valid than others. One result of this is the existence of a substantial new body of writing that, in the process of investigating whiteness, also makes it possible to see whiteness as neutral, as a respectable and nondangerous object of study. By subsuming the radical texts under the general heading of "whiteness studies," there is a real problem that the project of destroying white supremacy becomes contiguous with the banal activity of describing it. This collection represents our quest to discover unorthodox ways of knowing how white supremacy operates in the worlds that we have inherited and feel moved to change. We are not advocating one single methodology; we are cautious about appropriating the term "ethnography" and will keep returning to the central notion of epistemology, reminding ourselves as we go that the most valuable ways of knowing about whiteness are those that ultimately help to bring the whole system of race-thinking and its consequences to an end.

Here we consider a branch of methodology that certainly falls into the category of "unorthodox," if not disreputable as well. It centers around the testimonies of several writers who wanted to learn more about racism than they could discover from books and conversations. They were convinced that there was a different story to be told than the one that was already available to them and that the only way to really understand was to become someone who experienced racism rather than witnessing its effects on other people. In each case these men and women were motivated by a desire to feel for themselves the full impact of an economic, social, and political system based on the exploitation and terrorization of a racially defined section of the population. The articles and books that emerged from their experiences were intended not just to educate the public about the evils of racial prejudice, but also to disrupt the complacent ignorance that helped to maintain systems of White Power and social injustice.[2] The most significant stories that we have so far identified range across continents and take place over a span of forty years. But they are connected partly through the technique of investigation that each protagonist chose to carry out his or her mission. These tales have enough in common to form a genre of their own, not in terms of publishing, although that, too, cannot be discounted, but in terms of the curiosity and desire for vicarious excitement that they grew out of, the impulse to find and offer solidarity and empathy with the oppressed, the yearning to know and to feel the facts of extreme social injustice by risking their own lives in the process. The confusion, both wholesome and, some would say, unwholesome, that erupts from the pages of their books is itself a sign that these texts are worth reexamining for what they have to say about the construction and destruction of racial categories.

By offering a selective reading of their experiences, I will argue that these writers employ a "language of perspicuous contrast" that helps to illustrate, perhaps in rather an extreme manner, the value of adopting an interpretive view of whiteness. It is worth beginning with an account of the failure of social science to uncover anything like the truth of white supremacy in the American South. In 1959 the writer John Howard Griffin was commissioned by a sociologist at the University of Texas to investigate the relatively high proportion of young black male suicides in the South. As Griffin explains in his book *A Time to Be Human,* he distributed a questionnaire to black and white community leaders, teachers, professionals, and business people and prepared to collate the results of his survey. The replies from the white participants did not surprise him. Almost unanimously they scoffed at the idea that blacks ever committed suicide, since it was not in their racial nature to be anything other than happy-go-lucky. The whole premise of the study was ridiculous; one wrote that a troubled Negro was more likely to find himself a shady spot under a tree and sleep it off than to contemplate killing himself. Griffin was almost more taken aback to find that few blacks bothered to respond to the questionnaire and that those who did sent brief notes explaining why they had not completed it. One respondent wrote, "You probably can't help it, but you think *white. . . .* We don't believe it's possible for a white man, even one trained in the sciences, to interpret his findings without thinking white and thereby falsifying the truth."[3]

Griffin knew enough about racism to understand that the bias of class and culture made any reputable scientific survey a dubious venture, but he found this expression "thinking white" both "accurate and illuminating." Added to this, several other respondents told him that the only way he could ever hope to understand anything about racism was to wake up some morning in a black man's skin. Griffin had heard this many times before, but the charge that he might be unable to transcend the limitations of "thinking white" caused him to hear this advice in a new way. He began to doubt in fact that he had ever really understood the problem of racism "from the outside." He decided then and there that he would try to arrange doing just that, waking up some morning in a black man's skin.

Later that same year Griffin embarked on what he was to call his "experiment." With his skin temporarily darkened by a combination of medication, ultraviolet light, and stain, he spent six weeks traveling in the South, prepared to "live whatever might happen and then share that experience with others."[4] If pure reason was not enough to allow full communication between black and white in the United States, perhaps, thought Griffin, understanding might become possible at the level of shared experience. If the effects of racism could not be fully seen from the "outside," the only way to comprehend what it was like to be a victim of white supremacy in the United States was to move to the "inside." The results of his experiment were recorded the following year in *Sepia* magazine and then in the sensational international best-seller, entitled *Black Like Me,* published in 1960.

Griffin does not acknowledge, and quite possibly never knew, that another white journalist, Ray Sprigle, had carried out a similar case study a decade earlier. Working with the *Pittsburgh Post,* Sprigle already had made a name for himself as an undercover investigator: in 1938 he had won the Pulitzer Prize for revealing connections between a Supreme Court justice and the Ku Klux Klan, and in 1944 he had won another medal for his stories about the black market in meat, for which he posed as a butcher. Other exploits included working as a coal miner and as an attendant in several state mental hospitals in Pennsylvania. Clearly a man accustomed to unconventional but effective ways of delving into corruption and injustice, Sprigle made no claims to be impartial and evenhanded. In the first chapter of his book *In the Land of Jim Crow* he wrote: "Let me make clear at the start, too, that this is no complete and impartial survey of the race problem in the South. This is the story of a newspaperman who lived as a Negro in the South and didn't like it. . . . How can you correct evil until you find it? I deliberately sought the evil and the barbarous aspects of the white South's treatment of the Negro. It is of that only that I write."[5]

Although Sprigle wrote in the accessible style of a newspaper journalist, flavoring his accounts with brisk, vivid descriptions and organizing his material in short, easily digestible sections, his book does not appear to have caused the sensation that Griffin's was to produce later. This may have been because Sprigle was based in the North and because he was able to continue his life as a successful journalist working on a range of other unrelated issues. Southerners were, after all, used to northerners condemning their racism and segregationist ways from on high; it was not like one of their own had turned on them and made them look shockingly inhuman to the outside world. Also, during the eleven years that separated the two accounts, the mood in the South had changed dramatically, and the Civil Rights movement was under way by 1960. *In the Land of Jim Crow* may well have fallen on deafer ears because of the timing and because it was, for all its evidence of the evil of racism, less sensational and less ambitious than *Black Like Me*. In a foreword to Sprigle's book, Margaret Halsey describes it as "an unexpected glimpse into a mirror we had forgotten was there." She concludes with the following passage: "There are only two possible solutions to the problem of human relationships between white and non-white Americans. One is the ethical solution and the other is the unethical solution. It is too soon to be comfortably sure, as yet, in which direction the country will move, but there have been signs of late that the forces of progress are pulling ahead. If they are, some credit is certainly due to those American journalists who apply their techniques directly and without evasion to the American scene."

In the preface to *Black Like Me*, Griffin's language is filled with greater urgency than Halsey's, and his aims are less parochial. He offers his story as a universal one: "of men who destroy the souls and bodies of other men (and in the process destroy themselves) for reasons neither really understands";[6] he dismisses the idea that his methodology might be used to negate his findings by saying, "We no longer have time to atomize principles and beg the question. We fill too many gutters while we argue unimportant questions and confuse issues." His deep interest in the psychological effects of racism are revealed in the final sentence of his brief introduction to his book: "It traces the changes that occur to heart and body and intelligence when a so-called first-class citizen is cast on to the junkheap of second-class citizenship." Even in the provocative title of his book, Griffin demonstrates a very personal involvement in his project, an approach that Sprigle disowns from the start, as this extract shows. An early chapter, entitled "The Problems of Passing," begins: "I might as well be honest about this expedition of mine into the South. I wasn't bent on any crusade. All I saw at first was the possibility of a darned good newspaper story. The whole idea was pretty dreamy and nebulous."[7]

One of the greatest differences between the two projects undoubtedly lay in the manner of "becoming" a Negro adopted by each man. It could be argued that Sprigle's was the more radical and potentially subversive, since he made little attempt to alter his appearance other than obtaining a respectable suntan, and even that he found unnecessary once he started his journey. This portion of his story forms an important element of his testimony, since it deals in a most matter-of-fact way with the relationship between "racial" identity and skin color. Sprigle explains how he first thought that "the task of transforming myself into a working model of a Negro would be a comparatively easy one. . . . Remember all those romances you've read in which the hero disguises himself as a Hindu or Arab or one of the darker-skinned races?"

The intrepid journalist describes in detail how he was unable to get rid of his "white hide" without risking severe discomfort and even instant death. "Six months' searching and experimenting, the expenditure of a couple of square feet of skin (mine) and a couple of hundred dollars (my publisher's) and I was no nearer to getting away from the white race than I was the day I started." Somehow—he doesn't say—he came to realize that for his mission to succeed he had to gain the trust of blacks and that the best way to achieve this was to obtain a companion who could guide him through "every phase of the black world of the South." He contacted Walter White, the blue-eyed director of the National Association for the Advancement of Colored People, who had documented experience of passing as a white man in the South and knew exactly what it took to be identified or recognized as black. White provided Sprigle with a perfect companion who accompanied him on his four-week project, and all Sprigle had to change was his name. Nevertheless, the shock of moving across the color line was like being dropped on the moon, as Sprigle discovered when he "quit being white, and free, and an American citizen" as he took the Jim Crow Pullman car from Washington to Atlanta in his new guise as Brother Crawford. Only twice was his cover almost blown: once when he talked too much and another time when he walked through the wrong door.

This process of crossing over, of self-consciously seeking recognition as a member of another species of human being, provides the most problematic and contradictory section of this discussion, and I will return to it in more detail later. It is worth spending a little more time on Sprigle's account simply because, of all the case studies, he seems to have the least invested in self-discovery or in learning to see the situation differently. Yet, for all his hard-boiled reporter's insouciance, he was quick to recognize and condemn the "burden of the Jim Crow system, with its iniquitous pattern of oppression and cruelty and discrimination." When the time came for him to end his project and travel back to the North to recover his status as a white man, he registered the impact of his temporary transformation deep down in his new way of thinking: "We rolled out of Kentucky across that old Ohio River bridge into Cincinnati—into safety and freedom and peace. Again I was free, with all the rights of an American citizen. Again I was—no, not white. Not yet. It wasn't that easy. Down south my friends had done too good a job of making me into a Negro."[8] Sprigle's new consciousness kept him from entering a "luxurious restaurant with fancy food and prices and service and attention." He just could not bring himself to go in, choosing instead to find a lunch counter. It almost kept him from entering his hotel through the front door. Fearing that he might be wrongly identified, he decided to go around the block to telephone for a room in his real name, emphasizing the fact that he was a journalist from an important Pittsburgh newspaper.

In his final chapter Sprigle reflects on his own behavior as a Negro, acknowledging that his story could have been more sensational if he had returned with bruises and bullet holes inflicted by trigger-happy white supremacists. "I could have gathered them, all right. Just by getting 'fresh' at the right time and place. But for me, no role as hero. I took my tales of brutality and oppression and murder at first hand. And was mighty glad to do so." But he concedes that if he were to become a Negro for longer than four weeks, for the rest of his life even, there was one thing to which he could never harden himself, and that was the "casual way" that his new friends referred to slavery. Sprigle does not elucidate this point, though he implies that he found it shocking to be reminded that the barbarism of slavery in the South was so recent.

Sprigle ends his book with a "last word" from a Negro—"even though a temporary one"—to the "white man" in the South. This passage has a curious tone that I found hard to interpret. His message begins: "Don't be concerned about the Negro's seeking to rise to the status of manhood and American citizenship. Don't worry about him defiling either your hotels or restaurants or, above all, your race." He goes on to say that blacks of all classes whom he met expressed the opinion that they wanted as little contact with the "white world" as possible. At this point Sprigle takes advantage of his new double consciousness and explains the things that he learned to want as a Negro. He introduces his demands—or rather requests—almost apologetically, adding that they would not even dent white supremacy if granted. Just stop shooting at us, give us the vote, and let our children have the same education as yours. His last line reads: "We might even be of service to you."

The evidence provided in his book was a damning indictment of a system that dehumanized all its participants, organized under chapter headings such as "White Hospitals and Black Deaths"; "Fear Walks with Me"; "Life, Liberty and the Pursuit of Justice"; and "Pastoral in Blood." Sprigle had investigated lynching; individual and systematic acts of terror and intimidation; the exclusion of black children from schools; and the basic denial of services to blacks wherever possible (restrooms, eating places, hotels); he had documented his own shock, disbelief, and anger at his discoveries, both first- and secondhand. In a chapter entitled "Voters Don't Kill Easy" he wrote:

> Strangely enough, the Negro in the South doesn't hate the white man. It could well be that my four weeks in the Deep South fall grievously short in equipping me as an authority on the subject. But I'll still stand on my opinion. . . . Remember that I talked at length with the real leaders of the Negro. . . . I wasn't a white man interviewing them, remember, I was a Negro from the North, a friend of Walter White, executive secretary of the NAACP. . . . Frankly, why the Negro doesn't hate the Southern white is a mystery to me. Give me another couple of months, Jim Crowing it in the South—forever alert never to bump or jostle a white man—careful always to "sir" even the most bedraggled specimens of the master race—scared to death I might encounter a pistol-totin', trigger-happy, drunken deputy sheriff or a hysterical white woman—and I'm pretty sure I'd be hating the whole damn white race.[9]

In this passage Sprigle is honest about the distance between his response to white supremacy and the views expressed by his informants. Without wanting to lose his cover, he probed the men he met for their views on reform. He discovered that, despite the fact that the white man was always in a position to kill a black person in cold blood with impunity, black people's hatred was directed at the mechanisms that deprived them of their citizenship rather than at whites themselves. Above all, they wanted the right to vote without fearing that the successful black candidate was in danger of being shot.

The vote and adequate education for their children. These are the demands that Sprigle reiterates, in his own voice, at the end of his book. He ducks the question of how it could be possible to recognize some aspects of equality without overthrowing the whole basis of white supremacy, the legacy of slavery, on which it rested. If one read the last chapter first, one might miss the impatient sarcasm that is surely there between the lines, positively oozing from that final remark about being of service to the white man. Perhaps this is too generous to Sprigle, who was after all only doing his job and had, by the time he published the book, resumed his life in Pittsburgh, where he might have regarded the whole adventure in the South as a nightmare. The point is that, although *In the Land of Jim Crow* might exist as an interesting—though largely forgotten—historical document, it does not, on its own, reveal anything new either about the black experience of southern racism or about white supremacy. When the book was published in 1949, a wide variety of voices had testified to the barbarity of white supremacy and its effects on Americans, particularly in the South: Richard Wright's *Native Son* (1940), Gunnar Myrdal's *An American Dilemma* (1944), and Lillian Smith's *Killers of the Dream* (1949) are just three examples of different genres and voices available to a wider public. The reason for paying attention to Sprigle's work is that it needs to be read as part of a dramatic tradition of investigating the truth about white supremacy, a tradition that is marked by its unorthodox and unconventional methodology. This point will hopefully become clearer as I move on to introduce some other protagonists.

Black Like Me

John Howard Griffin needs little introduction, since his most famous book, *Black Like Me,* has enjoyed worldwide readership since it was first published in 1961, after a series of articles appeared in *Sepia* magazine. He had been asked to carry out the study of suicide rates that was to precipitate his *Black Like Me* project because he had established a reputation as a public speaker who knew about racism—he was also the author of two novels and an established writer of nonfiction. He invariably attributed his special interest in "race" to the fact that he had grown up as a boy in Texas. In *A Time to Be Human,* his diatribe against racism published almost twenty years later, he recalls his earliest consciousness of black people and his family's response to the idea of difference and discrimination. At the age of fifteen he left home to attend a school in France, where he was exposed to a different regime of race-thinking that began to challenge his childhood assumptions. Stranded in France in 1939 when war broke out, he became involved in the French resistance movement, helping to move Jewish children to safehouses when their parents were in danger of being shipped off to Nazi camps. This experience affected him deeply for the rest of his life, and he would often compare the German persecution of the Jews and the complicity of the French collaborators with the racism of his own country. It is also important to note that Griffin was an intensely spiritual man, drawn from an early age to the philosophy and theology of Catholicism, and throughout his life he regularly sought retreat in monastic life and solitary confinement. A ten-year period of blindness following a war injury gave him further insights into ideologies of racism and white supremacy, which became a preoccupation for the rest of his life. In his journal Griffin wrote that this combination of "past experiences, my religious encounter and academic studies came together with the personal experience of blindness, and the evil of racial discrimination was revealed by all of that in such a way that struck me a tremendous blow."[10] First, he came to realize the limitations of relying on physical eyesight, since a blind man "can only see the heart and intelligence of a man, and nothing in these things indicates in the slightest whether a man is white or black, but only whether he is good or bad, wise or foolish."[11] Added to this, Griffin had to contend with his new status as an object of pity; as a sightless man he was considered to be inferior and less than human.

Following his disastrous sociological research on black suicide rates, Griffin decided to take literally his respondents' challenge: to wake up in a black man's skin. From November 7 to December 14, 1959, he posed as a black man in the South, having darkened his skin through medication and staining. His book includes a detailed account of this experience, with a section on the aftermath of his experiment when his project received national publicity, and an epilogue added in 1976. A film was later made with the same title. Griffin became an activist during the Civil Rights movement, working as a writer, lecturer, and media commentator. He died in 1980.

Soul Sister

Grace Halsell wrote *Soul Sister* in 1969. For her "experiment" she turned her skin dark through medication and extensive sunbathing. She then lived and worked in Harlem and the South over a period of six months. In her account she explains how she was inspired to make her journey after reading *Black Like Me,* which she did not even hear about until 1968. Halsell was a journalist who had traveled widely in Asia and South America before taking up her post in the White House as a presidential aide. During the Vietnam War she became worried about her own ignorance of black people in the United States. She describes how she read *Black Like Me* and arranged to meet Griffin, who came from Fort Worth, Texas, as did she. As she read Griffin's book, she heard him talking to her "like an inner voice, calm, suggestive. 'I could do that . . . I could be black.'" In another book, published in 1986, she recalls how her Christian education had inspired her to become a "sojourner" in foreign lands, a pastime that she continued to enjoy long after *Soul Sister.* In this later book Halsell explains that her distress at witnessing President Johnson's disastrous handling of the Vietnam War caused her to ask questions: "Why, I kept asking, do we not see Vietnamese as people? How can I say to President Johnson and others, They are real—as real as you and me? Then I asked myself Were there other groups of people we did not see? As a white, growing up in Texas, I had never really seen black people. Was their being invisible the racism within me?"[12]

At the beginning of *Soul Sister,* Halsell speaks several times of her motives, sometimes asking herself why she was so set on the project: "Was this determination founded on an unconscious guilt feeling? Did it spring from my curiosity as a trained reporter who wants to find out the true facts at first hand? Why was I really going to do it? My emotions answered: I need this experience."[13] Although Halsell does not claim to be pursuing a fact-finding mission in her attempts to answer these questions, she does come to a very clear conclusion, which she reiterates several times toward the end of *Soul Sister:* "What did I learn? I learned only what we always forget: that there is no certitude, that we 'know' little beyond the fact that life is pain and life is a burden, and often insupportable for those who believe they can walk or live alone."[14] Halsell dedicated *Soul Sister* to her mother: "She knows suffering can bring understanding; that understanding frees one to love—without limits."

Halsell went on to work with Charles Evers (who endorsed her temporary transformation) on his autobiography, and wrote a book on interracial sex called *Black/White Sex.* In 1973 she published the results of another investigative project in which she adopted the identity of a Navajo woman in order to see from an "Indian" point of view what life would be like in a middle-class white environment. More recently she produced a book called *Prophecy and Politics* about the links between Israel and the U.S. Christian Right.[15]

Lowest of the Low

The Lowest of the Low, an account of Gunter Walraff's research, was published in German in 1985 and translated into English in 1988. He is a respected German left-wing journalist who had also infiltrated the Right in Germany. For his research into German racism he posed as Ali, a Turkish immigrant, for two years. His account is interspersed with extracts from the media, documentary evidence, and transcripts of interviews. The chapters are organized by his investigations into different kinds of labor and institutions—including his attempts to get baptized, to organize his own funeral, and to lead one of his employers into hiring illegal immigrants to carry out a highly dangerous job. The book is dedicated to Turkish friends. Over two million copies were sold in Europe by 1988, and an award-winning film was made of the book.

Gunter Walraff begins *The Lowest of the Low* by writing reflexively about his motives in deceiving people:

My disguise meant that people told me directly and honestly what they thought of me. By playing the innocent I became more cunning, and I was able to experience a life which gave me a new insight into the narrow-mindedness and coldness of a society which believes itself to be so clever, confident, perfect and fair. I was the fool to whom the truth is told.

Of course, I was not really a Turk. But one must disguise oneself in order to unmask society; one must deceive and dissimulate in order to find out the truth.[16]

Walraff's book ends with a dramatic plot in which he and several others "in the know" lay a trap for his employer, the industrialist Adler. The plan was to aid and abet Adler in recruiting several Turkish workers with uncertain status to carry out a lethally dangerous job at a nuclear power station. Walraff, who had been promoted to be Adler's chauffeur and chief procurer of illegal immigrants, set up the contract and arranged for the plan to fail at the crucial moment. Adler's enthusiasm for the project, his cynicism, and his total lack of sentiment for the individuals involved are carefully documented in chilling detail. However, the final paragraph of Walraff's book begs the reader not to make a monster out of him: "If this investigation has contributed to alerting the sensitivity of the public and the media to these secret worlds, then our efforts have been worthwhile. Adler isn't the real target here. His criminal energy and imagination are not above average. . . . He is one of many thousands who help to maintain and benefit from a system of boundless exploitation of, and disregard, for human beings."[17]

As Walraff explains at the start of the book, he is able to visualize the life of immigrants in West Germany: "The limitations on the right to political asylum, the racism, the increasing ghettoization—I knew about it but I had never experienced it." By the end of his experience of living as a Turkish man he is able know *what* has to be endured by the immigrant, which he has investigated and documented, but makes no claims as to *how* he managed to cope with "the daily humiliations, the hostility and the hate." The truth that he discovers in the course of his transformation is far worse than he could have imagined: what makes it so terrifying is that "a bit of apartheid" is "happening right here among us—in our *democracy*."

My Enemy, My Self

My Enemy, My Self, written by Yoram Binur, was published in 1989. Binur was an Israeli journalist specializing in Arab issues for a weekly paper.

The idea to transform himself into a Palestinian stemmed from his being constantly mistaken for an Arab, since he could speak Arabic fluently. He spent some time practicing and then embarked on a more serious "posing project" for six months. He took the official identity of a dead Jordanian soldier that fell into his hands a few months earlier, but used the different name of Fat'hi, by which he was known among Arab acquaintances, who had trouble pronouncing his Hebrew name. His book includes a confessional but not self-pitying account of his time in military service, enforcing curfews and controlling Palestinians, and is dedicated to "a better understanding among the Israelis and Palestinians." The book jacket comments that it echoes Griffin's *Black Like Me*.

In Binur's account there are traces of cynicism, which are noticeably absent from the others. Perhaps there is something in the opportunistic way that he devises his subterfuge after already being mistaken for an Arab in the course of his work that suggests a different approach. His political motives are harder to ascertain and his conclusions more guarded. Yet there is also something slightly refreshing in the way he straightforwardly refers to himself as an "impostor" and to his work as a "posing project." As the front cover of his book demands: "Why (on earth) would an Israeli Jew pose as an Arab? It was the best way I knew to get inside the mind of a Palestinian. . . . " Although this is a quote from the book, it was not really Binur's chief intention to infiltrate the Palestinian mind. In his introduction he describes how his original plan was to "offer a fresh perspective on our relationship with the Palestinians" by posing as a Palestinian and recording his own feelings as well as the reactions of other people toward him. In his final chapter he repeats his original intention to "look for the personal dimension, which is lacking in so many learned articles that analyze the Arab-Israeli conflict." Instead of drawing any far-reaching conclusions about the nature of this conflict, with which he was already familiar as a journalist, he wrote explicitly about the value of the experience for his own understanding:

> Posing was a tactic that enabled me to see the conflict in a different perspective and to experience it with a greater intensity. As an impostor, I was able to understand, for the first time, what it means for a man to feel afraid and insecure inside his own home when a military patrol passes outside his window. I had heard Palestinians tell of such things many times, and I had always regarded it as a slightly wearisome example that they were prone to give in order to embellish their arguments against the occupation.

But when I was gripped by that paralyzing fear myself, when I felt it in my guts, I grasped a dimension in their lives in a concrete fashion, in a way that I never really could as an Israeli journalist, however understanding I was of their situation. It wasn't a question of discovering new facts, but of discovering what it meant to feel the facts.[18]

To Learn the Truth

This discussion will focus on the four texts produced by Griffin, Halsell, Walraff, and Binur, though it will be embellished, where possible, by details from other examples of their work that I have been able to find. In that sense this chapter is both about the freestanding texts and about the need to place them within the context of the writers' lives and other related projects. These are not stories about passing in any conventional sense: there is no triangular theater of the dupe, in-group, and spectator described by Amy Robinson, for example.[19] The nature of these experiments demanded that the performances be at least as convincing to the people who considered themselves white (whether that be American, German, or Jewish Israeli) as they were to those whom the authors were trying to impersonate. It could almost be said that they were more anxious about how they looked to "their own kind," so to speak, in order to be passed by as not white. I shall return to this point later. Nor do they constitute some kind of racial drag or flamboyant cross-dressing— we see no playful distinction made between the phenotypic "race" of each performer and his or her assumed racial identity. In fact, their acts do not demand that the reader share the joke that, as Ralph Ellison pointed out, "always lies between appearance and reality, between the discontinuity of social tradition and the sense of the past that clings to the mind" in America or elsewhere.[20] There are few jokes indeed, even though whites are continually "duped," along with many of the victims of the oppression that is being described. If there are any figures of fun, the most likely candidates are the authors themselves. Both Griffin and Halsell, and particularly the latter, laid themselves open to mockery and derision among U.S. audiences accustomed to viewing any act of blackface with suspicion. Walraff and Binur, on the other hand, seem to have escaped such scrutiny—either because they were professional investigative journalists who used a range of different techniques to procure their material or because they took less drastic measures to change their appearance.

Collectively these books begin to describe the intricate contours of societies that are systematically structured by "race" and class and gen-der. The vantage points from which the authors speak are unique in that they invariably involve a self-conscious double take; in addition to learning to feel the impact of that outrageously unfair and cruel system, they are in a position to acknowledge their part in sustaining it in their previous lives. By changing their physical appearance they might merely cross the street or move across town to gain entry into what they first experience as a totally different world, but they are each at times pain-fully aware of what they bring with them that forces them to feel out of place. There are few illusions that they can ever become or be black, or Arab, or Turkish, or even hope to represent what they imagine it is "re-ally" like for those who inescapably are. What is more precious to these individuals is that they come to feel the spiritual, emotional, and physi-cal impressions of the hatred that they witness in their new daily lives: a hatred that they suspected of being there, but that they could not see, feel, or know before.

These may sound like great claims for escapades that were simulta-neously based on deceit and driven by arrogance, naiveté, and the reck-less pursuit of self-knowledge. By reading them together and seeing them as part of a newly invented tradition I am not trying to advocate their methodology as ideal or present them as antiracist heroes and her-oines. Nor am I denying the importance of viewing each book separately within its own historical and geographical context to appreciate the im-pact that it might have had when it was first published. Eric Lott, for example, has placed *Black Like Me* firmly in a tradition of American min-strelsy, arguing that "Griffin's narrative is only one relatively recent ex-ample of a blackface tradition that is fundamentally concerned with a forbidden 'lapse into familiarity' between black and white men."[21]

For Lott, Griffin's "earnest antisegregationist politics" is connected to the less noble impulse behind blackface minstrelsy to try on the accents of "blackness." As Lott has demonstrated powerfully and consistently in *Of Love and Theft,* one of the problems with blackface, whatever the mo-tives of the performer, is that it "reifies and at the same time trespasses on the boundaries of 'race.'" This doubleness, Lott continues, is "highly indicative of the shape of American whiteness." *Black Like Me* exempli-fies how the construction and reproduction of white American man-hood depend on the existence of "a racial other against which it defines itself and which to a very great extent it takes up into itself as one of its own constituent elements."[22]

Griffin's book is indeed highly troubling when it is held up to scru-tiny, not least because it was written almost forty years ago, at the dawn of the Civil Rights movement and before feminism. But I think it is important not to underestimate the huge readership that the book has enjoyed since it was published. How do we account for its audience of over five million people worldwide, and how can the effect of a book like that be measured among more than a generation of earnest antisegregationists both inside and outside America? The key word here is "earnest," for the power of the book lies largely in the desire it expresses to break down the brutal structures of racial supremacy, to demonstrate that we are all alike under the skin. It is also important to appreciate the fact that Griffin actually set out to chart the shape of American whiteness in the first place. He may have become morbidly fascinated with the fantasy of becoming a black man, but his aim, as stated in his original account and in the updated epilogue, was "to learn the truth": "Though we lived side by side throughout the South, communication between the two races had simply ceased to exist. Neither really knew what went on with those of the other race. The Southern Negro will not tell the white man the truth. He long ago learned that if he speaks a truth unpleasing to the white, the white will make life miserable for him."[23]

Almost twenty years later, reflecting on the circumstances and the reasoning that had motivated him to carry out this project, Griffin expanded on his original formulation:

> People often ask me what was my motive, my "real motive" for doing this experiment in blackness. I think it finally boiled down to the fact that I had three children. I knew without any doubt that my own formation, no matter how benevolent, had filled me with prejudices at deep levels that had probably handicapped me for life. . . . And I did not want my children, or the children of any person, white or black or any other color, to grow up in a climate of permissive suppression of fellow beings if I could do anything to prevent it. In other words, my deepest motive was simply to preserve my children and the children of others from the dehumanizing poison of racism.[24]

Unnatural Days

I only had to imagine myself black and then, for the first time, I saw myself white!
— GRACE HALSELL

So far I have tried to emphasize the common themes that tie these books together, but in doing so I do not want to overlook the idiosyncrasies of each story that also make them profoundly dissimilar.

Soul Sister is unlike the others in that it deals with the experience of a woman, and although Halsell makes no reference to feminism, she is sensitive to the difference that gender makes. The male writers, on the other hand, live mainly in a world of men in which woman are marginal.

It is important, too, to pay attention to the particularities of time and space out of which they emerged. Griffin and Halsell together spanned the Civil Rights movement; they investigated the American South—although in Halsell's case Harlem, too; they took dubious drugs to make their skins tan more quickly and intensively and used stain to hasten the process. Halsell acquired dark contact lenses, which she selected from a row of disembodied glass eyes; Griffin seemed to wear sunglasses constantly, possibly because his sight was still impaired. Both kept their own names and claimed to speak their own language, as though their dark skin alone was enough evidence to show that they were black (and their desire to go as dark as possible a sign of their lack of confidence about how to act black as well).

Walraff and Binur, although crossing similarly intractable lines of "race" and culture, did not have to take any medication to change their skin color, but instead paid close attention to clothing and many subtle details of outward appearance. Both had to speak and learn to think and react in a different language—Walraff used a kind of made-up "foreigner's German" that no one bothered to scrutinize, while Binur's life depended on his command of spoken Arabic. Walraff ordered customized dark contact lenses that he could wear day and night, prompting his optician to remark: "Now you have the penetrating gaze of a southerner." Binur took pleasure in picking out his new wardrobe and some of the "typical paraphernalia" of a typical Arab laborer, such as a cheap plastic shopping basket used by elderly Israeli housewives, like his own mother, and by Palestinian workers. The right newspapers, cigarettes, a red keffiyeh (the traditional Arab headdress), and an unshaven face helped to complete the disguise. Binur also made a note of Palestinian body language: how to hold a cup of tea, how to cross his legs when riding in a taxi or bus.

These different technologies of transformation are straight out of acting school, but the energy with which these impostors had to act out their roles depended partly on how they felt they looked from the outside. And to "see" themselves from without they had two options: to confront themselves in a mirror and to test the disguise in public. It is no coincidence that each protagonist felt compelled to carry out a kind of dress rehearsal, nor is it any surprise that Binur and Walraff omit any

mention of how they reacted to seeing themselves in disguise, since neither of them was obliged to look startlingly different. Binur makes a
powerful point at the end of his book when he describes the reactions
of his Jewish audience once his project had been publicized. Disappointed that so many professed greater curiosity about how he "did it"
rather than in the Palestinians themselves, he wrote: "My appearance
isn't Middle Eastern, and a native speaker of Arabic would have been
able to tell that I wasn't an Arab myself had we discussed issues that
required a measure of sophistication. . . . One of the things I learned was
that as long as I didn't upset people's expectations it was very easy to
mislead them. The risk of being discovered was much smaller when I
was posing as an Arab among Jews. . . . But then, why should a Jew sus-
pect an Arab of being a Jewish impostor?"[25]

One of the aspects of his story that differentiates it from the others is
the degree of intense danger he risked among both groups. While
Halsell, Griffin, and Walraff were aware of retributions from the racists
they were exposing, Binur also had to contend with the workings of the
Israeli secret service and the Palestinians' hatred of any kind of collabo-
rator. He knew that any mispronunciation, any slip of the tongue, would
cause certain death with no questions asked. Yet, as he explains, "I found
it relatively easy to establish myself as an Arab among them." The codes
that authenticated Arab identity were not so much visual as cultural.
Although the details of his outward appearance were important, it was
his grasp of particular ritual greetings and etiquette that enabled him to
be accepted.[26]

For Griffin and Halsell the physical change was much more profound,
and therefore disturbing, although they describe the transformation in
quite different tones of voice. Both accounts describe the search for medical expertise and advice as well as the process itself, but Halsell's is much
more detailed: she is enchanted and intrigued by her changing looks
and by how people respond to her as her skin darkens beyond a decent
tan. Determined to go for black rather than red or yellow, she swallows
her first tablet as if it was giving her new life itself: "That night I could
not sleep. The pill, in my imagination, was—in its entirety—sitting inside my stomach and almost had eyes and ears and was observing me! I
reached to feel it there, as a pregnant woman would feel the seed within
her. I felt (or imagined that I felt) the change that would occur within
me because of the change that would be made outside of me."[27]

The most shocking and distressing moment for Halsell comes when
she sees herself in the mirror after a week at the beach working on her
tan in idyllic surroundings. On the seventh day she stands before the

glass to inspect her creation, but instead of finding "precious, beautiful, black skin," she is horrified to find she has no face at all: "As I sit looking at that face with pale, accusing eyes—self-indicted as miserable, ugly, unloving, and unlovable, not myself, not another, a nobody, a nothing—the eyes condemn me, no longer able to see the person I have destroyed, only this unraveled, molting monster I have created." Before she is reassured by her black doctor that she is merely suffering from severe peeling caused by too much exposure to the sun, she is ready to confess that she has been seduced by a feminine weakness that already connects her to black women in an almost mystical sense: "I, black woman, white woman—human, female—ache. I am too alone! I envelop myself in a blanket of self-pity. I am ravaged by a sense of great loss—and weakness. I feel I have betrayed the pledge that women make: to keep our secrets, our understanding of deep mysteries, nobly and undefiled—because we know pain and we welcome pain."

Halsell uses the device of the prologue and the epilogue to articulate her altered sense of self after she emerged from her experience. She begins her book with an account of her recurring nightmare, demanding that the reader share her inner torment and make the journey with her:

> Night after night I have this dream—it is a busy street in mid-Manhattan and strong men in steel hats drill their power tools into the earth to lay more ducts and more sewers to create a greater New York. Buses and taxis screech and whirl; the subway grinds and hurtles; and thousands of people scurry, guided by lights, bells, signals: "Follow the green arrow," "Follow the red arrow." I am one of a mass of men, moving relentlessly, ceaselessly. And I pass a manhole and see the face of a child, a doll's face, large, white, round; and doll's eyes that look but see nothing. And I scream, "It is a child!" I reach but realize the doll-child is beyond my grasp, and the body floats past and returns in a liquid casing, appearing caught up in some underground eddy.
>
> The people run faster, and I scream "Help! Police!," and three policemen, strong and rough, bear down on me, heedless of the child and of my pleas for the child. They arrest me. I shriek, plead with them but I am helpless, and they carry me away to their jail. . . . [28]

Halsell interprets this dream as an index of the mental turmoil caused by the terror and helplessness that she felt as a result of her transformation. It is striking that she shares this representation of herself as a victim within this drama, forcibly prevented by "strong and rough" men from doing what she thinks is right and struggling to go against the tide of what might be called progress. It is less clear how we might read the symbolism of the infantilized white femininity that floats passively, but fatally, beyond her grasp. From her prologue it would seem that the most profoundly disturbing experience of all was the moment of her reentry into the "white" world of her Washington apartment. At the stroke of midnight she collapsed into uncontrollable tears as soon as she opened her door. But this was not distress that came from dejection or a loathing of familiar surroundings: she describes how the moment of unbearable grief erupted as she tried to cling to her perception of herself as a black woman, seeing herself in that instant standing on the threshold of a white woman's home, overwhelmed by the sense of comfort and security that engulfed her as soon as she saw her familiar possessions again. In this state she passed "unnatural days," feeling "neither black nor white, but a recluse," until rescued by her friend Roscoe, the black maintenance man.

At the end of her book, having taken the time to explain how she had reached this state, Halsell seems to have achieved a state of inner peace that allows her to connect all the different selves that she has known, including the privileged white woman who owns the comfortable apartment. She recalls how she was warned point blank by a black lawyer whom she met before she embarked on her journey that she would learn to hate her own people. She dismissed it at the time, but "had reason to remember it time and time again in the months that followed": "Yes, I can see the white people as 'my' people, but the Washington lawyer was wrong. I can hate them only if I hate myself. At one time I thought 'my people' were Koreans, another time Mexicans, and still another, Peruvians. I cannot escape the fact that I was born a Southern white. But nothing prevents me from feeling spiritually black—or brown, or yellow or red, for that matter. 'My people' abide in my heart and mind—and that is the reality that all people must come to know and recognize."[29]

Four years later, in her book called *Black/White Sex,* Halsell elaborated on this lesson as a way of introducing (and legitimating) her own viewpoint on the meaning of race in the United States. When a white neighbor, a respectable businessman, complained to her that he had been given hepatitis as a result of receiving some of that "black blood" in a recent transfusion, she told him, "I am black, you know."

> He looked stunned, momentarily, in the manner of one who has made a derogatory remark about the Jews and then discovered he

was talking to a Jew. I then told him that I had once turned my skin black with medication and sun and that I had lived for a time as a "black" woman, and found it an enriching experience. I argued that in this country, with so much mingling of the races, being black or white is a state of mind rather than a color. And I added that spiritually I felt I was black. He looked at me with increased interest, for when the white man says he hates niggers, he usually excludes the women.[30]

Throughout this book Halsell struggles to deal with the gaps that lie between minds and bodies. As we shall argue later, it was through encountering men's sexual desire that she came to articulate the theory that race was not so much in the eye, but in the imagination of the beholder. At the same time she is not able to explain how she is able to square her own inner sense of being "black" with the comforts and security afforded by the privilege of looking "white."[31]

Shadowy Realms

I felt the beginnings of great loneliness, not because I was a Negro, but because the man I had been, the self I knew, was hidden in the flesh of another.

— J O H N   H O W A R D   G R I F F I N

For John Howard Griffin, the trauma lay not in leaving his state of blackness, but in entering it. The initial change is more sudden than Halsell's and the shock of not recognizing himself acute. Not for him picnics on the beach, thrilling feelings of liberation, and the creative possibilities of a new life. Having decided to conduct the experiment, he confesses to being overwhelmed by loneliness tinged with a dread, and he is in a hurry to get going: "Outside my open window, frogs and crickets made the silence more profound. A chill breeze rustled dead leaves in the woods. It carried an odor of freshly turned dirt, drawing my attention to the fields where the tractor had only a few hours ago stopped plowing the earth. I sensed the radiance of it in the stillness, sensed the earthworms that burrowed back into the depths of the furrows, sensed the animals that wandered in the woods in search of nocturnal rut or food. I felt the beginning of loneliness, the terrible dread of what I had decided to do."[32]

It is tempting to interpret this passage as an expression of Griffin's associations of blackness with nature, animal instinct, and physical underground cultures, and so to catch his own unconscious racism that equates black with dark night, white with daylight. This theme runs through the whole book and, of course, is echoed in the title, which is taken from Langston Hughes's poem "Dream Variation." At the end of his experiment Griffin welcomes "the return to light and affection" symbolized by his reunion with his wife and children.[33] But night is when one is most alone with oneself, and Griffin's darkest moments occurred when the sun had gone down and he was tormented by rage and despair at the iniquities of racial injustice, prompted by the arrogant foolishness of white men and a new awareness of the mechanisms of power that deprived black men of their humanity. However, darkness provided Griffin with solace and refuge as well as nightmares.

One may speculate on whether his heightened sense of natural forces in the passage quoted was caused by an unease at going against nature, so to speak (by turning white into black), or by a genuine sense of panic felt by a man who had recently recovered his sight, a phenomenon that he later described as "more terrifying than the loss of it."[34] In Robert Bonazzi's biographical account Griffin speaks movingly of his fear that he might forget his sightless brothers and sisters as he left their world; as his sight slowly returned, he found the light almost unbearable, and he felt a "strange nostalgia" for the night: "And then to see all of this brightness, to see the scene change like a modulation in harmony. Is this what it is like to see? Is this the way other people see? If not, it is surely the way they were meant to."[35] To deny the impact of the extraordinary insights provided by a decade of sightlessness would be presumptuous on the part of those who have been able to take sight for granted. Yet since Griffin does not elaborate on his blindness in *Black Like Me,* the reader may also be forgiven for dismissing its significance.

Despite his conviction that he had no choice but to affect blackness to do his research, Griffin reconstructs his moment of resolve as the first of many personal crises that beset him during the course of the book. In doing so he situated himself firmly at the center of his project. His story becomes not his mission to discover "what was it like, really like, to be a black in the Deep South," as it is heralded on the front cover of the edition now in print, but rather an exploration of the shadowy realms in which blackness and whiteness coexisted in almost unfathomable relation to each other.

The section of the book in which Griffin describes his transformation contains some of its most notorious passages. Unlike Halsell, he does not monitor his metamorphosis in public. Only when he has shaved his head, has donned his costume and packed his duffel bag, and is ready to step out of the door does he steel himself to look in the mirror. When he encounters his own blackened face staring back at him, he is profoundly disturbed not to recognize himself. Expecting to see a sign of the John Griffin he knew, instead he encounters a hostile, unsympathetic stranger whose existence nullified his own. "The completeness of the transformation appalled me. It was unlike anything I had imagined. I became two men, the observing one and the one who panicked, who felt Negroid even into the depths of his entrails."

While Halsell was able to claim a mysterious sense of connection with black women through working on her face, Griffin was repelled by the intrusion of black masculinity into his own inner core. What he had attempted was so unnatural that, in making this change, he had killed part of himself: "I had tampered with the mystery of existence and I had lost the sense of my own being."[36] Lott has observed that Griffin's horror stems from his essentialist identification of dark skin with racial identity: "'White skin,' to play on Franz Fanon, is here obliterated by 'black mask'—a possibility only available to someone who imagines skin color in the way Griffin apparently does, as completely constitutive of identity and entirely divisive of the races."

But we see a contradiction here because Griffin's immediate estrangement from his mirror image suggests that he had not assumed that dark skin alone would make him black. As I have already suggested, his previous history of blindness had given him a fundamentally different relationship to the idea of visuality. In any case, he realized that he could never be black because he had not grown out of the same historical struggles against "the mark of blackness." Yet since the blackness of this man in the mirror reflected the outward signs of that history, he was truly a Negro. Now, when it was too late to turn back, Griffin recognized that it was impossible for a white man to retain the "powerful, life-preserving fixity" of whiteness, to borrow Lott's phrase, while taking on the outward appearance of a black man. Skin color was the visible sign of racial difference, but racial difference was more than skin color. The only alternative open to Griffin was to accept his own death, to renounce the freedoms he had known as a white man, and to step out of the door, "a man born old at midnight into a new life."

However, he had not gone very far before demonstrating the ludicrous impossibility of this solution. Before he was able to reach the door, the telephone rang, and he answered, marveling that the person on the other end of the line did not know that he was talking to a Negro. As soon as he walked out of the house into the darkness of his new world, he proved to his readers, if not to himself, that the old white John Griffin had refused to quit after all. Who else would be scrutinizing this newborn Negro with such acute sensitivity? How did he account for the "enormous self-consciousness," which caused him to recognize with "childlike naiveté" that the new Negro John Griffin's body perspired in exactly the same way as the old white one's?

As he became reassured that the people around him acknowledged him as black, he did indeed begin a new life, but not in quite the way that he had imagined—for the most striking aspect of this book, which connects *Black Like Me* to later versions, is the extraordinary position from which the author speaks. The self-consciousness that Griffin carried with him in the first hours and days of his journey provided him with a very particular lens through which to perceive and interpret his experiences. He had expected simply to change the color of his skin in order to test the reactions of his fellow Americans: a scientific project to determine "Were we racists or were we not?" His first discovery was the depth of that racism even within his own unconscious, a fact that he shared with his readers in order to emphasize his terror when confronted by his own ignorance and arrogance: "I prepared to walk into a life that appeared suddenly mysterious and frightening. With my decision to become a Negro I realized that I, a specialist in race issues, really knew nothing of the Negro's real problem."[37] Although his visceral panic soon evolved into a more manageable discomfort, it would be a mistake to spend time speculating on Griffin's newfound racial identity, which enabled him to continue and complete his experiment without becoming schizophrenic. To ask who he was and whether he was now black or white would be to perpetuate the ontological association of "race" with skin color. A better question, and one that applies to the three other "impostors" that we have been describing, would be simply this: where was he?

Ghoulish Conversations

[E]ach of us, helplessly and forever, contains the other—male in female, female in male, white in black and black in white. We are a part of each other. Many of my countrymen appear to find this fact exceedingly inconvenient and even unfair and so, very often, do I. But none of us can do anything about it.

— JAMES BALDWIN

The four protagonists that we have discussed represented their projects in different ways: as a quest for the "truth," a spiritual journey, a personal desire to feel and experience a different perspective. Yet there is an element of scientific inquiry running through each story. Griffin states explicitly in his epilogue, written in 1976: "The experiment . . . was undertaken to discover if America was involved in the practice of racism against black Americans."[38] Looking at their books in this light, it is appropriate to ask more theoretical questions about their methodology: were they attempting to achieve some form of objectivity by relocating themselves, and from where exactly were they gathering their data? Not being able to find a satisfactory term for the standpoints adopted by these very unscientific empiricists has not helped to improve the status of their research or of their discoveries. In their attempts to reposition themselves these individuals and others like them who have not achieved such notoriety have produced a disproportionate amount of what Zygmunt Bauman has, in another context, called proteophobia— "the apprehension and vexation related not to something or someone disquieting through otherness and unfamiliarity, but to something or someone that does not fit the structure of the orderly world, does not fall easily into any of the established categories, emits therefore contradictory signals as to proper conduct, and is behaviorally confusing; something or someone that in the result of all these foibles blurs borderlines that ought to be kept watertight and undermines the reassuringly monotonous, repetitive, and predictable nature of the life-world."[39]

These stories of men and women trying to relocate themselves in relation to "racial" and cultural categories also demand to be read from a feminist perspective. By this we do not mean simply that it is important to pay attention to the different experiences of gendered and "racialized" identity that each protagonist describes. In the process of acting out, or grasping for, an appropriate version of masculinity or femininity that is required for each situation the writers are also demonstrating both the continuity of these constructions across "race" and culture and their instability. In other words, by seeking to alter their "racial" identity they have also to reckon with the changing sense of themselves as men and women in order to interpret their new place in the world. This has the effect of both cutting them adrift from who they were before they began their journeys *and* providing them with a lifeline that allows them to feel safely human. The tension produced by this dilemma highlights the contrast between the material and psychological realities of racism and the contiguity of all socially constructed categories in a discursive chain. Gender helps to make sense and nonsense of "race" and vice versa.

To illustrate this and to demonstrate the importance of evaluating what we have referred to earlier as "a dramatic tradition in the history of truth-seeking about 'race,'" I have chosen incidents in which each author is forced to assess the utterly humiliating effects of a racism that is precipitated by his or her gendered, nonwhite bodies. We begin with Griffin's famous account of a journey through rural Mississippi.

As the heat of the day turned to the cool evening and he began walking along the road away from the coastal highway, he found to his surprise that he began to receive offers of rides from white men driving by. His surprise soon turned to disgust when he discovered that the motive for giving this black man a lift in the dark of night was to interrogate him about the sex life of the Negro. His motive in dwelling on this was to expose the total lack of self-respect or respectability with which these "decent-looking men and boys" approached him. Griffin was man enough to recognize that these "ghoulish conversations" bore little resemblance to the "bull sessions" that "men customarily have among themselves," which, "no matter how frank, have generally a robust tone that says: 'we are men: this (and here he does not specify what) is an enjoyable thing to do and to discuss, but it will never impugn the basic respect we give one another; it will never distort our humanity.'" The implication here is that a more natural and celebratory masculinity may be consolidated when the men involved in discussing sex (with women) are socially equal, but when white men try to engage black men about their sexual proclivities, the camaraderie turns into a relationship fraught with terror. Griffin accepts one such ride after another, finding himself back on the road each time he declines to take part in the pornographic exchange demanded of him. Finally, he climbs into a car driven by a young man who appreciates his articulate and scholarly tone. The conversation, however, drops to the same level as before:

> It became apparent that he was one of those young men who possess an impressive store of facts but no truths. This again would have no significance and would be unworthy of note except for one thing: I have talked with such men many times as a white and they never show the glow of prurience he revealed. The significance lay in the fact that my blackness and his concepts of what my blackness implied allowed him to expose himself in this manner. He saw the Negro as a different species. He saw me as something akin to an animal in that he felt no need to maintain his sense of human dignity, though certainly he would have denied this.[40]

On being asked to expose himself for the benefit of this young man's education, Griffin found himself unable to speak. In the silence that followed he regretted the reprimand that this implied, not wanting to judge the boy too cruelly for showing him "a side of his nature that was special to the night and the situation, a side rarely brought to light in his everyday living." When the young man tried to apologize for his curiosity, which had emerged out of a lack of opportunity to ask these questions, Griffin recounts the talking to that he gave him, once he had recovered his voice. The truth was that there was no basic difference in human nature between black and white: "We are all born blank." Environment and conditioning determined the character and behavior of men: "pigment has nothing to do with degrees of intelligence, talent or virtue."

Speaking for the black man, apparently in the voice of the black man, Griffin used this opportunity to deliver his verdict on the "truth" of racism. But humiliated beyond endurance by successive white men who failed to acknowledge his humanity, let alone his masculinity, he slipped back into being a "specialist on race issues," showing the youth a side of himself that he would not have revealed in daylight:

> Ignorance keeps them poor, and when a town-dwelling Negro is poor, he lives in the ghetto. His wife has to work usually, and this leaves the children without parental companionship. In such places, where all of man's time is spent just surviving, he rarely knows what it means to read a great book. He has grown up and now sees his children grow up in squalor. His wife usually earns more than he. He is thwarted in his need to be father-of-the-household. When he looks at his children and his home, he feels the guilt of not having given them something better. His only salvation is not to give a damn finally, or else he will fall into despair.[41]

Following this ride and this lecture, Griffin is rewarded when the next driver appears to be color-blind, and he is spared further humiliation. On reaching his destination, Griffin concludes this exhausting and wretched day by accepting the offer of an "elderly Negro man" to share his bed for the night. Overwhelmed by the poverty of the room, symbolized by the presence of only one book—appropriately a mystery—Griffin welcomes the chance to talk as a way of keeping his depression at bay. With no trace of irony or discomfort at betraying the old man's hospitality, he is soothed by the darkness of the night as it cloaks the differences between them. As the two men lie side by side, speaking and laughing about religion, family, and racism, he is obliged to listen to his companion's lecture on the need to love whites as God's children, "just like us." At last he is able to fall asleep reconnected to another human male with whom he can wholeheartedly agree: "None of it really makes any sense."[42]

Divided Self

Nothing in all my travels over the past two decades, nothing in my experiences, prepared me for going to the South as a black woman. The emotions I harbored belonged to two persons: a black woman and a white woman. I was cast in a twin, paradoxical role of oppressor and oppressed. I was a vessel of sorts for two personalities, two sets of eyes, two bodies. But the heaviest, and most unhappy, element in this strange container was a single human heart in conflict with itself.

— GRACE HALSELL

The episode chosen from *Soul Sister* represents an encounter that is absolutely integral to the history of white supremacy, and without which Grace Halsell's book would have had little redeeming value. While working as a maid for a white southern woman, she is nearly raped by the husband when he sneaks back home to have sex with her while his wife is out. This is not to suggest that Halsell sought this experience out of expediency, for she writes as though she was not expecting it to happen; in fact, she is brutally honest about her own fears before her experiment that it was the black man who was likely to be the rapist. But in fighting to defend herself from the lustful clutches of the white man, she comes to understand two truths: that her life would have been very different if she had been born a black woman and that "the problem is larger than black and white. It is man's inhumanity to man (and woman), always and everywhere."

Halsell prepares the scene for this incident by describing her attempts to find work in the South. Unlike Griffin, she stays with households who are aware of her project and who welcome her as an equal, but then she was driven by a different urge, to be accepted by blacks as a loved one. She, too, is invited to share a bed with her host, whom she refers to as Mrs. Tubbs, but this time there is no deceit or awkwardness, and she find immediate refuge and companionship with her, like a child in the arms of her mother. It is Mrs. Tubbs who counsels her on the white man's sexual abuse of black women and on the white woman's complicity in prolonging it. Halsell had already experienced two days as a domestic, working long hours for cold white women who refused to acknowledge her fatigue, her hunger, or her femininity. One had sat down with a cup of coffee and talked at great length of her husband's sexual inadequacy without offering her servant so much as a drink of water. While the woman spoke, "as if I am here and yet not here," Halsell reflected on the way that racism works by reducing a black people to a "non-person." "Even if I quote Newton's laws or Einstein's theories she will 'see' me only as she assumes me to be, a member of the caste system, a 'Nigra' not her equal and one who is supposed to do slave labor while a few like her are not supposed to work. And this system is this way because God ordained it that way."[43]

Any normal dialogue was out of the question because the woman had reduced her to a thing. But if she was not looking for any response from her silent listener, wondered Halsell, what did she get out of it? The healing powers of conversation were possible only if one gave and looked for compassionate understanding. But her employer's whiteness rendered her unable to conceive of the other person as a fellow human, let alone a woman.

Some time later, in another part of the South, Halsell is assigned more jobs as a maid by the state employment office. On entering the home of the Wheeler family, and noting the expensive luxury of the house and its furnishings, she observes that it has "an air of impermanence, with the kind of emotional kinship and stability you'll find in a hotel lobby."[44] Her employer drives off to work in the family store, leaving her to carry out her numerous chores on her own. The husband returns early, lures her to a bedroom by pretending to need her help, and grabs her in his arms, "muttering hoarsely about his need for 'black pussy.'" Halsell escapes by wrenching a large oil painting off the wall with a free hand, but as it falls on the man's head, she realizes that her life is in danger. The sound of the clock marking the hour brings him to his senses, and she is able to grab her coat and leave the house. Luckily she is able to get a ride back into town with a black family whose blackness allows her to breathe once more and whose sympathy, based on an instinctive understanding of the situation, makes Wheeler's "whitey world" momentarily bearable.

The dramatic tension of this episode is transformed by the reader's knowledge that the white man had been duped by Halsell's adopted identity. Although she was traumatized by the assault, she knew that it did not make her black. In struggling to articulate what she had learned from the experience, she chose to represent herself as being both black and white, knowing racism from both sides and temporarily unable to come to terms with the divided self that was produced.

Better to Play Dumb

Is it true that in Anatolia you can buy a woman for a goat?

— GERMAN FOREMAN IN *LOWEST OF THE LOW* (GUNTER WALRAFF)

Gunter Walraff's account of the way that German men attempt to humiliate southern migrant laborers by speaking about "their" women is written from the point of view of the almost detached observer. I say "almost" because Walraff's evident disgust at the behavior of a German coworker prompts Ali to "answer back," which unleashes a torrent of racist abuse. This in turn leads to a situation in which Ali is taken aside by a comrade and given advice on the best way to deal with these kind of experiences. Had Walraff not expressed a rather "white" response to the insult, he would not perhaps have uncovered the strategies adopted by Turkish and other migrant men to survive the daily negation of their masculinity.

The incident takes place while Ali is employed to carry out highly dangerous and difficult labor in a large steel mill.[45] During a break a German foreman comes over to his group and, identifying one of the workers as North African, starts to tell him of the wonderful holiday he enjoyed in Tunisia with his wife the previous summer. Yusuf, the worker, who is from Tunisia, is apparently pleased to hear positive interest expressed in his native country and invites the foreman and his wife to his home when they are next there on holiday. The foreman is pleased, but then continues: "You just have to get me a couple of addresses. You know what I mean. You've got such crazy women to fuck. It's incredible there. How much does it cost at the moment?"

The conversation, if it can be called that, goes on in the same vein: "those are hot women you've got there. Real wildcats. Once you've pulled the veil off, they're real goers. Don't you have a sister?" Yusuf tries to remain polite, reminding him that he would have his wife with him, but feeling completely humiliated in front of the other workers; eventually, he moves away with the excuse that he has to go to the toilet. The foreman then looks at Ali, asking him, "Is it true that in Anatolia you can buy a woman for a goat?" When Ali tries to turn away disinterestedly, he presses him: "It's true, isn't it? How did you get landed with your old dear?" At this Ali replies, "The Germans think always, money can buy everything. But the most beautiful things in the world not for money. That's why Germans always so poor with all their money."

This response produces an aggressive outburst from the foreman, denouncing Turkish "harem-ladies" as dirty. Afterward Yusuf takes Ali aside and tells him: "Is not good, that we learned and understand German. Always trouble. Better to play dumb." This was the strategy adopted in that workplace by many young Tunisian workers; they deliberately avoided learning any more German so that they could not understand the foreman and could always answer yes to anything he said without getting into trouble.

The form of racism involved in this exchange constructs the sexuality of the foreigners within a predictably recognizable orientalist discourse. The men themselves are not seen as highly sexed or threatening to the European, unlike black men, but "their" women are considered to be hot, wild, and cheap, once the tantalizing veil is removed. Alternatively, when these pleasures are denied, the women are referred to as dirty, covered in too much stuff, and little more than animals. At the same time, Walraff's representation of this incident implies that a central feature of the oppression of migrant laborers in Germany is the assertion of a particular kind of "white" German masculinity over a disempowered and humiliated "foreigner."

However, one of the problems with his interpretation of his whole experience posing as a Turk is that it renders the life of the migrant as overwhelmingly male, thus obscuring the existence of the migrant woman altogether. In his book Turkish and North African women either exist as fantasies in the minds of German coworkers or else occupy a significant but subservient place as wives and daughters of the "workers" who inhabit the world being brought to light by Walraff's investigations.

Extreme Humiliation

For them I simply didn't exist.

— YORAM BINUR

Yoram Binur is the only one of these four protagonists who actually experiences an intimate sexual relationship with "the enemy" during the course of his posing project. After being introduced to a Jewish Israeli woman called Miri, who is clearly attracted to him as a Palestinian, he decides to use the opportunity both to pursue his research and to satisfy his need for a woman, which he is convinced will cure his boredom and depression. The affair itself is enjoyable at first, but Binur confesses to feeling tired of his own deception when he realizes that his Arabness is a problem for Miri, as she has to conceal him from her Jewish friends. But he is also worried that he will talk in his sleep and give the game away, particularly after she recounts a dream in which she saw him come to visit her wearing a mask. He resolves that the best solution is to disappear, with no explanation: "It wasn't particularly pleasant to deceive someone as I was doing with Miri, but it was no use crying over spilt milk. At the time I wasn't capable of offering her much in the way of an explanation and to this day I don't believe that an explanation would have helped any."[46]

In order to analyze what purpose this episode serves in the book *My Enemy, My Self,* it is necessary to go back to an earlier incident that Binur himself describes as "the most degrading moment" in his entire "posing adventure." While working as cook and dishwasher in a small pub run by a Jewish Yemenite woman, in a kitchen measuring two by three meters, he begins to feel utterly sick of his role as Arab servant. One night, when he is clearing up dishes and preparing food for the next day, the owner's sister comes in with her boyfriend, and they start to kiss passionately, wedged in a corner between Binur and the refrigerator. Binur is surprised and lowers his eyes in embarrassment. As the couple's breathing becomes heavier, he decides to allow himself the pleasure of a quick peek. "Then a sort of trembling suddenly came over me. I realized that they had not meant to put on a peep show for my enjoyment. Those two were not the least bit concerned with what I saw or felt even when they were practically fucking under my nose. For them I simply didn't exist. I was invisible, a nonentity! It's difficult to describe the feeling of extreme humiliation which I experienced."[47]

Binur continues with his project for a short time after this, moving in with a group of Arab men who seem to lead bleak and joyless lives working long hours in restaurants and avoiding arrest by Israeli police at night. Disillusioned by his posing act and tired of being someone else, he decides to quit his job and have a break for a few days. Even that does not bring respite, since he is recognized as Fat'hi in the street and has to be on guard continually. Still more worrisome, he finds that he is beginning to forget who he really is: "It was important to go about as a Jew again for a few days; maybe I'd be able somehow to counteract the increasing domination of my Palestinian identity over my own personality."[48] Binur does not elaborate how his conflicting identities made him feel; instead he admits that he wanted to relieve his tension in the company of a woman. He reclaims his old car and returns to his home in Jerusalem, in the hope that his Jewishness will provide him with the tonic that he needs: "As an Arab impostor it hadn't been possible to form any sorts of relationships with women. Nor, I discovered was it even possible during my brief return to myself. I drowned my sorrows in the few bottles of brandy, vodka and arak which I had at home. For three days I didn't leave my bed except to go to the bathroom or to replenish my supply of drinks. The bottles piled up around me, together with cigarette butts, old newspapers, and other rubbish, creating a carpet of emptiness and despair."

A telephone call from his photographer friend, Yisrael, rouses Binur from his depression, and he is persuaded to try a different tack in his research, no doubt encouraged by the prospect of acting out a more pleasurable version of Arab masculinity. Dressing up in his fanciest clothes and relying now on the barest of props—cigarettes, a newspaper, and a keffiyeh—he goes out with his friend to hit the night spots in Tel Aviv. It is here that he meets Miri and suspects a mutual attraction. Pushed on by Yisrael, who has already been introduced as a hard man, Binur quickly sees his opportunity to try out an affair with an Israeli woman who thinks he is an Arab. But recognizing some of his own feelings as genuine, he is momentarily uncomfortable at the prospect of lying to someone he might care about. Still the opportunity is too good to miss, and Binur is able to carry on with his research, relieve his tension, and find himself again through asserting his masculinity.

It would be tempting to conclude here that it is through this action that he is able to come to terms with himself as being both Palestinian and Jewish. By the end of the book, when the Intifada has already begun and his project has to be terminated, he discovers that he does not have to even try and pose in order to be mistaken for a Palestinian. What is interesting about this revelation is that he appears to have forgotten that his ability to "pass" as an Arab had led him to carry out the project in the first place. What seems to have changed is his self-image: he now accepts that he will never be able to escape back to the comfort and security of his Jewish Israeli identity without remembering what it is like to live as an Arab, and, more than this, will have a sense of what connects them. It is largely through coming to terms with the various forms of masculinity demanded by his performance that he is able to move on to this realization. The intense humiliation that he suffered as an Arab caused him to lose track of himself; finding love in the arms of a woman (even under false pretenses) made him realize that, whether Jewish or Arab, he could prove to himself that he was still a man.

Detective Stories

You see, Deen, you have to keep pushing them back across that nigger line. Keep pushing! That's right. Kind of like it is with a dog. You have a dog, seems right human. More sense than most men. And you a lot rather be around that dog than anybody you ever knew. But he's still a dog. You don't forget that . . . God made the white race for a great purpose. Sometimes I've wondered what that purpose is. Between you and I, I've wondered—with all reverence—when God is going to divulge that purpose, for up to now, seems like we been marking time most ways, or making a mess of things. . . .

    — PREACHER DUNWOODIE IN *STRANGE FRUIT* (LILLIAN SMITH)

There are many ways of looking at these texts. We would argue that, if read together, and depending on the questions that are asked of them, they contribute to an understanding of how the multiple discourses of racism/whiteness/white supremacy can be invisible to those who are not able (for whatever reason) to "see" them. Significantly, they also reveal how the process of learning to "see" how those discourses operate must involve a measure of self-discovery and self-awareness that goes far beyond the capacity to recognize certain visual codes. This last point is a reminder that political vision is not limited to an ability to see, which, as these impostors show, is a highly unreliable form of evidence. Our aim has been to freeload off them to see what happens when individuals consciously, and dramatically, attempt to change their point of view through a literal transformation of their bodies and, in doing so, usefully evoke a "language of perspicuous contrast." The effort entailed in making profound connections between self and "other" within the confines of their own bodies suggests that theirs is no objective study of whiteness; nor are they engaged in pursuing a relativistic approach that seeks to explain or to understand whiteness on its own terms.

What are the implications of these inevitably troubling testimonies for a politics of active antiracism? As we have said, we are not advocating that we all go off and don disguises for the sake of subverting categories and investigating oppressive structures; nor are we making any general point about needing to feel or to experience oppression in order to understand or believe it. The hostile reaction that these texts have produced undeniably needs some attention. At what point does a healthy dislike of pretense and self-deceit become a reactionary form of proteophobia? How often do we hear ourselves repeat, when it suits us, "Let the White go to the White, and the Black to the Black?" as though it is possible to police the explorations, furtive or flamboyant, that individuals are moved to carry out in order to understand what race is or is not? The tactics adopted by the investigative journalist are not ideal; nor are they necessarily always successful in demystifying and denaturalizing what we are told repeatedly is immutable racial and cultural difference. Like bad detective stories, for the most part, they tell too much about the deficiencies of the main character, and the plot is always too overwhelming for the individual protagonists to resolve. But the books remain as historical documents of a particular genre of avowedly antiracist activism whose genealogy and influence deserve to be investigated. Both individually and together they offer the reader an extraordinary point of view, not of anything that can be called an authentic experience of being on the other side of the lethal divisions of color and culture, but of the callous, ignorant, and unfeeling actions of those who may not realize or care that they are helping to maintain a brutally unjust white supremacist system.

Les Back

4. WAGNER AND POWER CHORDS: SKINHEADISM, WHITE POWER MUSIC, AND THE INTERNET

The New York Police Department expressed concern yesterday at the number of Hairless Vagrant Youths hanging around underpasses, dark alleyways and latrines holding Personal Computers with the intent to Maim and Rob. One such unhirsute youth was questioned by reporters:

Our man in Brooklyn: So, Dave—can I call you Dave?

Dave: That's me name.

OMIB: So, Dave, you—hit people with this Personal Computer thing?

Dave: I do. Ram the screen down straight over their 'ead. IBM PC's work best, then the 'ole 'ead goes right down the cathode tube. Macintoshes only works on folks with small 'eads, like children and creationists.

OMIB: But . . . why don't you just . . . hit them. With your hands?

Dave: I'm a child of the Information Age.

This joke conjures up the image of a brainless skinhead for whom the only use for a computer is to inflict physical harm.[1] It is the quintessential stereotype of what a racist looks like—male, maniacal, the uncivilized "white-faced" minstrel of the antiracist imagination. But such lampoonery masks a deadly serious reality. The success of the White Power music scene today is in large part the product of the Information Age. The key exponents and distributors of White Power rock have utilized computer technologies to advertise, network, and market their products in unprecedented ways. In this sense the neo-Nazi moguls of the music scene are certainly the children of a digital era. Such current realities undermine any crude correspondence between ignorance or stupidity and racism or fascism. Technological advances such as the Internet have provided a means for contemporary fascists within Europe and the white diasporas of the New World to garner a digitally enhanced translocal culture in cyberspace and a truly international market. The Internet provides much more than just another publishing tool for propaganda, for it has offered an immediate and direct form of access to people with networked personal computers and a means to participate interactively in racist movements without face-to-face contact.

This chapter will explore the intersection between fascism and the technologies of a translocal whiteness. The focus here will be the emergence and growth of White Power pop music in the nineties. However, wider concerns about the ways in which the digital technologies and simulation are being utilized to articulate and embody racial absolutism within transnational networks will also be explored. Critical discussion of cyberculture has in the main focused on its potential to realize new forms of human subjectivity. Cyberspace illustrates the contemporary resonance of poststructuralist philosophy, which emphasizes *becoming* over *being*[2] and *performance* over *essence*.[3] Sherry Turkle has commented on how computer simulation demonstrated the relevance of French social theory:

> more than twenty years after meeting the ideas of Lacan, Foucault, Deleuze, and Guattari, I am meeting them again in my new life on the screen. But this time, the Gallic abstractions are more concrete. In my computer mediated world, the self is multiple, fluid, and constituted in interaction with machine connections, it is made and transformed by language; sexual congress is an exchange of signifiers; and understanding follows from navigation and tinkering rather than analysis. And in my machine generated world . . . I meet characters who put me in a new relationship with my own identity.[4]

It is here, too, that Sadie Plant and Donna Haraway have argued that within these virtual domains new utopian possibilities exist for women to inhabit a world beyond the constraints of gender.[5] All this stands in stark contrast to the profoundly essentialist arborescent quality of Net-Nazi activism. But such a possibility, in which digital culture might enhance rather than undermine modern fascisms, was anticipated by some of these theoreticians and particularly by Deleuze and Guattari.

In *A Thousand Plateaus*, Deleuze and Guattari argue that part of the nature of fascism is a "proliferation of molecular focuses in interaction, which skip from point to point, before beginning to resonate together."[6] This comment might well have been made about the lateral connectedness found in cyberspace. Rather than seeing fascism enshrined in a totalitarian bureaucracy, they argue that fascism was and is manifest in the micro-organization of everyday life. The power of fascist culture here is in its "molecular and supple segmentarity, [with] flows capable of suffusing every cell. . . . What makes fascism dangerous is its molecular or micro-political power, for it is a mass movement: a cancerous body rather than a totalitarian organism."[7] There is, however, little discussion in the theoretical literature on cyberculture that looks at the ways in which the extreme right has utilized the medium. On the other hand, the work produced by antifascist monitoring organizations adds little to the qualitative understanding of how virtual fascism might relate to its previous media incarnations.[8] In this sense there is a real gap between the politically engaged and empirically extensive forms of antifascist monitoring and the academic and theoretical work on virtual culture. This chapter situates itself somewhere between these ways of looking at the politics of cyberspace in an attempt to make critical theory speak to political realities and vice versa.

The cultural politics of racist youth culture is complex and challenges us to think again about the relationship between form and social context, between performance and the politics of style. The situated nature of racist culture and the connections between specific political cultures will be examined here through a discussion of the origins of skinheadism in England and its arrival at new destinations around the world. This will then be developed through an examination of the contemporary White Power music scene and its related subculture, networks, and simulated nature. This aims to try to unsettle some of the stereotypical ideas of what racism and white chauvinism look like, in an attempt to complicate our understanding of the politics of youth culture. Also, it points to the need for evaluating the changing morphology of whiteness in a technological age where, as Turkle points out, the modernist preoccupation with calculation is being superseded by simulation and invention at the interface between flesh and machines.[9]

Media, Fascism, and New Technosocial Horizons

The contemporary cultures of the ultra-right pose real difficulties with regard to definition and classification. A wide range of terms are currently used to describe these groups, including neo-Nazi, Nazi, Ultra, white supremacist, fascist, and racist. These labels are used to describe a complex range of ideologies, movements, and groups. For the sake of conceptual clarity I shall be deploying the notion of cyber-Nazis to speak about a range of subcultural movements in Europe, North America, and beyond. While these movements are diverse, they exhibit the following common features:

- a rhetoric of racial and/or national uniqueness and common destiny
- ideas of racial supremacy, superiority, and separation
- a repertoire of conceptions of racial otherness
- a utopian revolutionary worldview that aims to overthrow the existing order

In line with Umberto Eco's insightful comments we would argue that these diverse movements possess a "family of resemblances,"[10] while recognizing that it is not necessary for specific groups to hold to all of the social features outlined above.

For some conventional scholars of the far-right the current interest in the relationship of xenophobia, popular culture, and new technologies is little more than a fashionable intellectual chimera.[11] They caution that the "real issue" is what is happening in terms of the ballot box and the macroeconomic and political trends that underpin political mobilizations. Such a view misses the importance of vernacular culture—be it mediated by technology or other forms—in sustaining what Deleuze and Guattari call the "molecular nature" of authoritarian politics. Alternately, there is a tendency within cultural studies to politicize all aspects of youth culture, reading style as a prosaic statement of protest without establishing the connections among its symbolism, action, and political affiliation.[12]

In order to understand fascism, either in its generic or in its contemporary form, it is crucial to develop a sensitivity to the interconnection of politics, culture, and the mass media. The relative absence of a clear analysis of these issues in contemporary scholarship is somewhat at odds with the focus of some classical studies of fascist ideas and values. Walter Benjamin, for example, in his essay "The Work of Art in the Age of Mechanical Reproduction," commented that new technologies, like photography, enabled the mass character of Nazism to be captured in unprecedented ways: "Mass movements are usually discerned more clearly by a camera than by the naked eye. A bird's eye view best captures gatherings of hundreds of thousands. And even though such a view may be accessible to the human eye as it is to the camera, the image received by the eye cannot be enlarged the way a negative is enlarged."[13] From this perspective the medium *and* the message are important if we are to understand the dynamics of these movements. This is no less true today. In this sense Benjamin's suggestive comments about the potential of technology to express aesthetic politics in a new dimension can usefully be applied to simulation, style, and digital culture. The simple point that follows from this is that it is both important and necessary to map the matrices of contemporary fascist politics through their specific forms of cultural expression.

It is for this reason that it is important to combine an analysis of the politics of racism and fascism with a focus on the ways in which racist ideas and values are expressed through particular cultural modalities.[14] The first of these is the technosocial.[15] A particular technology has no inherent ideological orientation. Rather, the relationship between form and content is found at the interface between particular technologies and their utilization. In the context of Nazism the technosocial modalities of photography and film contributed to the mass choreography of moral indolence. They provided a way for state authority to be embodied and a means by which individual conscience could be dissolved in the *volkish* reverie of mass art.[16] As Benjamin rightly argues, this is made possible by the form itself, along with the historical forces that put it to work. This approach stresses the realm of possibilities that are opened up by the deployment of a particular technology in the context of racist cultures. The key point to emphasize here is that the Internet and other related media allow new horizons for the expression of whiteness. In fact, as will be argued, the rhetoric of whiteness becomes the means to combine profoundly local grammars of racial exclusion within a translocal and international reach, which is made viable through digital technology.

From this perspective the Internet, subcultural style, and pop music each constitute a particular kind of cultural modality that needs to be evaluated within its own technical apparatus and form. The second element identified here is the mechanisms of circulation and their spatial distribution. In particular, this means identifying how these cultural forms of expression address particular audiences and their spatial patterns of reception. The last element focuses on the way symbolic and linguistic elements are combined within particular technical modes. For example, it seems possible, within the White Power music scene, for staunchly nationalistic sensibilities to be maintained while common images and icons and musical forms are shared among subcultures throughout the world. The syncretic dimensions of these processes are best exemplified by the internationalization of skinhead culture. Before discussing the developments within cyberspace further, I want to look at the genealogy of skinhead style in all its complexity, its diffusion, and the peculiarly English forms of authenticity deployed in its global manifestations.

Trads, Boneheads, and Soulies: The International Emergence of Skinheadism

Just watch the way a skinhead moves. The posture is organised as carefully as the length of the red tags or the Sta-prest or the hair. . . . The head twists out as if the skin is wearing an old fashioned collar that's too tight for comfort. The cigarette, tip turned in towards the palm, is brought down from the mouth in an exaggerated arc and held behind the back. It's a gesture reminiscent of barrack rooms and Borstals, of furtive smoking in parade. That's the dance of the Skin.

— DICK HEBDIGE,
"THIS IS ENGLAND! AND THEY DON'T LIVE HERE"

Skinhead style has its origins in Britain and, more specifically in London in the working-class districts to the south and the east of the capital in the mid- to late 1960s. Characterized by cropped hairstyles, braces, Doc Marten boots, and tight Levi jeans, this style utilized industrial working-class imagery to produce a conservative masculinity in a period of political, economic, and cultural upheaval. Skinheadism really came of age in 1969, in an era when urban protest, gay politics, feminism, and a host of other social movements were emerging. Early writers viewed this style as an attempt symbolically to resolve the social transformations and communal breakdown taking place within working-class districts in postwar Britain.[17] This was achieved through the assertion of a white working-class identity, albeit in a burlesque form. Skinhead style was understood as deeply imbued with the domestic semiotics of class, masculinity, race, and power. The whole nature of skinhead performance was predicated on the embodiment of a very particular masculine culture. "The dance of the Skin is, then," commented Dick Hebdige, "even for the girls, a mime of awkward masculinity—the geometry of menace."[18] Anoop Nayak, in an excellent discussion of skinheadism, has emphasized that this form of identity is a tightly choreographed performance.[19]

While skinheadism was imbued with heterosexual, masculinized, and conservative class symbolism, this did not confine its attraction to white straight men. The style from its very inception had an ambivalent gender politics. Women skinheads, referred to as "rennes," would combine styles considered to be masculine (Ben Sherman and Fred Perry shirts, penny loafers or monkey boots) with women's clothing (miniskirts, fishnet tights). In fact, this complex male/female stylistic composite was best expressed in "The Feather," a hairstyle that combined the "short croptop" style worn by men—usually number two or three razor setting—with a feathered fringe that fell down over the eyes and neck. Equally, the masculinity expressed through dance—often resulting in large groups of men dancing together bare-chested—possessed a kind of homoerotic quality, and from the very beginnings of the skinhead culture a small number of gay skinheads set up their own scene, particularly in the working-class districts of inner London. Murray Healy, in his excellent study of gay skins, quotes one gay skinhead's account of club night held at the Union Tavern in Camberwell in the late 1960s: "Tuesday night was skinhead night and you could walk into the pub and there'd be a sea of crops. Fantastic! And everyone was gay! We'd dance to reggae all night, you know, the real Jamaican stuff, and all in rows, strict step. It was a right sight seeing all those skins dancing in rows. The atmosphere was electric."[20] These connections complicate the idea that this was a simplistically chauvinistic culture.

Two very particular maxims held the skinhead movement together in the early days—namely, the recovery of *Englishness/Britishness* and the preservation of *authenticity*.[21] This is not to say that the culture of first-wave skinheads did not assimilate the black registers of metropolitan multiculture. What is interesting here is the coexistence of a kind of opaque hybridity alongside open racism and racial nationalism. Roger Hewitt recounts a story offered to him by a skinhead of a conflict in 1969 at a dance hall called the Locarno in Streatham, south London. The skinhead gave his version of the racialized dynamics of the respective scenes, a white fantasy of urban dominion:

> [Skinheads] formed a big massive movement. We had control of a place called the Locarno, it's up Streatham. There were thousands of skinheads come from all over the place. And the Old Bill never touched us. And one night the nig-nogs came up. They were called "soul boys" then, the niggers them days, and they came, about five hundred of them, from a place called the Ram Jam. Do you know Geno Washington and the Ram Jam Band? Well that was their scene—Brixton. And our area was Streatham—a white man's area. And we run that place, doing the *Skinhead Moonstomp and all that*. And they came up and reckoned they wanted to take it over. Our place. So we said, "Fair enough." The word got around London and thousands of skins drove down. By nine o'clock there was 1,000, 500 in. By ten o'clock there were 3,000 skins. The nig nogs started then and we ran them all the way to Brixton and we walked through Brixton after that. We didn't touch their area before but we ran through Brixton and you couldn't see a nig-nog on the street. Any nig nog walked on the street was dead. We could smash em to pieces. That's the way it should be today.[22]

Such a fantasy of racist street power seems unthinkable in the context of contemporary Brixton, a place where a black community has established itself and where popular racism has been muted. Perhaps the accuracy of this account, even in its day, was questionable, but this particular skinhead embodied some of the complexities and ambiguities in the culture. Hewitt comments: "He was a mandarin of Nazi books and pamphlets. He was a committed racist. He was also Jewish and wrestled with some fierce demons. 'Them' and 'Us' were within him as well as without, a syncretism in desperate need of relief."[23] This discordant hybridity is retained in the style itself at another layer beyond Hewitt's insightful account. The skinhead moonstomp, invoked in the story as the dance of the whiteskin tribes of London, was in fact pounded out on dance floors to records by Jamaican and black artists. Jamaican forms of music (like ska and bluebeat) were adopted by the white devotees of the style, producing a genre that came to be known as "skinhead reggae."[24] A black Jamaican group called Symaryp cut "Skinhead Moonstomp," which defined the attitude of the genre: "I want all you skinheads to get up on your feet, put your braces together and boots on your feet and gimme some of that ole moonstomping."

A small number of black skinheads were involved in the scene. Elsewhere in south London, clubs like the Galaxy in Lower Sydenham played Jamaican music to audiences of black and white club goers. For these people their involvement was caught between the style's putative racism and what it symbolized from the outside view. Darryl, a black skinhead from Bournemouth, commented on this syndrome: "I've had it from all sides. Some skinheads don't believe I should be one because of my colour. Then I get black people coming up to me and saying, 'You're a disgrace to your race.'"[25] These complications were part of this youth style from the very beginning. In the 1970s and early 1980s multiracial elements seemed to be superseded as skinhead style converged with neofascist politics through the British Movement and the National Front, which openly courted them as foot soldiers in their "race war." The political affiliations of skins were signified by the color of the laces worn in their characteristic Doc Marten boots: white laces indicated support for the National Front, and red laces attested British Movement affiliation.[26] This was mirrored in the musical tastes with the emergence of the postpunk Oi! music scene with bands like Sham 69 and the Cockney Rejects, while the National Front sponsored White Noise Music Club, set up by two key young fascist activists, Patrick Harrington and Nick Griffin, and British Nazi musician Ian Stuart Donaldson in 1979.

While London has been the focus for much of the account of the rise of skinheadism, its provincial development took a range of different forms. There were skinhead scenes in the Midlands of England and northern towns and also a significant scene in Scotland. As the racial politics of the music scene unfolded, there was a convergence between some aspects of the skinhead scene and the soul dance music cultures in the industrial towns of the Midlands and the north of England. By the early 1970s soul clubs and all-night venues had been established at the Twisted Wheel in Manchester, Va Va's in Bolton, and the Torch in Stoke on Trent.[27] The phrase "northern soul" was coined by *Blues and Soul* writer Dave Godin as a way of capturing the distinct soul culture of the north of England and the Midlands. The scene was built on the seemingly inexhaustible supply of black music and unknown great soul records largely recorded in Detroit and Chicago and drawn from labels like Okeh, Ric Tic, Sansu, La Beat, Revilot, and Backbeat. Many of the top disc jockeys (DJs) built their reputations by seeking out rare soul records in American ghetto record shops and dusty warehouses. Ironically today there are probably more great northern soul records in Britain than there are in the United States. The best-known venue was the Wigan Casino, which featured DJs Russ Winstanley, Richard Searling, and John Vincent. The Wigan Casino opened its doors in 1973 and staged regular all-night soul extravaganzas for up to 1,500 fans.[28] The patrons of the scene were predominantly young, sharp-witted, stylish, white working-class kids.

The dress of the day incorporated and adapted aspects of skinhead style, which for men consisted of Spencer's soul bags (trousers), Ben Shermans, bowling shirts, red or Lime green socks, and loafers or brogues, while women wore long, flowing full-circle skirts, Mary Quant look-alike fashions, and sandals. The loose-fitting style was perfect for the flamboyant and acrobatic forms of dancing that were invented inside the scene. Fans would throw talcum power on the floor to lessen the friction on their leather-soled shoes. The "niters" were peaceful and a complete alternative to the glitz of mainstream seventies pop culture. Looking back, soul fans reflect on what made northern soul attractive and appealing. In these accounts we find a complex story that reveals the inclusiveness and working-class aesthetics at the heart of the scene. "It was such a big fuck off to record companies and clothes companies and all these folk that were trying to sell you something and tell you the way you should be," comments Keb Darge. "Everyone was so pleased to have something that was theirs, that was created by them."[29]

Keb was first exposed to soul music at a disco on a local Royal Air Force base in his native Elgin, Scotland. Soon he joined the ranks of thousands of Scottish soul fans—or "Troups"—who regularly visited the English northern soul clubs. His first trip to England was to attend the

Black on white: Jeff's tattoo of Gene Chandler (photograph by Elaine Constantine)

Wigan Casino. "We got on this local coach and there was Dundee boys on there who had moved to Bolton to live so that they could go to the all-nighters. This gives you an idea of what the northern punters were like." Keb continues the story: "There was a couple of young Northern boys sitting at the front of the coach and three or four of the local thugs were picking on them. One of the Dundee boys shit into this paper bag on the back of the bus, ran up and smacked it into this thug's face and said in his strong Dundee voice 'You yer fucker.' I thought 'Whey, this is a great big family thing.' You felt you belonged!"[30]

Women have always been centrally involved in the scene, but it is the men who are the main collectors and DJs. "Women can be just as obsessed with vinyl as the men but on the whole the boyfriends buy the records and spend the women's hard-earned cash," suggests Elaine Constantine with a wry smile.[31] Elaine was first exposed to northern soul at school in Bury and later became a devoted soul fan after becoming disillusioned with the Scooter scene. She continues, "I saw one guy out-

Soul diving, 6 Ts All Nighter, 1000 Club, London (photograph by Elaine Constantine)

side The Ritz in Manchester a few months ago and he had scratches all over his neck. They were that deep that they'd gone green. I said to him, 'Oh what happened to you?' He said, 'Oh me wife attacked me and she burnt all me dancing shoes so I couldn't go to any more niters.' I looked down at his feet and he was wearing carpet slippers."[32] Many women on the scene said that one of its attractions is that it is a safe place to go alone. Sue Henderson comments, "I could go down to niters by myself and different people would talk to me. But I am not going to get some drunken slob come and chat me up because I'm a girl sitting by myself. I can't think of anywhere else which is like that."[33]

The 1970s were characterized by violence and a crisis around popular racism. Soulies looking back now speak of the enduring friendliness within the scene, which also offered a relatively safe place for black fans to get involved. Collector and fanzine writer Tim Ashibende, from Stoke, recalls, "For me socialising in general during the seventies wasn't the safest thing to do as a black person. That's what I loved about the northern scene—if you were into the music that was all the credentials you needed. I don't doubt there were a whole bunch of racists on the scene but I've never actually had any problems."[34] Yet traveling to venues could be dangerous, particularly since the local pubs would be turning out just as the all-nighters were about to begin. Dean Anderson, a black fan and well-known DJ from Newark, remembers a particularly harrowing journey to the Wigan Casino: "I was always very paranoid about stopping at service stations. In the old days on the M62 you'd always get coach loads of football fans. This night we stopped and I was playing on one of the pinball machines close to the entrance. Clive who was mixed race was across the room. All of a sudden the doors opened and these lads walked in, must have been twelve blokes, and they took one look at me and in unison they started chanting 'Sieg Heil, Sieg Heil, Sieg Heil.'"[35]

Dean and his friend made for the crowded restaurant in the hope that they would be safe there:

> One by one each of these blokes came up to us right in our faces and said things like "We don't want to beat you up lads, we want you to come outside so that we can kill yer." It was as if it was rehearsed and saying everything under the sun, they thought they could terrorise us into going outside. My white mates were just ashamed. They'd never experienced anything like that and they really felt as black as we did when we were sat at the table. When they realised they couldn't get us they turned to one of the white lads, got him by the scruff of the neck and said "Don't mix!" Those words just ring in my mind.

He continued:

> There was a table behind us and there were two ladies and two men. The lady was from Liverpool. She stood up in the restaurant and she said "Are you people in this restaurant so weak, have you seen what these two lads have been through for the last fifteen minutes? Is anyone willing to stand up with them?" The whole restaurant went quiet. She said, "Look lads, we'll be with you, we'll walk you out to your car." Honestly, for ten minutes we didn't dare go anywhere. Ten minutes we plucked up the courage and they said, "Come on we'll walk with you to your car." So there was these two women from Liverpool with their husbands and they walked with us to our car. They were the only people who spoke up in the whole restaurant and they dragged their husbands and said, "Come on are you going to walk out with these lads? If they get it, you get it." They walked with us to the car. It was the worst moment in my life, that whole half an hour seemed like a day and I went to the all nighter and I don't know what happened that night. It wasn't the first night I'd been to the Casino luckily because if it had have been I wouldn't have gone again.[36]

This incident evokes powerfully a cultural politics of 1970s Britain in microcosm. The racist skinheads confront and attack not only black people, but also "race traitors," who are admonished for their "mixing." Also, the white onlookers in the service station choose to be silent bystanders until two women from Liverpool break the spell of white complicity. Through embarrassing their husbands into action they sanction a moment of brave antiracist concert.

Similar processes of transcultural dialogue were also manifest around the second-wave ska revival, which took place during the late 1970s with the emergence of bands like the Specials and Selecter. This racially mixed music scene came to be known as "2 Tone"—after the record label of the same name—and took transracial dialogue to new levels.[37] It was also met with hostility by racist skinheads both inside the scene and outside.[38] It was at this time that expressly White Power rock bands were also emerging as an offshoot of the more ambiguous connection between skinheadism and white chauvinism. Key in this development was Ian Stuart Donaldson, who broke away from the National Front's White Noise Music Club and set up under the name Blood and Honour. Stuart Donaldson's career bears closer discussion because as a leading figure in the European racist rock scene he is unrivaled.

Stuart Donaldson was born in Poulton-le-Fylde in Lancashire in the late 1950s. A fan of the Rolling Stones and other blues-inspired sixties rock bands, he formed a band called the Tumbling Dice in the mid-1970s, which played the local workingmen's clubs.[39] In 1977 the band changed its name to Skrewdriver and released its first record, entitled "You're So Dumb." The band veered away from the anarchism of the punk scene toward racist politics and a heavy metal/hard rock sound. Skrewdriver covered Lynyrd Skynyrd's "Sweet Home Alabama" as an expression of redneck sympathy, missing the nuances contained within the song and its defense of a more complicated southern whiteness.[40]

The significance of Skrewdriver is hard to overstate: it became a touchstone of racist authenticity and established the heavy metal sound as *the* form among white supremacist bands. Skrewdriver also toured, making connections with racist music scenes in East and West Germany, Holland, Belgium, Sweden, France, Canada, Brazil, and Australia.[41] Indeed, the international networks evident in the racist rock scene today were mapped initially through Skrewdriver's international circuit of live gigs. In 1984 Skrewdriver signed a contract with the German record company Rock-O-Rama Records.[42] Stuart Donaldson saturated his songs with racial mysticism and pan-European white rhetoric of survival, separatism, and rebellion. What was important about Ian Stuart Donaldson was his view of the potential for music to unite racists across Europe through guitars and sound, without the cumbersome apparatus and regalia of political parties. The following passage from his *Blood and Honour* magazine renders these connections explicit:

> Our fight begins in Europe and will spread all over the White World. There are certain moments in our lives when we grasp the magnitude of our task. I have walked from Antwerp during the first hours of the night when the nationalists gather in pubs. The marvellous architecture of the cities of Flanders embodies the soul of Europe—sunset in Rotterdam when the lights of the city glitter and we are made welcome by our friends—afternoon in Stockholm, frost on the ground and thereafter a journey to Gothenburg where the Swedish and Nordic beauty is hypnotising.[43]

During the late 1980s and 1990s racist skinheadism was exported to Germany, Czechoslovakia, Poland, Holland, Russia, Switzerland, Sweden, Brazil, Norway, and the United States.[44] Its proliferation challenges previous explanations put forward about the relationship between its character and the local conditions of its initial formation.

In the diffusion of racist skinhead style, two things have remained constant: its appeal as a translocal emblem of national chauvinism and white pride, and the transposition of a language of racist rhetoric and style from a variety of European contexts to specific local concerns. Hilary Pilkington shows, in her account of the emergence of what she calls "designer skinheads" in Russia, that racial epithets assimilated from England were used against Azerbaijanis. She argues that, rather than being the product of Soviet modernization, designer skins are "more the product of the post-modern culture of global borrowings and displacements. Their style and language is littered with globalisms: white laces in Doc Marten shoes borrowed from German skins to show hatred of foreigners; phrases such as 'Ausländer raus' and 'Skins on your bikes' decorate speech; references to the Australian cult film *Romper Stomper* abound; positive political preferences are orientated to the French neo-right around Le Pen."[45] While the translocal elements of this white chauvinism are clearly evident, something distinct remains in these national manifestations. Pilkington goes on to discuss the deep sense of ambiguity that the young skinheads she interviewed had with regard to postcommunist Russianness. A Moscow skin told her that he would never attack a "Negro" because "their civilisation is higher than ours . . . especially if a Negro is an English person or an American."[46] What is interesting is the combination of translocal elements within racist culture and local ambiguities and insecurities. It seems telling here that part of the "higher" civilization of Negroes is the notion that they have entered modernity through their status as English or American citizens.

While the global dispersion of racist skinhead style was at its highest point, the culture was being transformed in its metropolitan cradle. Since the 1980s the style has become increasingly popular among gay men in London. As mentioned previously, there have been gay skinheads from the inception of the culture, but during the 1980s and 1990s the style became ubiquitous in gay nightclubs. Murray Healy argues that the gay appropriation of skinhead style is a complex combination of homoerotic desire, kitsch, and a masculinization of gay culture. The nuances of his argument are beyond the present discussion, but he claims that the pervasive gay adoption of skinhead style is starting to change the associations in London at least. He quotes a gay skinhead who is an active member of the White Power music scene, Blood and Honour: "When I first became a skinhead and was walking down the street, you might get a bit of hassle from people, you know, 'Nazi Bastard,' that sort of thing. Nowadays they say, 'Batty man.' It doesn't matter who you are—they've never seen you before, you could be covered in White Power tattoos—that's their first image. You get that reaction from straight blokes. For me, the gays have fucked up the Nazi skinhead image."[47]

Such combinations of sexual transgression and racial authoritarianism are no less complex than the Jewish Nazi discussed earlier. Healy argues that the growing public awareness of gay skins has corrupted the association between skins and a conservative, white racist, straight masculinity. It is interesting that the skin quoted above invoked the association between skin style and gay London through the Creole homophobic epithet "Batty man." The fear of being identified as gay is augmented here because these associations are being directed at white skins from a black location. It may be that, just as skinheadism is being globalized, its hypermasculine straight image is being decoupled at "home." However, this may well be confined to London, and there is little evidence to suggest that skinhead style has lost its currency as sartorial racism elsewhere in Britain.

In summary, throughout this section a complicated picture has been sketched of the racial politics of skinheadism. Before moving on to discuss how this culture has entered cyberspace, I want to reiterate two points. First, skinheadism has a complex hybrid history even though some of these traces remain opaque, be it in the form of the blues roots (via the Rolling Stones) of the White Power group Skrewdriver or the Jamaican rhythms that bring the skinhead moonstomp to life. What I

want to stress here is that white people may carry the traces of otherness alongside overt racism in their everyday lives without a necessary
contradiction. This was in fact brought into sharp focus during an
argument I had with a fifteen-year-old skinhead from the English Midlands during the early 1990s. Daniel was not a follower of Skrewdriver,
but rather a devotee of rave and house music. I tried to use the fact that
this music was crucially influenced by black gay DJs in Chicago before it was imported to Britain. Something of an antiracist pantomime
ensued in which, like the pantomime dame, I insisted, "Oh, yes, it is
black," and Daniel replied, "Oh, no, it isn't." I cautioned Daniel that if
he threw all black people out of the country, then his music would go
with them. A moment of silent reflection ensued, and Daniel cocked his
head to one side. It felt like a long time, but it was probably just a few
seconds. Then he replied: "No, because we will still have the tapes, won't
we!"[48] Black culture, without black people: problem solved. It struck me
afterward that this was a kind of a triumph and perversion of Benjamin's
famous ideas about the possibilities of the mechanical reproduction of
culture.

Second, and conversely, following from the notion of the mechanical
reproduction of culture, skinheadism need not be a product of any particular set of economic, social, or political circumstances. In this respect
skinhead style has been severed from its British roots, constituting something more promiscuous and akin to a white rhizome of translocal inter-
connections. As I have tried to argue, the politics of this culture needs
to be evaluated carefully in terms of time and place. But it is not just the
racist incarnations of skinheadism that have been globalized; its complexities, which have remained hidden from public view, have also been
offered up to the forces of global dissemination. Germany, where young
people have embraced some of the styles of English chauvinism, has
become something of a Mecca for racist skinheads and has also imported
some other aspects of the skinhead legacy. On a cold December night in
1997 I made my way—somewhat in disbelief—to a northern soul all-
nighter in East Berlin. Arriving at the Volksbühne, a Brechtian theater
on Rosa Luxembourg Platz, I found a dance floor full of young Germans,
Turks, and Africans immaculately turned out in Ben Sherman shirts, Fred
Perrys, Crombies, Levi jeans, and Mary Quant styles. At the end of a long
and inspiring night I remember walking out in the dazzle of daylight.
Through the mist I could see the red and white television tower that
dominates the East Berlin skyline. This was northern soul a long way
from Wigan.

Finally, the purpose of this section has been to offer a more compli-

cated account of the status of skinhead youth culture as a cultural modality of racist expression. Cyberspace has provided a vehicle for accelerat-
ing the processes of global traffic in skinhead culture. More than this,
virtual culture has provided an arena in which the meaning of skinhead
style and racist culture more generally can be both articulated and contested. On the Internet there has been a profusion of "Trad" sites, which
lay claim to traditional skinhead style as an emblem of multicultural
working-classness. Here Trads argue openly with racist skinheads—or
Boneheads—over skinhead authenticity and history. In a recent debate
on the alt.skinheads newsgroup the skinhead ethos was defined variously as "the sartorial expression of white racism" or an "irreverent anti-
bourgeois class consciousness" or an "anti-fascist urban multiculture."[49]
I will return to the role of on-line activity, but first I want to look specifically at the role of the Internet in the growth of the White Power music scene.

Resistance through Digital: George Burdi and the Birth of Cyber-Nazis

At its most basic the Internet is an interconnected computer network
that enables hyper forms of communication, which compress the relationship between time and space. Its origins go back to 1969, when the
Defense Advanced Research Project Agency (DARPA), a part of the U.S.
Defense Department, developed a method of exchanging military research information among researchers based at different sites. By the
mid-1980s these computer networks were expanded by another U.S.
government agency, the National Science Foundation (NSF). The NSF
established supercomputer centers whose resources were required to be
accessible to any educational facility who wanted them. The NSF network was gradually refined and evolved into what we know as the Internet. Evidence first appeared in the 1980s that electronic mail and bul-
letin board systems (BBSs) outside of the Internet were being used by
neofascists. Since 1995 the level of right-wing Internet activity has increased dramatically.

Resource pages on the World Wide Web (Web) are closest to a broadcast model of propaganda. They enable White Power groups to circulate
articles, CD catalogues, images, and symbols. Rick Eaton, of the Simon
Wiesenthal Center, sums up the pace of change: "At the time of the
Oklahoma City bombing there was one white supremacy page on the
web—that was Don Black's page, Stormfront. Now there are literally
hundreds and there's new ones that come up all the time."[50] Estimates
of exactly how many sites there are vary, and the transient nature of

these pages makes it difficult to establish an exact figure. There are around two hundred white-supremacist websites, but some estimates put the number of hate sites as high as six hundred. These include Hammerskin[51] sites and music dedicated pages, most notably Resistance Records, originally based in Detroit. Eaton concludes: "The Internet was one factor in giving new life to that music scene. The skinhead movement in general was in decline three years ago. Now it is international and big business. Resistance Records brought it all together and through their web site established an international market."[52] The Web has been particularly effective for advertising White Power music available by mail. Previously the music could be bought only at concerts or through advertising in skin-zines, but through the Web, CD catalogues potentially reach millions.

Resistance Records was founded in 1994 by George Burdi (a.k.a. Eric Hawthorne) and Mark Wilson, both of whom were in their early twenties. The label's twelve bands sold fifty thousand CDs in their first eighteen months of business. By 1996 the label made a profit for the first time, with total sales of $300,000. The label also sold its own glossy magazine called *Resistance,* which had a circulation of fifteen thousand. Its webpage was highly sophisticated, including sound samples of each band that could be downloaded and heard on-line. Burdi, formerly of the Church of the Creator, is also the lead singer of RAHOWA (RAcial HOly WAr), one of the leading American Nazi bands. His voice is evocative of Roger Waters, from the English progressive rock band Pink Floyd, providing another example of how particular images of Englishness are utilized within white musical authenticity.

Burdi's story is interesting precisely because he is an example of a middle-class and highly media-literate youth being drawn into the White Power scene. The son of an insurance broker, he grew up in a suburb of Toronto. His upper-middle-class family was not known for espousing racist views. A bright child, he received his first computer at the age of ten. Mark Potok, of Klanwatch, comments: "The music scene is important because—along with the Internet—it has helped The Movement reach people it has never reached before, specifically, middle-class and upper-middle-class teenagers. Kids who live in their parents' two and three and four hundred thousand dollar homes."[53] Currently, in America, racist recruitment is focused more on the suburbs than the working-class trailer parks. Potok concludes: "There was a great deal of interest in the 1980s in recruiting thugs, your typical racist skinhead. There's a lot less interest in that now and a lot more in recruiting college-bound or college-educated upper-middle-class bright kids because they are looking for strategists, not street soldiers. It's not about beating people up in bars but looking for the leaders of tomorrow."[54] For a while it seemed that in Burdi one such leader had been found. Articulate and charismatic, Burdi gave the White Power Movement a new face and an underground youthful attraction. In 1995 he told Kevin Alfred Strom:

> People—especially young people—are attracted to things that are off the beaten path. If something has an underground flavour, or image of being forbidden, the youth are naturally attracted to it. Now, in the past this is something that has harmed our young people . . . examples would be race mixing or the use of drugs. The mainstream media have made everything OK except being proud of your race and culture, and this tendency of youth is now having a very undesired effect from the perspective of the mainstream media giants because these young people are now interested in the new forbidden thing; and that is being proud to be white.[55]

The use of music within fascist movements has been widely documented,[56] but what is interesting about the racist rock scene is its attempts to package and exploit "low culture." Racist ideologues like George Lincoln Rockwell, John Tyndall, and Harold A. Covington invoked classical music and composers like Wagner as the staple of the "European spirit." In the early 1990s the Ku Klux Klan made an abortive attempt to set up a symphony orchestra to be based in Atlanta. The Triple K Symphony Orchestra was to start touring in November 1990 under the management of Charles Calhoun. An advertisement offered musicians $1,500 plus $60 a day food allowance and stated the Triple K Orchestra's "initial purpose is to improve the image of the Ku Klux Klan and foster a kinder, gentler attitude towards this historic American organization. . . . Musicians must be willing to perform wearing official KKK robes. Protection and anonymity guaranteed. Equal opportunity employer. Strings, brass, woodwinds and percussion sections to be filled." This attempt to harness classical music to the cause of making the KKK respectable and attractive amounted to nothing.

Resistance Records has located itself in the space between organized fascist politics and musical subcultures. In an interview in the *New York Times,* Burdi claimed that music would address hearts as well as minds: "The reason that the so-called movement has been struggling over the years is because it has operated on a rational—not emotional—level. George Lincoln Rockwell was successful because he could stir people's emotions."[57]

The White Power rock music scene marks a partial break with the

Advertisement for the KKK Symphony Orchestra

enchantment with racially pure "high culture." This was rendered explicit in Burdi's interview with Kevin Alfred Strom that was broadcast on the National Alliance's radio station. After playing an excerpt from RAHOWA's "The Snow Fell," Strom put it to Burdi that "some older patriots . . . are completely opposed to rock music. They see it as a destructive and degenerative influence on white youth. . . . Some of them think that the artistic expression of the pro-white movement should not include rock. What would you say to them?"[58] Burdi's response is worth quoting at some length:

> What is important for these people to realise is that the history of our race includes a very, very diverse musical influence. There are times throughout our history when we have had different types of music being played. We have not just always played baroque classical music. We have not just always played folk or country music. We have made different styles of music during the last three or four thousand years, many of which these same critics would not very much like. For instance, the ancient Vikings used to make as large a racket as possible: banging on drums, smashing things to make as much noise as they could. This form of ritual dance and music was intended to summon the gods. They believed that they would waken the gods by creating *thunder.* In many ways, if you compare modern skinhead culture and even the wider culture of pro-white music, you have a lot of it that sounds very noisy, that sounds very heavy, and very loud. And it is meant to be played loud. It is warrior music. It is the new Viking music. This is not a time of peace when we can sit back and put on sweet violins and contemplate the cosmos. This is an era in which we are being forced into a life-or-death struggle for the survival of our people. And music that is hard, music that awakens the warrior spirit in these white people, within these white youth, which stirs up barbarian rages in them—is healthy. It is a natural, instinctive response to the darkening of our world. We are ready for Ragnarok once again.[59]

Rock music and skinheadism are seen as the current manifestation of an ancient white racial lineage, the cry of the barbarian devoid of any modern traces of black music because these have been bleached from the form and its history—although there remains a concern about the racial purity of rock. Strom's next question was "You would agree, though, that some rock music—though not the music you sell—does have a Negroid sound to it and some Negroid influences?" to which

Burdi replied: "I would have to agree with that. You can take any genre of music and you can blend it and cross it with other genres, and you can spoil it. This has even been done with baroque classical pieces. They have taken compositions by Vivaldi and put rap drumbeats to them and they've *rapped* to them. You can go into dance clubs and you can hear these bastardised versions of these beautiful compositions which have been ruined by including rap lyrics."[60] Strom responded with a strain of anxiety: "But the artists who perform pro-white music have pretty well strained out any of these Negroid influences from rock, haven't they?" Burdi promptly assured him:

> Absolutely. As a matter of fact, one of our bands, Bound For Glory, one of the most famous white power bands in the world—the guitarist, Ed, from this band, whenever asked about from where his influences come for his music writing, says Wagner is his number one influence. He takes a lot of his chord progressions right out of Wagner's compositions and simply plays them on guitar. There is a direct similarity here. This is an evolution of music. We are simply using guitars to play a form of classical progression in a new music that does have a very *heavy,* powerful sound—for a reason.[61]

A converted Strom brought the broadcast to an end by pouring praise on Burdi and Resistance Records: "I am proud of what you are doing for white youth, I'm impressed with your capabilities, I'm impressed with the music I've heard. May you have all success in your endeavours."

This dialogue highlights the ways in which issues of racial authenticity, culture, and musical form are managed. Here Burdi offers an aetiology of rock brutalism that goes back to a barbarian Nordic past. This version of rock history conceals any intercultural traffic with rhythm and blues or with jazz, while at the same time these two fascists are compelled to address this issue directly. White Power music has "strained out" the "Negroid influences," replacing them, in Burdi's account, with the old classical masters of German romanticism: the bizarre fusion of *power chords* and *Wagner.* Musicologically this claim is hard to verify. The music of Bound for Glory seems a very long way from "The Ride of the Valkyrie." But this is interesting as a rhetorical move, in that it attempts to blur the distinctions between "high" and "low" culture, while claiming and promoting the idea of a racially pure form. Some racist bands attempted to fuse progressive rock with neoclassical forms of instrumentation, the use of the harpsichord, and orchestral arrangements.[62]

Despite these moves, the genre has been in large part dominated by heavy metal/post Oi! guitar band sounds. There are some exceptions to this. One of the most popular CDs that Resistance sells is Johnny Rebel's *For Segregationists Only,* containing segregationist country music recorded in the 1950s and 1960s.[63] There have also been attempts to use rockabilly styles, which combine rock and country, through groups like The Klansmen, which featured Ian Stuart Donaldson.

The dominance of metal and rock has been bemoaned by racist women for its masculinity. In a essay on white women in music Cindy MacDonald expresses her disapproval of the androcentric nature of racist music: "There is nothing I find more discouraging than browsing through a catalogue of white racist CDs and finding *NO WOMEN ARTISTS!* Sure, racist music is racist music. The message is roughly the same whether a man or *woman* sings the song. But, I like to hear *women* singing too. And those *female* voices just aren't out there in racialist music. *Women* need to harness music's power."[64] This article is striking in the way it invokes a kind of brummagem feminism, while at the same time disavowing the women's movement.[65] It is part of a wider webpage, Her Race, aimed at white women. The logo of the page invokes a feminist icon and promotes a strange combination of themes around white women's emancipation and a kind of racial ecology that fixes white women's destiny in a state of nature. There are sections on career advice for white women, abortion, tattooing, women's birth stories, a Women's Hall of Fame (including Brigitte Bardot, Queen Elizabeth I, and Alessandra Mussolini), and links with the webpages of Women for Aryan Unity and the World Church of Creator's Women's Frontier. MacDonald continues:

> The potential market for racist *women* music groups is larger than it is for men. *An all-female band* would have far less trouble in terms of anti-racist violence at gigs. All-male bands have problems. They are far more restricted in terms of the types of clubs they can get into. That limits their audience. But with *women* artists, protestors would be a little less aggressive than they would be toward male musicians; also, concert goers might be curious at why women would be singing racialist songs. It's a good selling point— *women* racialist musicians. It allows more potential concert goers because some *women* music fans are turned off by ultra-aggressive testosterone-laced performers. A racialist *woman* singer would be an excellent role model which might attract women into our cause.[66]

This version of female "empowerment" self-consciously seeks to undermine both the masculinized image of the male "racist thug" and the masculine quality of the white racist pop music scene.

Women for Aryan Unity

There are very small numbers of women involved in white racist bands. The Italian group ADL122 has had a female musician in its lineup, the British group Lionheart has had two different female singers in the group, and Razor's Edge has a female bass player. MacDonald, in her article, invokes nonracist women in pop music as an example. Sinéad O'Connor is said to have the "right hair," but the wrong "leftist politics." Madonna is presented as the confused "material girl" and offered the admonition "Race is more important than money, honey." Country star Terri Clark, the all-women band The Go Go's, Alanis Morisette, and Annie Lennox are invoked as credible examples that racist women musicians might follow. MacDonald ends with an appeal for greater variety in racist music: "What is lacking in the racist music scene is a variety of styles. Too many bands are into metal music. In mainstream society, the public is choosy about what styles of music CDs they buy; there should be many racialist music styles to suit all tastes. For example, 'folk' (i.e. acoustic guitar), traditional, dance, and country music are all lacking representatives in the racialist music scene."[67] In particular, she appeals to the idea that country music has a particular potential: "Since most country fans are white, country fans might be interested in hearing the racialist message if it were sung by a *woman* to a country beat. In order to market the racialist message in a variety of music styles, we need to take a peek at what's out there in the mainstream music-land and see what's been done."[68]

However, the attention to racial authenticity so carefully manufactured in the rhetoric of George Burdi and other White Power bands is impossible to sustain in mainstream music. This was demonstrated in the response of Harold A. Covington, the general secretary of the American National Socialist White People's Party, to an article on the black musical influences on country music published in the *Chicago Tribune* on September 16, 1998. In an e-mail posting entitled "New PC: Niggers Invented Country Music," circulated on the *Resistance*-moderated mailing list, he complained: "One of the goals of Political Correctness is that white, European males must have NOTHING of our own. Credit for EVERYTHING we have ever done, invented, or accomplished must go to non-whites or women and history must be re-written accordingly."

White racist rock has established itself within the rhetoric of a hermetically sealed racial authenticity. As Cindy MacDonald rightly complains, this has been maintained through a preoccupation with metal and other rock genres that are coded in hypermasculine ways.[69] When Stuart Hall and Tony Jefferson published *Resistance through Rituals* in 1976,[70] the analysis of youth culture was connected with an antihegemonic politics of "the popular." It is not without some irony that over twenty years later the chief exponent of fascist music should have stolen the language of "resistance" in the name of popular racism. White Power rock is a form of ritualized resistance, but it has been ritualized in ways that the early cultural studies writers would not have anticipated. In the United States Resistance Records has been successful in constructing a well-packaged and alluring form of media-generated racist rebellion. This music has garnered an international market, and its appeal in different national contexts is varied and driven by contrasting social forces. In Britain, White Power music may be an appeal to a racist notion of proletarian authenticity; in America, it may be invoked by middle-class kids to shock their parents' pretensions to liberal multiculturalism; in Sweden, it may be used by rebellious young people to goad the nation's Liberal Democratic self-image. It is to these points of connection between racist activists in America and in Europe that I now want to turn.

Early on, Resistance Records forged connections with *Nordland* magazine, published by an equally sophisticated group based in Sweden. Sweden, in particular, has provided an example where media marketing has

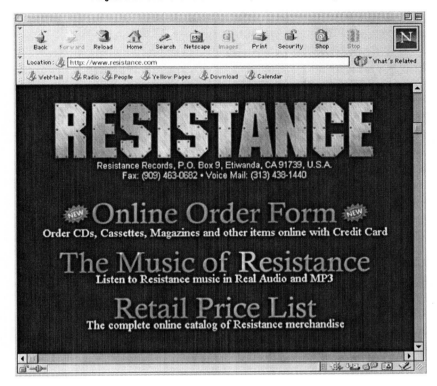

White Power music on-line: Resistance Records

brought White Power music to a wide youth audience.[71] Stephane Bruek-feld, former executive officer of the Swedish Committee against Anti-Semitism, was involved in a 1997 survey of eight thousand young Swedish people between the ages of twelve and nineteen. The study showed that 12 percent of the young people listened to White Power rock "sometimes or often."[72] Nordland Records developed its own website in September 1996, advertising CDs for sale. Initially, it worked in close association with Resistance Records. Both pages offered subscriptions to a virtual newsletter, providing readers with news of releases and concert promotions. In 1997 Resistance Records offered some seventy-one CDs, along with back issues of its *Resistance* magazine, patches, white fist and "88" pins, Ian Stuart Donaldson postcards, and Nazi flags. By comparison, in 1997–98 Nordland Records boasted the largest White Power music catalogue available on the Internet at the time, including some 135 CDs, and a range of White Power name-brand T-shirts, patches, bottle openers, stickers, and even cigarette lighters.

The success of these companies in America and Sweden brought them to the attention of the police and legal authorities. On April 9, 1997, the Michigan authorities raided the Resistance Records offices in the Detroit suburb of Highland Township to investigate possible tax evasion. At the same time Canadian authorities arrested Burdi at his home in Windsor, Canada, just across the river from Detroit. Some two hundred thousand CDs and cassette tapes were seized along with business records, computers, and newsletter subscription information. Burdi was charged with promoting hatred under the Canadian Criminal Code along with Joseph Talic, age 26, and Jason Snow. The case against Resistance Records was quickly settled with a fine. Significantly, the global nature of its market saved Resistance from a more serious tax prosecution because most of its customers were out of state and the income they provided Resistance was not taxable in Michigan. The arrest of Burdi and his Canadian associates has had a more enduring effect.

While awaiting trial Burdi sold his stake in the company to Willis Carto. Carto published the Washington, D.C.–based right-wing *Spotlight Magazine* and is a former associate of the Holocaust-denying Institute of Historical Review. Resistance Records was relocated to Eitwanda, California, near San Bernardino. The company was owned jointly by Carto and his business associate Todd Blodgett. Blodgett, a right-wing Republican, had been a minor figure in Ronald Reagan's White House staff. The key problem for Carto and Blodgett was that the two magazines had very different readerships. *Spotlight Magazine* was oriented toward a middle-aged audience, while *Resistance* appealed to the lifestyle racism of the devotees of White Power rock. Carto, amid legal and financial struggles, declared bankruptcy and sold his share to Dr. William Pierce of the National Alliance.

In late April of 1999 Blodgett and Pierce agreed on a strategy for working together, but their partnership was short-lived. In the summer of 1999 Pierce took control of Resistance Records and relocated the company to his headquarters in Hillsboro, West Virginia. In the autumn of 1999 Pierce also purchased Swedish competitor Nordland Records. BBC News reported in its film *Hate on the Net,* broadcast in January 2000, that the quantity of mail arriving at Pierce's retreat in the mountains of West Virginia was such that the local post office had been expanded. Pierce has a warehouse on the grounds of his compound used to store nearly 80,000 CDs, reflecting an estimated 250 titles.

Nordland and Resistance took Nazi merchandising to a new and unprecedented level, and the authorities found it very difficult to act against them. In addition, others have followed in their footsteps. In 1998, the Aryan Graphics page, for example, offered a whole range of

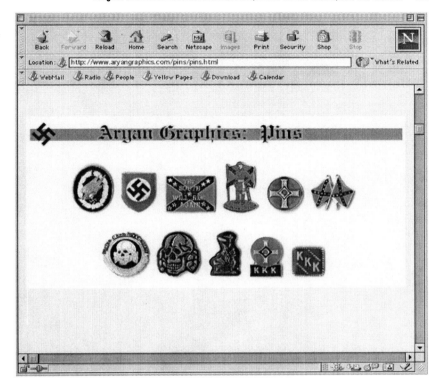

Nazi e-commerce: racist pins advertised on the Web

Nazi merchandising that included T-shirts, pins, and patches, all of which could be viewed on the Web along with their mail-order catalogue. The SS Bootboys White Power page offered free graphics files (.gif files), which, with viewer software, could be used to generate flyers and posters. Readers were invited to "Print 'em out! Put them up in your room! Put them [in] your schools! Spread the word." These images manifest the full range of racist stereotypes, striking out at Jews, blacks, and so-called white race traitors. On its webpage SS Bootboys stated boldly its faith in a digital future: "The damage and corruption drilled onto [*sic*] the heads of three generations of white America is nauseating to say the least, but not irreversible. There is now the Internet; the interactive utopia. Articles, visuals, and audio which can be seen over and over again. We are telling the other side to the story. This movement will never stop. Read our articles, view our links, and support the movement! If nothing else . . . think about it!"

What is uniquely important about the Internet is that it is not merely

Racist flyer from SS Bootboy's webpage

a means of disseminating propaganda. Rather, cyberspace offers a relatively safe space where people can participate in an interactive way in a largely autonomous, although not hermetic, racist Net-world. Here social networks and aspects of the everyday life of racists can be carried into cyberspace and sustained. In the late nineties the United Skins Webring provided a good example of this kind of networking. It enabled skinhead pages to be entered as part of a connected circle of websites. However, not all skinheads were invited. "Baldies, commies, queers and trads [i.e., traditional skinheads] that can't admit they like Skrewdriver need not apply." Another highly sophisticated site was Micetrap's White Pride Network. Its webpage provided a library of 250 White Power tracks that could be downloaded through a form of sound file compression called mp3, which makes it possible to record a whole song in a file that takes up only a few megabytes of memory. The webpage also offered links to the home pages of bands like Berserkr and Intimidation One, music reviews, and sections dedicated to racist jokes and White Power video retailing. When you opened the NS88 page, messages appeared beneath the logo: "Welcome to NS88 Websites/The best in white power video/committed to the highest quality." As each message flashed on the screen, the sound of a whip being cracked would be heard on the speakers.

The combination of intimacy and distance found in cyberspace provides a new context for racist harassment through abuse or digital tools like "mail bombs." It also provides a context in which racism can be simulated. Elsewhere I have talked about the use of computer games that offer the "pleasure" of simulated racial violence.[73] These modalities make new types of racist behavior possible. They combine all of the fruits of the digital era to produce interactive visual forms that are alluring and attractive to a particularly youthful audience. Virtual forms of racial violence relate to chilling lived experiences, while remaining in the "other world" of computer simulation. They are politically slippery because they blur the distinction between social reality and fantasy.

This issue was brought sharply into focus in April 1996, when a photograph of a young black man, lying facedown on the floor and being beaten and kicked, was posted on the Skinheads USA website. The site was maintained by twenty-eight-year-old Dallas resident Bart Alsbrook, known by his on-line name, "Bootboy." Another photograph, entitled "Mexican Getting Smashed," showed two men beating a bleeding victim. The incident was reported in the local newspaper.[74] The Dallas police examined the possibility of using the images as evidence, and since this incident the website has been closed down. Mark Briskman, a director with the Anti-defamation League, commented at the time: "It reminds me of Nazi Germany and the way they meticulously documented all their atrocities in stills and on film."[75] This incident is a dangerous example of the use of the Internet to celebrate real incidents of racist violence. The tension between national chauvinism and the increasingly transnational matrices of neofascist culture can be managed within cyberculture. It seems possible for staunchly nationalistic sensibilities to be maintained while common images and icons are shared. The syncretic dimensions of these processes are best exemplified by the internationalization of skinhead culture mentioned earlier.

The World Wide Web also allows the symbols and regalia of racist youth culture to be displayed and disseminated. The Hammerskin Nation page includes a rogues' gallery of racists displaying their tattoos as examples to assimilate and reproduce. But, more than this, these cyberstudios produce incarnate portraits of skin and bodies marked by whiteness. This highlights two further points: first, that racialized bodies are an achievement, rather than a given, and are acted upon in the creation of whiteness; and, second, that the processes of simulation and authenticity are being combined within these cultures. To have tattoos is the ultimate mark of White Power authenticity; this indelibly marks and fixes light skin in racialized terms. However, these images are being digitally disseminated, producing fascist cyborgs that can be downloaded and admired narcissistically as artifacts of racial authenticity.[76] Anne Miller's article on "Racialist Tattoos," posted on the Aryan Dating webpage, argues that ancient Celtic tattoos might be more appropriate for "main-stream racists": "Why get a Celtic design instead of another kind? One reason is acceptance. There are other racialist symbols that are viewed as extremist by today's society. The symbols could affect your job security and middle-of-the-road friends might avoid you if your *tattoo* is too wild. But a Celtic tattoo would say to the World, 'I'm proud to be white' without causing too much fuss with your boss or friends (and it looks neat too!)."[77] Examples are also provided on this page in digitally enhanced color. The Internet fosters a kind of closet form of white supremacy that people can participate in from the privacy of their computer terminals.

Newsgroups are an important interactive aspect of the medium. They operate within USENET and offer forms of exchange, debate, and chat concerning particular themes and special interests. Articles and responses are sent to newsgroups by electronic mail. Racist Internet activists have established their own groups within the alternative or "alt." areas of USENET. The most important of these newsgroups are alt.politics. nationalism.white, alt.revolution.counter, alt.skinheads, and alt.revisionism. The newsgroups become a context in which racist sentiments can be countered by antifascist activists or nonracist skinheads, but they also allow for networking and the exchange of information and correspondence between White Power music fans. This can vary from posting lists of CDs for "tape trade" to advertising or simply posting information about new websites or channels for Internet relay chat and on-line discussion groups. One recent posting to the alt.skinheads newsgroup offered a list of 340 Oi! and White Power CDs and vinyl recordings for trade, along with an offer to make copies of an additional 163 tape recordings.

In 1996 former Net-Nazi Milton J. Kleim made application to establish a mainstream White Power music newsgroup within the recreation or "rec." part of USENET. Although USENET has no formal governing body, there is a requirement that additions to the "big seven" newsgroups (i.e., comp., misc., news., rec., sci., soc., talk.) be sanctioned by the wider Internet community. So, in order for rec.music.white-power

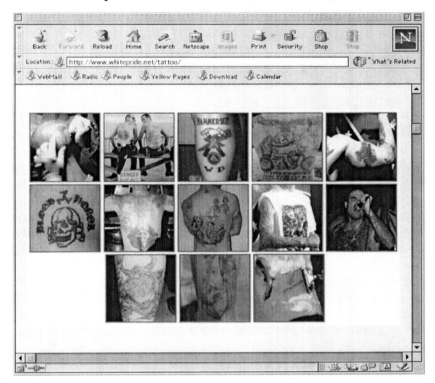

Inscribing whiteness: racist tattoos

to be established, it had to pass a vote open to all USENET users. The vote, which took place between February 26 and March 18, 1996, gave insight into the numbers of active Net-Nazis. The vote was organized by the USENET Volunteer Votetakers, a group founded in 1993. In total, 592 votes were cast in favor of the White Power music newsgroup and a massive 33,033 votes against, with 6,200 invalid votes. Resistance Records' mailing list was made available to the campaign, and George Burdi put his support behind it. Regardless, the campaign failed to muster more than 600 votes.

It is very difficult to estimate exactly how many people are drawn into racist activity on-line. Recently, Alex Curtis—self-proclaimed "Lone-Wolf of Hate" from San Diego and producer of the extremist magazine *The Nationalist Observer*—claimed to reach "100s–1000s of the most radical racists in the world each week."[78] However, it is dangerous to overestimate the level of activity. The number of white racists regularly involved in the Internet globally is somewhere between five and ten thousand, divided into ten to twenty clusters. It is impossible to offer anything other than an educated guess. The number of "hits" on a web-page, for example, need not indicate "sympathetic inquiries." Rather, they could include opponents, monitoring agencies, and researchers. The key point is that these relatively small numbers of people can have a significant presence.

Attempts have also been made to combine Internet activism with "real-world" association. In 1998 the RaceLink webpage offered a list of activists' contact details and locations. It aimed to put racists in contact with each other. It is no longer on-line, but when active, it included mostly American links and also provided contact e-mail addresses and post office boxes in Canada, Germany, Portugal, South Africa, and the United Kingdom. The Aryan Dating webpage offered a contact service for white supremacists. Entries were listed for men and women, some-times including pictures. While most of the profiles were American, there were also personal ads from a range of countries, including Brazil, Canada, Holland, Norway, Portugal, the United Kingdom, Slovakia, and Australia. In June 1998 the page included 140 advertisements from white men, of which 80 percent were from the United States and 15 percent from Canada. There were also 60 personal advertisements from white women. Again, these were mostly American (68 percent), but the page also linked to a considerable number of white South African women (17 percent of all ads) through a mailing list compiled by Zunata Kay. The Aryan Dating page was pushed off the Internet server that carried it in 1998, and today it has been assimilated and reconstructed on Don Black's Stormfront webpage, where it has been renamed "White Singles."

One of the interesting things about scrolling through the personal ads was that the faces that appeared were nothing like the archetypal image of "The Racist." There were very few skinheads with Nazi tattoos: these white-supremacist "lonely hearts"—mostly in their twenties and thirties—looked surprisingly prosaic. Take thirty-six-year-old Cathy, who lived in Pennsylvania, but who was "desperate to move to a WHITE area!" She appeared in the photograph in a rhinestone outfit with glitzy earrings: "The picture of me is a little over done," she explained. "I had photos down with the girls at the office. I am really a blue jean natural gal, but I look like an Aryan Princess when I get dressed up. But I am really the girl next door type."[79] Or nineteen-year-old Debbie from New England, who wrote: "I am [a] young white power woman who seeks someone seriously devoted to the white power movement. A person whose commitment is undaunting. I am a member of several WP organi-zations, and would like to speak with men who share the same values as I."[80]

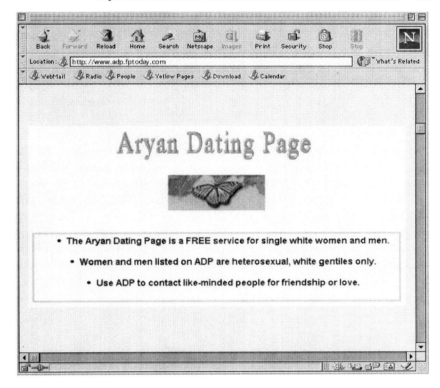

Lonely hearts for "white gentiles only"

The male ads provided an equally unexpected set of portraits of white supremacy. Frank, a forty-eight-year-old, divorced single parent from Palo Alto, California, wrote: "Today I'm a responsible parent and have my views but don't go out of my way to let it be known unless confronted, I have tattoos, and am down for the Aryan race. So hope to hear from you fine ladies in the near future. PS know how to treat a lady and that's with love and respect."[81] Here Frank presented himself as a kind of white-supremacist "new man." This is contrasted with the ad of John Botti, a twenty-five-year-old from Los Altos who presented himself as a kind of preppy, "going places" nineties man. He wrote: "I am looking for someone who is as conservative and pretty as hell. Equally as important is someone with a quality education."[82] These are images of fascism in the Information Age that bear little resemblance to previous incarnations. This was brought home very powerfully by the image of Max, a thirty-six-year-old Canadian, who described himself as a "long-time Movement activist." He listed his interests as anthropology, Monty Python's humor, the *Titanic* story, Celtic music, and Civil War reenacting.

Max chose to have his photograph taken at his computer keyboard, where he presented himself as the picture of technological proficiency. This struck me, the first time I saw it, as a very appropriate image of the face of late-twentieth-century white supremacism.

Through these accounts we glimpse the ways in which these people move between mainstream society and the world of the cyber-Nazi and White Power movements. This is signaled by Cathy's mention of having photographs taken with the girls from the office and Frank's description of picking up his seven-year-old daughter from school and keeping his views to himself "unless confronted." In this sense the different cultural modalities discussed in this chapter allow different types of whiteness to be inhabited at various times. In one moment the mainstream whiteness of the school or workplace—coded here as normality—is occupied, while at other times the public privacy of the Internet digitally facilitates the communion with a whiteness that announces itself openly. The technological clothes of these identities provide an ontological milieu in which the interplay between symbol and self can be established in new time/space coordinates.

"White Pride World Wide"?

The circuit of this international system is made possible by a shared translocal notion of race. This is reflected and enshrined in Don Black's slogan "WHITE PRIDE WORLD WIDE," which has been used by Resistance Records as a title for their compilation albums of White Power music. Racist rock fans belong to distinct national settings, yet they can all position themselves within a shared translocal racial lineage. These connections are rendered explicit; consider this passage from an e-mail sent to Stormfront: "I am a 20 year old white American with roots in North America dating back 300 years and then into Europe, Normandy, France. Well anyways, I am proud to here [hear] of an organization for the advancement of whites."[83]

The Internet provides a context to trace these genealogies, fostering a transnational notion of whiteness that unites Old World racial nationalisms (i.e., in Europe and Scandinavia) with the white diasporas of the New World (i.e., in the United States, Canada, South Africa, Australia, New Zealand, and parts of South America). New connections are being established among ultra-right-wing sites in North America, Western Europe, and Scandinavia at a considerable pace. Yet it is still the American websites and newsgroups that are the most sophisticated. A survey of Stormfront's archived letters shows that 70 percent of all correspondence comes from the United States and Canada, with only 14 percent from Western Europe and Scandinavia.[84] Similarly, most of the activity on the Web, be it the Aryan Dating site or the Hammerskins site, is predominantly American in focus.

Computer simulation and transnational information networks provide a key context in which the theoretical and political tensions between the ethnocentric and Eurocentric elements of contemporary racism can be worked through. In this sense it is necessary not only to explore the impact of technological change on racist cultures, but also to reconceptualize how racism works within and beyond the boundaries of particular nation-states. Ethnocentric forms of racism seem to be targeted at particular minority groups depending on the specific national context and their histories of migration and racialization. Similar patterns of substitution and commensurability apply to the understanding of ethnocentric racism within the context of the Internet. The nationalists in Germany focus on the Turks, whereas their compatriots in Britain will demonize Afro-Caribbeans and South Asians. The processes of racialization are commensurable even though the complexion of the racial "other" varies.

The international Jew is an omnipresent figure of hate within the cultures described here. It seems that the preexisting histories of anti-Semitism in North America and Europe are being given a new lease on life within cyberculture. Anti-Semitic ideas are enhanced by the Internet's global framework precisely because these discourses have historically been articulated through a notion of an international conspiracy. This may go some way to explaining the high level of anti-Semitic sentiment found within the neofascist Internet world. The cover of a White Power music compilation *Leaderless Resistance* represents the Jew as a serpent preying on a shackled white man. Taken from the Resistance Records website, this extreme anti-Semitic image reinvigorates the historical legacy of the Jew represented as a predatory subhuman. Similarly, a cartoon that was posted on the White Aryan Resistance website showed the Jew as a parasite to be exterminated, the caption reading:

> They sting like a bee
> Dart like a flea
> Strip you bare like a locust
> You, too, will make a ready meal
> If you remain unfocused
> Stand up! Take arms!
> Defend yourself . . .

Like the heroes of the past
When the Kikes come crawlin'
Just send them sprawlin'
With a dose of poison gas!

These are images that are not in themselves new, since they have been part of anti-Semitic ideas for some time and were articulated in a different form by the Nazis in their attempt to dehumanize Jews. Sophisticated digital technology is enabling these products of the racist imagination to be circulated in an unprecedented way.

It might be possible to talk here about an emergent elementary structure that can describe this translocal whiteness. Picking up the point made by Deleuze and Guattari at the beginning of this chapter, these networks possess a supple segmentarity that combines recombinant, molecular qualities with lateral connection. They operate through the boundaries of nation-states and national particularity, while at the same time these supple white rhizomes possess a series of discursive strands. First, this notion of whiteness promotes a *racial lineage* that is plotted through, and sustained by, cyberspace. This transnational technology, which in many respects has come to personify the permeability of human cultures, is used here to foster and articulate an ethos of *racial separation*. The racist Internet world itself becomes the embodiment of this ideal, with individuals at their computers projecting themselves into a simulated "racial homeland"—this, despite the fact that it is almost impossible to maintain a hermetic digital world without the potential intrusion of "outsiders." At a deeper level many extreme-right users of the Internet are also concerned that their enemies have access to the very technology that they are using. In a posting to alt.politics White Power leader Reuben Logsdon articulated a key concern: "The main problem with racial separation is that with all this damn communications technology, Jewish media can still be broadcast into the country to corrupt whites, and whites can still meet marriage partners over the net from outside Greater White Amerikkka."[85]

Such views reflect the very real ambivalence that extreme-right activists feel in supporting the right to "free speech," but within the present political climate it is also clear that their strongest defense is to argue for unhindered access to the technology that they also see as a threat to their notions of racial and cultural purity. An essay posted on Stormfront in 1996 by L. R. Beam warns of "The Conspiracy to Erect an Electronic Iron Curtain." The author states that any attempts at censorship will be met by what he calls "acts of random electronic violence." He then goes on to compare attempts at censorship to "a sort of information cleansing of the Internet" and quotes one activist as saying "I'll give up my information when they pry my cold dead fingers from the keyboard."[86]

Second, this notion of whiteness has a relational "other," or more accurately a gallery of "others." Through the processes of substitution the image of alterity can take on different forms depending on local circumstances (that is, Turks in Germany or black people in America). However, representations of particular racial minorities within this international framework are commensurable with each other in that, depending on circumstances, they can be substituted without changing the elementary structure of this translocal whiteness. In this sense the "other" is designated as a *social contaminant* both in the racial body and within the wider society.[87] Through these figures of otherness the threat of race/cultural miscegenation ("immigrants," "slaves," "guest workers," "race mixers") and/or sexual difference ("gays," "lesbians") is named and attributed to particular people. In addition to the coupling of *otherness* and *contamination* there is articulation between *alterity* and *conspiracy.* This is the field in which the figure of the international Jew looms in these white looks. As Susan Zickmund points out: "Thus the Jew is constructed as the agent which lies hidden within institutions possessing hegemonic power, structures which they then use to manipulate society. The government, the media, and even the spread of academic knowledge or ideological doctrines may emanate ultimately from this source."[88]

Finally, there is the *minoritization of whiteness* within the rhetoric of White Power activists. Here whiteness is seen to be under threat, to have been superseded demographically on a global scale. This is exemplified in the White Power band New Minority, whose recording "White, Straight and Proud" complains that white men have become a lesser part in "their" world. George Burdi, who signed this band to the Resistance Records label, reinforces this lament: "Look at the global population levels. Whites account for only 8% of the planet's population. Only 2% of the babies born last year [1995] were white. . . . It's WHITE PEOPLE that are the 'new' minority."[89] This form of discourse is not confined to the digitally assisted whiteness found in the digital domain. Cindy Patton has outlined a similar process in the writing of the New Right in the United States. She outlines the specific minoritarian identity discourse, expressed in periodicals like *New Dimensions,* that is opposed to both the rainbow coalition of gays/blacks/feminists and far-right white supremacists. While New Right campaigners profess a nonracialized identity as "real Americans," their claims to minority status are based on a set of premises similar to those of White Power groups. Here the image of the all-pervasive Jewish conspiracy or ZOG (Zionist Occupation Government) is replaced with the idea that the institutions of the media and the state have been captured by black, gay, and feminist "special interest" groups.[90] Taken together, these elements constitute the core ambient factors in a whiteness that is sustained in cyberspace and within which racist activists from a range of national contexts locate themselves.

While the Internet is making it possible for these forms of fascist activity to take on a new shape, the compression of time and space also brings racist activists into extreme forms of contact. This seems to have accelerated the tendency toward factionalism, which has mercifully haunted postwar fascism. The vituperative on-line feud between Harold A. Covington of the American National Socialist White People's Party and William L. Pierce of National Alliance, and their respective sets of supporters, is perhaps the best example of this syndrome. In March 1998 Covington, reflecting on what he referred to as "The Future of the White Internet," wrote:

> First off, we need to look at the PRESENT of the White Internet. I do not have to tell you that a) It is a tremendously valuable tool and an immense amount of good has been worked out of the Net; while, simultaneously b) The Net is being viciously and tragically abused by a shockingly large number of either bogus or deranged "White Racists" . . . I think it is too early just yet to quantify just how the lunacy interacts with, counteracts and affects the impact of the serious political work. It is like panning for gold in a flowing sewer; both the raw, and toxic sewage and the gold are there, and the question is how much gold any individual can extract before the fumes and the corruption drive him off—or until he keels over and falls in and becomes part of the sewer system.[91]

Cyberspace offers new possibilities, but it also accelerates the long-standing tendency toward attrition and division within the neofascist movement. The Information Age is changing the relationship among time, space, and form in racist culture. New territories of whiteness exceed the boundaries of the nation-state, while supplanting ethnocentric racisms with new translocal forms of racial narcissism and xenophobia.

Vron Ware

5. MOTHERS OF INVENTION: GOOD HEARTS, INTELLIGENT MINDS, AND SUBVERSIVE ACTS

Obviously, no amount of writing by radical intellectuals can stand in for a freedom movement in which ideas can be tested. But it is nonetheless incumbent on those of us who have argued that seeing race as socially constructed is a vital intellectual breakthrough to suggest where we think that breakthrough may lead politically.

— DAVID R. ROEDIGER

David R. Roediger suggests quite rightly in the above epigraph that this expanding body of written work on whiteness cannot really be tested until it has been put into practice,[1] which means that it is vital to discuss the forms of political agency that might flow from a radical analysis of race-thinking. This sense that the work might have important consequences for activists must surely motivate many people who take the trouble to read it. In our case, forced by virtue of living outside the United States to translate the many insights and theories under discussion there to a different setting, we have had to consider the transnational application of this new scholarship in the absence of much parallel work that addresses the historical construction of whiteness in a British context. But to what extent is it feasible to adopt political strategies from one national setting and make them work in another? Can specific histories be made to speak to each other?

One example that comes to mind is the campaign to attack the racist platform of Pauline Hanson's One Nation Party in Australia. In the period preceding the 1998 general election actors, comedians, musicians, and other entertainers adopted the tactic of savage parody to combat Hanson's white supremacist views. Drag queen Pauline Pantsdown used voice-clips from Hanson's speeches to make fun of her attacks on Asian immigrants and aborigines, and Pantsdown's single "I'm a Backdoor Man (Why Can't My Blood Be Coloured White)" was taken off the air after One Nation won a court injunction—but not before it had sold ten thousand copies.[2] Pantsdown, whose real name is Simon Hunt, also stood as a candidate for the Senate, the upper house of federal parliament in Australia, against David Oldfield, the strategist behind the One Nation Party. It is impossible to assess what part this cultural broadside played in the party's resounding defeat in the election, but in Britain at least the activities of antiracist campaigners in the period preceding the election received almost as much media attention as the despicable Hanson herself. But we must ask these questions: Could these particular vaudeville tactics travel? Could they be translated to other places with different cultural repertoires and turned against local targets to the same effect? Or to put it another way, how effective is satire as a means to undermine and dismantle the forces of white supremacy within a global as well as local context?

Using the transatlantic abolitionist movement as another, entirely different resource, it is possible to find numerous ways in which individuals and organizations in Britain and America exchanged ideas, provided inspiration, gave and received both practical and financial support—and conducted furious arguments and feuds. The volumes of surviving correspondence between black and white abolitionists provide ample evidence of this traffic. Yet this example triggers further questions: Is it appropriate to make comparisons between the international movement against racial slavery in the nineteenth century and resistance to white supremacism in its local and global forms that we face at the start of the twenty-first? Can we move at random between different historical periods as well as between countries in this quest to develop—or test—a renewed politics for social justice? Because it is taken out of context, Roediger's statement has the unfortunate effect of suggesting that a line can be drawn between the way that radical intellectuals comprehend "race" today and the ways that it has been understood in the past, however recent or long ago. This has further implications for the kinds of politics that might emerge from this new, postmodern symposium, since it infers that it would not necessarily be useful to look to the past for examples of successful strategies. I want to argue for the necessity of compiling genealogies of resistance to white supremacy in the interest of testing and refining appropriate and effective political responses to race-thinking by those categorized as white.

Although it is always important to specify time and place in any analysis of whiteness, we believe that it is also necessary to carry out cross-cultural, comparative studies of the many inventive, subversive, and possibly even futile methods used to contest it. In order to focus this rather ambitious project, I will center it around the question that Malcolm X was frequently asked when he toured the United States giving lectures in the 1960s: what *can* a sincere white person do?

Apart from his status in his own country, Malcolm X was a hugely influential figure in other parts of the world, particularly in Africa and other colonial settings. His speeches and publications were extraordinarily important to activists fighting white supremacy in different locations in the second half of the twentieth century, a fact that helps to underline the importance of keeping an internationalist and a historical perspective. I will examine some American responses to this question, but first I want to turn to the history of struggle against apartheid in South Africa to discuss some of the ways in which this question was dealt with there. This comparison between these two countries is particularly appropriate because historians have been able to show important connections between the system of segregation—"the highest stage of white supremacy"—as it operated there and as it was structured in the American South. John W. Cell, for example, has examined both countries during the period from 1890 to 1925 in order to compare the "evolving matrix of race and class relations in two societies that are widely regarded as being the most pervasively racist in the world."[3] His thesis is that the system and ideology of segregation represent an essentially revolutionary form of social control that arose out of racial slavery and colonialism. He argues that apartheid and Jim Crow did not evolve inevitably from these histories, but were systematically created in both places. He contrasts this view with that of George Fredrickson, whose own book *White Supremacy: A Comparative Study of American and South African History* places a different emphasis on "the slave and frontier past" in his explanation of the historical origins of segregation.[4] This literature demonstrates the value of a comparative approach to the historiography of whiteness and provides further motivation for thinking creatively about traditions of resistance.

Looking outside academic texts the symbolic figure of Mohandas K. Gandhi can be used to bring some of these links to life. First, it was in South Africa that Gandhi developed an analysis of British colonialism and white supremacy, which he was able to apply to his native country, India. Second, the fact that he was not of African descent, and in South Africa was classified as Indian, helps to undermine the binary constantly implied by a focus on whiteness. The project of racial classification may have had the desired effect of holding those defined as white at the opposite end of a spectrum from those defined as black, but this did not mean that the other racially defined groups did not serve equally important functions in holding that system in place. A third reason why Gandhi is such an iconic figure in this genealogy is, of course, that his philosophy and tactics of nonviolent resistance, *Satyagraha,* refined and practiced in the Indian struggle against British colonialism, were adopted by freedom movements worldwide, most notably by the African National Congress in 1952 and by Martin Luther King Jr. across the Atlantic.

A Way of Telling a Story

We, the people of South Africa, declare for all our country and the world to know:
That South Africa belongs to all who live in it, black and white, and that no government can justly claim authority unless it is based on the will of the people;
That only a democratic state, based on the will of the people, can secure to all their birthright without distinction of colour, race, sex or belief;
And therefore, we the people of South Africa, black and white, together equals, countrymen and brothers, adopt this Freedom Charter. And we pledge ourselves to strive together, sparing nothing of our strength and courage, until the democratic changes here set out have been won.

—FROM THE FREEDOM CHARTER, 1955

Non-racialism is not just a bland thing. It is not just an absence of racism—that's empty. In fact, the reality of developing a non-racial culture in South Africa is much richer than that. It is much more active, more dynamic. It includes language, song, it includes dance, movement, it includes laughter, a way of telling a story, a way of making a political point. I enjoy seeing a way of working that maybe takes a little longer, but involves people much more. It has a richness, a strength. It is popular in the sense of being people-oriented, people participatory.

—ALBIE SACHS

In a remarkable book entitled *The Unbreakable Thread,* Julie Frederikse charted the concept of nonracialism in the history of South African politics. Drawing on interviews with leading activists, documentation from key organizations, and transcriptions from legal proceedings she worked collaboratively with the Popular History Trust in Harare to produce a history that could be of service to democratic South Africans and their antiapartheid supporters, who were at the time of publication (1990), still struggling to overthrow the government. The book begins with quotes from representatives of several national organizations, such as the African National Congress (ANC), the Mass Democratic Movement, and the Institute for a Democratic Alternative for South Africa, each making connections between the struggle for democracy and the principle of nonracialism.

An extract from Nelson Mandela's first public address after his release from prison expands on this in greater detail: "We call upon our white compatriots to join us in the shaping of a new South Africa—the freedom movement is a political home for you, too. Universal suffrage on a common voters' roll in a united, democratic and non-racial South Africa is the only way to peace and racial harmony."[5] This speech was broadcast in many countries and had an immeasurable effect on the anti-apartheid movement worldwide. In her introduction, Frederikse explains that "non-racialism" is a word that is used repeatedly in the history of South African demands for justice: "In an era of pat slogans, sung and shouted at mass meetings and headlines in leaflets and banners, this word stands out precisely because it is not glib." Echoing Albie Sachs's assertion that nonracialism represents a dynamic and "people participatory" goal that signifies far more than an absence of racism,[6] she makes the claim that the demand for a nonracial South Africa is the common ground that unites a wide range of forces for change. "To be democratic," she asserts, "the future South Africa must be non-racial: that premise is fundamental."

The book is divided chronologically into five parts, beginning in 1652 with the early European colonization of South Africa, the introduction of racial hierarchies, and documented resistance to the divide-and-rule tactics of the colonizers. The second and subsequent sections deal with the post-1950 period and the attempts of the apartheid government to repress all forms of opposition to the regime. The book's title refers to the way that the ideal of nonracialism, enshrined in the Freedom Charter adopted at the foundation conference of the South African Congress of Trade Unions (SACTU) in 1955,[7] survived the murder and mass imprisonment of thousands of its believers and the competition with the different movements for black autonomy and African nationalism. From the historic Rivonia trial in 1964, which culminated in the imprisonment of Nelson Mandela, Walter Sisulu, Govan Mbeki, Ahmed Kathrada, Raymond Mhlaba, Andrew Mlangeni, Elias Motsoaledi, and Denis Goldberg, until the early 1980s, the Freedom Charter remained more of an underground document than a publicly available manifesto. This meant that many whites were ignorant of the aims of organizations like the ANC and often demoralized by indecision and confusion over what their most appropriate political response to the regime might be. The interviews bear living witness to the bitter arguments over the role of whites in these struggles. The demand for black autonomy, the influence of Marxist analysis, and the role of the Communist Party are some of the most important factors that determined the political choices adopted by individuals and organizations. There is far too much detail to compress here, but there are two constant themes brought to life in this book that might help to illuminate key issues within this ongoing history.

The first concerns the arguments over autonomy versus integration and the idea that there was an undeniable logic in favor of working in mixed organizations against a system that defined people by color. In his Rivonia speech Mandela defined the main aims of the ANC in fighting, first, for an end to poverty in South Africa through redistribution of its wealth and resources and, second, for political rights for all its citizens. Outlining the history of his own ambivalent relationship to Marxism and the Communist Party, he made it clear that the ANC was prepared to fight alongside any committed organization that recognized the artificiality of political division based on color. However, the Black Consciousness movement, founded in the 1970s, condemned the notion of racial integration, asserting that it would inevitably entail the domination of blacks by whites.

Using language and arguments that can be linked directly to the American Black Power movement, this extract from a policy manifesto produced by the separatist South African Students Organisation (SASO) in 1973 explains the need to exclude whites:

> SASO believes that:
>
> a) South Africa is a country in which both black and white live and shall continue to live together;
>
> b) That the white man must be made aware that one is either part of the solution or part of the problem;
>
> c) That in this context, because of their privileges accorded to them by legislation, and because of their continual maintenance of an oppressive regime, whites have defined themselves as part of the problem;
>
> d) That therefore we believe that in all matters relating to the struggle towards realizing our aspirations, whites must be excluded;
>
> e) That this attitude must not be interpreted by blacks to imply "antiwhitism," but merely a more positive way of attaining a more normal situation in South Africa.[8]

Pandelani Nefolovhodwe, a founding member of SASO, explained the thinking behind this new development:

> From 1960 up to about 1966 there was a lull in this country, but as early as about 1967 some people got involved in trying to shape a new direction. We were debating issues like the disaffiliation from NUSAS [National Union of South African Students], as part

of this new mood which wanted to get away from liberalism as a form of struggle.

At that stage we were in a state where we were searching for our own identity. We had to liberate ourselves from this psychological oppression, and to do so the argument was that you have got to be away from the people who on a daily basis infuse you with an idea of their superiority, because if you continue to be with them you will forever not be able to extricate yourself.[9]

This notion that Black Consciousness was a necessary stage in the development of a more inclusive movement for democracy occurs repeatedly in these interviews. Many younger activists were incarcerated during this period, and those who found themselves in the notorious Robben Island prison discovered internees from an earlier generation of struggle whom they knew little about. Patrick Lehota, another founding member of SASO, was sentenced in 1976 along with eight other Black Consciousness leaders. He assessed this earlier part of his life in relation to the education he subsequently received in prison: "I regard my days in SASO as my formative years, politically. We saw the struggle strictly in terms of one race versus another race. We were deprived of the wealth of the heritage of struggle which others who had gone before us had already amassed. We moved into this as virgins, completely. We were bound therefore, to commit mistakes, in terms of judgment."[10]

It was during the course of his discussion with Mandela and other freedom fighters that he broadened his understanding of the issues involved in fighting for a free, nonracial, and democratic South Africa. For many younger activists in his position the involvement of people like Joe Slovo, Ruth First, Denis Goldberg, and Bram Fischer provided conclusive evidence that whites were prepared to play an active role in the ANC, and their example was a very important symbol of nonracialism in practice. But Lehota himself rejected this view in favor of a more radical adoption of ANC principles: "All of us who embrace the non-racial line do so not because there are some white people participating in the struggle—we embrace the non-racial line, first and foremost, because we consider it to be right. . . . The participation of white democrats in the struggle in our country is only evidence of the correctness of our non-racial approach—not that the correctness of non-racialism is predicated upon them participating."[11] The correctness that Lehota refers to here stems from the revelation that separatism entailed fighting apartheid on its own terms: if the system distinguishes between people purely on the basis of skin color and a spurious notion of race, then no movement that accepts this arbitrary division will prevail. Many activists during the late 1970s and early 1980s spoke of their sense that the regime was far more threatened by and punitive toward those organizations like the ANC that were mixed, while showing a greater degree of tolerance toward those that worked along separatist lines. Steve Tshwete, sentenced to fifteen years in prison for Umkhonto we Sizwe sabotage activities in 1964, spoke of the conviction shared by ANC members that the Black Consciousness movement was ultimately an obstacle to national liberation:

> We knew it was the responsibility of the revolutionary movement to direct the Black Consciousness Movement into more progressive positions. I mean, we certainly knew that BC could give problems in the long run, by reason of it being colour politics. Colour politics are dangerous. They are just as bad as tribal politics, you know. That's why we know that the imperialist countries were very much interested in boosting Black Consciousness, knowing that the politics of the skin are going to blunt the revolutionary drive of the working class, and in particular, the anti-imperialist nature of the struggle.[12]

The second theme that emerges from Frederikse's collection concerns the ways that whites saw their own roles during this period from 1950 to 1990. Again, this is far too complex and fragmentary to compress here, but I want to give some examples of strategies and tactics that were found to be particularly effective in the struggle against apartheid. I have already mentioned the symbolic importance of the most outspoken leaders like Slovo, First, and Goldberg. Along with many others they risked their lives working alongside blacks to undermine the system and to persuade others through action and analysis.[13] But it is not these examples that concern me here.

Many of the interviews indicate that white activists were often unsure as to their most effective role, and they often speak of the debilitating effects of guilt and shame in their own and others' attempts to work in mixed organizations. One of the most famous of these was the Black Sash group, an organization of women founded initially in 1955 as the Defence of the Constitution League to protest at the removal of "coloureds" from the common voters' roll. The organization began to set up advice centers and to arrange bail funds to support hundreds of black women who were imprisoned for refusing to apply for passes. Their concern for individuals suffering through the destruction of their families echoes the activities of women abolitionists in the United States and in

Britain over a century earlier, where hundreds of women were persuaded to campaign against slavery upon being told about the violation of family relationships under plantation slavery.

According to Sheena Duncan, Black Sash members retained this concern, but developed a broader understanding of the structures and ideologies at work under apartheid, and this was reflected in their changing strategies:

> We've moved from our naive belief that if you could convey to people such as English-speaking businessmen, the human suffering involved in migrant labour, if you could convey that to them, they would do something to get rid of it. Our whole attitude has toughened considerably in that respect because we discovered that people, on the whole, are not moved by human suffering, and that you therefore have to find political pressures that will start hurting them enough to make them move. If profits are threatened, that is when you get white people in this country to act. . . . What moves them is what hurts them, not what hurts other people.[14]

The accompanying photograph of a Black Sash protest, showing a row of respectably dressed white women, with hats, handbags, and placards, standing shoulder to shoulder in the street, casts a different inflection on these words. It suggests that the impact of this particular organization stemmed partly from the apparent incongruity of middle-class white women taking a militant stand against a political system that ostensibly served their interests.

The awareness of many Black Sash members that arguments alone could not persuade many whites to renounce the privileges afforded to them by white supremacy was shared by other groups of activists, who nonetheless struggled with their own sense of having grown up with access to a university education and professional training. Many did consciously give up these unearned privileges by refusing the opportunity for well-paid careers to work in the struggle, while some of these tried to use their training to more subversive ends. Dave Lewis, a trade union leader during the 1980s, explained that the problem of white guilt caused some whites to keep a low profile in predominantly black organizations, embarrassed by their ability to understand and articulate:

> How I, as a white, function, is important, there's no doubt about it, and how I, as a white, relate to black workers is important, but my position as an intellectual is actually a more interesting

contradiction that has to be resolved. . . . My ability to write and articulate the way I do has been a function of the kind of privileges that have been granted to me because I'm a white South African, and I still think that my primary way of paying back some of this is to use that, is to say, "Look, I've great respect for your organisation, but I think you're heading in the wrong direction. I may be right or I may be wrong in my assessment, but nevertheless this is what I think, based on sort of ten years of reading Althusser and Lenin and bloody newspapers." I think that part of the guilt of being a white South African is that the minute you get involved in realpolitik, you feel you can't say anything because you haven't really experienced it, and you are, after all, part of the oppressors. I don't buy that.[15]

The combination of guilt, state harassment, discouragement in the face of black separatism, and other key factors prevented many whites from organizing politically in the 1970s. In 1982 trade unionist and medical doctor Neil Aggett became the first white political prisoner to die in Security Police custody. Shortly after this Barbara Hogan was sentenced to ten years in prison for gathering information for the ANC. According to Frederikse, both these events had a profound impact on the "white left." David Webster, a social anthropology lecturer at the University of the Witwatersrand, and a friend of Hogan, recalls his own response: "We all developed politically at that time, because up until then it had been rather an abstract kind of game, and then suddenly it was the real thing: torture and life and death. I helped form the Detainees' Parents Support Committee (DPSC) and Detainees' Support Committee (Descom). By working in the detention field, one learned in a very empirical way what you were up against: the ruthlessness of the state and what it is capable of, in terms of its raw power. It was an alarming thing—I was quite naive until then."[16]

Webster also makes a point of mentioning the influence of Helen Joseph, who had been unbanned in 1982 and immediately went onto university campuses to talk about the aims of the ANC and "this glorious non-racial past." He continues: "With this lack of knowledge about the ANC and its policies, broadly, whites hadn't heard of the Freedom Charter until about 1981—it was a forbidden topic. She was a point of entry, because she looks like a granny and she is so reasonable and sweet. She was critical in raising a whole white generation's consciousness about the non-racialism of the struggle in the old days."

Although it is very hard to do more than select a few statements reflecting moments in this extraordinary history of opposition to the apartheid regime, I want to end this section with another contribution from Black Sash. Speaking of an occasion when group members were called to a township police station by a community organization, Molly Blackburn, Port Elizabeth Black Sash leader, described how "by some strange quirk" they found themselves witnessing a young black boy being whipped as he lay on the blood-soaked floor, handcuffed to a table. Since they were able to give very clear details of the incident, it actually made the headlines, but seemed to have little impact on public opinion. This story prompted Frederikse to ask: "Which do you see as more important: going to the black areas and standing up for rights there, or making changes amongst your own community of whites?" Blackburn replied:

> I don't think it's possible to make changes amongst the white community without black involvement, and by that I mean not only taking terrified whites over to the other side to go and look at the community problems and showing them that really they don't need to be so fearful, but I also mean that it's important to bring articulate, sensitive, clear-thinking black leadership over to this side to talk to the whites, and let them question and cross question. These sorts of meetings which we've had with them have been very, very productive and useful.[17]

It is important to note here, however, that Blackburn's interview is followed by a discussion about the toll that this outreach work took on black leaders. A conversation with the Reverend Frank Chihane, general secretary of the Institute for Contextual Theology (ICT) from 1983 to 1987 and Transvaal United Democratic Front executive member, reveals that "[i]t is painful to speak to white audiences, to help them out of the heavy propaganda they have been subjected to, but I feel I have to do it, even if it is only a few who become committed." All racially defined groups living in South Africa are victims of apartheid, and all are battling to come out of the system. The fact that whites belong to the ruling group does not disqualify them from dissent: "my theory makes allowance that there would be a few people—I'm not expecting a lot of whites to come on our side, but a few—who become committed and give their lives to be part of that struggle. It is a matter of them participating and proving their genuineness in action more than trying to theorize about the possibility of their participation."

This discussion of nonracialism in the context of the recent South African past argues for the necessity of taking both a historical and a comparative approach to questions of resistance to white supremacy. Although it is always relevant to demonstrate the local manifestations of race-thinking and the particular conditions set by the specific context in which it takes effect, here I want to stress the continuity, however tenuous or disjointed, of ideas, strategies, and experiences of those challenging the operations of White Power in widely differing places and historical periods. In the next part of this chapter I want to return to my earlier question about the type of politics that might emerge from the new scholarship on whiteness, which is being produced mainly in the United States. This will involve a discussion of some of the more programmatic ways that writers and activists have proposed to undermine (or at least damage) the edifice of white supremacy, acting both on their own and collectively, under and outside the more traditional heading of "anti-racism."

"Honest Black/White Brotherhood"

"What *can* a sincere white person do?" The emphasis that Malcolm X gives this question in his autobiography implies that the sincerity is genuine, but also suggests a desperation induced by not knowing exactly what to do. I am less concerned with his actual reply in the 1960s than with the representation of his political position in more postmodern times. The film *Malcolm X,* directed by Spike Lee, came out in 1993. The opening section purports to show Malcolm's earlier life as a hustler in New York, taking drugs, dancing and sleeping with white women, and leading the dissolute life of a petty criminal. Following Malcolm's conversion in prison and his renunciation of hedonism and crime, white women disappear from the story with the exception of one scene that I have reproduced below, with the help of the published transcript. A young white woman, a college student, approaches Malcolm on his way to deliver a lecture at the Harvard Law School. Flanked by several male companions and bodyguards, Malcolm stops briefly to listen to what she has to say. She asks:

> Mr. X, I've read some of your speeches and I honestly believe a lot of what you say has truth to it. I have a good heart. I'm a good person despite my whiteness. What can the good white people like myself, who are not prejudiced, or racist, what can we do to help the cause?[18]

Malcolm stares at her and then answers, "Nothing," before walking away. The young woman is left "crushed," according to the script, and runs away in tears.

The predominantly young, black audience in the north London cinema where I saw the film hooted with laughter at the white student's humiliation. But this scene represented a similar episode in Malcolm X's autobiography, where he describes a young white woman who tracks him down to ask him the same question, to which he gives the same reply. However, in the autobiography the encounter is made more complex for two reasons. First, it comes after Malcolm has given a historical account of the white woman's role in slavery, and, second, the conversation takes place in Harlem, an area where few white people would dare to go, rather than on the grounds of a white, privileged university, where the student was able to speak to Malcolm from a "safe" vantage point. Malcolm's own version also conveyed a degree of compassion and reflection absent from the film:

> I will never forget one little blond co-ed after I had spoken to her at her New England college. She must have caught the next plane behind that one I took to New York. She found the Muslim restaurant in Harlem. I just happened to be there when she came in. Her clothes, her carriage, her accent, all showed Deep South white breeding and money. . . .
>
> Anyway, I'd never seen anyone I ever spoke before more affected than this little white college girl. She demanded, right up in my face, "Don't you believe there are any *good* white people?" I didn't want to hurt her feelings. I told her, "People's *deeds* I believe in, Miss—not their words."
>
> "What can I *do?*" she exclaimed. I told her, "Nothing." She burst out crying, and ran out and up Lennox Avenue and caught a taxi.[19]

Later in the book Malcolm referred back to this incident when reflecting on his revised aims and strategies, developed after extensive travel throughout Africa and Western Europe. He wrote specifically about the way that his attempts to work toward "a society in which there could exist honest black/white brotherhood" were being dogged by his earlier image as a black separatist—"my old so-called 'Black Muslim' image." In his speeches and interviews he stated clearly that, in the United States at any rate, the struggle against the white man's racism was a human problem and that both races, as human beings, had the "obligation," the "responsibility," of helping to correct America's human problem. He distinctly outlined the tasks that white people could engage in to support this struggle and acknowledged that he was frequently bombarded by whites asking, "What can I do to help?" In his reflections he recalled the young white woman who had first asked him that question:

I knew, better than most Negroes, how many white people truly wanted to see American racial problems solved. I knew that many whites were as frustrated as Negroes. I'll bet I got fifty letters some days from white people. The white people in meeting audiences would throng around me, asking me, after I had addressed them somewhere, "What *can* a sincere white person do?"

When I say that here now, it makes me think about that little co-ed I told you about, the one who flew from her New England college down to New York and came up to me in the Nation of Islam's restaurant in Harlem, and I told her that there was "nothing" that she could do. I regret that I told her that. I wish that now I knew her name, or where I could telephone her, or write to her, and tell her what I tell white people now when they present themselves as being sincere, and ask me, one way or another, the same thing that she asked.

. . . I tell sincere white people, "Work in conjunction with us— each one of us working among our own kind." Let sincere white individuals find all other white people they can who feel as they do—and let them form their own all-white groups, to work trying to convert other white people who are thinking and acting so racist. Let sincere whites go and teach non-violence to white people! . . . Working separately, the sincere white people and sincere black people actually will be working together.[20]

This reflection does not appear in the film, an omission that is all the more puzzling because it is represented in the published version of the script. The missing scene acknowledges Malcolm's conscientious recollection of the "little co-ed" by setting up a similar encounter with a young white woman toward the end of the film, when Malcolm has left the Nation and is engaged in trying to set up his own organization. The young woman's question is framed deliberately to evoke the earlier episode:

I have a good heart. I'm a good person despite my whiteness. What can the good white people like myself who are not prejudiced do to help the cause of the Negro?

The script instructs Malcolm to pause before he replies: "Let sincere white individuals find other white people who feel as they do and teach non-violence to those whites who think and act so racist." And he adds: "Let's all pray without ceasing. May Allah bless you."[21]

The decision to cut this scene was presumably based on expediency, since the film was considerably overlength and had to be further cut back before it was passed for general release. However, I am not going to be drawn into speculating here on Lee's motives for this excision. I want to argue instead that it helps to create the powerful impression that destroying white supremacy is a task for black people alone, despite the suggestion toward the end that white men who are Muslim might have a supporting role to play. By excising a scene that would neatly reinforce Malcolm's radically altered political strategy of working toward "honest black/white brotherhood," the film turns away from the opportunity of engaging with a more complex politics of race—and, I think, gender. The white woman who wanted to "help" is left as a laughingstock; she becomes irrelevant to the more serious business of brotherhood, consigned to the world of decadence and mindless pleasure suggested in the opening sequence.

It is hard to assess the educational impact of a film such as *Malcolm X* on younger generations, both within and outside the United States, who do not share living memories of the 1960s. If it inspired many to go back and read the autobiography, it may well have introduced them to more complex and challenging ideas than the movie was able to supply. Yet the movie was clearly intended for the widest possible audience. In a conversation with Arthur Jaffa, bell hooks deals with the fact that this film about one of the most important African American political figures begins with him having sex with a white woman. "Well, I totally relate that to the position of white women as consumers in this society and the fact that in any kind of activity, whether it's bookselling or filmgoing, white women are the top of the list for the consuming audience. And they're seeing themselves at the very beginning, as though they are where this powerful black man's life begins."[22] If she is right that Lee was demonstrating his awareness of what lures people into the cinema, then it seems reasonable to ask why he did not offer these same consumers a sense of how they might connect politically with the ideas of Malcolm X, assuming that he was interested in those ideas in the first place. By humiliating the white figure who declares a commitment to fighting white supremacy, the film returns us to the prescriptive view of Rudyard Kipling: a man should, whatever happens, keep to his own caste, race, and breed.

Despite the bleak scenario offered to global audiences through the vehicle of *Malcolm X*, versions of the same question remain a recurrent motif in North American culture. The most recent example that I have found is contained in a comprehensive academic reader entitled *Critical White Studies*, edited by Richard Delgado and Jean Stefancic and published in 1997. The volume contains over one hundred contributions and reprints from a wide range of mostly contemporary authors, bringing an immensely valuable collection of perspectives to bear on the subjects of whiteness, white supremacy, and U.S. culture. Many of the articles deconstruct the concept of "race," while others pay more attention to the effects of racial hierarchy in political or legal institutions, for example. Authors address the question of biology and "pseudoscience" as well as examining the phenomenon of white supremacist groups in the United States. As a whole *Critical White Studies* represents a fair cross section of opinion and scholarship, which is to say that it spans the political divide between those who argue for the abolition of whiteness and those who propose the forging of a "positive white racial identity."[23]

In order to guide the unwary student approaching this book without a sense of direction, the editors have written a short introduction to each of its eleven sections. It is the final section that concerns us here. Under the heading "What Then Shall We Do? A Role for Whites" the editors outline the diverse positions that follow by asking some pertinent questions: "Whites may—and should—study race, including their own. That is the whole premise of this book. But suppose a white person wants to do more—wants to be an agent for change, wants to challenge and blast the systems of racial privilege and exclusion that bring so much misery to all those on the other side of the color line? What can a white person do? Is there a role for him or her in improving the fortunes of people of color?"[24]

Turning to the end of this section, effectively the end of the book, on a page with notes on suggested readings, there is a brief paragraph headed "From the Editors: Suggestions and Comments":

> Do whites have any role to play in liberation movements for blacks, Puerto Ricans, and other nonwhite groups? Or is it their most appropriate role working among their own people, raising consciousness and preaching racial tolerance? If a white person wants to be helpful to blacks, should he or she first come to terms with their own whiteness—and if so, what does that mean? If you are white, should you be a "race traitor" who goes round challenging the white point of view at every opportunity? Is every white— perhaps every person in our society—an unconscious racist, as a number of our writers assert? If so, should we all give up—or try harder?[25]

I found it very depressing that these should be the questions to emerge at the end of such an exhileratingly cacophonous assembly of voices. This concluding paragraph demonstrates perfectly the way that potentially radical and subversive scholarship on "race" and culture can become utterly meaningless when subsumed under the general heading of "whiteness studies." This may sound harsh in the face of this selected evidence, but these brief extracts reflect a basic hermeneutic problem that betrays the writers' lack of objectivity in assessing their material and locates them within a particular tradition of antiracism that is resolutely impervious to the claims of much new writing on whiteness.

Their first mistake is to imply that white supremacy, or "systems of racial privilege and exclusion," does damage only to those on "the other side" of the color line. They seem to be suggesting that whites ought to take an interest in race insofar as they benefit from the structures of power and privilege that flow from their categorization as white and they ought, if they want to "help" the victims of racism, to think about the best ways to improve themselves and to be more tolerant. This discourse renders invisible, or inaudible, the arguments of those (on both sides of this apparently unbreachable barrier) who have consistently demonstrated that "race" itself is a social construct and that whiteness is intimately and automatically related to blackness. The complex processes through which different ethnic groups entered the United States and achieved membership in the "white race," despite some inauspicious beginnings, are evidence enough that whiteness has historically been acquired at a price.

As several writers in that volume have painstakingly shown, this perspective on whiteness results in a different interpretation of U.S. history which documents precisely when and how the brutal strictures of capitalism, patriarchy, and white supremacy have seduced and press-ganged people into servitude. For example, Kathleen Neal Cleaver's review of Roediger's *The Wages of Whiteness,* entitled "The Antidemocratic Power of Whiteness," hardly paints a picture of whites standing idly by, cocooned in their protective coatings, while the rest of humanity was excluded and immiserated on "the other side."[26] Here she argues that "a widespread failure to acknowledge that whiteness conveys internal meanings at the same time it fulfills anti-black functions helps frustrate programs that seek to eliminate racism's pernicious legacy." Applauding Roediger's approach, she cites the same quote from W. E. B. Du Bois that he uses in order to emphasize the point that whiteness does not just entail "skin privilege": "Du Bois wrote that though 'the consequences of [racist] thought were bad enough for colored people the world over,' they were 'even worse when one considers what this attitude did to the [white] worker. . . . He began to want, not comfort for all men but power over other men. . . . He did not love humanity and he hated niggers.'"[27]

The second problem raised by the editors of *Critical White Studies* is that to ask what a "white person" should do to be "helpful to blacks" does not necessarily "help" the student of whiteness to move beyond the simple binary viewpoint, which paints one group of people as the perpetrators of evil and the other as the victims. This question does not suggest that whites themselves would benefit from eradicating what John Howard Griffin has called "the dehumanizing poison of racism"; instead it summons up images of hand-wringing, produced by guilt, rather than of hand-holding, produced by nonracial solidarity. Are all whites racist? This question threatens to suck readers deeper into the swamp of epistemological stickiness, which, as we have argued earlier, characterizes much of the recent writing and thinking on whiteness. The option of giving up, which also figures on the list of possible things to do, seems a strangely unserious proposition in this context, while the counter act of trying harder may actually be more dangerous when you are floundering in a swamp.

A third problem raised by the questions found at the end of *Critical White Studies* is that they suggest a somewhat ahistorical view of racial discourse, as though no one had attempted either to ask or to answer them before. As I have already argued, the histories of abolitionism and anticolonial struggle contain countless examples of women and men struggling to find different ways of distancing themselves from the barbarities of white supremacy, and instructing others how to do so. To take a less celebrated example, was it self-interest or pity that prompted scores of British women to persuade their neighbors to boycott slave-grown sugar and cotton on the grounds that these products polluted their homes or to urge others to identify with black women enslaved and abused by white men? Or was there some degree of responsibility involved, which led to a refusal to be complicit in such an inhuman system? The answers to these questions will depend on how the evidence is interpreted, but this is just one example of the value of keeping a historical perspective in mind when considering "What can a white person do, if anything?"

A final criticism that seeks to avoid the paralysis likely to be induced by this question is that it misses what is surely the fundamental point of focusing on whiteness as a means to understand race-thinking and its effects. In our view a radical analysis of whiteness means more than shifting the focus away from those who experience racism toward those who perpetuate it, knowingly or not. As so much of the best scholarship has shown, it entails not only marking the intricate ways that blackness has been and continues to be connected to whiteness, but also pointing to ways in which that *relation* might be used to promote new dialogues on the basis of nonracial solidarities. In other words, the study of whiteness can, in conjunction with other kinds of politics, open up new insights into patterns of social and political injustice, which may in turn lead to different kinds of alliances dedicated to combating them—alliances that make nonsense out of this question: what role is there for whites?

"Things to Be Done"

Writer Lillian Smith was notable for her insistence on dialogue throughout her career. Born in 1897 in the small segregated town of Jasper, Florida, she lived in relative affluence until 1915, when her father's business collapsed and the family was forced to move to their summer home in the mountains of north Georgia. Their new home in a rural area with high levels of poverty provided few opportunities to earn a living, but in 1917 she was able to escape to Baltimore, where she enrolled at the Peabody Institute to study music. When she was twenty-four, she gave up the idea of a career in music and accepted an offer of a teaching job in China, where she spent several years. This proved to be a formative period of her life, since she was exposed not merely to a completely different culture, but also to the corruption that marked the final years of the prerevolutionary regime. The experience helped her to make sense of international politics in her later life and to motivate her to work within organizations such as the United Nations. Obliged to return to Georgia to care for her parents, she became involved in running a summer camp for young women. Together with her partner, Paula Snelling, who was also employed to work there, she developed a distinctive regime aimed at reeducating and politicizing the girls who attended the camp, most of whom were from white middle-class families. Smith is mainly remembered as a writer and activist who played an important role in southern politics. A book of collected correspondence—significantly entitled *How Am I to Be Heard?*—illustrates the passion with which she hated all forms of white supremacy and other legally sanctioned injustice in her own country. It also describes an extraordinary cultural and political world to which she was connected through friendship, politics, love, and disagreement.[28] Her most well known work was written during the 1940s in the context of the war against fascism in Europe and Asia, and it is this period that concerns me here. However, Smith continued to write, lecture, and campaign during the Civil Rights movement until her death from cancer in 1966, and the rest of her life deserves to be examined in greater detail than I can attempt here.[29]

In 1942, in the process of writing her best-selling novel, *Strange Fruit,* Smith compiled a list of "Things to Do" in a piece entitled "Address to Intelligent White Southerners."[30] This was basically a set of instructions aimed at those who felt paralyzed by the situation in the South, over-awed by a sense of guilt and frustration at the impossibility of change and the likelihood of conflict. Although this essay demands to be judged in the specific historical and social context in which it appeared, it is important to remember not just that there was a war being waged on several continents, but also that the process of decolonization was al-ready under way.

Smith addressed her piece to southern women and men in the knowl-edge that, as individuals, they were powerless to overturn the underlying economic and political forces that produced and sustained the iniqui-tous situation in the South: "forces which have no doubts, no inner con-flicts. They know what they want. Childlike, savagelike, ruthlessly, they go after it; without scruples to hamper them, without conscience clut-tered with guilt and good-will to sap their energies, with no long range wisdom to trip them up with its questions. . . . " In a letter to fellow author Richard Wright the following year she wrote that she was not in the least bit interested in political movements, nor was she tempted to become a reformer or political leader.[31] Anticipating his agreement on this matter, since she was well aware of his relationship to the American Communist Party, she suggested working together to encourage other writers to think creatively about "our cultural problems" without any ideological ties.

Her dislike of organizations did not mean that she was not committed to radical change, however. Her motive seems to have been to encourage people to break free from inertia and complacency; she defined her audi-ence as those who felt they were caught up in a system from which they did not directly profit, but by which they were not apparently harmed—"not daring to face and acknowledge our unconscious desires, nor indi-rect gains from these more ruthless activities of the 'powers,' and our identification with white supremacy; not daring to turn away and face the necessities of survival itself and the implications of that good-will which we now use to shield us from the future and its new patterns." But in reaching out to well-meaning white southerners, she also casti-gated those who comforted themselves with the idea that it was safer for all concerned, black as well as white, to remain "loyal to the strict, steel-like code to which we, since birth, have been trained to bend."

Smith was concerned primarily with the psychological development of white racism in the South, the subject of her later book *Killers of the*

Dream. In a brief introduction to her list of proposals she made it clear that it was not only black people who experienced the traumas of white supremacy: "From childhood to old age, the sensitive white southerner whips himself with this cutting fear of doing harm until, humane impulses worn out, decency exhausted, courage bruised and flabby, he learns to move through his southern way of life like some half-dead thing, doing as little harm (and as little good) as possible, playing around the edges of great life issues, blinding himself to the ever-increasing misery, the ever-increasing frustration which his very lethargy is bringing to his land."

Individuals needed to open their eyes, she wrote, and to stare at the misery of "our people, at the gullied land and gullied culture, until our imaginations begin to see what we have done to all our people and ourselves by *not* acting." There were jobs that everybody could do, from the weakhearted to the more revolutionary-minded, suiting those who were less concerned for their own safety and more courageous and those who possessed the necessary skill, intelligence, and resourcefulness. The suggestions for action were arranged in three sections, and the first heading was "The Simple, Undramatic Things We Can All Do." The underlying theme was education: the necessity for each well-meaning individual to learn what was going on around her or him. Tasks included reading books and articles by black authors and white authors covering the history of the region; Smith also recommended Jawaharlal Nehru's *Toward Freedom* as one of the best books on the white man and the black man in the South ever published—even though "written by a Hindu about India."

This process of self-education was to be complemented by entering the world of the Negro—reading black publications; subscribing to black journals; visiting black colleges, hospitals, or public schools; even becoming good friends with individual Negroes—"for the sake of peace and a new world order, for the sake of our own souls." However, the chasm that appeared to lie between the two groups of people was not to be bridged solely by self-improvement. Smith gave detailed instructions on how to challenge any manifestation of white supremacy: through talking with friends, correcting racist language, or writing letters, particularly to local institutions like newspapers, libraries, and the church or to local and regional politicians. Explicit gestures were recommended, such as addressing black people by courtesy titles, treating one's cook with more consideration, paying her a fair wage and shortening her hours, or taking any opportunity not to be segregated. Finally, individuals were encouraged to "find some racial project that fits your temperament and talents": working for better health care, education, and recreational facilities for Negroes, for example, or campaigning for the abolition of the poll tax and the white primary. None of these activities, wrote Smith, was in bad taste or too difficult for the average white southerner to undertake, but "done by tens of thousands . . . they would change the South." This change, she added, would "begin to take place where it must take place first: in a man's own heart and mind."

Amid this first set of instructions there was an exhortation to spend some time thinking how it must feel to be a Negro in the South at that time; Smith described this as the least outwardly dangerous of all the proposed activities: "you will not lose your friends, nor your prestige, nor your job, nor will you cause a race-riot, by thinking . . . thinking about the Negro and the white man in the South in 1942." This appeal to the imagination—and Smith provides examples of the kind of situations readers might want to imagine themselves in—connects to our earlier discussion of the "language of perspicuous contrast," advocated by Charles Taylor in his discussion of the ethics of ethnography. Here it can be argued that Smith was offering her readers the opportunity to make sense of the dichotomy between self and other by urging them to go beyond the information available through the printed word, to silently put themselves in the shoes of the people they had been trained to fear and hate. In effect, she was advocating a program of self-awareness—urging her readers in fact to rouse themselves from a "half dead" position induced by the southern way of life—that also entailed an invitation to demonstrate the undemocratic nature of white privilege, eventually by any means necessary. The enormous value of this document is that it began to frame a different kind of politics that confronted unequal power relationships in everyday life. She offered all her readers a chance to feel involved in a wider struggle, encouraging them to go to the limits of their own capacity in the interests of wider social and political goals.

The next section of the "Address" was directed at those who had more time, more imagination, and more energy. The first instruction underlined the context in which Smith was writing: "We can all begin to train our children now to be, not little Nazis, but democratic world citizens. We owe this to them, in order that they may adjust harmoniously and without psychic conflict to the new world democracy which we now dream about and know is coming toward mankind." This meant more than training children to respect people regardless of race or economic status; it also entailed giving them what Smith called "a sensitive appreciation of human personality" and "awareness of their identification with all children of the whole earth." Shifting the emphasis from the regional conflict of the South to an international arena had the effect of underlining the common humanity shared by black and white southerners, but it also contrasted the Jim Crow system with the Nazi enemy fighting for survival in Europe. Smith repeatedly drew attention to the fact that many young black men in the United States were preparing to fight fascism on behalf of their own country, which did not recognize either their humanity or their claims for full citizenship. Once the evils of white supremacy in one part of the world were shown to be similar to its catastrophic effects in another, the alliances of people dedicated to fighting it could be enlarged and strengthened on a global basis. After this instruction to target the education of American children on the evils of narrow racism, Smith urged her readers to insist on new textbooks for schools that would help "develop global attitudes of mind, stretch imaginations and loyalties to include the whole earth and its needs." This would entail an enormous amount of writing and rewriting, but "[t]hink of the sheer adventure of working out a curriculum for our Georgian, our Southern, our American children who are also to be citizens in a world democracy!"

Smith's third instruction involved more practical advice on becoming a "troubleshooter for democracy." This was particularly addressed to "well-bred" southern white women, who, Smith explained, are especially suited for such roles: "A bus driver who speaks undemocratically to a Negro passenger can be quietly rebuked by a white southern woman. Due to our southern defensiveness, it might not be wise for a northern woman or man to attempt it, but any white southern woman of tact and dignity can protect a Negro passenger on train or bus or street car, can ease tension and avoid incidents—with no harm to herself and with assurance of no bad effects upon the Negro race."

Smith went on to describe such an incident when a white woman from Atlanta acted to defuse a situation on a bus traveling to Columbia, South Carolina. When a white passenger objected to taking the only available seat, since it meant sitting next to a black women who defiantly refused to move to the back of the bus, the white woman quietly moved to sit beside her, much to the relief of the bus driver and many other passengers. Smith commented: "Such an act requires imagination and sympathy, tact and good-breeding, but many southern women have these in abundance. It is time now to use such gifts in fields where they are so badly needed." Every act like that, she added, whoever carried it out, was "a triple victory for racial democracy, Christianity, and for the United Nations in this war."

Here women are addressed as potential agents for change in ways that emphasize their particular, locally inflected femininity, but at the same time their unequivocal actions against the stubborn pride and false deceit of white supremacists are revealed to be all the more effective, since they do not involve violence. Their relative powerlessness renders the men whom they shame even more inhuman and deluded as to their own importance, and their quietly subversive acts constitute a revolt against the so-called chivalry that ought to inspire the white man to offer his seat to the white woman, in public at least. Smith's appeal to women "of good breeding" to act in ways that accentuated their traditional qualities rather than jeopardizing their elevated position in southern society refers indirectly to the work of the Women's Interracial Committee, founded in 1920, and the Association of Southern Women for the Prevention of Lynching (ASWPL), founded in 1930 by Jesse Daniel Ames and active until 1942. As Ames's biographer, Jacquelyn Dowd Hall, points out, Smith saw herself as emerging from this specific history of white southern women who came together to protest the atrocities and exploitation being carried out in their name.[32]

In *Killers of the Dream,* published at the end of the decade, Smith wrote about the "lady insurrectionists," who "had the power of spiritual blackmail over a large part of the white South."[33] She traced the first stirrings of revolt among middle-class women of her mother's generation: women who had witnessed years of humiliation at the hands of their husbands and fathers and who had begun to ask how it was that segregation "cleaved through white women's tenderest dreams. . . . How could they sit in the audience and applaud their own humiliation?"

> So, learning these answers to their questions, they climbed down from the pedestal when no one was looking and explored a bit. Not as you may think, perhaps. They were conventional, old-fashioned, highly "moral" women, who would not have dreamed of breaking the letter of their marriage vows or, when not married, their technical chastity. But their minds went a-roaming and their sympathies attached themselves like hungry little fibres to all kinds of people and causes while their shrewd common sense licked old lies around until they were popping like firecrackers.[34]

Smith repeatedly emphasized the contrast between the covert insubordination of the early women rebels and their demure, almost cozy performance of conventional femininity. These women wrapped "innocence around them like a lace shawl. They set secret time bombs and went back to their needlework, serenely awaiting the blast." Domestic chores provided a screen behind which black and white women could discuss matters of great importance to both of them. The women involved in the Women's Interracial Committee during the 1920s were "too prim and neat and sweet and ladylike and churchly in their activities" to be dismissed as communists or bolsheviks; in any event their fundamental loyalty to the South and their fear of radical change prevented them from doing more than a basic "house-cleaning of Dixie." Those who campaigned against lynching and attacked the Ku Klux Klan (KKK) followed a "sound feminine intuition" and often worked with great bravery, but so unobtrusively that many could not be identified.[35]

Without actually naming individuals and organizations that had contributed to the campaigns against lynching in the 1930s, Smith urged "intelligent" white southern women to continue this tradition of working quietly and with feminine composure to oppose the worst excesses of segregation and thereby help bring about a new, democratic way of life. Her advice covered other aspects of women's lives, urging them to do what they could to end segregation and discrimination in department stores, clubs, and missionary societies, for example, and to organize social occasions such as international lunches so that black and white could simply eat together according to basic Christian precepts. All these activities could be carried out without heroism or drama, with no threat to personal standing or safety; in fact, added Smith, forcefully addressing the other half of her audience, for a man to refuse to eat with his black brother while daring to take Holy Communion amounted to nothing less than blasphemy.

Toward the end of her life, as she struggled with the pain of cancer, Smith often complained of the fact that she felt ignored by the literary establishment and trapped by this very stereotype of the demure and responsible southern white woman following her faith: "they say I am not creative, not talented, not a 'writer' just a nice woman helping Negroes find for themselves a better life."[36] This verdict was all the more crushing because she was resolutely unconcerned by public opinion and throughout her life more interested in the wider dynamics of human development rather than simply in the well-being of black people. The final part of Smith's injunctions, reflecting this more holistic view of southern society, was directed at the few who were not only braver, but also in possession of vision, self-control, and skill. What was needed was a greater number of white southerners who were prepared to break "the twin taboos of silence and action" by speaking against segregation and demonstrating their unequivocal opposition to it in public. They would face accusations of bad taste and criticism even from some black people, and they would run the risk of losing jobs and friends. The forms of action needed here were more collective than individual: organizing protests against segregation in churches, in labor unions, and in political institutions was essential if any kind of "shock treatment" was to be administered effectively.

Smith returned to the theme of education; assuming a different degree of awareness on the part of those who fell in this third category, she spoke of the need to educate both the "healthy-minded" (by using "skillful modern forms of propaganda as to the urgency of swift and non-violent change") and the "mentally ill," who would have to be "color-weaned" by forcing them on the defensive. Acknowledging that changing consciousness was not enough, she urged that "[l]abor union pressure, Constitutional amendment, new laws, and Presidential war decrees" would be needed to alter the economic basis of southern racism. Again, the war against fascism being fought in Europe provided a different context, first because it signaled wider global changes that were beyond the control of the South—in particular, the anti-imperialist movement of the colonized world: "The world situation, the pressure of war needs, the global hunger for human freedom, the changing economic patterns, have pushed the South into a new situation which cannot be dealt with in old traditional ways. Freedom is ringing its bell—in Harlem, in India, in Detroit, in Burma, in Atlanta, in Jackson, Mississippi . . . and it is making a music the whole world likes and is moving up close to. . . . "

Second, the war provided an opportunity for more radical social and political change than could happen in peacetime. During the last war, for example, American women had won the vote; during this war, Smith asserted, "the Negro and the poor white can win the vote." Committed to nonviolent and democratic change, she ended her appeal by reiterating the desperate urgency of the situation: "We are now in the midst of a total world war and a total economic race-revolution. Things are happening; things are going to continue to happen. We can sputter and break a blood vessel or we can roll up our sleeves and get to work to make them happen smoothly and harmoniously. The choice is ours only in *what we do about it;* not in the changes themselves."

It is impossible to assess what impact this document had on its readership and whether it was successful in shifting public opinion against segregation. Doubtless it inspired individuals to take a braver stance against the injustice they encountered in their daily lives and prompted many to feel personally connected to a process of fundamental social and political change in the South. Its overriding value for students of whiteness today is that it tries to break down in detail the main sites and structures of routine white privilege and to offer practical ways of challenging, subverting, and denouncing it. It anticipates and answers the question "What can a sincere white person do?" in ways that were more radical and extensive than the options suggested by Malcolm X two decades later. When he exhorted white supporters to "work among your own kind," in conjunction with but separately from black people, he reinforced the principle of segregation by color and undervalued the power of dialogue and social exchange between groups fighting the same enemy. Smith's recognition that whiteness was experienced differentially through gender and social class also showed that she had a different understanding of the phrase "your own kind." Malcolm X reminded his readers of the role of white women under slavery, but did not indicate how this might be exploited in the fight against white supremacy in the 1960s. It is especially curious that the editors of the *Critical White Studies* should formulate their suggestion that whites should perhaps work "among their own people" without endeavoring to qualify this phrase at all.

The Most Subversive Act?

It is time now to consider what a contemporary version of Smith's "Address" might look like, and to ask ourselves where a student of whiteness might find a direct answer to this question: if I am to be categorized as white, what can I do to end white supremacy? The *Race Traitor* initiative, founded by Noel Ignatiev and John Garvey, has provided the most direct and explicit set of instructions under the heading "How to Be a Race Traitor: Six Ways to Fight Being White," which can be usefully read against the historical background provided by Lillian Smith.[37] The authors' assertion that "treason to the white race is the most subversive act that I can imagine" echoes the sentiments of Smith in another essay, where she equated the betrayal of white supremacy to a form of "disloyalty to civilization," a phrase effectively borrowed by Adrienne Rich in her own inspiring analysis of gender and racism.[38] Before analyzing the *Race Traitor* manifesto, it is worth pausing over the phrase "to fight being white" in order to clarify what this implies. First, it plays on the contradiction between "being" as ontology and "being" as behavior or performance. By raising the possibility that one can stop being white, this phrase suggests that the socially constructed raciality of the would-be traitor can be unpicked from her or his physical and psychological identity and discarded. This business is not, then, about reformulating a different, nonracial or antiracist version of whiteness; it is about finding the will and the courage to change oneself from a white person to a not-white person. We will return to the implications of this statement in due course.

The first of the six points can be read as a summary of much of Smith's more detailed proposals: identify with the racially oppressed, and violate the rules of whiteness in ways that can have a social impact. Ignatiev provides a little more detail as he continues: oppose white privilege in schools and in the labor market, and oppose the police and courts, which define black people as a criminal class; target not the racist individuals but the mainstream institutions that reproduce the color line. Do all these things in such a way as to disrupt their normal functioning. To be a race traitor means identifying with Smith's third category of activity: the final instruction urges readers to "go beyond socially acceptable limits of protest" in order to distinguish oneself from the "good whites" who stay firmly within. Only one of the six points gives a precise example of how to behave differently in order to distance oneself from whiteness: "Answer an anti-black slur with. 'Oh, you probably said that because you think I'm white.'" It is this point that differentiates Ignatiev's approach from both earlier historical and other contemporary examples of antiracist discourse.

I know of one example where a young woman used this tactic to repudiate a racist comment addressed to her by a stranger as she was preparing to cross the road. Her retort evidently perplexed and annoyed the man, and history does not relate whether it caused him to think twice before making the same casual assumption about the propensity of blacks to commit crime. On this occasion the young woman who tried out this response felt it to be an effective way of refusing complicity with a racist sentiment, although she risked incurring the anger of a strange man who had expected to solicit her agreement—she did not say whether she delivered the softening follow-up sentence suggested by Ignatiev: "That's a mistake people often make because I look white." One of the interesting things about this situation is that it returns the onus of challenging racism back to the individual: this is not primarily about working through organizations and institutions or making a public stand. It concerns those moments when, usually, no one is looking and the individual has only her or his own conscience to deal with. In fact, it is as much about changing one's own orientation as it is about striking a blow against white supremacy and social prejudice. It represents a creative and nonviolent alternative to the other options so often taken in that kind of situation: being stuck for words, delivering a lecture, shouting abuse, or even hurling the old inflammatory chestnut: watch what you say, I'm married to one.

Although this particular injunction has greater relevance to the more private moments of social exchange, it also presents the best opportunity for examining the theoretical—epistemological—basis of the position set out in *Race Traitor*. For this attempt to force a separation between physical appearance and political identification suggests an analysis of "race" that is definitely not shared by many other antiracist activists and scholars of whiteness. As Ignatiev explains, most scientists and social scientists now accept that "race" is a historically constructed concept, with no basis in biology. However, understanding how this category is reproduced in the modern world is not enough: the point is to abolish it. It is significant that here Ignatiev begins to refer exclusively to the "white race," which, he asserts, functions like a private club that grants privileges to certain people in return for obedience to its rules. "It is based on one huge assumption: that all those who look white are, whatever their complaints or reservations, fundamentally loyal to it."[39] It is this assumption of unthinking loyalty that contains the seeds of the system's destruction. If more people realized that they were not obliged to retain membership of this club, and could be persuaded to leave it, the club—the white race itself—would eventually cease to exist. Being a race traitor effectively means disobeying the rules of whiteness, renouncing the privileges that membership entails, and identifying with those who are not allowed to belong. The only way that whiteness can be destroyed is from within, which is why "so-called" whites have a special responsibility to work for its abolition.

Ignatiev makes it clear that committing acts of treason to whiteness is not the same as antiracism. Attacking the basic premise of whiteness is different from employing more moderate or reformist strategies, since it is aimed at eliminating the causes of white supremacy rather than at alleviating its effects. Race treason involves a more radical and bold approach, and some of the tactics might be classed as "unreasonable" or "provocative" because "they fly in the face of all contemporary reasonable opinion."[40] Race traitors need to act as a kind of vanguard in order to undermine the public currency of whiteness and to expose the heavy price being paid by its unwilling or agnostic collaborators. When a critical mass has been reached, the white race will undergo fusion, and "former whites will be able to take part in building a new human community."[41]

Although they are aware of the global implications of this statement, the editors of *Race Traitor* address themselves almost entirely to the situation in the United States. Adopting the New Abolitionist Society as the title for their project, they make a conscious attempt to situate the initiative in the context of the best traditions of U.S. radicalism: Ignatiev has described how he developed his insights after studying pre–Civil War abolitionism, inspired by activists like Wendell Phillips who went far beyond criticizing slavery on moral grounds to making connections between slavery and free labor.[42] In the context of contemporary society, whiteness and blackness exist as mutually exclusive political categories. Where the former expresses a willingness to seek a comfortable place within the system of "race" privilege, blackness functions as its opposite: a "total, relentless and implacable opposition to that system."[43] So-called people of color are defined in relation to the line between black and white, although, as Ignatiev suggests, some ethnic groups demonstrate a more complex and ambivalent relationship to both whiteness and blackness and have historically been eligible to move between the two. Any attack on the integrity of "the white race," any flagrant violation of the rules of membership, is a step toward dissolving the hateful line that separates people on the basis of white supremacy.

This is the basic philosophy that lies behind Ignatiev's programmatic advice. He invariably explains the principles of the New Abolitionism in an unequivocal and no-nonsense fashion, suggesting a take-it-or-leave-it approach to destroying white supremacy. Judging from many of the contributions published in *Race Traitor* and the reactions of its correspondents, the project has generated a significant number of enthusiastic supporters, many of whom are evidently empowered by the knowledge that they are not alone in their desire to "commit unreasonable acts" in the cause of abolishing whiteness. But while there may be a solid constituency of people who sympathize with the broad aims of the journal, there are many other critics of whiteness who are less than convinced by the rhetoric that demands its abolition. Our question is this: does the manifesto published by *Race Traitor* offer effective strategies for both understanding the operations of white supremacy and contributing to its demise?

There are three broad areas of what we have called epistemologies of whiteness that need to be examined in order to do justice to this inquiry. The first concerns the central topic of "race," and how it is defined. In the spirit of *Race Traitor*'s accessible and forthright style this discussion may run the risk of oversimplifying what are extremely complex and contested arguments in the interest of trying to clarify some important basic precepts. As we have seen, whiteness and blackness are understood as political categories that have been historically constructed on the basis of the European belief in "racial" supremacy—the notion of "race" being also socially constructed on the basis of perceived differences in the body's appearance. In Ignatiev's view, the idea of "race" is applied to whites in such a way that blacks are left outside; any serious attempt to undermine the idea of the white race will subvert the notion of race in general. It is only whites who are attached to the idea of "race," since they are the ones who benefit from it. Blackness in fact symbolizes "implacable opposition" to the concept and practice of race privilege. It ought to follow then that to be black entails an opposition to the whole idea of racial particularity and "race" privilege.

There are two problems that initially flow from this. For a start, as Roediger argues in his book *Towards the Abolition of Whiteness,* whiteness may be socially constructed, and it may function as a contentious political category, but this does not reduce its power to mobilize profoundly undemocratic currents in contemporary U.S. life:

> Whiteness exercises such political force despite its thorough dis-crediting as a "cultural colour," despite its having become the fair game of standup comics who reflect on the vacuity of "white cul-ture" in a nation in which so much that is new, stirring, excellent and genuinely popular—in music, fashion, oratory, dance, vernac-ular speech, sport and increasingly in literature, film, and nonfic-tion writing—comes from African American, Asian American and Latino communities. We face, in short, a mad and maddening sit-uation in which the appeals of whiteness are at their most pitifully meager and the effectiveness of appeals to whiteness—from How-ard Beach to Simi Valley to the ballot boxes—are at a terrible height.[44]

This observation is in keeping with Ignatiev's comment that "the white race does not voluntarily surrender a single member, so even those who step outside of it in one situation find it virtually impossible not to step back in later, if for no other reason than the assumptions of oth-ers."[45] Far too many people share investments in the material and psy-chological benefits of race privilege to give up on whiteness without a bitter and protracted struggle. But are all these people white? This is the second question that emerges from the *Race Traitor* position. While there is a certain logic to the idea that the concept of "race" will wither away when it ceases to have any redeeming value to those who have formerly benefited from it, the position rather conveniently overlooks the invest-ment that all those who are not categorized as white have made in their own "racial" uniqueness or prowess—even if they have formed their own historical countercultures in self-defense. Yet black identity, for example, cannot, within this discourse, ever amount to an expression of "race privilege," despite the assertions of some black supremacist groups. This is one area where a direct comparison with the recent history of South Africa is especially valuable. It is pertinent to recall Mandela's speech at the Rivonia trial, shortly before he was sentenced to life imprisonment in 1964: "During my lifetime I have dedicated myself to this struggle of the African people. I have fought against white domination and I have fought against black domination. I have cherished the ideal of a democratic and free society in which all persons live together in harmony and with equal opportunities. It is an ideal which I hope to live for and to achieve. But if needs be, it is an ideal for which I am prepared to die."[46]

This brings us to another problem in the way that *Race Traitor* represents blackness and returns us to questions of methodology with which we began. Treason to whiteness may be loyalty to humanity, but humanity is not yet a political category in the United States, and the ideal of nonracialism may not be deemed appropriate to that situation. In a discussion of whiteness and contemporary U.S. racial politics, Howard Winant situates these new debates in a context where "race continues to play its designated role of crystallizing all the fundamental issues in U.S. society"; he adds that "[a]s always we articulate our anxieties in racial terms: wealth and poverty, crime and punishment, gender and sexuality, nationality and citizenship, culture and power."[47] Does this mean that persons who disassociate themselves from whiteness have nowhere to go but black? Is Ignatiev playing on the idea of blackness as a political color, divorced from its association with African American culture, when he asserts: "To the extent so-called whites oppose the race line, repudiating their own race privileges and jeopardizing their own standing in the white race, they can be said to have washed away their whiteness and taken in some blackness"?[48] Perhaps this is an echo of Audrey Lorde's invitation to "reach down into that place of knowledge . . . and touch that terror and loathing of any difference that lives there," cited by Mike Hill in his discussion of "white critique." This is unlikely, since Ignatiev goes on to say that "a black person" should not accept "a white person's claim" without first watching to see how that white person acts. Blackness then is a quality automatically possessed and defined by a black person—that is, a person who has never belonged to "the white race." To be against whiteness means more than identifying with black people; it requires an excursion into rather inhospitable theoretical territory that no one quite knows how to define. This is a very difficult question to resolve, and the squelching of the epistemological stickiness can be heard louder than ever, threatening to drown out all further discussion.

One way that critics of the New Abolitionism project have dealt with this awkward situation is to connect race treason with blackface minstrelsy, as though an explicit desire to disconnect with whiteness automatically suggests a desire to become black. In a critical review article entitled "Uncolored People" David Stowe discusses this problem at length.[49] After asking a perfectly valid question—How does one recognize a race traitor?—he suggests that it is within the realm of popular culture that the majority of the project's enthusiastic supporters can be found:

> There are the white devotees of hip-hop, who, if they exhibit too much enthusiasm for black culture, may be reviled (or honored) by peers as "wiggers." And there are the white ethnics who have embraced black culture: Italian-American "guidos," for example; or the many who contributed their talents to the making of jazz or rock'n roll. The history of American popular music looks like one long succession of race traitors from the Jewish songwriters of Tin Pan Alley to Benny Goodman, from Elvis to the Beastie Boys.[50]

This characterization of would-be race traitors as mainly young white men drawn instinctively toward the black or ethnic "other" by their music does not allow for the possibility of individuals being drawn to aspects of revolutionary or creative cultural forms on the basis of respect and admiration. Nor does it allow much room for the supporters of *Race Traitor,* who are engaged by more obviously political concerns. Stowe's assessment was possibly inspired by reading the anecdote at the very beginning of the *Race Traitor* anthology, which is told as an example of "fracture" occurring in the white race in the rural Midwest. Several white schoolgirls, calling themselves the "Free to Be Me" group, were attacked by some of their male counterparts in their almost all-white school when they chose to identify with hip-hop culture through wearing their hair in braids and dressing in baggy clothing. The girls were physically and verbally abused by male students, and a Klan rally was held at their school. Opposition to the Klan was demonstrated by many more students braiding their hair and wearing "Free to Be Me" buttons. After several of the girls appeared on a black-hosted talk show, which aired nationally, their harassment increased further. The story does not have an ending, as the girls were still battling over their right to wear headbands in school and suffering appalling physical threats as a result of their actions. *Race Traitor* comments that this incident reveals, "among other things, the tremendous power of crossover culture to undermine both white solidarity and male authority." It does a disservice to the courage of the young people involved in this example to dismiss them as white youngsters who merely hankered after black identity. Their slogan, "Free to Be Me," was expressive of a more interesting and creative tradition than that, and the gendered implications of their protest demand a more detailed consideration.

Moving into a critical discussion of the recent scholarship on the history of blackface, Stowe focuses on Eric Lott's book *Of Love and Theft*. He connects this work with the arguments of Roediger and Ignatiev almost as if he was trying to trip them up. "It would seem," he suggests, "that within every white Negro lurks a race traitor struggling to break free. Or is it the other way round?"[51] He frames another question that follows directly from his narrow perception of race traitors as "wiggers": if some of these new scholars of whiteness are engaged in excavating a history of American minstrelsy in order to investigate the interface between whiteness and blackness, where exactly does one draw the line between blackface (which, in his view, the abolitionists consider to be bad) and race treason (which they advocate as good)? His charge is that the abolitionists cannot have it both ways and that their own moral(ist) reasoning betrays a deep ambivalence when it comes to popular culture. Stowe's own opinion is that it is not possible to uphold any distinction between good and bad elements of cultural exchange, whatever the circumstances in which they take place. What matters is that American culture is recognized as being hybrid, "something different from any of its original ingredients, a creole stew for which Africa provided the essence." Conflating the critics of blackface, who have written about cultural borrowing in terms of appropriation, with the proponents of abolitionism, who regard it more warily as one possible step toward race treason, Stowe accuses them all of political moralizing: "One never knows if one is helping undermine the currency of whiteness or adding to the long history of blackface. The cultural tourist is easy to mistake for the freedom fighter. Fretting too much over these distinctions leaves one in a state of hyper-consciousness, like a gawky kid at an eighth-grade prom."

This reference to the stirrings of awkward sexuality leads to another area of discussion that the *Race Traitor* project leaves somewhat neglected. Stowe might have taken an altogether different tack if he had spent a little more time reading the correspondence at the back of the journal, some of which has been reprinted in the anthology. Under the heading "Devil's Advocate" one contributor raises the issue of a more historical form of race treason that is not part of the *Race Traitor* repertoire, but that nonetheless touches many people in her (or his) community: "in my neighbourhood 'race treason,' as I understand it and as it has been defined historically by the racist right, is rampant. Young women and couples can be seen carrying babies more often than books, and in recent memory I can't remember when one of those babies *wasn't* mixed."[52]

The writer acknowledges that it would not be appropriate to advocate this form of race treason, which does not even touch on the analysis of whiteness offered by the journal. But it remains an important point that, in the eyes of an active white supremacist, the worst crime is for a white woman to have sex with and breed with a black man: the visual image of the race traitor is invariably the white woman clutching a dark-skinned baby. Race, in this context, can be understood as embodiment and containment. The history of the attempts to control white femininity in order to avoid the dilution of the "white race" is just one example of the futility of trying to keep "race" and gender apart in any sustained analysis of white supremacy. Yet the editorial reply is noncommittal, responding to the letter as a whole rather than answering this particular point: "The stories you tell about race treason in your community are great. It is those things that make it a center of rebelliousness. If RT can give voice to that tendency, so much the better." The "Free to Be Me" anecdote mentioned earlier is another instance where *Race Traitor* flags the connection between male authority and white power, but makes no attempt to analyze why this powerful challenge to both has been the cause of so much agitation and violence. Though they rightly deny the charge that they ignore forms of oppression based on something other than race, the six-point program that has formed the starting point for this discussion does not address the possibility of specifically gendered forms of resistance. Where Lillian Smith specifically appealed to white southern women to fulfill their role as the traditional moral and spiritual guardians of society, *Race Traitor,* in this truncated manifesto, takes a possibly postfeminist line by not mentioning women at all. Other examples of correspondence in the journal provide evidence of a fairly mixed constituency, but neither the critique of abolitionism—as evidenced by Stowe—nor the leadership itself is able to offer a more complex understanding of "race" or whiteness in relation to other kinds of divisions and hierarchies, most notably gender, sexuality, and sex.

So far we have pinned this critique of the *Race Traitor* position on the door of Ignatiev's six-point plan without paying much attention to the function of the journal, which has been appearing at regular intervals since 1992. Although critics like Stowe might not feel connected to the "wiggers," who he imagines are its biggest fans, the journal itself claims to have a significant readership that ranges from "university professors to skinheads who resent nazi attempts to appropriate their culture."[53] It is important to acknowledge the project's role as a place for exchanging political ideas, served mainly by the publication (and including its website), which evidently provokes healthy dissent, encourages individual and collective activism, and plays an educational role among its readers. It is all the more surprising then that the *Race Traitor* manifesto does not mention the necessity of self-education or the importance of listening to others in the interest of cross-cultural dialogue; either of these, and preferably both, would have been an appropriate addition to the six points. For Lillian Smith this was where the absolute beginner was advised to begin treading the long path from a guilty conscience all the way to a life dedicated to militant opposition to white supremacy: read a book, talk to somebody black, spend some time thinking. These tasks were set in order primarily so that the individual might start to make connections between her or his own situation and behavior and those of black fellow citizens, deprived of their human rights by the Jim Crow system. Bearing in mind that it is a historical document and that it is written in ways that might sound dated or even patronizing today, Smith's "Address" offers an unusually clear and detailed exposition of both the power and the weakness of white supremacy as it operated in private and in public life.

This comparison between these two sets of instructions has allowed us to test and extend some important methodological questions that flow from a radical critique of white supremacy. One of the greatest values of Smith's "Address" is that it serves to illuminate a moment in an ongoing struggle almost fifty years before *Race Traitor* was first published, and it demands to be read in the light of the history that separates the two publications. Smith's awareness of similar struggles against fascism and colonialism in other parts of the world provides another dimension that secures it against a parochial understanding of Jim Crow, disconnected from the global operations of capitalism and white supremacy. *Race Traitor* has emerged from this tradition, and its aims and strategies are all the more inspiring where they are able to feed from and develop the insights gained in earlier periods.

Les Back

6. SYNCOPATED SYNERGY: DANCE, EMBODIMENT, AND THE CALL OF THE JITTERBUG

The music of my race is something more than the "American idiom." It is the result of our transplantation to American soil, and was our reaction in the plantation days to the tyranny we endured. What we could not say openly we expressed in music, and what we know as "jazz" is something more than just dance music. When we dance it is not a mere diversion or social accomplishment. It expresses our personality, and, right down in us, our souls react to the elemental but eternal rhythm, and the dance is timeless and unhampered by any lineal form.

—DUKE ELLINGTON

Far from Harlem, from Chicago, from New Orleans, uninformed and naive, we served the sacrament that verily knows no frontiers. . . . I can see them in their longish skirts, dancing and "dipping" in the taverns of remote villages, with one fan always standing guard at the door, on the lookout for the German police. When a *Schupo* appeared over the horizon, a signal was given, and all the *krystýnky* and their boyfriends, the "dippers," would scurry to sit down to glasses of green soda-pop, listening piously to the Viennese waltz that the band had smoothly swung into. When the danger had passed, everyone jumped up again, the Kansas riffs exploded, and it was swing time once again.

—JOSEF SKVORECKY

In 1931 Duke Ellington published an article—his first—in the pages of a British dance-band magazine called *Rhythm*. He emphasized that the culture of jazz is infused with the experience of dislocation and oppression, but also stressed the timeless, nonlineal nature of jazz dance. He commended his British readers for their appreciation of his music, but ended his first excursion in print with a caution: "Remember that your most important asset is your rhythm."[1] By the 1930s and 1940s European dance halls were no longer the exclusive province of the waltz and the foxtrot. A generation of young Europeans had assimilated the sounds, movements, and sensibilities of swing. The passage of swing into Europe was complex. For some it constituted an exotic pleasure only to be enjoyed, but for others it provided a starting place to question authority. Jazz—a music born out of what Ellington called the "white heat of our sorrows"[2]—provided a resource for self-expression and dissent among young Europeans both inside Nazi Germany and elsewhere in Europe. It was the age of jazz, the jitterbug, and generic fascism.

Nazis propagandists found jazz simultaneously both threatening and useful. Jitterbugging youngsters drawn to the likes of Benny Goodman, Count Basie, Nat Gonella, Django Reinhardt, and Duke Ellington became the focus of an anxiety about preserving the racial and national spirit. Swing could also be represented in propaganda as the exemplary symbol of decadent non-Aryan *Entartete Musik*—part African, part Jew, part Gypsy—the mongrel creation of the American metropolis. Concerns about the politics of swing were not confined to the Reich. Jazz had established itself in Britain long before the outbreak of World War II. In 1919 the Original Dixieland Jazz Band, a white ensemble from New Orleans led by Nick La Rocca, opened the Hammersmith Palais de Dance, attracting 5,800 dancers on its opening night.[3] Dances originating in black America, like the Charleston and the Black Bottom, had been introduced to Europe in large part through the fame of Josephine Baker, who performed at the Folies Bergères in Paris from the mid-1920s.[4] Equally, the new forms of jazz dance being pioneered at the Savoy in Harlem started to make their way to Britain and Europe via the already established jazz subcultures in London.[5] But it was from 1942 on, with the presence of American GIs on British soil, some of whom were black, that the introduction of black dance accelerated. The displays of breakaway dancing outside the meter of "strict tempo" posed a serious moral dilemma for the military and the political elite. There were sincere concerns about the import of the "American race problem" and even antipathy toward the bigotry of white southerners. Yet interracial jitterbugging—black soldiers dancing with white English women—revealed uncomfortable similarities among Jim Crow, John Bull, and the racial phobias of Nazism. I will look at the ways in which swing made these racial harmonies audible. At the same time I will examine how the jazz subcultures that took hold in Europe registered dissonance within the demesne of race and culture. The reactions to swing exposed the normative whiteness at the center of the Allied and the Nazi causes. Encoded in the aesthetics of swing style was an ambivalent cultural revolt against both liberal democratic and fascist forms of white supremacy.[6]

In America swing had provided the context for the first racially integrated dance halls. For black people the opportunities for public dancing were few and confined to the after-hours "jook houses," private parties, and the dance halls that served the black community. The Lindy hop was created by the black dancer George "Shorty" Snowden in 1928 during a dance marathon in New York. Snowden had developed a breakaway technique that involved separating, allowing for individual improvisation while holding onto the dance partner with one hand. He named the step, which was danced to a 4/4 syncopated beat, after Charles Lindbergh's successful transatlantic flight. In the 1930s Lindbergh was an admirer of the Nazis. Ironically, the Reich would later brand the new step named after him degenerate and racially corrosive.

The Savoy Ballroom on Lennox Avenue in Harlem provided the context where these techniques were practiced and developed.[7] The dances innovated in "cats corner" at the Savoy Ballroom were not simply a response to the music of the time. The movement of the dancers affected and inspired the musicians on the bandstand. Complex forms of call and response developed, giving the interrelationship between music and dance an organic and antiphonic quality. The Savoy in Harlem provided one of the first contexts where dancers could enjoy an open dance floor in front of large audiences. Swing brought black dance out into the public domain in unprecedented ways.[8]

The Savoy Ballroom was racially integrated, and white dancers learned their steps—sometimes with black partners—on the dance floor.[9] The exact relationship between the Lindy hop and what came to be known as the jitterbug is the source of some contention. Some authors suggest that it is basically the same dance,[10] while others argue that the jitterbug has a more complex genealogy and marked a specific white adaptation.[11] Terry Monaghan has argued that white swing enthusiasts—referred to as jitterbugs—developed their own style of dancing to swing called the collegiate/shag. This was "a descendant of the first form of Lindy when it was still clearly influenced by the Charleston. By the 1930s it had evolved some fast kicking steps executed by both partners but it didn't really 'swing.' It was often danced in a bouncy upright fashion. Students from Yale used to travel to the home of the Lindy Hop—the Savoy Ballroom—each Sunday afternoon to demonstrate 'their' dance—the Collegiate/Shag."[12] The controversy over the different nuances and distinctions between these steps is further complicated by the insistence of black American dance innovators like Mama Lu Parks and Frankie Manning that the Lindy and the jitterbug are one and the same. There are certainly distinctions to be made between these forms as they evolved, emerged, and crossed over into white usage. The fundamental point of agreement, regardless of emphasis, is that both steps share a common lineage.

The "white jitterbugs" prompted a significant moral panic.[13] By the late 1930s some localities in the American Midwest banned the dance, prohibiting contact to be broken beyond arm's length on the dance floor. But the hedonism of the jitterbugs also offended some swing partisans who saw the dance culture as shallow in terms of its musical appreciation. The impulse that drew young whites to the ghetto dance halls was complex. Malcolm X in his autobiography describes these encounters as a combination of white voyeurism and sexual adventure.[14] David Stowe, in his study of swing in "New Deal" America, concludes: "For the moralists, jitterbugs combined two unsavoury tendencies in American culture: the hedonism and uninhibited exhibitionism of African-American culture coupled with the mindless 'mass man' behavior symptomatic of and conducive to totalitarian societies. 'Bugs' thereby conflated a racial and a political threat."[15] Ironically, it was precisely the expressive nature of swing dancing that made it alluring to young people living within the totalitarian cultural universe of Nazism. The rhythms of Nazism insisted on a different beat.

The Choreography of Nazism

Adolf Hitler did not and could not dance. He frowned on social dancing, particularly when it involved the women that he took into his jealous and suspicious guardianship. Hans Peter Bleuel, in his insightful study of sex and society in Nazi Germany, described one such relationship, which involved his niece, Geli Raubal. Geli enjoyed dances, but Hitler permitted her to attend only under the surveillance of his cronies and with a curfew. Her uncle's strict rules and repressed desires created tension between them. These longings were never realized, as Hitler presented himself during the prewar years as being married to the German people and by implication to all German women. Bleuel comments on the erotics of Hitler's appeal to women and describes the response of German women to Hitler's call for devotion and domination as almost orgasmic. This union, however, proved fatal for Geli. After a quarrel with the Führer, the content of which is not known, Geli shot and killed herself. Eva Braun, the woman that Hitler eventually married on April 29, 1945, in his Berlin bunker, was also a keen dancer. But, like her predecessor, Eva, who enjoyed dancing at home, lived in "constant dread lest [Hitler] learn of the gay soirees in which she indulged during his frequent absences, innocent but with an aching conscience."[16] Why was Hitler suspicious of Geli's and Eva's penchant for a dance-floor embrace?

These private anxieties point to a larger unease within the Nazi vision of the Aryan woman—the womb of the nation—and her place within society. During the Third Reich dance took its place within the pageant of Aryan purity. It became a public, mass activity in which the German Girls League would be put through their paces in front of huge audiences. Dance was not a matter of individual pleasure or expression, but a collective entertainment and a demonstration of the national spirit and will. Events like the opening-night spectacle of the 1936 Berlin Olympics presented a national community unified through its allegiance to Hitler.[17] Some German dancers found this spectacle of mass adoration a step too far. Martha Graham, for example, was asked to perform, but she refused. The Olympics and its festivals and symbolism provided an international stage to advertise and entrench the regime.[18] Through such spectacles a model of Aryan masculinity and femininity could be exhibited. The mass dance of the Third Reich attempted to present an image of Aryan Germans into which the individual could project himself or herself. These mass forms of dancing were not achieved through the invention of a new Nazi aesthetic of the body and movement; rather, the "nazification of art"[19] involved the recombination of German dance.

Unlike the case in other forms of art, the majority of the leading dancers and choreographers—including those who were exponents of modernism—remained in Germany after Hitler took power in 1933. There were some notable exceptions. Martin Gleisner, who was Jewish, escaped to Holland, and Kurt Jooss, who had left-wing affiliations, fled to Dartington Hall in England.[20] While the Reichskulturkammer (RKK) attacked modernism in art and painting, the leading exponents of German dance were accommodated within the new regime. Susan Manning has commented that twice as many leading dancers remained in Germany and collaborated with the National Socialists as did not.[21] This, she argues, disrupts the widely held belief that Nazism cut short the development of modernism within Germany. The reasons why figures like Rudolph Laban and Mary Wigman remained and worked with the Third Reich are complex. While some key figures became exponents of Nazi dance, in the main modernist or expressionist dance under Hitler occupied an ambiguous position.

During the Weimar period expressionist dance, or *Austdruckstanz*, drew its followers from amateur students who were devoted to *Tanz-Gymnastik* (dance gymnastics). Within *Austdruckstanz* Laban blurred the distinction between professional and amateur dance and developed improvisational techniques that enabled new forms of mass participation. This combination provided the members and audiences for Laban's movement choirs (*Bewegungschor*), which were organized through a unique notation system called "labanotation" or "kinetography." During the 1920s movement choirs were established in association with unions, political parties, and religious organizations. Although the expressionist movement embraced mysticism and antirationalism, later to be exploited by the Nazis, from its inception the form was not explicitly connected with a particular ideological position. For example, expressionism was critical of the regulated nature of ballet and its internalized discipline. Equally, new German dance challenged the distinction between professional and amateur, performer and audience. Laban's dream was to emphasize community through dance and to establish movement activity at the center of the life of every citizen regardless of his or her class, gender, and age group.

Initially, the new regime seemed to express compatible aims. Laban was the director of dance and movement for the Prussian State Theaters in Berlin, and he immediately became an employee of the Nazis when Hitler took power. However, as Valerie Preston-Dunlop points out, his relationship with the fascists was ambiguous and complex. Laban found little in the ideologies of Nazism attractive; he had Jewish friends and was in a relationship with a Jewish girlfriend.[22] He was a Rosicrucian, a member of a sect that emphasized a culturally eclectic spiritualism and promoted personal growth along with an ethos of not judging others. Within this worldview it is understandable that he naively thought it possible to serve his ideals within the regime.[23] However, tension became apparent between his vision of expressionist dance and the Nazi dictates on movement culture. Dance became almost solely a female activity, as the male membership of the movement choirs declined. Mass dance performance became the context in which the Aryan ideals of womanhood were represented and celebrated. Through the naked Venus in "Night of the Nymphs," the athletic heroine in "Festival of the Amazons," and the wholesome peasant mother of community festivals, the gendered and racialized archetypes of Nazism were choreographed and set in motion.

Men's involvement in dance was relegated to folk dancing. Directives from the *Fachschaft Tanz* (Dance Department) of the *Reichstheaterkammer* (RTK) espoused and encouraged particular dances; they invented new Aryan steps and aimed to eliminate all non-Aryan and "degenerate" influences.[24] Dance schools had to comply with these directives if they were to stay open. Gymnastic components of *Tanz-Gymnastik* were emphasized at the expense of Laban's commitment to self-expression. Under these circumstances it proved ultimately impossible for Laban to continue his work. He was investigated and offered an ultimatum to join the party or resign. He refused, and after two years in the wilderness, he eventually fled from Germany to Paris and ultimately to England to join Kurt Jooss at Dartington Hall.

Mary Wigman, a Laban apprentice and the most prestigious German dancer of the period, also felt that Nazism offered a possibility to extend her art. Like Laban she was ultimately to fall from favor. Wigman is an interesting and enigmatic figure precisely because Nazism initially appealed to her ideas about expressing German nature through movement. Hedwig Müller[25] argues that in order to understand Wigman's reaction to Hitler it is necessary to locate her philosophy of dance within a wider intellectual context. Wigman adored Goethe, and she saw herself on a Faustian quest for truth and knowledge. She was also influenced by the ideas of Nietzsche, particularly the notion of becoming a spiritual and philosophical being. Through her dance she embraced spirituality and irrationalism as part of a collective tradition of national consciousness: "This struggle turns on the essence of existence, of man and his fate, on the eternal and the transitory. This struggle opened up the path to the primeval source of existence. . . . Because this dance had the courage to confess to life, to life as the eternal mystique of weaving and working, because this dance searched for God and wrestled with the demon, because it gave form to the old Faustian desire for redemption as the ultimate unity of existence—because of all this, it is a German dance."[26] It is not surprising that Wigman was fascinated with Hitler's charismatic and demonic persona. In many ways she identified with the Faustian quest to realize his vision of a new German Reich.

She was disgusted, however, by the anti-Semitism that raged in 1933. The book-burning and violence she saw as a result of baser instincts being unlocked in revolutionary times. Like Laban she had Jewish friends and students and fought to defend them. At the same time the emphasis on individualism and self-expression within new German dance came into direct conflict within the Nazi imperative of mass control. The Nazis wanted dance to be a diversion from—not a confrontation with—experience and emotions within everyday life. Ultimately, artists like Wigman were caught between the desire to further their art and the necessities of placating their political overseers. The result was that German dance was reduced to the choreography of obedience and submission: "Choric dance no longer served to promote *Gemeinschaft,* community, but *Volkgemeinshaft,* the fascist community based on the spirit of the German *Volk.*"[27] Wigman became disillusioned and marginalized, and it was only her deeply felt love for Germany that prevented her from leaving.

While the dancers and choreographers who stayed were certainly complicit with the nazification of German dance, they were not always willing collaborators. Goebbels's insistence on submission, escape, and entertainment came into direct conflict with the philosophy of self-actualization through dance, which was at the core of the modernist movement. The vision of inclusive community within *Austdruckstanz* and movement choirs was lost in its vapid Nazi counterpart. The artifice of Nazism was its ability to ensure that politics was collapsed into popular aesthetics.[28] Preoccupied with organizing people within rows and circles, these mass dances enforced a political as well as a physical line. Nazism produced an image of the German *Volk* where individuality could be dissolved and where human conscience could be lost in the stenciled order of mass kinematics.

As the nazification of German culture reached its height, physical exercise took on a kind of messianic fervor. Nazi dance organized its participants within a geometric discipline: "It place[d] a grid over the mass of bodies, which both arranged individuals and separate[d] them from one another. Clear lines confine[d] them to their places and prevented them from escaping."[29] Within the starkly gendered universe of Nazi aesthetics women were given nice ballet and happy folk dancing, while men were assigned to folk dancing and the marching ground. The spectacular rituals of mass dancing and the display of storm troopers marching in perfect cohorts through the Brandenburg Gate anchored Nazism in the rhythm of the body. Through these choreographed rituals identities of race and gender were both embodied and publicly worshipped, producing a kind of racial narcissism. Bleuel concluded that, in this climate, personal awareness, so much at the center of the expressionist dance of the likes of Laban and Wigman, was effaced by national anaesthesia.[30] These demonstrations were Hitler's rejoinder and stood as an answer to the very different rhythms that occupied the metropolitan nightclubs, where his *volkish* reverie was less secure. The mute call of black culture—whether practiced by white or black musicians and dancers—was answered in Germany with unexpected consequences.

"Negro Tribes Do Not March": German Youth and Swing Subculture

For the propagandists, jazz, or more correctly the big-band dance genre of swing, stood in contrast to the wholesome Aryan idyll. Swing and the jitterbug were the "mongrel creation" of the American city, the mark of a modern civilization in the advanced stages of cultural decline. In contrast, the rural folk dancing and Nazi festivals were presented as the mark of national purpose, cultural health, and racial authenticity. The Nazis filtered out the expressive elements of modernist German dance, but swing offered a compensatory resource to young Germans. I want to suggest here that there is a connection between Rudolph Laban and Duke Ellington. This is made less tenuous by the work of black dancers like Katherine Dunham and Talley Beatty, who combined modern dance influenced by Laban with the musical scores of jazz.[31] In both cases dance provides, in Mary Wigman's words, a means of "perfecting the dance personality as an individual; and on the other hand, blending this individuality with an ensemble."[32] I am not suggesting any simple correspondence between these forms. Laban in his piece *The Night,* performed in 1927, utilized a caricature of jazz to form the sonic backdrop to his representation of the depravities of city life.[33] The sensibilities of the piece were not very far from the image of jazz in the big city so deftly utilized by the Nazi propagandists. The swing subculture, unlike the institutionalized forms of expressionist dance, was altogether more difficult to regulate and control. What was lost in the nazification of *Austdruckstanz* was nurtured and developed in the dance halls where the saxophone and syncopation reigned supreme.

Nazi musicologists attacked jazz and justified their opposition to it by arguing that its rhythm was unsuitable. They complained that, unlike Germans, "Negro tribes do not march."[34] This was coupled with an attempt to show that jazz was the product of an abominable collaboration between "Negroes" and "Jews," with racially corrosive implications for Aryan Germans. The Nazi assault on jazz was not centralized and absolute. Goebbels himself was inconsistent on the matter. On October 12, 1935, he banned jazz from the airwaves, proclaiming: "Today I declare a total ban on Nigger-jazz on the whole broadcasting system. We want the German people to rejuvenate their cultural and moral life. We reject hot music and all elements of jazz. National Socialism condemns those who worship syncopation and the sound of the saxophone."[35] He condemned the "degeneracy" of jazz, but he paid little attention to it. Jazz subcultures in Nazi Germany were consequently subject to cycles of persecution and harassment followed by periods during which the regime was dismissive of their significance. While characterizing jazz as another form of "degenerate culture," the Nazi propagandists attempted to develop their own saccharine form of swing.

By the middle of 1937 new forms of swing dancing inspired by the Lindy hop had been introduced into Germany and elsewhere in Europe through the popularity of Hollywood films such as *Broadway Melody* and *Born to Dance.* Through its newspaper called the *Black Corps,* the Nazi

"Entartete Musik" at a Nazi exhibition of "degenerate culture"

military elite offered the Party line on the dance. The article used a picture of a black Lindy hopper as evidence of the folly of America's flawed attempts at racial democracy: "On the one hand the equality of all men; on the other, the Lindy Hop—a mixture of cannibalistic abdominal contortions and obscenity. Such a reckoning simply does not balance."[36]

The RKT social-dance instructors set about providing an alternative to the "foreign dances." They planned to expunge the foxtrot, Charleston, and Lindy hop, which they saw as inspired by "niggers" and Jews and connected with lurid expressions of sexuality. The RKT revived long-outdated German dance forms that "stressed the desired communal animus at the expense of individuality and eroticism."[37] Through organizations like the Hitler Youth, state-sponsored dances became the Party-sanctioned version of youth culture. These wholesome Aryan capers included the *Deutschländer*—predictably performed in groups—and the *Marsch*, which was performed in pairs. Added to these were the staple polka and waltz and a more wooden version of the foxtrot called the *Marschfoxtrot*. These steps were danced to the accompaniment of the mandolin, zither, harmonica, and recorder. This vapid Nazi dance did little to turn young Germans away from swing. Local dance divisions of the RTK in Gau Essen and Düsseldorf circulated ordinances that banned the jitterbug. Other areas, like Osnabrück and the Ruhr Valley, later followed this example. Ultimately, state and Party agencies, including the Weirmacht, RAD, SS, Deutsche Arbeitsfront (DAF), Nazi student organizations, and Hitler Youth, joined the condemnation of swing dancing.[38] All of this disapproval fueled the attraction of the jitterbug to nonconformist youth.

Swing was particularly popular in the city of Hamburg. This Hanseatic metropolis was a port town with a long history of cosmopolitanism. The participants in the jazz scene were often drawn from wealthy and middle-class homes, and some had traveled abroad with their parents. The swings were anglophiles; they utilized English rather than German as their prestigious vernacular. They would greet each other on the street with the phrase "Swing high!" or "Hallo Old Swing Boy," and they took up nicknames drawn from American films. Swing style for men took the form of a caricature of the "English spiv" and included sports jackets, crepe-soled shoes, extravagant scarves, "Anthony Eden" hats, an umbrella on the arm regardless of the weather, and a dress-shirt button worn in the buttonhole, often with a jeweled stone. Women styled their hair long, shaved their eyebrows and penciled them, dressed in flowing luxurious gowns, and wore lipstick and lacquered nails.

The swings were scrutinized by the Hitler Youth, who compiled "ethnographic" reports on their un-Aryan behavior and sexual degeneracy. One such account of a swing festival in Hamburg in February 1940, attended by five to six hundred young people, reveals the considerations of these youth spies:

> The dance music was all English and American. Only swing dancing and jitterbugging took place. . . . The dancers were an appalling sight. None of the couples danced normally; there was only swing of the worst sort. Sometimes two boys danced with one girl; sometimes several couples formed a circle, linking arms and jumping, slapping hands, even rubbing the backs of their heads together; and then, bent double, with the top half of the body hanging down loosely, long hair flopping into the face . . . when the band played the rumba, the dancers went into wild ecstasy. They all leaped around and joined in the chorus of broken English. The

band played wilder and wilder items; none of the players were sitting down any longer, they all "jitterbugged" on stage like wild creatures.[39]

The introduction of Hollywood styles of feminine beauty was viewed as particularly abhorrent by the Nazis and posed a serious challenge to the femininities associated with Nazi ideology and the state youth organizations. The body became the site for the expression of these gendered styles. Young women wore their hair long and flowing and openly rejected the homespun braids and German-style rolls. Equally, young men's urban style challenged the dominant uniform of Nazi masculinity, which combined the Aryan warrior hero with images of the responsible peasant patriarch.

In the midst of this hedonistic dance culture there was an important challenge to what Bleuel referred to as the "edifice of tyranny by wholesome popular sentiment."[40] This revolt was not just around style, but, through these "forbidden steps," focused on issues of sex and sexuality. While the Nazis attacked bourgeois prudishness, they were equally appalled by the sexual permissiveness of the swings. The police explained their conduct as the result of "sexual license stimulated by dancing to highly syncopated music."[41] By the early 1940s stories of dance-hall decadence and orgies of group sex were being circulated in reports composed by the authorities. The official statistics recorded a dramatic increase in juvenile delinquency, with more than twice as many cases recorded in 1941 as before the outbreak of war. Detlev Peukert concludes:

> They carried over features of the music, and their response to it, into their everyday behaviour. Relaxed surrender to the rhythms; spontaneous bodily movements instead of coached dance-steps; unexpected discords instead of conventional harmonies—all these were expressive of a loose, easy-going attitude to life in general and a desire to escape from the rigid demands of social order, school discipline, the paramilitary drill of the Hitler Youth, the "keenness" of Nazi officials and the ever-present call of duty. Their aim was to spurn the duties laid down by those in authority, to throw off inhibitions of behaviour, and to defy sexual taboos.[42]

The swing subculture was not a self-consciously radical movement, despite the vicious suppression meted out to them by the Gestapo and the Hitler Youth. It was estimated that from 1942 to 1944 seventy-five swing youths were sent to concentration camps by the SS, who classified them as political prisoners. For many it was only as the prison cell door slammed shut that they realized that their music and dance—which they loved in equal measure—amounted to a ritualized form of opposition.[43]

Within the context of the metropolitan nightclubs the jitterbug allowed for counterhegemonic forms of bodily expression and individuality, so emphatically repressed within Nazi popular culture, music, and dance. Josef Skvorecky, a Czech writer and jazz musician who lived under the shadow of both Nazism and Stalinism, has argued that for this reason totalitarian regimes aim their ideological guns against those who dance to the song of the saxophone.[44] That is not to say that young Germans were attracted to jazz because of an overt political impulse or agenda. These style revolts were ultimately about nonconformism and individual expression, which had no necessary attendant political ideology. In Germany the jitterbug produced a culture-quake of racial fears, but the same is true for its reception in Britain.

Chocolate Soldier, Vanilla Jitterbug: Black GIs, Military Segregation, and Jazz Propaganda

Swing went to war through Glenn Miller's band of the Allied Expeditionary Force (AEF), but it also exposed one of the deepest flaws at the heart the American dream. In Europe black GIs served in segregated units, but outside their military bases the color bar was not observed. Indeed, in Britain the responses of military and political figures to young British women dancing with black American GIs revealed racial trepidation reminiscent of their professed enemy. Integrated dances, where black and white mixed and swung together, also invoked double standards within imperial Britain. The jitterbugging dance halls became a context where these tensions were manifest, but they also enabled a momentary and alternative vision of kinship and intimacy to emerge beyond the color line within sound and motion.

The Allies and the Nazis put women to work during the war. With these new financial opportunities came partial escape from male authority. Women on both sides of the conflict became increasingly self-reliant; they had their own resources, and many women exerted this newfound independence in matters of sex as well. Bleuel illustrates this by quoting from an account of a young German soldier's Christmas leave, 1943–44: "New Years Eve was frightful. The streets swarmed with females chasing field-grey uniforms. Many of them carried bottles containing their extra *Schnapps* allocation and broke the ice by asking to borrow a corkscrew. If the soldier didn't have one, they produced one from their handbag.

They weren't just young women either. There were forty- and fifty-year olds among them."[45] The war had brought the sexualization of community life in ways that threatened the *volkish* ideal of German family life. The Nazi authorities mourned this situation, but took little action except when this promiscuity involved German women crossing the barriers of race and nation. There were many thousands of foreign indentured laborers working in Germany. German women who were caught having sex with French prisoners of war or Polish laborers were viciously pilloried, often having their heads shaved publicly and being sentenced to severe prison terms. For men caught having sex with foreign women workers, their punishment was at most a verbal condemnation. The bodies of women and their sexuality became the sites for concerns over "miscegenation" and "racial hygiene." This was no less true in Britain.

British women were conscripted into the war effort through the opening up of industrial jobs that had been until then the province of men. The presence of American GIs on British soil added another dimension to the processes of sexualization that Bleul identified in Germany. The dance halls became the focus of concerns about the sexual probity of the GIs and also the effect that their presence was having on English women and the culture as a whole: "For older women during the war, dances, even before the Americans arrived, were oases of pleasure in a wilderness of work and worry; for younger women, after the GIs poured onto the dance floors, they became sheer fairyland."[46] Britain was particularly well equipped with dance halls. The prewar years had been the heyday of English dance bands, popularized by their regular broadcasts on radio.[47] The most famous ballroom was the Hammersmith Palais in west London. The hallowed Covent Garden Opera House was also converted into an elegant dance hall. Like their German counterparts, American soldiers found themselves surprised and a little thrown by the female assertiveness that the conflict had seemed to foster. Norman Longmate quotes an account of a "fantastic dance in Cricklewood" by a white airman from Plymouth, Massachusetts: "Even a poor dancer like I was could do well. When they had a 'Ladies Excuse-me' dance [in which women invited male partners to dance] it was chaos. You hardly had time to introduce yourself to the girl before you were tagged by someone as lovely or lovelier."[48] The war had suspended some aspect of male power. In this context women were exploring quite new forms of autonomy in all matters from spending power to sex.

From 1942 until the end of the war some 130,000 black American troops were stationed in the British Isles. Graham Smith, in his groundbreaking history of the experience of black GIs in wartime Britain, has shown that the general public often reacted in a positive manner to, as one popular song of the time put it, the "Chocolate Soldier from the USA."[49] Despite this, the American command imposed a rigid system of racial segregation that transformed the English countryside. Military segregation was acute and actively enforced in East Anglia, where important combat units and air bases were located. Here black GIs were stationed and served as engineers, truck drivers, and ordnance workers. The U.S. Army decided that the innocently named River Dove, which flowed through East Anglia, would provide the geographical expression of the color line. All areas east of the river were out of bounds to the black GIs who were stationed at Eye and Debach and in Haughly Park near Stowmarket.[50]

For black and white GIs alike the social center was Ipswich, which boasted 150 public houses, of which fewer than 10 were set aside for black soldiers. Black GIs formed swing bands and hosted their own dances. Graham Smith has argued that the politeness of black GIs and events like these made the black soldiers extremely popular with the local people. While the U.S. Army attempted to impose racial segregation, these integrated dances brought white English women onto the dance floor, and within this informal social arena young white English men were introduced to the culture of black America. Black GI swing bands staged daytime performances and invited local children to "post parties" to hear Count Basie and Duke Ellington tunes rendered in the heart of the English countryside. Each unit had its own band. For example, the black unit of the 923rd Regiment of the Aviation Engineers formed a swing band called the 923 Reveilleers. In addition to concerts on their army base, they performed in local venues in and around Ipswich.[51] West Indian band leader Leslie "Jiver" Hutchinson also took his London-based All-Coloured Band to play at the black GIs' dances. Peter Powell, a jazz devotee who traveled and became close friends with these West Indian musicians, recalls the reception Hutchinson's band received: "Remember large numbers of the American centre-board were always Negroes, so the Leslie Hutchinson Band was very acceptable. They loved Leslie because he played American style, you know Count Basie and Tommy Dorsey. There would be one night somewhere in the middle of Suffolk or Norfolk or somewhere hidden away in Kings Lynn. There was a lot of mixture between American Negro soldiers and English women and one saw it on the dance-floor."[52]

Informal forms of segregation persisted in the dance halls. The manager of the Dorothy Dance Hall in Cambridge effected the exclusion of black troops by maintaining that his floor was "not suitable for jitter-

Censored steps: multiracial dancing in Ipswich, 1943

bugging."[53] Other dance halls, including the converted Royal Opera House at Covent Garden, put up "No Jitterbugging" signs, but dancers mostly ignored them, and they did not discourage white GIs from attending. Black culture was embraced, albeit through white dancers, musicians, and bandleaders. Many of the popular orchestras of the period were white, like the big bands of Glenn Miller, Benny Goodman, and Tommy and Jimmy Dorsey. "In the Mood," arguably Miller's most famous tune, was composed by black reed instrumentalist and arranger Joe Garland.[54]

Through the jitterbug, forms of dance that had their origins in black America had an unprecedented impact on English culture. As Brenda Deveraux remembers: "American boys were the master of the Jitterbug craze. We English girls took to it like ducks to water. No more slow, slow, quick, quick, slow for us. This was living."[55] The white GIs and their English dance partners elevated the jitterbug from a cult interest to a general fashion: "In the process they changed the whole nature of the dance-hall phenomenon. Where formerly there had been graceful, circular movement of dancers around the floor, now there were wild gyrations of hip cats who pecked, trucked, leapt and dived."[56] Black music and dance could be tolerated and even loved within mainstream American and English cultures, with some reservations, but when it came to black people themselves, this was quite another matter.

Walter White, the civil rights activist, came to Britain during the war years and described what he saw in his book *A Rising Wind*. White was light-skinned and could pass in white society. On entering a London cab, he asked to be taken to the Liberty Club, which was near the British Ministry of Information. The driver, believing him to be white, responded, "You mean the Rainbow Club of the American Cross, don't you, sir?"—the latter being a white club. Once the confusion cleared, the driver agreed to take him "where the coloured boys go." London's night life was effectively divided up like a kind of racial checkerboard.[57] The color-coded hermetics of this geography were not, however, complete or absolute. On arriving at the Liberty Club, White struck up a conversation with a white GI from Georgia, who had made friends with black peers whom he could not meet comfortably in other clubs. He writes: "I asked him about the continuation of these friendships when he returned to America. Ruefully he spread his hands, palm upward, and shrugged his shoulders. 'I don't know,' he said sadly."[58] Other white GIs also found the import of American racism all too close to the ideology of their fascist opponents.[59] In the main, white American troops found the presence of black soldiers threatening, and spontaneous violence—usually instigated by whites—was commonplace.[60]

The British, confronted with this specter of racist violence and the institutionalized military segregation, more often than not took the side of the black soldiers. Walter White concludes that the brightest note in all the stories told by his black countrymen was the friendship with the British people:

> One had told of the distinguished British family inviting a group of American soldiers to their home for dinner and dancing. Everything moved smoothly during the meal, but when one of the Negro soldiers danced with one of the English women, he had been assaulted by a Southern white soldier. A free-for-all followed in which the British took the side of the Negroes.
>
> And there was the story of the pub keeper who had posted a sign over his entrance reading "THE PLACE FOR THE EXCLUSIVE USE OF ENGLISHMEN AND AMERICAN NEGRO SOLDIERS."[61]

White figured that this could be explained by the sensitivity to material hardships shared by British working people and black soldiers—three-quarters of whom came from the rural South. This stood in stark contrast to the cocky garishness of the white GIs. He concluded that, for many black GIs, coming to England resulted in their first experience in being treated with respect and friendship by white people. The stumbling block, however, was the issue of relationships between black soldiers and white English women, which the Americans and the British condemned equally.

On August 12, 1942, a whole meeting of the Bolero Combined Committee was given over to the "Problem of American Coloured Troops."[62] Attending the meeting were representatives from the War Office, the Ministry of Home Security, the Ministry of Information, and the Foreign Office. The minutes of the meeting are very revealing in that they show clearly the priority the members placed on the issue of potential relationships with British women. After a preliminary discussion General Williams, representing the War Office, said: "The only problem that remained was the question of the association of colored American soldiers with British women."[63] To this General Venning added that the possible repercussions of such relationships would be threefold: First, American opinion would be affected if "British women were acting in a way that Americans by their upbringing, could only regard as grossly immoral." Second, British public opinion may be affected if the government was seen to be subscribing to "an undemocratic American attitude to the color problem." Finally, Venning pointed to the possible effect on the morale of British soldiers "if they heard reports that the white women at home were associating with colored men."[64] A suggestion was made that British women might be discouraged from "such associations" if an open statement was made by the government on the dangers of venereal disease. This was quickly and strongly opposed by the representative from the Foreign Office, since such a statement would "be regarded by the progressive elements in the United States as a slander on the American Negro." The general consensus was that they would not intervene directly. General Venning concluded: "[T]he problem should be tackled without using the weapon of fear; in some way the historical background of the American attitude to the color problem should be explained to the British public, the implication being that, since this was based on years of experience, the British attitude should be the same."[65]

What is implicit in all these accounts is that race and nation are coupled—in American and British cases—and coded as white, while there is some reticence on the part of the British to commit wholly to this shared view in terms of wider public opinion. The end result was that the committee concluded there could be no official sanction against these relationships, although it was agreed that a draft statement on the

"Color Problem" would be distributed to men and women in the British Armed Forces. Without official restrictions and in the context where military segregation was at best minimal, the dance hall became a new social sphere for integration.

Life magazine published a story on the Lindy hop and dubbed it "a true national folk dance born in the U.S.A."[66] The photographic essay accompanying the Lindy hop story include no pictures of interracial dancing. White and black dancers appeared, but they were shown dancing as "same race" couples. These images stood in stark contrast to the scenes of black servicemen in racially integrated dance halls in Britain. In 1943 several American newspapers and *Life* magazine published photographs of black GIs dancing with white English women. The response of the American military's Bureau of Public Relations was prompt. It ordered the censorship of any photographs that portrayed interracial dancing and social mixing. Black soldiers could sacrifice their lives in the fight against fascism, but they could not be seen dancing with the natives! Toward the end of the war this policy was slightly modified after the protest of black troops both in Western Europe and in Italy. This issue even attracted the attention of General Eisenhower, who countenanced the general principle behind the censoring of these photographs and who proposed a compromise. Black GIs could post photographs home as long as they were stamped "For personal use only—not for publication."[67] Black troops confronted with racial violence and military segregation were rendered publicly invisible through these forms of censorship. As I will show, the Nazi propagandists found the undoubted hypocrisy of the Allies over the question of race particularly useful. The meaning of jazz itself became an emblem of a wider struggle over the opposition between liberal democracy and fascism.

One of the paradoxes of the Nazi terror was that SS officers themselves demonstrated a fondness for swing. They went so far as to encourage the formation of jazz combos in the concentration camps of Terezin and Auschwitz, where prisoners performed swing tunes for the officers' pleasure.[68] Mike Zwerin, in his exploration of jazz under the Nazis, described a Luftwaffe pilot who switched on the BBC, hoping to catch a few bars of Glenn Miller before bombing the antennae from which those forbidden sounds were being broadcast.[69] Allied propagandists recognized the potential for exploiting the contradictory allure that jazz possessed within Nazi society.

The sound barrier of 1944 was marked on the one hand by the music of the Nazi marches and on the other by the big-band swing of Glenn Miller. The Allies attempted to exploit the popularity of swing inside

Germany. On October 30, 1944, Miller's swing tunes were aimed at German soldiers through the American Broadcast Station in Europe (ABSIE) in an effort to persuade them to lay down their arms. The music was transmitted under the title "Music for the Wehrmacht" (that is, German armies). Major Miller addressed German soldiers in their own language with the assistance of Ilse Weinberger, a German compere and translator. Ilse introduced Glenn Miller as the "magician of swing," and through a strange act of cultural alchemy, tunes like "Long Ago and Far Away" and "My Heart Tells Me" were rendered by vocalist Johnny Desmond in German.

Miller's Wehrmacht sessions included a number of extraordinary exchanges between Ilse and the major. In one program he denounced "Nazi gangsterism" and claimed that "there is no expression of freedom quite so sincere as music." He presented the cultural diversity found among the musicians in his band as a microcosm of the American way of life: "Today they are true Americans sitting side by side with their buddies, no matter who they are or where they came from. This is a true picture of the great melting pot, America, and a symbol of unity in the fight for freedom." Through a clumsy summary of these words Ilse unknowingly touched on a profound tension in the relationship among Glenn Miller, jazz, and this image of America. Her German translation characterized the AEF band as "[a] true symbol of America, where everybody has the same rights—it is all equal regardless of race, color and religion." True, Miller's band was made up of the sons of immigrants from Germany, Russia, and Italy and even included some Jews. But this microcosm of American freedom was not extended to include the very black musicians who had played a vital role in the development of swing.

Miller's musical gift transcended mere pastiche. Yet his music was invoked as an icon of American justice at the very time when racial segregation in the Allied armed forces was prevalent. The war had a devastating effect on African American jazz musicians, many of whom were drawn into the armed services not as prestigious musical tribunes, but as common foot soldiers. Fearing military racism, some attempted to evade conscription. Buck Clayton, virtuoso trumpeter in Count Basie's band, tried unsuccessfully to escape induction by eating soap and drinking Benzedrine, and almost killed himself. Clayton later claimed that white officers treated German prisoners better than black Americans. This is borne out by the experience of bandleader Horace Henderson and singer Lena Horne, who cut short a tour after finding that in Camp Robinson, Arkansas, black soldiers were not permitted to see the show, while Nazi prisoners of war were welcomed.[70]

Nazi propagandists hit back by proclaiming jazz the product of an inferior black race. Prior to the D-Day landings posters were plastered over Dutch billboards representing the "Allied Liberators" as the bearers of a dangerous cultural heritage. American troops were portrayed symbolically as an "uncivilised Frankenstein" that had jitterbugging apes for its torso, a face hidden behind the mask of the Ku Klux Klan, and black arms sporting a boxing glove on one hand and a jazz record in the other. The posters also tried to invoke racial fears among the peoples of occupied Europe by spreading the rumor that black American soldiers would play a prominent part in the invasion. Goebbels's Ministry for People's Enlightenment and Propaganda produced a pamphlet entitled "Greetings from England—The Coming Invasion." Written in Dutch in the form of an Allied communiqué, it stated that the Germans had been duped into wrongly expecting a sea invasion and that half a million "Negro paratroopers" would spearhead the attack: "It will be an enormous humiliation for Hitler, the prophet of racial theories, when his warriors will be driven from Western Europe by the black race. Dutchmen, your co-operation will be counted . . . make your old jazz-records ready, because at the celebration of liberation your daughters and wives will be *dancing in the arms of real Negroes*" (emphasis added). Jazz was equated with blackness and the presence of black soldiers on mainland Europe with miscegenation.

Aerial propaganda dropped by the Nazis in the first days of the invasion picked up these themes, but targeted white and black GIs separately. A "hold to light" card targeted at white American soldiers began with an image of a dead American soldier in the foreground. As the card was exposed to the light, a bedroom scene was revealed, showing a white woman on all fours with a naked black man having sex with her from behind. The caption read: "White Plays, Black Wins." Equally, black soldiers were targeted. The Nazis dropped "certificates" in both English and German guaranteeing safe conduct to those presenting them to the Germans. One card presented images of smiling, well-fed black GIs who had surrendered. Another showed two black babies with this commentary:

THEY WANT YOU BACK ALIVE
Well what chance have you to survive? Hardly any at all! Remember, back home the colored man always had to do the dirty work. On the front it is the same—Uncle Sam's colored soldiers are just CANNON FODDER.
YOU HAVE ONLY ONE CHANCE
If you are fed up with the fighting, join the other colored boys who are now waiting for the end of the war in modern sanitary

LIBERATORS

Monstrous regiment: Nazi poster portraying the GI as a jitterbugging marauder, Holland, 1944

GROETEN UIT ENGELAND

DE KOMENDE INVASIE

ONRUST DER DUITSCHERS
OMTRENT ENGELAND'S NIEUWSTE WAPEN.

De Duitscher is altijd een slecht psycholoog geweest. Hij denkt zijn Engelschen tegenstander te kennen en verwacht dezen zomer een landing aan de Noordzeekust.

De gedachte aan deze mogelijkheid heeft den anders zoo zelfverzekerden mof kennelijk onrustig gemaakt. Het O.K.W. (Oberkommando der Wehrmacht) gaf daarom bevel, de Westkust in staat van verdediging te brengen. Onze heldhaftige piloten lachen echter in hun vuistje, wanneer zij het zenuwachtige gewriemel van de Germaansche stakkers gadeslaan. Zij weten, dat niets de komende invasie zal kunnen tegenhouden, zij kennen het nieuwe wapen,

„de donkere wolk".

De Britsche generale staf heeft thans toestemming verleend, hieromtrent enkele nadere bijzonderheden te vermelden. Sedert het begin van dit jaar zijn meer dan een half millioen negers uit Amerika naar Schotland gebracht, waar zij een speciale opleiding ontvangen in het afspringen met valschermen. Een interessante bijzonderheid is nog, dat hun valschermen gemaakt zijn van donkergrijze zijde. Daar gewoonlijk de bewolkte lucht boven Nederland ook donkergrijs is, maakt deze handige camouflage het den Duitschers onmogelijk, het valschermlegioen af te schieten. Voor Hitler, den propheet der rassentheorie, zal het de grootste vernedering zijn, wanneer zijn strijders door het zwarte ras uit West-Europa worden verdreven.

Nederlanders, op Uw medewerking wordt gerekend bij de komst van het zwarte legioen. Leg Uw oude jazz-platen klaar, want op het feest der bevrijding zullen Uw dochters en vrouwen dansen in de armen van echte negers. Grillige puinhopen zullen een fantastischen achtergrond vormen van het bevrijdingsbachanaal, waar blank en zwart zich zoo innig zullen vermengen, dat het voor de bewoners van Nederland een prettige herinnering zal blijven aan de invasie van de donkere wolk.

Nederlandsche meisjes en vrouwen, hier ligt voor U een mooie en aangename taak, waaraan U zich geheel dient te geven zonder eenige terughouding, teneinde het rassengedaas van Hitler te logenstraffen.

DUITSCHE LEUGENS
over den handelsoorlog.

Groot-Brittannië is dezen oorlog ingegaan met 20 millioen ton handelsscheepsruimte. In den loop van dezen oorlog is daar 10 millioen ton aan Noorsche, Belgische, Nederlandsche, Fransche, Grieksche en andere scheepsruimte bijgekomen. Eigenlijk beschikt Groot-Brittannië dus over 30 millioen ton scheepsruimte.

Volgens sommige berichten (U behoeft niet te vragen uit welke bron) zou hiervan reeds 23 millioen ton door oorlogshandelingen zijn verloren gegaan. Dit is een gemeene leugen.

Volgens het Amerikaansche blad „Navigation Statistics" van 1 Juni 1942 bedroeg de door duikbooten, mijnen en vliegtuigen tot zinken gebrachte Britsche Handelstonnage slechts 3 millioen 6 honderdduizend 3 honderd 54 ton en geen ton meer. Laat U dus niet door Duitsche leugens misleiden.

"Greetings from England: The Coming Invasion," Nazi pamphlet circulated in Holland, 1944

prison-of-war camps. They are being treated decently like all the
prisoners-of-war. They are getting good food and Red Cross par-
cels. They may write home and receive mail regularly. Above all
they know AFTER THE WAR THEY WILL BE SENT HOME TO
THEIR FOLKS AS SOON AS POSSIBLE

The Nazi propagandists scorned American racism as a means to exploit racial injustice and to get black GIs to turn away from the conflict.

For both sets of propagandists swing provided the symbolic mecha-
nism to ridicule the racial fears of the opponent. The Allies, through the
big-band sound of Glenn Miller, attempted to capture the hearts and
minds of the jitterbug-loving Germans. The Allies attempted to mock
the Nazi prohibitions against jazz, but in doing so, they sidelined the
black musical innovators of swing and censored all trace of black GIs
in Europe. The Nazis for their part used swing to expose American democracy as a sham. They flaunted the blackness of the jitterbug as
means to invoke fears about miscegenation. White women would be
"dancing in the arms of real Negroes," or worse. Ironically, the Nazis
used the racial apprehension of white men to expose American and European racisms.

Fleeting Pathways and the White Imaginary

A rapid turning movement makes the surrounding objects vanish in the whirl, and
the dancer with his inner wrestling seems alone in the world as if on an island, so
dance—like thinking and feeling brings about a consciousness of one's inner most
self. The fleeting pathway of the dancer is filled with ethical spirit. The trace, the
pathway, the movement are the result of struggle, they represent the victory of an
endeavour which, gentle and restrained or wild and abandoned, contains the gift
of ethical understanding. . . . Dance is no static picture, no allegory, but vibrant life
itself.

—RUDOLPH LABAN

Dancing enhances.

—DIZZY GILLESPIE

The music of swing was answered emphatically on the dance floors of
Europe during the war years. As the jitterbugs hopped, dived, and
turned, they found a rhythm that clashed with the time signature of
totalitarianism. Nazi dance filtered out the expressive dimensions of *Austdruckstanz,* leaving a coercive racial culture that assigned specific gendered archetypes to men and women: submission was made obligatory
and individuality impossible. The swing subculture offered young Ger-

mans an alternative to the state-sanctioned youth institutions and a ritual means to express contrasting gender identities and sexual mores. Thorsten Muller, a Hamburg swing, reflects: "The swing music was the first step on my way to resistance. So, later a Gestapo man said to me, when he saw me for the second time: 'Agh, this I could have promised you. Your kind of high treason began with a tune by Duke Ellington and ends with a plot against the Führer.' I think he was right, I think he was right. The swing music was my first step on this way. And finally, I got involved with a resistance group called the White Rose."[71] But why did this culture resonate so powerfully within the context of Nazism?

Paul Connerton has written that collective memories can be conserved in bodily automatisms and passed on in nontextual and noncognitive ways.[72] Perhaps even in translation the jitterbug traced a living and embodied memory that went back to the slave master who exercised his chattel by making them dance under the whip.[73] It is the transcendence of rupture, terror, and suppression that is embodied within swing dance. This is why it was so attractive to the white jazz nonconformists who lived under Nazism. In those sounds and motions they discovered a living response to the terrorizing racism that lurked in the shadow of modernity, and it found its expression within the Third Reich. As the dancers spun, broke away, and turned, they discovered an ethical understanding that valued the individual "off beat"—a syncopated sensibility.

This is not to say that there is any simple correspondence between political resistance and style or dance. There is no necessary relationship between the rejection of racism and racial ideology and musical cultures like swing jazz and its associated dance forms. Jazz was conscripted to the Allied cause, which showed little consideration toward translating the rhetoric of freedom and democracy into racial justice. Without any seeming contradiction, capricious racists—on both sides of the conflict—could be jazz fans. The jitterbug brought these tensions into focus where the dance floor offered a place for interracial contact and sociability between black men and white women. These fragile associations were subject to scrutiny and censorship by politicians and the Allied military. Swing dancing was feared because it might lead to interracial sex and ultimately miscegenation. The experience of black GIs in Europe was to raise expectations that would ultimately flower during the postwar Civil Rights movement. The period of the war in Europe provided a glimpse of the coming loosening of segregation; yet at the same time brutal forms of Jim Crow racism were brought to bear. Black GIs were vulnerable to both vengeful attacks by their white peers and accusations of rape. From 1942 until the end of the conflict eighteen American soldiers were hanged under U.S. military law at Shepton Mallet Prison, Somerset. Six of that number were hanged for rape, and all of these men were black.[74]

Himmler gave the directive that the swings be rounded up for "jazz crimes." He ordered them to be tortured, brutalized, and subjected to hard labor for up to two to three years. Inga Madlong and her sister Jutta were taken to the concentration camp at Fuhlsbuttel in April 1943. She remembers: "Lots and lots of older women over 30 just simply died like flies. And people committed suicide who just couldn't bear it anymore. But then I developed scarlet fever and they made me look into the sun and something burnt away in the back of my eye and from that day on I couldn't see anymore."[75] For the next twenty-seven years she had only 10 percent of her eyesight. The cost of her love of these forbidden sounds was her sight. There is something deeply profound and telling in this testimony because it alerts us to the important distinction between the visual regimes of racism and whiteness and the utopian possibilities of sound.

Detlev Peukert has argued that National Socialism unwittingly paved the way for modern forms of youth leisure.[76] The history of the swing subculture in Europe and North America certainly disrupts the established wisdom that sees youth culture as a product of postwar consumerism.[77] Equally, this experience disrupts some of the ways in which the white orientations to black music and culture are understood. This issue will be addressed more directly in chapter 8, but the point here is to appreciate the significance of the political context in which the identification and assimilation of black music take place. To embrace jazz music in a situation where it could cost you your life is clearly different from a whimsical stroll through the jazz section of a record store today. The point here is simply to suggest that the "black through white" cultural dialogue will have different qualities depending on the historical, social, and political contexts in which it occurs.

In 1946 the cartoonist Stil published a series of cartoons that heralded a generation of young English women as sexually knowing and fully initiated in American popular culture and style. One entitled "Tommy Comes Home" showed a dance floor full of airborne Lindy-hopping women. Their newly demobbed English partners stood rigid, stuck to the floor and unable to follow their steps. The caption read "What happened to you Myrtle—you never danced like that before I went away!" The war had increased the spending power of these women, and the wartime dances had allowed them to explore areas of self-expression and autonomy that had previously been unthinkable. This all changed again as they were forced to give up their jobs and sacrifice their Saturday-night freedoms. While Britain knuckled down to postwar austerity, the jitterbug, increasingly known as the jive, was driven off the ballroom dance floors. Yet public reaction to these humble steps during the war revealed the distinct, but commensurable racisms that lay at the center of both liberal democracy and Nazism. Future generations would answer the call of the jitterbug and its cognates in new and indeterminate ways.

By the early fifties a new moral panic had emerged, this time focused on immigration, interracial contact, and deviant urban mores. The figure of the black GI had been supplanted by the figure of the black immigrant. A report published in 1951 in the *Sunday Graphic* observed a "be-bop club" in London's Soho:

> In a corner five coloured musicians, brows perspiring, played be-bop music with extraordinary fervour. I watched the dancing. . . . I counted 28 colored and some 30 white girls. None of the girls looked more than 25. Girls and colored partners danced with an abandon—a savagery almost—which was both fascinating and embarrassing. From a doorway came a colored man, flinging away the end of a strange cigarette. He danced peculiar convulsions on his own, then bounced to a table and held out shimmering arms to a girl. We went outside. I had seen enough of my first bebop club, its coloured peddlers and half-crazed, uncaring girls.[78]

This could have been an excerpt from the pages of the Hitler Youth ethnographers who spied on Hamburg's jazz fraternity ten years earlier. Such reactions reveal the recurring articulation of sex and race at the center of racism's white imaginary.

Vron Ware

7. GHOSTS, TRAILS, AND BONES: CIRCUITS OF MEMORY AND TRADITIONS OF RESISTANCE

Every English landscape is full of ghosts. . . . So many things have happened in England, that all we English are in a sense strangers who have to come back to our own country and learn the traditions of our ancestral house. But, when we do, we are surrounded by ghosts that are friendly as well as heroic and polite.

—EDWARD SHANKS

On several occasions these young people expressed the belief that the white English "brought black people over [to England] as slaves," but that black people had somehow managed since to rise to a position of dominance now threatening whites. It was well established among them as an historical account and seemed to be a confusing melange of school economic history and racist resentments.

—ROGER HEWITT

In his research into adolescent racism in an area of London that had seen three racist murders of young black men in three years, Roger Hewitt encountered many examples of this "confusing melange" of inaccuracy and prejudice that so often passes for history. The idea that "blacks," who were originally brought into the country as chattels, were now becoming more powerful and wealthier than "whites" was clearly a major cause of the bitterness felt by many of the racist young people targeted in the survey. Entitled *Routes of Racism: The Social Basis of Racist Action,* Hewitt's report observed that the articulation of unfairness was a "radical new theme" in the way that white people, young and old, talked about race issues: "By this we mean that, although there is a greater awareness of racism and the agendas of multiculturalism, there exists also a contrary bundle of related opinion and beliefs."[1]

According to Hewitt, the various antiracist and multicultural policies and practices of the previous decade had helped produce a dangerous consensus among the majority white population of this area. Ethnic minorities were seen to be getting "too much attention," and the parallel concerns of whites about issues such as policing, schools, and health care were being overlooked. This profound sense of unfairness not only was a major obstacle in promoting an awareness of racism, but also deflected attempts to tackle it.

Hewitt cited an earlier critique of antiracist practices in education and youth work, published ten years before his own, which had also drawn attention to the clumsy, ill-thought-out model of multiculturalism that assumed "there is uniform access to power by whites, and a uniform denial of access and power to all blacks."[2] While this damning report received only brief attention in the national media, the research carried out by Hewitt has been incorporated into a new discourse on the crisis of English national identity. In the eyes of many commentators the bored teenagers who were actively selected by Hewitt because of their racist views symbolize an alienated, urban, and, above all, white England that not only has lost, but also is being deprived of any legitimate claim to a positive ethnic identity.

Ann Leslie, a right-wing journalist who served as a foreign correspondent in the former Yugoslavia in the early nineties, and who uses this experience to argue for the psychic benefits of a strong sense of national identity, provides a good example of this. She cites Hewitt's research in her advocacy of a positive reevaluation of Englishness and concludes: "If it is necessary to build up the self esteem of young blacks (which it is), that should not be at the expense of the self-esteem of young whites. English people should be proud of ourselves for our real achievements, past and present. This is not a recipe for rampant chauvinism. It is quite the opposite. It is a prophylactic against it."[3]

Here we have two interrelated crises: the first stems from a serious critique of the dominant models of multiculturalism, and the second is expressed as a desperate attempt to redefine what it means to be English at the end of the twentieth century. The link between them is echoed in the words of a young woman featured in Hewitt's survey: "I don't like blacks, full stop, right. We brought 'em over 'ere for slaves. . . . [T]hey should go back to their own country."[4] The "we" in this statement expresses a white supremacist worldview, indicating the failure of antiracist education, but at the same time it evokes a sense of pride in England's past achievements that might indeed be called "rampantly chauvinist" and in need of redirecting. The idea that it might be rather difficult to distinguish between a positive white English identity and its even more unpalatable manifestations seems to have escaped those who share Leslie's vision. The call to recognize "the real achievements" of the (white) English as a way of countering the "unfairness" of a multiculturalism biased against whites sounds like a highly dubious invitation to fall back on the segregated patterns of race-thinking. In this fantasy figures like Shakespeare (especially in love), Charles Dickens, Jane Austen, William Blake, and the Beatles are coded as the property of something called English culture, which is defined as white and handed down at birth. Conversely, those who are not fair-skinned, and who do not necessarily self-identify as English despite being born in the country, are disqualified from claiming such a distinguished heritage, although they are presumably entitled to boast another kind of cultural package derived from the "real achievements" of their ancestors who came from elsewhere.[5] Thus, understanding inherited culture as being both an index and a consequence of racialized difference only compounds the opportunities to rank the multiple cultures that are so unevenly celebrated in schools. Meanwhile, the project of antiracist education is reduced to making moral or even political demands on young people who do not always have the resources to counter the allure of separatism.

The underlying link between the perceived failure of multiculturalism and the desire to reinforce the whiteness of English national identity is provided by a shared notion of the role of history. Where multicultural education has sought to include some aspects of minority history and culture as an adjunct to the mainstream curriculum, the nationalists believe that history can be taught to discrete groups of people as a way of defining what is special and worthy about their past. In both cases the past is approached as a source of evidence for the differences among national, ethnic, or even racial collectives.

How would a critical analysis of whiteness offer a more constructive view of history that would muddy the artificially clear waters of radicalized difference? The short answer is that any theoretical approach based on the understanding that "race" is a socially constructed category will logically argue for the importance of showing how categories like whiteness and blackness have been produced historically, in relation to each other. The problem with this formulation is that it does not always take into account the work that has to be done in order to make that relation visible. The "confusing melange" quoted above is a good illustration of the way in which racism effectively denies black people any history of their own, beyond the fact of slavery. Likewise those who are anxious to promote a renewed sense of white English ethnicity can choose to overlook the fact that there has been a black presence in England since the sixteenth century. A radical analysis of whiteness therefore demands an active political engagement with this "historical forgetfulness."[6] It requires a political counteroffensive to seize whatever resources come to hand in the present in order to swirl those unnaturally clear waters of false memory and social amnesia.

While this argument has particular resonance in postcolonial Britain, it will also be familiar within other national contexts shaped by centuries of white supremacism. This point underlines the importance of looking beyond national borders in order to make sense of this history and demonstrate the connections between different places. Finding appropriate resources with which to demonstrate these connections and crosscurrents requires an acknowledgment that there are at least two layers to this inquiry. The first concerns ways in which dominant ideologies of "race" have operated in struggles to define nations and to determine who belongs to them. The second consists of the oppositional practices and strategies devised to counter the destructive forces of white supremacism. Here the question of "race" may be seen from the perspective of those who are marginalized by dominant historical accounts, but who nonetheless compile their own counterhistories of agency and resistance as part of a political struggle for survival. But identifying these two layers is absolutely not another way of saying that there are simply dominant white histories and insubordinate black versions, both of which need to be challenged. The project of analyzing and deconstructing whiteness also demands a critical treatment of those strategies of resistance, looking for signs of cooperation and solidarity across the imposed divisions of race, color, gender, religion, and nationalism. The failures and shortcomings of multiculturalism suggested above need to be placed within a much more valuable tradition of opposition to white supremacy, a tradition that is only enhanced by being seen as a historical phenomenon that possesses its own genealogy.

One way of addressing these issues is to consider the importance of heritage and the public commemoration of people, places, and events whose memories may be interpreted in the light of the histories of opposition to slavery, apartheid, colonialism, and everyday, routine race-thinking. Later in this chapter I hope to show how a shipwreck off the coast of southwest England can be used to address these two layers of historical inquiry, both to argue against an exclusionary definition of Englishness and to demonstrate the value of cross-cultural solidarity. But before turning to the heritage of this particular historical accident and the possibilities it offers for a political antirace agenda in the present, I want to revisit an established memorial site wearing the hat of an eager tourist intent on exploring the legacy of the transatlantic social movement against slavery.

Physical Traces of the Past

Following the Black Heritage Trail in Boston, Massachusetts, brings the visitor face to face with solid and tangible evidence of the bitter constraints endured by free African Americans in the nineteenth century. It begins on the edge of Boston Common at the memorial dedicated to the 54th Regiment of the Massachusetts Volunteer Infantry and its commander, Robert Gould Shaw. Shaw, who was descended from a wealthy Boston family, volunteered to lead the regiment, the first to which blacks were recruited after President Lincoln conceded to abolitionist pressure in 1863 and allowed black soldiers to join Union forces. Shaw's correspondence with white and black abolitionists provided important background information for Edward Zwick's film *Glory* (1989), which has helped to confer a mythic status on the whole episode. As the film graphically illustrates, the regiment was almost destroyed after an assault on enemy positions in Charleston, South Carolina; Shaw was killed alongside his men, and Sergeant William Carney was awarded the Congressional Medal of Honor for his heroic attempts to save the Union flag from capture. The regiment also deserves to be remembered for its refusal to accept salaries lower than those of their white counterparts, a struggle that was vindicated after eighteen months when Congress increased their pay retroactively. The brochure that accompanies the Black Heritage Trail explains how the memorial came to be built:

> This high-relief bronze memorial to Colonel Shaw and the 54th regiment was erected through a fund established by Joshua B. Smith in 1865. Smith, a fugitive slave from North Carolina, was a caterer, former employee of the Shaw household, and a state representative from Cambridge. The sculpture is by August Saint-Gaudens, and the architectural setting by McKim, Mead and White. The monument was dedicated on May 31, 1897 in ceremonies that included Carney, veterans of the 54th and 55th Regiments, the 5th Cavalry, and several speakers, including Booker T. Washington. The inscription on the reverse side of the monument was written by Charles W. Eliot, then president of Harvard University.[7]

The sculpture is an extraordinary example of civic art that seeks both to recall and to celebrate a momentous battle for freedom in American history—freedom not just from slavery itself, but also from the forces of segregation and discrimination that continually compromised the ideals enshrined in the Constitution. It takes the form of a relief image depicting Shaw and his men marching from left to right, a robed angel hovering over their heads. Shaw's figure dominates, since he is astride a prancing horse, while the African American soldiers make their way along the entire length of the frieze, bayonets over their shoulders, heads held high. Today it might be read as an example of traditional public art: the white male hero on a horse, the glorification of military combat and male solidarity. But the histories represented by this monument—and here I include its construction and inauguration, too— touch on themes that have rarely been immortalized in this traditional format. The sculpture and its inscription bear witness to an interpretation of national history that values gendered solidarity across the bitter social and political divisions of "race" and class. The white man on the horse is clearly in charge of the marching column, but this did not prevent him from facing death in battle alongside his troops in the cause of abolishing slavery. The black soldiers are fighting not just for the right to bear arms for their country in the war against slavery, but also for the right to be paid a wage equal to that paid whites. In his study of nineteenth-century war memorials Kirk Savage explains how this panel "broke the mold" of the standard soldier monument, despite having been created by a man who held standard white supremacist views. According to Savage, this memorial "treated racial difference openly and with dignity, asserting a 'brotherhood' of man. And yet it registered, compellingly and beautifully, the transcendence of the white hero in that brotherhood."[8]

Who knows what inspired someone to balance a bunch of flowers on Shaw's lap on the day that I visited the site? The trail continues away from the park toward Beacon Hill. From this point the stories about individuals and incidents attached to particular buildings and spaces help to reconstruct aspects of American history that do not figure in the official versions and that, depending on the narrative powers of the guide, can successfully evoke the extraordinary combination of fear, courage, and resistance that sustained the small community during this period. Since Boston was one of the centers of the abolitionist movement from 1820 to the Civil War, this area of the city was particularly significant as a refuge for those fleeing from slavery or facing persecution for their outspoken views against it, whether they were black or white, women or men. However, the primary function of this particular heritage trail is to document African American history, not to try to tell the story of cooperation, solidarity, and conflict that marked the movement in its local forms.

There are frequent indications that the individuals being commemorated were involved in larger organizations and networks—the Underground Railroad being the most significant. The accompanying brochure refers to various abolitionist organizations, for example, and describes one black householder, John Coburn, as a follower of "Garrisonian principles" who named his adopted son Wendell. This is one of several references to Wendell Phillips, who, like William Lloyd Garrison, was white and who developed an analysis of slavery that connected it to the exploitation of free workers and to the oppression of women.[9] Documents from this period indicate that Phillips was highly respected among more radical circles and that he was critical of the program for moderate abolitionism, which sought to alleviate the worst excesses of the system rather than bringing about immediate emancipation. In the course of researching her *Key to Uncle Tom's Cabin* in 1853, Harriet Beecher Stowe was brought to meet Lewis and Harriet Hayden, who introduced her to a company of fugitive slaves sheltering illegally in their home. The brochure mentions that Stowe was brought to the Haydens by contacts at *The Liberator*, the abolitionist paper founded by Garrison. Garrison's statue stands alone in another part of the city, and his name does not otherwise feature in the Black Heritage Trail.

When I took this walk, I was fascinated by the recovery of the extraordinarily rich local history, which contrasted sharply with the highly affluent appearance of the place today, and our guide, a young African American student working over the summer vacation, took extra care to address the children in our party, all of whom were descended from slaves. However, when we reached the final destination, the African Meeting House, "the oldest black church structure in the U.S.,"[10] I began to feel increasingly frustrated by the rather prescriptive accounts of abolitionist history that we were being given. My question about the whereabouts of *The Liberator's* office, for example, was brushed aside, despite the fact that the brochure mentions that Garrison had founded the New England Anti-slavery Society in the same building. Nor was it possible to find out if any of the active female abolitionists, black or white, had spoken at the meeting house or to ascertain if any of the more well known white abolitionists had lived in the vicinity.

While the brochure referred to numerous personal and collective acts of cooperation between black and white abolitionists, including the fact that funds for the African Meeting House had been raised among black and white communities, the narrative of the memorial trail that day did not permit any comparative evidence of or interest in this history. It was hard not to conclude that the concept of heritage was being greatly oversimplified in order to serve the interests of the present. Where the monument to the 54th Regiment testified to a tradition of collaboration between black and white abolitionists, even though this was a complex and delicate balance of interdependence, the rest of the trail was informed by the need to celebrate and affirm aspects of African American autonomy. What does it mean to represent a movement against slavery as though it was organized separately along lines of color? But what would a public commemoration of abolitionism as a social movement look like, and how could it do justice to the conflicts that characterized its often difficult and unresolved history?

Architectural writer Dolores Hayden has also visited Beacon Hill in her discussion of the public presentation of historic urban landscapes.[11] Combining the incentives of architectural and environmental preservation with the demands of social historians is rarely a straightforward process in any event, but the process of collaboration might be made more rewarding if there was an acknowledgment of the cultural resources both produced by and reflected in the history of particular places. Using the concept of "place memory," she emphasizes "the importance of finding new, community-based ways of working with the physical traces of the past beyond its preservation as museums or adaptive use as real estate." Although the Black Heritage Trail clearly demonstrates the value of "place memory" in the reconstruction of African American history, it suffers, in her view, from neglecting certain aspects of local participation and planning: "Visitors come away with a sense of the active presence of African Americans in the city for over two centuries, although more material showing that the free black community included women who made important contributions would be welcome. Visitors also get a sense of urban history, although it could be more resonant if it addressed how black residents interacted with Irish and other European residents who were crowded into tenements at the edges of this area at the end of the nineteenth century."[12]

As Hayden argues in the context of her book *The Power of Place*, the process of carrying out research into the memories of specific places can prove an empowering experience for those involved, particularly if these "interpretive projects" are planned and run cooperatively. This means leaving room for stories that show failure as well as success, conflict as well as solidarity, sacrifices and disappointments as well as rewards and achievements. But the memory work that this openness requires is all part of developing political links in the present. It is also a way of creating countertraditions that can help to inspire oppositional consciousness among younger recruits.

The vast literature on the transatlantic abolitionist movement offers countless examples of these stories. William Lloyd Garrison provides an example of a complex figure whose record as a committed radical opponent of slavery and an outspoken supporter of women's rights deserves commemoration. His remarkable statement "My country is all the world; my countrymen are all mankind," engraved on his statue in Boston, shows him to have been an internationalist and progressive thinker. Yet he was clearly a difficult man to work with, as Frederick Douglass discovered when they disagreed over the manner in which the former slave acquired his legal freedom—allowing himself to be "bought" by abolitionist sympathizers in England. Nor was Garrison always respectful of the black women and men with whom he worked, as Sojourner Truth found when he abandoned her without warning at the beginning of what was supposed to be their first tour together.[13] As long as these details are available, it is important not to gloss over the personal and political differences that bedeviled and, in some cases, fueled the alliances among activists working broadly for the same cause.

The same is true in relation to the Civil Rights movement in the United States and to the struggle against apartheid in South Africa. Both these movements are accessible to living memory, and, therefore, some of the coals of disagreement and resentment laid in previous decades smolder alongside a more celebratory or even nostalgic overview held today. In the case of South Africa, of course, the memories of working collectively against the apartheid regime are interspliced with the problems of trying to build a new kind of society that can come to terms with the gross inequalities and injustices of the recent past, but that has legacies that remain very much alive. Nonetheless, just as it is a central part of the new scholarship on whiteness to chart the formation of racial categories in different places and at different times, so this investigation must be extended to histories of dissent in which women and men made clear their opposition to the various barbaric regimes that divided and ruled in the name of race.

Becoming European

This last point is a reminder that movements against white supremacy in different parts of the world have invariably relied on international support from sympathetic governments, organizations, and individuals. The policy of sanctions against South African goods is one example of this, since it helped to bring the subject of apartheid right into homes and workplaces outside South Africa as well as having economic repercussions for the apartheid regime. This point underlines the spatial dimension of history and therefore the need to take geography into account when compiling genealogies of white supremacy and traditions of opposition to it. Before returning to England to consider a specific site of commemoration, I want to maintain a connection between the invaluable historiographical work being carried out in the United States and the corresponding excavations being carried out beyond its borders, specifically in Europe and its former colonies. In the American setting Matthew Frye Jacobson has shown the following:

> The saga of European immigration has long been held up as proof of the openness of American society, the benign and absorptive powers of American capitalism, and the robust health of American democracy. . . . But this pretty story suddenly fades once one recognizes how crucial Europeans' racial status as "free white persons" was to their gaining entrance in the first place; how profoundly dependent their racial inclusion was upon the racial exclusion of others; how racially accented the native resistance was even to *their* inclusion for something over half a century; and how completely intertwined were the prospects of becoming American and becoming Caucasian.[14]

As the tortuous history of this process of "becoming Caucasian" in order to "become American" comes to light through the investigative powers of historians of whiteness, it will hopefully help to change the ways that Americans see themselves and their national past. While this is of great importance to those working within (and outside) the U.S. context, it is also worth emphasizing the interrelationship between the "alchemy of race" in the New World and the development of parallel ideologies and identities in the Old World. Jacobson argues that, on both continents, the early prescientific discourse on human origins and human difference, until the late eighteenth century, relied on a "logic of 'civilization' versus 'barbarism' or 'savagery,' or of 'Christianity' versus 'heathendom.'"[15] This logic helped to propel, inform, and justify Euro-American practices of conquest, genocide, and slave-trading, but it was not until the emergence of a new genre of scientific writing that sought to "enumerate, describe, and ultimately to rank the world's peoples" that the epistemological basis of whiteness altered significantly.[16] The fierce debates that took place over the concept of monogenesis, for example, raged back and forth across the Atlantic as well as between thinkers in different European settings. Modern raciology worked to explicate and consolidate economic, political, and social hierarchies among humans within the different but related contexts of European and American colonial expansion, before and after the abolition of racial slavery and during the onset of industrialization.

Contemporary debates on the discursive production of whiteness in the United States need to maintain that sense of interconnection with wider political processes in order to synchronize elements of a broader, possibly even global, struggle against the manifestations of raciology today. A specific example of where better communication is needed can be seen in the changing use of the term "European." Until recently this has functioned as a geopolitical category that incorporates a large number and variety of northern peoples who enjoy diverse ethnicities, but who generally regard themselves as "white" in relation to other non-European groups. Although twentieth-century European history testifies to the instability and volatility of that consensus, the term "European" has retained its associations with whiteness—in fact, it can provide a convenient cipher for notions of ethnic and even racial whiteness that refers back to earlier patterns of race-thinking. In the United States, for example, "European" is often used to distinguish "white" people from African Americans, Chicano Americans, Asian Americans, and so on, although there is also evidence that some groups of European descent prefer to distance themselves from this category because of its association with white privilege.[17] While there may be some historical justification for this particular conflation of northern, white, and Christian, the same discourse now operates within postcolonial Europe to differentiate those who struggle against mechanisms of exclusion from both national and regional collectives on the basis that they are foreigners, "auslanders," outsiders. These mechanisms range from concerted state regulation of migrants, refugees, and visitors from outside European borders to violent hostility from organized neofascist groups and the routine and pernicious metaracism that persists within the context of individual states.

In the same way that the ethnic reputations of immigrants arriving from Europe were measured against notions of Anglo-Saxon civilization before becoming unevenly and gradually united in the alchemic substance of American-flavored Caucasianism, so the concept of "Europe" itself rests on an endlessly complicated and contested historical process whereby people from different ethnic groups "became European" or were repelled at its shifting borders. This history demands a similar degree of investigation and scrutiny if we are to comprehend and intervene in the discourses of European politics today. This is partly a reminder that any new political initiative against white supremacism is likely to be less effective where it is contained within national borders and when it loses sight of what we have identified earlier as "new trans-local forms

of racial narcissism and xenophobia." The struggle of postcolonial settlers to claim new European identities that are not exclusively and automatically white must be acknowledged by U.S. scholars and activists
who continue to use the term "European" to indicate a kind of indigenous and hereditary whiteness that is simply not appropriate now, if it
ever was. Conversely, opponents of race-thinking in each European state
have to be constantly vigilant in their efforts to undermine dominant
sagas of becoming and belonging, forcing categories open by reminding
citizens of histories not just of fascism and colonialism, but also of slave-
trading and slave-owning before that. Only through these kinds of interventions will the category of "European" be able to expand to take on
and appreciate the pluralism that many of its inhabitants experience in
everyday life.

England, Whose England?

Whole forests have been destroyed to comment on and attempt to salve
England's national identity crisis, brought about by the end of empire
and the country's changing status in world trade and global diplomacy.
In the 1980s Patrick Wright was one of the first to provide a critical
analysis of what he saw as a morbid fascination with particular elements
of the national past in the name of heritage, exacerbated during conservative rule under Thatcher: "here is a strategy that would freeze the
whole of social life over, raising a highly selective image of British particularity to the level of Absolute Spirit and presenting it as the essential
alterity of the betrayed nation to which we must all return."[18] In his
book *On Living in an Old Country* he argued for a close investigation of
"this Conservative nation" with a view to discovering "other possible
articulations of cultural particularity, articulations which are respectful
of the heterogeneity of contemporary society and also capable of making
a coherent political principle of difference. Perhaps we should start in
the knowledge that the 'national past' doesn't exhaust or fully express
everyday political consciousness, and that everyday nostalgia therefore
has a critical and subversive potential as well."[19]

Defining the national "peculiarity" of the English is clearly a highly
charged ideological pastime, which has exercised many a government
minister and cultural critic.[20] In more recent times the Labour government, which came to power with an overwhelming majority in 1997,
adopted the language of advertising and public relations in an attempt to
promote the more inclusive notion of Great Britain as a youthful, forward-
looking, and innovative nation. Demonstrating that the heritage-driven

past could be read differently, not for evidence of cultural homogeneity or imperial greatness, but for proof of boundless creativity, originality, and cleverness, government advisers promoted the idea of "rebranding" Britain. The project was aimed at shattering the tired images of interminable industrial and imperial decline associated with seventeen years of Conservative rule and was designed to reflect the proposed changes that New Labour (the "old" Labour Party having undergone a similar transformation) was about to introduce to the rejuvenated nation. At the same time, it was made explicitly clear that this makeover was intended to attract new customers and investors in an expanding global market. National identity, as Geoffrey Cubitt has argued in *Imagining Nations,* has become something of such fundamental importance in the postmodern world that it manages to touch the lives of individuals as well as influencing wider outer-national concerns: "The concept of the nation is central to the dominant understandings both of political community and of personal identity. . . . Notions of national distinctiveness and of international competition or comparison have become intrinsic to the ways in which we think and speak about matters as varied as economics and topography, art and climate, sport and literature, diet and human character."[21]

As Benedict Anderson has argued, imagined communities that form the basis of the modern nation-state rest on a shared view of history and geography. Where one nation ends and another begins may be determined to some extent by border controls and checkpoints, but as Cubitt suggests, the essence of nation identity is a far more elusive quality, "often cast . . . as essentialist impressionism":

> For Stanley Baldwin, for example, the essence of England was most accessible "through the ear, through the eye, and through imperishable scents"—the tinkle of the hammer on the anvil, the sound of the corncrake on a dewy morning, the sight of the plough team coming over the brow of the hill, and other uniformly rural impressions, right down to the smell of "that wood smoke that our ancestors, tens of thousands of years ago must have caught on the air when they were coming home with the results of a day's forage"—the olfactory proof of the continuities of a nation's existence.[22]

These kinds of images of seamless continuity rely on an Arcadian view of the relationship between the English and their living environment. They seem quaint nowadays, since the technologies of the blacksmith and the plow horse are visible only on heritage sites and the sound of the corncrake has been almost silenced by years of pesticides and the pervasive noise of traffic. Yet the relationships evoked in Baldwin's vision have merely shifted into the national memory banks as evidence of a predominantly rural England that apparently once existed, even if it has been drastically modernized since that pre-1939 era. If the particular essence of national identity is communicated by certain indigenous smells, sounds, and sights, it is also the inevitable product of a harmonious social ecology, in which everyone and everything know their places. The combination of ephemeral, intangible impressions on the senses can suggest that the essence is fragile, vulnerable, and pure. In an imperial world, in which human relationships are organized according to strict hierarchies of race, class, and gender, this purity can easily be rendered as whiteness when defined against the dark, filthy chaos of the city, polluted by industry, commerce, and foreign bodies.

In his book *A Dream of England,* exploring the photography and landscapes of tourism, John Taylor remarks that "Englishness, which is a set of relationships, is not only in tension but always in flux."[23] It is still difficult for many outside the United Kingdom to comprehend the difference between Britishness and Englishness. While these are overlapping categories, it is important to understand how both have come to be contested in particularly important ways in this postcolonial era. Stuart Hall gives a lucid account of the changing definitions of Britishness and Englishness in an essay entitled "New Cultures for Old": "One only has to think of the regional, cultural, class, gender, 'racial,' economic and linguistic differences which still persist within its boundaries, of the tensions which now accompany the idea of a 'united' kingdom, and of the role of 'Englishness' as the hegemonic culture in relation to the other 'nations' within the kingdom—a fact which irritates many Scots, Welsh and Northern Irish people, and which fuels nationalist sentiment and aspirations in different parts of the UK."[24]

The United Kingdom has to be seen as a "composite nation," and the job of the national culture is to produce a "sense of belongingness," which might unify the different elements. The role of "Englishness" is clearly crucial to the national culture as a whole, as it has a "quintessential" relation to Britishness. The contingencies of imperialism brought under British jurisdiction many different ethnic groups that continue to retain an affinity with the country, either through direct settlement here or through structures such as the Commonwealth—but this does not automatically permit the members of these groups to identify themselves as English, even if they are born and brought up in the country. The fiftieth anniversary of the docking of SS *Empire Windrush,* one of the first ships to bring a significant contingent of Caribbean workers to postwar Britain, provided a valuable opportunity to examine new identities across two generations of black settlers. This recent history of migration and settlement, which also incorporates the experiences of people from India, Pakistan, Bangladesh, Hong Kong, Malaysia, Nigeria, and other former British colonies, can be read as an invasion that threatens to overpower the normative codes of Englishness that were supposedly refined and passed down from the ancestors sniffing the wood smoke. Without a sense of that continuous relationship between England and the peoples whose countries were explored, raided, occupied, and ruled, this image of the hostile takeover is able to influence the way that the beleaguered nation sees itself. To put it even more crudely, conservative and imperialist versions of English national identity have produced a nostalgic version of England that is white by birth and by right. This means that a great deal of subversive labor has to be undertaken in order to cast England in a different light and as more resilient to the allure of purity and essentialism that is intrinsic to race-thinking.[25]

Taking Patrick Wright's lead, other writers have begun to unearth important historical details that help to explain the relationship between landscape and Englishness. Using photography and the tourist's eye as its source, Taylor's work is invaluable in helping to document this claim: "The need to sustain the rural idyll derives from the need of the English to define themselves and remain united as a nation."[26] Geographer Stephen Daniels underlines the historical process by which landscapes have come to "provide visible shape" to the mental images of the nation. "As exemplars of moral order and aesthetic harmony, particular landscapes achieve the status of national icons."[27] Yet, he continues, there is "seldom a secure or enduring consensus as to which, or rather whose, legends and landscapes epitomize the nation. . . . [E]ven apparently singular histories and geographies may be open to varying interpretation, even appropriation, by those once marginalized in, or excluded from, the dominant national culture."[28] Far from always being a censored composition of dominant hierarchies and invisible social misery, the landscape of rural England has shown itself to be extraordinarily articulate when it has been "appropriated" by those who have found themselves to be marginalized or excluded. The work of photographer Ingrid Pollard is particularly relevant here. Whether she explores the socially mediated concept of nature in the wilds of Wordsworth country or documents the forgotten histories of remote trading ports in the north of England, her combination of images and words powerfully evokes, and challenges, the invisible restrictions of Englishness beyond the metropolitan centers.

Although Daniels is writing about the use of landscape imagery in the articulation of national identity in the United States as well as England, there are important distinctions to be made between discourses of belonging and exclusion within each "imagined community." Where race has been the primary means for dividing and organizing populations in the United States, it has played a far more furtive role in the context of English history; rather, the relationships between race and class have been distinctively dissimilar. The corresponding tasks of investigating and interpreting histories of whiteness demand different tactics, ones that can tackle the construction (and subversion) of the national essence on its own ground. An important aspect of this work is the contestation of national memory. This may require the manipulation of what Wright calls the "critical and subversive potential" of nostalgia, for if, as he also argues, "'the past' is there to be dug up and visited,"[29] then it is important to pitch in on the excavation to produce alternative kinds of evidence.

"Every English landscape is full of ghosts," but are they all friendly, heroic, and polite? The chance discovery of a long-forgotten grave in southwest England provides a chance to intervene in contemporary debates about national identity and the misrepresentation of the country's past. By telling this particular story I hope to show that the concept of heritage and the recovery of forgotten strands of history can be put to work in support of a political agenda that is dedicated to shattering all illusions of racial or cultural purity.

Local History

This next part of the argument moves backward and forward in time, since it concerns an episode from the past that needs to be interpreted in the present, but it also tries to keep a sense of the dynamic spatial history of capitalism and white supremacy that links together places that are geographically far apart. In February 1997 the national media became alerted when human bones were discovered at Rapparee Cove, near Ilfracombe in Devon, in the southwest of England. An archaeological dig quickly discovered the remains of a mass grave at the foot of the steep cliffs, which had been rapidly eroding after a seawall had collapsed a few years earlier. Local historians, who had been monitoring the area for some time, had already compiled an inventory of eighteenth-century coins found on the beach. They had traced these findings to a British transport ship called *The London,* believed to have wrecked in the cove in October 1796. Opinions were divided over the cargo of the unlucky ship and the origins and status of the victims. Pat Barrow, who had been

carrying out research on this particular route since 1970 and who organized the first excavation, was certain that the bodies buried in the walls
of the cove were those of black prisoners taken from the Caribbean island of St. Lucia as a result of the war between France and Britain that
began in 1793. Having been freed from slavery by the French in 1783,
the inhabitants of St. Lucia found themselves under attack from the British, since the island represented a strategic point in the Caribbean. They
were well aware that if the British overran the island, they would be
enslaved again, and they managed to repel the British for three years
before being defeated. Known as "Brigands," the prisoners were brought
back to Britain in large numbers to an uncertain fate, along with a large
quantity of coins and jewels. Despite Lord Mansfield's historic pro-
nouncement in 1772 that slaves were free once they reached English soil
and that no former slave could be compelled to return to the West Indies, there was still a great deal of money to be made by flouting the
law. Barrow's book *Slaves of Rapparee,* published in 1998, provides an extraordinarily detailed account of all the available evidence relating to
The London, interwoven with a description of local, national, and international interest in the site.[30]

One of the many mysteries surrounding the wreck of *The London* on
the night of October 9, 1796, is why the bodies were buried on the beach
and not in a marked graveyard. Barrow cites a local source, *Old Times in
the West Country: Stories, Legends, and Highwaymen; Traditions, and Rhymes
of Old North Devon,* published almost a century later, which gives an eyewitness account of the wreck and of the behavior of the local residents
who witnessed it. It is worth quoting at length not just because it evokes
a vivid picture, but also because it confirms the status of local legend,
which the incident had undoubtedly acquired by the late nineteenth
century.

> It was late in the evening when a gun was heard faintly booming
> in the distance. A fine vessel was seen in distress. . . . An Ilfra-
> combe pilot bravely ventured out in response to the signal, but
> was not allowed to board her. "Where are you from?" demanded
> the pilot. "From hell bound for damnation," was the awful answer
> given by the ruffian captain, who had on board such invaluable
> treasure—a cargo of human life with gold and specie, the worth
> of which none shall ever answer. "Pilot away," exclaimed the cap-
> tain. "We want no assistance, we're bound to perish," and soon
> the assertion was realized, and the noble vessel sank beneath the
> gurgling waters amidst the agonizing cries and shrieks of those on

board, thus ruthlessly and desperately deprived of precious life. In the morning the beach was covered with the bodies of the unfortunate Negroes, washed up by the tide: and amongst them, a strange and pitiful exception, like a pearl among rubies, was a lovely creature, a youthful lady. A naked lily fair, lying dead and cold. Whether it was the body of a captive, or the captain's wife, none could ever tell, but the sea had made no distinction between black and white victims.

As the waves moved the sand on the beach, heaps of shining coins in gold met the sight of the astonished inhabitants, who were busily removing the dead bodies to the outhouses of the Britannia Hotel. The sight was a wondrous and not unwelcome one. Eagerly they rushed to the treasure. The cry was raised by someone, "Stop, first bury the dead." They hesitated, but the inward voice of conscience re-echoed the mandate, and they returned to their work, and the bodies were hastily buried in the hillside, this being the most convenient spot near at hand, there to rest until the resurrection morn.[31]

Other descriptions cited by Barrow recall the efforts of locals to rescue the drowning crew and captives, but there are no other accounts of the portentous body of the lily-white woman. This image, once encountered, is difficult to efface: it conveys a sorrowful awareness that the distinction that people made between human beings on the basis of skin color, and for the purpose of profit, had no currency in nature. It helps to add an almost mystical element to this disastrous and shameful tragedy, compounded by the eagerness of the locals to put their own interests before Christian duty. There is no mention of proper or different funeral rites being accorded to this woman, who might herself have been a captive, since in the rush to collect the gold coins any respect for humanity was all but abandoned anyway. Whatever the origins of this account, and its dubious authenticity, it is significant that in 1873 it was this powerful imagery that was chosen to convey the story of that particular shipwreck, and thus to keep its memory alive in another historical period.

In his introduction Barrow prepares the reader for the controversy that began with the suggestion that those who died in the wreck had been slaves, destined for sale in Bristol, further up the English coast:

> I became aware of an increasing hostility as my research began to uncover details which it was obvious some people would rather I had left alone. While the motive for transporting black prisoners

from the Caribbean islands to a Bristol prison intrigued me, it appeared to infuriate the powers-that-be. The media seized upon the idea that this was a slave ship, yet it was never that simple. I was encouraged to describe the victims as prisoners-of-war as they were clearly freedom fighters embroiled in the Napoleonic revolutionary wars which at the time were raging in the West Indies.

Barrow states his own careful position here, always scrupulous to avoid jumping to his own conclusions and anxious to give the dead bodies the commemoration that they deserved. From his research he was convinced that the prisoners on board the ship were black captives of one kind or another, but he was also critical of the media, on the one hand, who wanted a simplistic, sensationalist approach and of skeptics, on the other, who cast doubt on the evidence that he had assembled with the help of historians from Britain and the Caribbean. More to the point, in some ways, was the fate of those who escaped drowning on that fateful night. Whether they were captured as slaves or defeated as freedom fighters, the prisoners were inevitably destined for captivity of one form or another when they arrived in Bristol: "Yet these people had fought heroically to avoid slavery, and had been captured by the British. So what of the survivors, what became of the people who did not perish in the wreck of the London? Were they ultimately treated honorably, as prisoners of war—or as slaves?"

The discovery of the grave received national attention, not so much when it was first uncovered, but when Labour Member of Parliament Bernie Grant, who is of Caribbean descent, traveled to the site to demand a memorial to the captives. As he examined the fragments of bone, some of them thought to have belonged to children, he was reported as saying: "I feel very emotional about it. I feel that there is a need for there to be some reburial together with some sort of a monument which would let everyone know what has transpired. What we want is for the truth to be told, warts and all."[32] Grant had paid a visit to Ilfracombe on behalf of the African Reparation Movement (ARM), which campaigns for compensation for slavery and in particular for the return of artifacts plundered and stolen from African people. In this case, he explained, compensation was a secondary issue compared to an apology; what was needed was a gesture of public recognition that something terrible had happened there. Grant told reporters that before visiting the area he had felt that the remains at Rapparee Cove should be returned to their home country, but he now supported the local view that there should be a memorial and a historic grave.

Grant's arrival on the scene precipitated a number of controversial reports in the media, since he personified the politics of race. His national reputation as an outspoken and combative figure had been secured over a decade earlier when he was the leader of the local authority in the same area of north London, earning the nickname of "Barmie Bernie" in the pages of the tabloid newspapers. Shortly before he visited Ilfracombe, he had been involved in an exchange with a museum in the nearby city of Exeter regarding the return of some African artifacts dating from the colonial era. As news of Grant's interest in Rapparee spread, Barrow began to find himself pressed to supply evidence for his views on the origins of the bones. He was astonished to read categorical statements establishing the "racial" origin of the captives in some papers and dismayed by the hostility he encountered when he maintained his position that the bones belonged in Rapparee until further evidence could be obtained on their source. The fact that so many journalists were interested in proving that the captives were slaves rather than prisoners of war indicates that this was the more immediately sensational account and corresponded neatly with the newsworthy and highly symbolic entrance of Bernie Grant onto this unlikely stage set.

The intense media attention received by this extraordinary excavation was short lived, however, and the local authority insisted on waiting for more evidence of authenticity before it made the arrangements necessary for a public memorial. Grant was entirely justified in demanding that the remains of *The London*'s captives rest in Devon, since they were already so far from anywhere that could be called home. Rapparee Cove can be seen as a point on a circuit that linked the three continents of Africa, North America, and Europe. A distinctive yellow gravel embedded in the sand of the Devonshire bay is thought to have originated in St. Lucia before being loaded into the hold of *The London* to act as ballast. If Barrow is right about this extraordinary detail, which can be corroborated through the writings of an eminent nineteenth-century naturalist, the image of the differently colored stones being churned by the surf emphasizes the ecological and geographical dimensions of the stories we need to know about the past.[33] The remains of the women, children, and men who drowned in the wreck, held by chains in the ship's hold, may constitute one tiny piece of evidence of the inhumanity of the international slave trade, but the very local discovery of their bones in a remote corner of England has created an opportunity to make sense of and intervene in that country's multicultural present.

Overlapping Territories

The episode needs to be understood within several different sets of arguments connected by the thread of identity politics, whether national, individual, or collective. First, there is the inescapable discourse of heritage, which, as we have seen, is already highly politicized by the mythical history of English nationalism.[34] A commemorative site is likely to become a potential feature of a tourist itinerary, which will in turn influence the way that it is presented to the public. This requires an interpretation of historical evidence that is sensitive to the line between entertainment and education. How does this story "fit" into the bigger picture of the nation's invincible seafaring past? How does national heritage treat episodes that remind visitors of the shameful elements of history rather than the glorious ones? Second, the reminder of slave-trading operating through British ports offers a longer term of the black presence in the country. It helps to counter the image of postcolonial settlers as inhabiting the metropolitan areas of Britain within the last fifty years, as being connected only to urban centers, and as being without history themselves. The story of *The London*, whom it was carrying, and how they were disposed of is testimony to the interconnected histories of England and Africa over several centuries. Third, the fact of the bones being held in a secret unmarked grave for two hundred years serves as an appalling metaphor for the way that the land itself bears traces of history that ideology, indifference, and guilty conscience have tried so hard to conceal. This last point can be connected back to the first question about heritage and the representation of the national past, since the iconography of the English rural landscape has been powerful in articulating "The Spirit of England."[35] Finally, both the process of authenticating the material evidence and the campaign to commemorate those who died form the basis of an "interpretive project" that might help to compile one more chapter in the genealogy of resistance to white supremacism.

This is a project that entails not the "discovery" of a hidden variant of English history so much as the recollection of certain material and ideological processes that helped bring the country to the state it is in now. But perhaps this is a dangerous undertaking, since the commercial power of postmodern heritage has effectively undermined the authority of one version of history as opposed to another. Can the two-hundred-year-old bones tumbling from an eroding cliff in a remote part of the country really be called to speak about English national identity in this climate, in which history has become commodified and marketable?

Even if a memorial to the prisoners aboard *The London* is set up by the local authority in conjunction with the town museum, what are the chances of this spot remaining an interesting detail on a tourist map, a place of pilgrimage for a few, a matter of indifference to most?

One way of answering this question would be to treat the grave as a unique accident without making any concerted attempt to establish the networks within which *The London* plied its trade. This would undoubtedly diminish the symbolic power of this particular site and reduce its ability to articulate other kinds of memory—or forgetfulness. But what other resources are there that might enable the story of *The London* and its shipwrecked cargo to take on a new life in the present? Are there ways of commemorating these particular dead that elicit hope, optimism, and creativity as opposed to guilt, recrimination, and shame? How would a politics that seeks to deconstruct and demystify whiteness handle with due respect the tangible remains of such a complicated international event?

This list of questions returns us to the different sets of arguments relating to the formation of individual, collective, and national identities that I outlined earlier. Clearly there is a case for compiling a regional history of slave-trading from ports in the southwest of England. Nigel Tattersfield's formidable history *The Forgotten Trade* provides a detailed account of slave ships operating from an area known as "The West Country," more commonly associated with rocky beaches, picturesque countryside, pony-trekking, cream teas, and other particularly English pastimes.[36] The evidence that he has unearthed not only casts the region in a slightly different light, but also paints a portrait of English radicalism that differs from conventional accounts. In a foreword to the book, novelist John Fowles, author of *The French Lieutenant's Woman,* which was set (and filmed) in Lyme Regis, one of the main ports featured in Tattersfield's book, recalls his shock at encountering this material:

> When I first read an early draft of Nigel Tattersfield's sharply revealing book, it was like some innocent stepping into a familiar next room, only to discover he had plunged out into empty space. What had caused this fall? My own almost wallowing in the illusion that in the seventeenth century and the first decades of the next all good, religious, political and ethical, had lain with Dissent, the complex aftermath of the Puritan movement. Had its Baptists, Independents, Quakers and the rest not heroically battled against the barbarous persecutions and the stifling authoritarianism of the last Stuarts? Wasn't the bravest movement in Lyme's

own history the withstanding of the Royalist siege in 1644? Where else did the obstinately free spirit of England, that quintessential "againstness," or contra-suggestibility, spring from? ... My romantically canonized "saints" of Dissent were only too like those gaudy plaster images that generations of militant Protestants once despised and hated the Catholics for worshipping.

But this regional history of the southwest would make sense only when placed in a wider international nexus connecting other ports on the English, Welsh, Scottish, and Irish coasts to the west coast of Africa, the Caribbean, and the east coast of North America. In many of these English seaside towns there is little evidence left to show that they were once thriving hubs of global commerce. The different demands of industrialization created a new network of urban centers that often supplanted the smaller docks that were once ideal for trading by sea. Through the recovery of elements of seventeenth-and eighteenth-century history that have long been forgotten, places often regarded by urban dwellers as provincial, monocultural, and out of the way can be brought back into a more cosmopolitan network generally associated with metropolitan centers and urban discourse. Barrow's account of the controversy produced by the discovery of bones at Rapparee Cove includes visits to the site not just by a Member of Parliament and representatives of the ARM, but also by the High Commissioner of St. Lucia and a number of West African, Caribbean, and black British visitors who came to learn more about the excavations and commemorate the dead. Within the imagined geography of England, with its exclusively white rural idyll set against its polluted towns and cities, a cultural event in a remote part of the countryside involving members of the African diaspora seems positively shocking. The fact that the event enabled some Devonshire residents to meet and talk with black people for the first time in their lives can be explained by geographical factors such as patterns of settlement and travel within the country. However, the idea that blacks belong in the cities along with (and contributing to) endemic urban problems is a standard feature of English race-thinking that is not limited to the countryside. An appropriate commemoration of the site might address the contingencies of local "place memory" and in doing so serve as a mnemonic device to recall earlier histories of interaction.

This emphasis on the significance of places within a wider regional context might be one approach to keeping the memory of past events and relationships alive and giving them meanings relevant to the politics of everyday life. However, safeguarding the heritage of sites like Rapparee Cove is likely to be ineffective as a tool to challenge the normativity of whiteness unless it is firmly connected to other kinds of history. The local details of Britain's imperialist activities and networks need to be accompanied both by the careful reconstruction of the black presence in Britain's national past and by rigorous accounts of movements to abolish slavery. This first task relates to the point we made above about the importance of establishing the heterogeneity of England's past in current debates about cultural identities. Peter Fryer's extraordinary work *Staying Power* (1984), which charts the history of black people in Britain, might now be read retrospectively as a contribution to an emerging study of the social construction of whiteness within the British context. Its opening sentence—"There were Africans in Britain before the English came here"—effectively jolts the reader into imagining a time before England existed and therefore preempts the whole question of national origins. Fryer goes on to explain how a soldier of Moorish descent, most likely born in north Africa, found himself stationed on Hadrian's Wall, helping a colonizing power from southern Italy defend its territory from the warlike tribes who inhabited what we now call Scotland. Although migration to Britain from the southern Mediterranean ended after the Romans had abandoned this outpost in the fifth century, the peoples who subsequently inhabited the island also came from outside—gradually to intermingle and settle in different parts of the country that was to become England.

It is important to consider also that London preceded England. In 1993 the Museum of London held a major exhibition called "The Peopling of London: Fifteen Thousand Years of Settlement from Overseas," which set out to document the cosmopolitan history of the city over several centuries. Beginning with an imagined site in the Stone Age, the successive panels and artifacts attempted to show that there had never been an "us," an original homogenous body of people who distinguished themselves from "them," the constant influx of visitors from abroad. The agenda of this exhibition was explicitly to promote and celebrate the idea of cultural diversity as a historical process. In an introductory essay published in the exhibition catalogue Nick Merriman and Rozina Vizram attempted to outline the extraordinary range of ethnic backgrounds, languages, and cultures that have combined to produce London today: "London was founded by people from overseas and the Roman town was cosmopolitan from the outset. Since then immigration from overseas has been a persistent theme in the city's earliest history."[37] One of the illustrations of this essay was a quote from "The Prelude" by William Wordsworth, written just a few years after the tragedy in Rapparee Cove. The poet wrote that in London, amid the "endless stream of men, and moving things," he could:

See—among less distinguishable shapes—
The Italian, with his frame of images
Upon his head, with basket at his waist
The Jew, the stately and slow-moving Turk
With freight of slippers piled beneath his arm!
. . .
As we proceed, all specimens of man
Through all the colours which the sun bestows,
And every character of form and face:
The Swede, the Russian from the genial south,
The Frenchman and the Spaniard; from remote
America, the Hunter-Indian; Moors,
Malays, Lascars, the Tartar and Chinese,
And negro ladies in white muslin gowns.[38]

This view of London as an international center underlines the city's complex relationship to England, let alone the larger entities: "British Isles," "Great Britain," and "United Kingdom," all of which include Scotland, Wales, and Northern Ireland. While London may have its own history of cosmopolitanism, which makes sense for a city that was once head of a world empire, this image is at odds with a more pastoral version of England that was constructed almost as an antidote to the chaos of nineteenth-century urban life.

Peter Fryer was by no means the first to provide a historiography of black people in Britain; *Staying Power* belongs to an expanding body of historiography that began with the publication of Kenneth Little's *Negroes in Britain* in 1948. This was followed by the work of Michael Banton, a student of Little, whose book *The Coloured Quarter* documented social life in an area of London called Stepney in the early 1950s. In 1974 Folarin Shyllon wrote the classic *Black Slaves in Britain,* followed by *Black People in Britain* in 1978. It is not possible to do justice to this body of work by summarizing it here, since it includes work by professional historians, photographers and artists, filmmakers, and writers of historical novels. It is also important to note that the term "black" here is in danger of obscuring the significant historical presence of travelers and settlers of non-European descent who were simultaneously caught up in circuits of trade and captivity and who were also regarded as black, heathen, and/or exotic. There are also a number of eminent figures like Olaudah Equiano, a noted abolitionist, writer, and historian, who pub-

lished autobiographical accounts of their life in England. Equiano, originally from a region of west Africa that is now Nigeria, was living in Cambridge at the time of the wreck of *The London,* having married an
Englishwoman with whom he had two daughters.[39] In *Reconstructing the
Black Past,* one of the most recently published volumes in this area,
Norma Myers attempts to fill in some gaps in the existing historiography
by focusing on the black poor who lived in Britain at the turn of the
eighteenth century. The evidence that she provides can also be read as
an important corollary to the remains left by the wreck of *The London.*

Myers attributes the rise of historical studies of blacks in Britain to
several factors: the expansion of research into African history in the
1950s, the development of black studies in the United States, and the
impact of E. P. Thompson's *The Making of the English Working Class,*
which provided a radically new model of historiography.[40] She does not
mention the extraordinary amount of feminist scholarship, produced
during this same period, devoted to producing new historiographies of
women's lives and to developing analyses of gender and class in British
(and U.S.) history, which was similarly inspired by Thompson's work as
well as by liberation movements in other parts of the world. Nor, more
important, does she mention the influence of C. L. R. James's inspira-
tional work *The Black Jacobins,* which was one of the first volumes not
just to examine a history of resistance to slavery but also to do so from
the perspective of the slaves themselves. Myers does, however, make the
rather facile point that black settlers have contributed to this expanding
history of blacks in Britain in a search for "their own roots and culture."

While this may be a convenient shorthand for the complex processes
of identity politics engaged in by the descendants of post-1945 settlers
from the Caribbean and South Asia, it makes the point that this body
of knowledge that focuses on blacks as both agents and subjects of British history can be made to serve an important function in the present. Yet it is not enough simply to assert that a significant number of
black people have lived on British soil as a result of the transatlantic
slave trade and European colonialism. As Michel-Rolph Trouillot argues,
"Even when the historical continuities are unquestionable, in no way
can we assume a simple correlation between the magnitude of events as
they happened and their relevance for the generations that inherit them
through history."[41] Using the hastily buried passengers of *The London* as
an example once again, the controversy produced by the possibility of
their having been authentic slaves is met by an almost universal condemnation of slavery. But as Trouillot also emphasizes in a slightly different context, "[T]o condemn slavery is the easy way out." Although he

was referring to the representation of African American slavery in a historical theme park proposed by Disney, his comments are apposite here: "The denunciation of slavery in a presentist mode is easy. Slavery was bad, most of us would agree. . . . What needs to be denounced here to restore authenticity is much less slavery than the racist present within which representations of slavery are produced."[42]

Trouillot is concerned with the way that certain histories are produced or silenced as much as with the knowledge that results. For him the processes of authenticating, celebrating, and interpreting historical narratives are likely to be the crucial factors in making different pasts meaningful in the present. This brings us to a third angle of approach to the possible commemoration of the St. Lucian prisoners. We have already seen that their fate can be read within a wider geographical context that recognizes the role of slave-trading in the economic history of the area and that this historical narrative can be used to intervene in representations of English provincial and rural life. In order to connect this past with more urgent themes arising in the present, I have argued that this local history needs to be spliced with a reconstructed black British past that demonstrates themes of agency, integration, and acceptance as well as victimization, exclusion, and exploitation. But how else does this relate to the scholarship and activism that arise from the deconstruction of whiteness in the present?

My final point is that the excavation of the bones themselves provides a pointer toward an appropriate way of interpreting the fate of the murdered captives in such as way as to look forward to the future rather than dwelling on an abominable past. The actual task of excavating and authenticating the archaeological remains provides a useful analogy for the division of labor required to unearth the layered deposits of White Power and to interpret the findings in the light of a politics of resistance and dissent in the present. The rather haphazard but ultimately productive conversations and connections among people from very different backgrounds recorded in Barrow's book demonstrate the possibilities of thoughtful solidarities that result from a shared sense of accountability to the victims of a white supremacist capitalist enterprise, whether they were slaves or prisoners of war. That is not to say that disagreements did not take place among some of the interested parties and experts, but rather to emphasize that those individuals who felt a genuine respect for the dead and a desire to know as accurately as possible where the prisoners came from and where they were bound were able to collaborate constructively both to fit together the pieces of the jigsaw and to discuss appropriate forms of commemoration.

A far broader and wide-ranging history of this cooperative process can be illustrated by the abolitionist movement in England, Scotland, Ireland, and Wales in the first half of the nineteenth century. A local history of southeast England might uncover a compelling account of local activism that stretched beyond the old slave port of Bristol, where the Quaker network of radical antislavery organizations was particularly strong, to the neighboring counties of Somerset, Devon, and Cornwall. Clare Midgley's account of women's involvement in abolitionist campaigns lists a number of groups formed in the West Country between 1825 and 1838.[43] From 1839 until 1868 there were no less than fifteen groups from the region of Somerset, Devon, and Cornwall who donated to the British and Foreign Anti-slavery Society. Local historians might well be aware of or be able to uncover significant links between the economic history of the area and the location of these groups. It is also possible that African and African American activists visited the West Country during this period on speaking tours or simply while visiting old friends. Frederick Douglass, for example, stayed with Helen Bright Clark, daughter of abolitionist Member of Parliament Joseph Bright, in the small Quaker town of Street in Somerset when he paid his second visit to Britain in 1886–87. It was here that he met another Somerset local, Catherine Impey, who was partly inspired by this meeting to launch *Anticaste*, a journal "devoted to the interests of coloured people." Her subsequent visit to Douglass's home in Washington, D.C., led directly to her introduction to Ida B. Wells, whom she invited to England in 1893 to help launch the Society for the Recognition of the Universal Brotherhood of Man and who was also a guest at her home in rural Somerset.[44] Moving farther north, William Wells Brown wrote in his autobiography of his extensive travels in England, which included a rather hazardous trek on the back of a donkey in the Lake District during a visit to Harriet Martineau.[45]

It is not that these journeys themselves are particularly remarkable, especially considering the relatively small number of radical, usually middle-class activists working against slavery and the racist regimes that superseded it. Given the ideological shifts of the intervening decades, the presence of leading African American activists in nineteenth-century rural England is hard to imagine now. Like the image of a black MP visiting a small town in Devon on behalf of his north London constituents, this earlier presence also suggests a combination of characters and politics in settings that seems quite incompatible today. The recovery of the spatial networks that operated in earlier times demands a rigorous questioning of the way that places are represented; this investigation requires an analysis of class as well as race and the deconstruction of national as well as regional identities.

Signposts and Paradigms

One other current story from the West Country serves to illustrate the way that the economic and cultural histories of racial slavery leave traces that often pass unrecognized but that occasionally surface as a means to negotiate crucial questions in the present. In January 1998 it was brought to the attention of the national media that a small fishing town on the west coast of Cornwall enjoys an annual festivity known as "Darkie Day."[46] Local residents of Padstow are described as blackening their faces and roaming the streets singing snatches of minstrel songs on public holidays following Christmas and New Year's Eve. Opinions on the origins of the tradition vary, but it is thought to have been carried out for at least a hundred years in some form or other. Following the media attention, the chair of the Cornwall Council for Racial Equality condemned the practice as offensive and spoke of the town being "defiled." The views of Member of Parliament Bernie Grant were sought once again: he was reported to be shocked that the practice of white people dressing up as black people was still allowed to continue, and he demanded an explanation. The town mayor, however, defended the tradition and criticized outsiders for stirring up controversy; the sole local black resident commented that it was no big deal, that he had never experienced racism in the area, and that black people had far more important things to worry about, like schools and proper housing.

Clearly the reporting of this event raises in a microcosm the issues of memory, place, and tradition in relation to whiteness. On one level it is essential that due historical research be carried out to ascertain where the practice comes from and what has contributed to its mutation over the years. In this instance local historian John Buckingham has been working on the connections between older Cornish traditions of guise dancing and later-nineteenth-century forms of minstrelsy, which seem to have been assimilated into the former. In his view Padstow is a town that is infused with a culture of tradition: it holds a spectacular celebration of Mayday every year that attracts many tourists and visitors from outside the area.[47] Buckingham's analysis of the music used in the festivities indicates that the participants perform a medley of verses from old minstrel songs that appear to date from the 1920s. Although the participants and their supporters have made it clear that they do not intend any offense toward black people, the problematic act of blacking up is exacerbated by the use of the word "nigger" in their songs. Since this is not a dispassionate matter that can be explained or excused by historical evidence, the participants in the festivities, who feel they are carrying on important traditions left to them by their parents and grandparents, have been placed in a position where they have to negotiate with those who disapprove of or who are offended by the very idea of Darkie Day. In other words, the local, public memory of the custom and what it stands for is being contested in the light of contemporary sensitivities to questions of "race" and representation. The world has moved on, and what passes as tradition has to be constantly reinvented.

The journey from southeast London to Beacon Common and from there to Rapparee Cove and Padstow Harbour is not so long as it might at first seem. The connection between the abolitionist movement in America and the operations of slave traders between the Caribbean and England is self-evident; the legacy of nineteenth-century minstrels is not confined to small fishing ports in the West Country. By focusing on particular places, it becomes possible to document and interpret the different scales of movement, collaboration, and resistance brought about by that deathly combination of capitalism and white supremacy. This chapter has argued for the importance of mapping the historical evidence that emerges in such a way that it can be used to inform and strengthen a politics for social justice today. This is partly an argument about historiography, but more specifically here it is about the need to connect seemingly different strands of history and social memory. It is difficult to overestimate the effort required to counteract the "confusing melange" of ideas about the past, the sheer ignorance and selective amnesia induced by the discursive production of whiteness in the present.

The British Broadcasting Corporation's (BBC's) 1998 adaptation of Thackeray's *Vanity Fair* for television can be used to provide a final illustration here. This novel of early-nineteenth-century manners offers an extraordinary range of attitudes toward black people, slavery, and empire held by different classes of English men and women. *Vanity Fair* was said to have inspired C. L. R. James to understand the English. The television version was excellent in many respects, but inevitably suffered from being compressed and cleaned up to suit the requirements of a more sensitized audience. Mr. Sambo, the black servant who is featured on the first page of the book and who is a significant member of the Sedley family, does indeed play a highly visible role in the first episode—but it was difficult to catch his name when it was uttered just once in the following one. The mulatto plantation heiress, Miss Swartz from St. Kitts, is offered to George Osborne as a bride by his father; in the book he declares that he does not like her color, whereas in the film he merely focuses on his love for another woman. Reading the novel after viewing the adaptation, it is astonishing to discover how many allusions there are to slavery and empire, providing what Edward Said has termed "a structure of attitude and reference" to the emerging culture of imperialism.[48] Although the BBC frequently comes under criticism for its period costume dramas, partly because of their lavish expense and partly because of their association with a nostalgic, English-heritage view of the past, the ability of such productions to rekindle interest in classic novels is undeniable and in most cases to be entirely welcomed. The problem arises, however, when the narrative is drained of this "structure of attitude and reference," so that the audience is discouraged from connecting the England of the novel—at war with the French, consolidating its empire in India, still enjoying the profits of the plantation system—to the cultural legacy of that period today.

In the introduction to *Culture and Imperialism* Said makes a general political argument relating to the study of the past, urging that we use "the prerogatives of the present as signposts and paradigms."[49] In this chapter I have focused on the history of slavery, but my arguments apply equally to imperialism and historical memory of empire. Emphasizing the "interdependence between things" that necessitates integration and connection between past and present, colonizer and colonized, culture and imperialism, Said continues: "So vast and yet so detailed is imperialism as an experience with crucial cultural dimensions, that we must speak of overlapping territories, intertwined histories common to men and women, whites and non-whites, dwellers in the metropolis and on the peripheries, past as well as present and future; these territories and histories can only be seen from the perspective of the whole of secular human history."

The contribution of historians of whiteness to Said's project is the addition of new strands to the intertwining of common histories rather than the construction of separate parallel narratives. This task demands that fixed categories produced by race-thinking be constantly wrenched open and allowed to connect with one another, both in the past and in the active present.

Les Back

8. OUT OF SIGHT: SOUTHERN MUSIC AND THE COLORING OF SOUND

The sun was setting on the parking lot of 3614 Jackson Highway, once the home of the Muscle Shoals Sound Studio. Here, deep in the rural heart of the Bible Belt, country music is heard on virtually every radio station. I turned off the car stereo, cutting Reba McEntire off in full flight. The fascia of this strange building, briefly used as a casket ware-house, looked like a collage of tombstones. Yet it was in this unlikely setting that countless rhythm and blues hits were recorded in the late 1960s and 1970s. The studio garnered some of the biggest artists in soul and funk, with black producers like Al Bell bringing his Stax artists to Jackson Highway to record with the studio's all-white house band.

When I pulled into the lot on June 18, 1996, the old studio was no longer used for recording. Freddy Parish, then the building's owner, ran his used washer-drier business from the premises. Stripped to the waist, he looked up from his barbecue grill where he was cooking hamburgers. "Y'all wanna see my buildin' don't cha?" He looked at me like he had seen my kind before. I nodded enthusiastically and we walked inside. Entering the small studio, you could still see the vocal booth where Ma-vis Staples exhorted the lesson "No hatred will be tolerated" on the Staples Singers' classic "If You're Ready (Come Go with Me)." The floor space where this and countless other hits were cut was occupied by row upon row of white front-loading washing machines. Freddy allowed me to take some pictures. I sat in the control room at the back of the studio. To the left there was the drum booth, and, looking out onto the studio floor, I imagined where the musicians would have been set up and beyond to the vocal booth from which Mavis Staples gave her righteous cues.

3614 Jackson Highway, Sheffield, Alabama (photograph by the author)

What was I, so obviously out of place, doing in this shadowy corner of the rural South? The visit was the culmination of a long sequence of events that started with the intense scrutiny I had given to the sleeves and labels of my favorite records. Since my youth I had been a fan of 1960s soul, initially associated with the Mod movement in Britain.[1] Like other soul fans I consumed every scrap of information on the records themselves, including songwriting and production credits, the label, catalogue numbers, and musician credits. It was through this vinyl archaeology that I first heard of the musicians and songwriters who form the central focus of this chapter.

As a musician I had labored over the guitar parts found on these records, in an often vain attempt to replicate their extraordinary sound and feel. The contribution of these musicians was hidden by the acclaim given to artists like Aretha Franklin, the Staples Singers, Wilson Pickett, and Percy Sledge. Record labels like Fame, Stax, Atlantic, Bell, Goldwax, and American Group Productions (AGP) were synonymous with the music that in many respects provided the sound track for the Civil Rights movement. As I learned about where and how these records were made, it was clear that a small number of white musicians and songwriters had been crucially involved in the making of this music. Their story was not widely known. Over a period of five years I contacted session players as they passed through London on tours or on recording visits. Then I went

Inside the old Muscle Shoals Sound Studio, 1996 (photograph by the author)

to Alabama to find out more about the racially integrated studios where soul music was made in the shadow of racism.

In this chapter I want to use this particular moment and context as a vehicle to develop a general argument about the relationship between white musicians and black music and what has been termed the "black through white" syndrome.[2] My initial point is that the identification of white people with black music too often is reduced to the binomial of pernicious envy and vicarious exoticism. There is a strain of this logic in Brian Ward's otherwise fascinating history of the politics of rhythm and blues, *Just My Soul Responding.* He argued that the constructions of blackness with which whites were identifying harbored dangerous racial essentialism: "For many whites, blacks embodied the sensual, spontaneous, creative and sharing side of human nature with which they themselves were rapidly losing contact."[3] The white preoccupation with black authenticity meant "that many white Rhythm and Blues fans missed, ignored, or dismissed as inauthentic, a whole range of black moods and preoccupations, styles and sensibilities, which did not appear, or were but faintly inscribed, on the ancient mental map by which whites habitually navigated black culture."[4] This observation undoubtedly carries more than a grain of significance, but the bold confidence with which it is asserted both fixes and ossifies white orientations toward black culture without any attempt at qualification or sociological support.

Critics and writers seem obsessed with reducing white involvement in black music to a very limited range of archetypal possibilities. This relationship is characterized variously as the return of the black-faced minstrel,[5] jazz-obsessed hipsters and white Negroes[6] who want "to be black," or latter-day hip-hopping Wiggers (i.e., "white niggers") who dream of the Hood from the safety of the vanilla suburbs.[7] Another archetype relevant to the focus of this chapter is the conniving and parasitic whites, record producers and company executives, who cream off the profits and exploit black creativity.[8] My initial point is that such prototypical images of love and theft conceal the diversity of white involvement in black music. It has been all too easy to characterize the encounters and dialogues involving white musicians in such terms. Distinctions among musicians, studio owners, producers, and songwriters are elided within the language of appropriation.

Recovering the heteroglot and composite nature of American culture has become a hallmark of the literature on whiteness.[9] But the possible orientations of whites to black cultural expression are disappointingly familiar, not to mention the tired and seemingly compulsory citations of Jack Kerouac's account of a stroll one "lilac evening" into Denver's colored section, Mezz Mezzrow's jazz adventures, or Lou Reed's desire for black transformation. If I am honest with myself, I went to Alabama looking to find a happy idyll of people getting together under the same groove, but cultural revolts against whiteness are rarely so straightforward. "Where exactly," writes David Stowe, "does one draw the line between blackface (bad) and race treason (good)?"[10] Walter Benn Michaels questions the underlying racial logic that defines to whom blues, rhythm and blues, and soul belong. He points out that when whites learn from blacks, this is understood as *imitation*, but when blacks learn the same chords, it is automatically a matter of *inspiration* in which their heritage is claimed.[11] Thus, the imitation/inspiration way of thinking about learning music reinforces a kind of genetic logic that defines which sounds belong to particular groups. This way of thinking about music Benn Michaels defines as a form of cultural geneticism. The result is the assertion of a crude correspondence between racial attributes and musical property.[12]

Anthony Appiah suggests that it is a mistake to view black people in America as defined by a singular culture, music, or language. He is critical of the view that "jazz or hip hop belongs to an African American, whether she likes it or knows anything about it, because it is culturally marked as black. Jazz belongs to a black person who knows nothing about it more fully or naturally than it does to a white jazzman."[13] Appiah argues for a "less scripted" notion of racial identity that is more open to the possibility of dialogue and transculturalism. The arguments against cultural geneticism need to be combined with a careful appreciation of the way in which racism and whiteness are manifest within the music industry itself. At what point is it possible to think about the heteroglot nature of musical expression without marginalizing the contribution of black musicians—or some white musicians, for that matter—without promulgating a saccharine multiculturalism in which complexity, ambivalence, and racism are sidelined?

My starting point is to stress the limitations of making general propositions about the relationship between musical form and race. The crucial point of departure is to situate musical encounters across the color line within particular social spheres, historical moments, and local circumstances. Equally, the existing ways of writing about black music do not allow for the possibility that the orientation of white musicians may have changed over time. Rather, their desires, identifications, and motivations are fixed and reduced to the couplet of love and theft. The point here is that such a logic makes little sense in the context of American southern music in general, and Muscle Shoals rhythm and blues (R&B) in particular, if one is to engage seriously with the contexts and situations in which white involvement in black music took place. The focus of this chapter is to carefully evaluate the ambivalent dialogues that took place in sound and produce a sensitive account of the people who produced R&B and lived the conditions of its creation. Through attention to these details one can see the limits of the terms of the debate about the "black through white" syndrome in music. Beyond this the chapter will examine the role of black musicians in country music—understood today as a quintessential white form—arguing for the importance of desegregating the understanding of southern culture. It is the tension between inimical racism and the fact of multiculture garnered in southern music that makes it particularly significant with regard to the concerns of this book. I want to argue that examinations of the relationship between music and race have been too preoccupied with "the visual." The result is that the culture of sound is interpreted only through the visual lens of racial difference. This, I want to suggest, has limited our understanding of the relationship among sound, culture, and racism. It is with this focus in mind that I want to return to Muscle Shoals and a key moment in the development in rhythm and blues.

Do Right Woman: Country Boys and the Queen of Soul

After being converted from a warehouse, 3614 Jackson Highway became a recording studio specializing in country music. It was owned by Fred

Beavis, a local song leader at the Church of Christ. In 1969 it became the home of the Muscle Shoals Rhythm Section. The band was composed of drummer Roger Hawkins, bassist David Hood, guitarist Jimmy Johnson, and keyboardist Barry Beckett, and it formed the rhythmic heart of one of the premiere funk factories in black music. They developed an ability to work fast and sympathetically with their clients. At the height of their relationship with Al Bell and Stax the band cut fifty-two rhythm tracks in one five-day period. "There is a great paradox in all this," reflects Atlantic Records executive Jerry Wexler from his home in East Hampton, New York.[14] "You had all these country boys brought up on farms and brought up on country music. They didn't always like to admit it but some of those influences came through when they played rhythm and blues." Wexler, brought up in a Jewish New York family, cautions, "What you need to understand is that these white Southern musicians did not learn to play this music from copying records. The reason that they play it so superbly is because they learned it by living it. They were of the same matrix, the same environment as the black players. When they walked the earth the same mud was between their toes." Muscle Shoals, this small rural community, located in a "dry county," in which alcohol was illegal, produced a generation of gifted songwriters and studio musicians. White musicians with a deep love and feel for rhythm and blues contributed to some of the most important recordings of the soul era.

Alabama was a focal point for the defenders of racial segregation. In 1963 George Wallace, then governor, physically blocked the entrance to Foster Auditorium on the University of Alabama's campus in an attempt to stop a presidential envoy serving a court order demanding an end to racial segregation.[15] No one could segregate the airwaves. This chapter is concerned with the deterritorializing properties of sound and the role that the radio, records, and music played in blurring the distinctions made between people on the basis of the visual regime of "race."[16] My essential argument is that the contribution made by these players to soul music cannot be reduced to their whiteness, but, paradoxically, in order to make sense of this story, it is necessary to know that these musicians are white.

Occasionally, the musicians would be credited on sleeve notes, but more often they were neither named nor pictured. Yet everything they played on bore their own unique signature. Their fame reached not only Britain and Europe. In the early 1970s Idrissa Dia was a part-time disc jockey (DJ) in Dakar, Senegal. He was also a fanatical soul music fan, and he has been credited with introducing this music to Senegal. The spread and impact of this music through the traffic in records put a different spin on the notion of globalization. These networks were outside the control of the record companies themselves, as fans and DJs circulated this music within new audiences. Today he is a journalist for the *Voice of America,* but he remembers the impact that southern soul had on him: "I liked the Memphis and Muscle Shoals music but I didn't like what Motown was doing: Motown was too white. The wonderful thing about the Muscle Shoals musicians was that they really play bluesy. It was wonderful. I mean, I thought these musicians were Afro-Americans before I met them."[17] Jimmy Johnson, guitarist with the band, recalled the first time he met Idrissa: "He told us that he used to call our names on the radio there in Dakar in Senegal as brothers. We were kind of a talking point, you know 'our African brothers in America' kind of thing. He wrote me a letter saying this amazing thing, that we'd done more for relations between Senegal and America than any of the ambassadors. The music had tied people together."[18]

Idrissa remembers his sense of disbelief when he found out that the Muscle Shoals musicians were not black. "When I learned that they were all white I could hardly believe it. The way they played sounded very black. From the sound you could only think in your mind that they were black because they were backing up all these great African American singers. It seemed to me that Motown were trying to bleach the music. In Alabama it was wonderful because despite the fact that they had a really racist governor in George Wallace, these white boys were really bluesy. I loved the music and the way they played. Now they play these tunes as a kind of nostalgia in Senegal."[19] Reducing the artistry of these players to pastiche or failed attempts of "white boys to play the blues" grossly simplifies their contribution to black music.[20]

This part of northwestern Alabama extends 150 miles along the banks of the Tennessee River. Within soul music lore the area is known as Muscle Shoals. It is, however, made up of four hamlets: Florence, Tuscumbia, Sheffield, and Muscle Shoals. These small places played a vital role in the development of black music. The area is incredibly rich in jazz and R&B history despite the fact that it has a relatively small black community, mostly concentrated in Florence. Today the black population is around 17 percent of the 36,462 who live there.[21] W. C. Handy, thought by many to be the father of the blues, was a native of Florence. Sam Phillips, who later founded Sun Studio in Memphis and launched the careers of B. B. King, Elvis Presley, Roy Orbison, and Johnny Cash, spent his early life in Florence, where he earned a living from making sound recordings of weddings and functions and selling them to local people.[22] Muscle Shoals takes its name from the freshwater mussels that could be found along the banks of the Tennessee River. The government opened a dam in 1927 that ended both the mussels and the shoals, but the name and its strange spelling endured. Today Muscle Shoals is much the same as it was thirty years ago. Some of the cotton fields have been replaced by malls, but through these changes the area has remained an important recording center.

The day after my visit to 3614 Jackson Highway, Roger Hawkins met me at the plush riverside building where the studio was relocated in 1978. The "new studio" was formerly a Naval Reserve building, and in the 1950s and 1960s it was the best local venue for bands to play live. Both he and Jimmy Johnson had played this venue many times, with their band, the Del Rays, playing tunes like "Annie Had a Baby," "Snake-Eyed Mama," and "Mama Lucie." This soft-spoken man revealed some of the truth of Wexler's observations as we walked along the banks of the Tennessee River. He talked about the crucial role of the church in providing a common reference point for whites and blacks in the South. "A lot of the musical influences in my playing come from the Pentecostal church."[23] Here Roger was introduced to gospel rhythms that he would later use so effectively on Aretha Franklin's recordings. "There were black drummers that I saw that influenced me too. I admired Al Jackson, the great drummer from Memphis. Some I did not even know their names, musicians I saw in shows. I said to myself 'too cool man, the guy looks like he's ridin' a bicycle.'" Roger Hawkins's list of recording credits reads like a who's who of soul music—among them Wilson Pickett's "Mustang Sally" and "Land of a Thousand Dances" and almost all of Aretha Franklin's most important sides from "I Never Loved a Man" to "Respect."

For Roger Hawkins it was not a matter of strenuously identifying, for whatever reasons, with black forms of expression at a distance. It would be misleading to claim that these musicians were merely the same in all respects as their black counterparts.[24] The problem with much of the writing about this period of southern music is that the contribution of white musicians is either erased from the pantheon of black genres[25] or explained as an adjunct to black authenticity, so that the artifice of the "barefoot redneck" becomes a southern emblem of pale-native exoticism.[26] The impulse to authenticate white musicians through the latter strategy might well be a response to the way in which they have been written out of the history of black music. However, this in itself produces a kind of reductive distortion of their lives and artistic careers. While it is certainly true that these musicians were part of the same "matrix," to use Jerry Wexler's evocative phrase, their musical artistry was as much a

Fame Studios, Muscle Shoals, Alabama (photograph by the author)

process of creative becoming as a product of southern authenticity. Before every session at Muscle Shoals Sound the rhythm section would listen and learn from the incoming artist's previous record.[27]

The studio at 3614 Jackson Highway was not the first in the Shoals area to make its mark on black music. These musicians served an apprenticeship with the local record business maverick Rick Hall, who owned Fame (Florence Alabama Music Enterprises) Studio. Hall is an extraordinary figure. He had grown up in rural poverty, but could relate to black performers and artists in a period when association with black people as equals raised attention. However, he was not a student of black music, and he was initially slow to catch onto the growing influence that black music had on young white musicians and songwriters. Hall was a former country fiddler and bass player who broke into show business as a member of a group called the Fairlanes, named after the battered Ford he used to drive. But his ventures into rhythm and blues caught the attention of Jerry Wexler, who by the mid-sixties was looking for a new source of inspiration. But for many of Atlantic's artists the journey south meant facing painful memories of segregation that for many was the very reason that they had traveled north.

As Wilson Pickett looked down at the tiny airport runway, little more than a dirt track, he saw not his musical future, but a stark reminder of a disturbing past. He was born in Prattville, Alabama, in 1941. "I looked down out the plane window. . . . And I see black folks pickin' cotton, and I say, 'Shit, turn this motherfuckin plane around, ain't no way I'm going back there.'"[28] You could see the cotton patch from the Fame Studios. Walking the red Alabama soil for the first time in years, Pickett's disbelief was palpable as he looked at Hall's pale wiry frame. "Look just like the law. Look mean. How did I know Jerry Wexler gonna send me to some big white Southern cat? Woulda never got on that plane. And I would have made the biggest mistake of my life. Rick Hall made things grow down there. What happened was beautiful."[29] While Rick Hall certainly made sounds grow in the shadow of the cotton fields, Roger Hawkins credits Wexler with the foresight to bring Atlantic's R&B roster to the white rural South.

"Jerry knew exactly what he was doing," says Hawkins,[30] reclining in his office chair. "Look what he had to do. He had to convince black artists to come to the South, more than likely artists or persons who had fled the South for all the obvious reasons. And then figure out how to make that person feel comfortable in the South and then how to make the Southern white boy feel comfortable playing with black people. All of that had to go through his mind. It is amazing what he did do to make it happen at Muscle Shoals. It's incredible what he did and the perception and the love of it. The absolute love of it. A connoisseur of music." Wexler was not merely a musical epicure, but also a wily businessman. The move to Muscle Shoals was in part the result of a souring of the relationship between Atlantic and Jim Stewart at Stax Records in Memphis, where Wilson Pickett had recorded hits like "Midnight Hour" and "634–5789." The success of Percy Sledge's "When a Man Loves a Woman," which was recorded by Jimmy Johnson in Quin Ivy's Quinvy Studio in Sheffield,[31] sealed Wexler's decision to shift emphasis to Muscle Shoals. There were, however, particularly in the early days of integrated music at Muscle Shoals, moments of tension in the studio, where an emergent transcendence of race in sound came into conflict with the enduring traces of Jim Crow racism.

The flashpoint came when Aretha Franklin and her husband, Ted White, came to Fame on January 27, 1967, soon after Atlantic had signed her. Five years prior to that she had languished on the Columbia label. Like Pickett, she was returning to the South. She had been born in Memphis in 1942, but was brought up by her father, the Reverend C. L. Franklin, in Detroit. As Ralph Ellison wrote, that migration north was to step "from feudalism into the vortex of industrialism simply by moving across the Mason-Dixie line."[32] While the racialized modernity of New York, Detroit, and Chicago could be impoverished and dangerously disorienting, it also offered opportunities: "Here a former cotton picker develops the sensitive hands of a surgeon, and men whose grandparents still believe in magic prepare optimistically to become atomic scientists."[33] Returning meant having to face memories of a painful past and an incomplete escape. "No-one knew who she was," remembers Donna Thatcher-Godchaux in between sessions at the riverside studio. Donna began her career as a background vocalist while still a student at Sheffield High School. Donna went on to sing at many sessions, including the Elvis session at American Studios in Memphis that produced "Suspicious Minds" and "In the Ghetto." In the early 1970s she was the first and only female member of the Grateful Dead touring and recording extensively. "I remember there was a board at the studio [Fame] where the session bookings were chalked up. I was looking at this name—Arrr . . . Aritha . . . Aritha Franklin? We couldn't even say her name. We sure knew who she was after she'd sat at that piano and hit the first chord."[34]

The rhythm section was composed of Hawkins on drums and a white bass player from Memphis called Tommy Cogbill. Cogbill had originally been a jazz guitarist. He crossed over to the electric bass, where he developed a unique fast-fingering, funky playing style, in part made possible by the fact that in between takes he would dip his picking fingers in a tub of Vaseline that he kept next to his chair in the studio. On rhythm guitar was Jimmy Johnson, and the lead guitarist was Chips Moman. Moman, originally from La Grange, Georgia, had become an established songwriter and later was to be a studio owner and producer in his own right in Memphis.

In order to engender a more inclusive atmosphere in the studio, Wexler asked Hall to hire a racially mixed horn section,[35] as black musicians Gene "Bowlegs" Miller and Aaron Varnell were regular visitors to Fame. However, Hall ended up hiring a completely white band, including the horns, with Charlie Chalmers on tenor saxophone, Ed Logan on baritone sax, Ken Laxton on trumpet, and David Hood on trombone. This decision was to prove fateful. Linden "Spooner" Oldham, a local white songwriter and keyboard player, was hired to fill this last spot, at the piano. Spooner's nickname came from a childhood accident when he pulled a scalding hot spoon from a cooking pot, blinding himself in one eye. He was exposed to black gospel music through sitting outside a small church in nearby Center Star and listening to the congregation. He was involved in the Muscle Shoals music scene from the very beginning, and he played organ on Arthur Alexander's "You Better Move On."

Oldham is an intuitive player, known among his peers for both his creativity and his reputation for never playing the same riff twice. At his home in Rogersville, Alabama, just a few miles from where this recording was made, this quiet man, normally possessing a languid and measured manner, remembers the session with uncharacteristic verve: "I just loved meeting [Aretha Franklin] and playing that music. I walked in that day and in the back of the room in the right corner was a stand-up microphone set up. That'd never been there before. I remember asking Junior Lowe 'I wonder what that's set up there for.' But it was so loose in the studio no one told me what to do. I assumed that I'd be playing piano. But when I heard her hit those chords I just said 'I wish you'd let her play that thing,' so I played with her and listened to what she was doing and tried to add something on the organ."[36]

Aretha seemed comfortable in the studio, and they got straight to work. Wexler commented in his autobiography: "Aretha's response was no response. I never should have worried—about her. She just sat down at the piano and played the music."[37] First up was a song she had chosen by Ronnie Shannon from Detroit. "I Never Loved a Man (The Way I Love You)" is a complex, bittersweet love song in which the protagonist is a defiant critic of her "no good heart-breaker" lover, but nonetheless unable to break herself from her desire. While the song had strong lyrical content and melody, it lacked meter or groove. Initially, no one on the studio floor could connect with precisely what Aretha was looking for. "There's always that scary moment when you're presented with a song and you feel like everything is on the line, your life, your career, your family—everything is at stake in this moment," reflected Spooner.[38] It was at that moment that he came up with a simple three-finger rhythmic figure. This provided the song with a groove. "Sometimes," Spooner concluded, "the key to soul music is about holding back a little and letting go a lot."[39] Chips Moman was quick to recognize it, and all the other players fell in behind. The arrangement quickly took shape; Spooner's opening riff on the Wurlitzer electric piano laid down the basic groove for the rest of the band to follow, augmented by Aretha's piano in the second verse. By the middle of the afternoon the song was almost complete, and spirits were running high.

"They cut 'I Never Loved a Man' before anybody got settled good," remembers Dan Penn. Penn, a songwriter and singer, is something of a seminal figure in the Muscle Shoals scene. Sitting on the couch of his Nashville home in overalls and chewing a toothpick, he reflects on the events of that first Aretha session in listless southern tones. "It was a knock out. They just cut that. And at that time, you know, great stuff

Spooner Oldham in the studio (photograph by Dick Cooper)

broke out. Boy, wow and everybody's just having a big ole time, after a couple of hours of drinking and everybody patting each other on the back and 'Who is this woman?'"[40] Penn was raised in the tiny rural town of Vernon, Alabama, about an hour's drive from the Shoals. Black music reached this community through the high-powered radio stations, like WLAC in Nashville, and in particular through white DJ John R. (Richbourg), who broadcast rhythm and blues to a youthful audience, both black and white, all over the South. By the time Penn entered the emerging Muscle Shoals recording scene, he knew as much about contemporary black music as any of his peers.[41] While there were very few black people in Vernon, like many rural communities it harbored a culturally diverse heritage, and Penn's own family included native Americans.[42] Memphis guitarist Reggie Young, who played many sessions in Muscle

Shoals, described him as "the most soulful white man I ever met. The thing about Dan Penn is that there's not a fake bone in his body—he is the real thing."[43] By 1967 Dan Penn, whose full name was Wallace Daniel Pennington, had established himself as a songwriter and performer of some note.[44]

After successfully committing the first side to tape, the session needed another song. Dan Penn and Chips Moman had an unfinished song called "Do Right Woman" that had caught Wexler's attention. "So it's at that time that Wexler brings up 'Do Right Woman.' He comes to me and he says [Dan switches to a parody of Wexler's nasal New York Jewish accent] 'I dig this song, baby. But we got a space here where there's nothing going on.' I am going 'yeah, yeah,' and I am listening to him. Chips is playing the song on the session so he ain't talking to him, he's talking to me. So Jerry says [switches again to a high-pitched nasal New York voice] 'We need a little re-write here, baby.' I am sitting there watching him and I says 'You know you're right.' He said, 'Can you do it now?' I said, 'yeah, I can do it right now.' I said, 'You wanna he[l]p me?' He said 'Yeah.' He grabbed Aretha and he said 'come on 'retha.'" The three of them disappeared into a closet that ran under the stairway that led to Rick Hall's office. Confined in this space, a New York Jew[45] from Washington Heights, an emerging black superstar, and a white southerner put the finishing touches to one of the greatest of all soul ballads.

The song was complete apart from the bridge. "We go under the stairway going up to Rick Hall's office and underneath that there is a cloakroom. A pretty good cloakroom with no cloaks. Anyway, we go in this room, shut the door and it is Aretha, Jerry and me. And so we're singing the song, I am slapping the wall and she's picking it up a little bit, and eh, you know I believe I said, 'You know I believe it's a man's world' because I loved James Brown's 'It's a man's, man's world.'" Jerry Wexler picked up the story: "My contribution was the line 'You can't prove that by me' which had a certain Jewish cadence to it."[46] As Penn recollects, Aretha added the line "As long as we're together baby, show some respect for me." This line captured a kind of audacious statement of feminine respect that had terrible resonance in her own life. Her marriage to Ted White had not been without personal sacrifice and emotional hardship. Dan remembers, "That was it. We stayed in that closet approximately twenty minutes. We came out, well, we came out and I knew we had a better song."[47]

Amid this moment of musical interchange, the atmosphere of the session was starting to sour. In the euphoria of the initial success of the session the jug was passed around and everyone was drinking. There was a moment of uproar when Ken Laxton made a derogatory remark about Aretha and Ted White responded by getting into what Jerry Wexler recalled as a "dozens" duel: "They were ranking each other out while drinking from the same bottle. A redneck patronizing a black man is a dangerous camaraderie."[48] Memories are vague surrounding the exact nature of the exchange. On top of this the second tune was not going too well. Aretha was having problems with the song: she could not produce a performance from the lead sheet, and it was clear that she would need time to assimilate the song. Dan Penn was asked to do a guide vocal. This was a common practice, and while Penn, a very talented singer, could sometimes tempt the artist to better his attempt, it didn't work. After showing such initial promise, the session was grinding to a halt. Dan Penn summed up his feelings: "At the end of that day I just felt like 'I wanna go home.' They got me to sing in her key. Which put me singing like a little bitty lizard. I didn't wanna party nor nothing and I didn't feel any of the friction, there was none at the studio. I left immediately after they cut the track and believe me I felt bad because that track consisted of Roger Hawkins hitting the drum every once in a while, Spooner just playing on the organ and it was kinda out of tune, and every once in a while Cogbill would go 'thunk' on the bass, and between there was just me there squealing like the worse singing you ever heard."[49]

The session ended in a tirade. Ted White made loud complaints about the whiteness of the session band. Wexler voiced his disappointment that Rick Hall had not delivered a mixed horn section. At the climax of all the tension Ken Laxton is said to have made another disparaging remark about Aretha, and some suggest that he was physically abusive to her. Hall fired the trumpeter, but it was all too late. The session broke up amid acrimony that was in part racialized. Wexler tried to smooth things over and hoped that heads would be cooler in the morning. Rick Hall decided not to go home, frustrated that the day's session had finished so disappointingly. He got into an argument with Ted White that was continued back at the hotel, and harsh words were exchanged.[50] Hall's regret today is palpable, but the outburst, replete with racist epithets, was enough to make certain that Aretha Franklin would never return to Muscle Shoals. The next day the musicians turned up for work only to find out that both weeks had been canceled. Jimmy Johnson said, "We came back to the Studio and we were locked out but Rick's car was outside, he'd been up all night. No-one told us what had gone on."[51]

Aretha would never again return to the rural South, but Wexler's response was simple: he would merely bring the funky young southerners north. Within days of returning to New York Wexler had a dub made of "I Never Loved a Man," and the response from DJs was unprecedented. "I had a smash record but I didn't have a B-Side let alone an album," he remembers.[52] Always the astute businessman, Wexler got on the phone to Hall and asked him if he could spare his musicians to play on an album with King Curtis, eventually entitled *King Curtis Plays the Great Memphis Hits*. All of the members of the session band made the trip to New York. On arrival at Atlantic's studios Dan Penn discovered that his rough demo of "Do Right Man" had flowered into a B-Side to rival "I Never Loved a Man." The musicians involved in these sessions talk about the exceptional energy that was evident in the studio.

For Roger Hawkins, just a teenager at the time, the impact of communicating musically with Aretha, reaching over the color line, is as immediate today as it was over thirty years ago:

> It was just the electricity . . . the total electricity of it. Listening to her. I was sitting not more than six feet from her on a small drum riser with some baffling but I am looking down, I am about eight or nine inches off the floor, she's sitting on the floor at the piano. There's Aretha Franklin singing and playing and I am playing *with* her. I am playing music with her, not sitting and playing a drum part, there was a mental connection even though we never sat or had dinner together. When the session was over, Aretha went her way with her husband and spoke with Jerry and I guess talked about what was going to be recorded the next day. We went back to the hotel or walked around the city. But in that studio it was like electricity. Jerry had the ability to know when the electricity was turned on and what to do to make that happen.[53]

This electricity was quickly turned into record sales. In the seven months following its release "I Never Loved a Man" sold 3.5 million records.[54] Aretha became the voice of black America. Summing up her ascent, *Ebony* magazine characterized the summer of 1967 as the "summer of 'Retha, Rap [Brown], and Revolt."[55]

"It was an exchange," concludes Roger Hawkins, as his languid voice softens.

> It was a wonderful, beautiful, honest exchange and we "got off" on each other. Some look at it as the white man exploiting the black person's music and that may be true on a record company level, but never the human beings that we all were—the Wilson Pickett, the Solomon Burke, the David Hood, the Jimmy Johnson,

Roger Hawkins (left) and King Curtis (right) in Muscle Shoals Sound Studio,
Alabama (photograph copyright Tommy Wright; all rights reserved)

the Aretha Franklin, the Tommy Cogbill, the James and Bobby
Purify. Man, it was people just having the best fun that I've had
in my life and it was honest fun. If it was manipulated by someone
above us, owners of studios, owners of record companies, whatever, they had the vision on what they wanted to do, what they
wanted to put together to make these things happen. We were
musicians enjoying ourselves—it was as innocent as that. It was a
very innocent, wonderful time.[56]

This exchange was confined to the studio floor; very few people outside
the industry knew who the players on these records were, and it was not
until 1969, with the release of the compilation album *Aretha's Gold,*[57]
that pictures of the band members were shown.

To conclude, these historic sessions captured in microcosm the dialogue, transcendence, and ambivalence at the heart of southern soul
music. White musicians were crucially involved in making Aretha Franklin's early recordings so compelling. Equally, racism and the looming
political crisis in the wider society disrupted the nascent integration

achieved among musicians. The tensions that surfaced between Ted White and Rick Hall were one such moment. In response, Jerry Wexler took the transracial synergy that was captured in the studio and simply relocated it north. The tensions surrounding the Aretha Franklin sessions at Fame Studio did not stem the flow of R&B artists to Muscle Shoals.[58] Hall would go on to cut many hits for black artists such as Clarence Carter, Wilson Pickett, and Candi Staton. The fate of southern soul was to be influenced not in the studio, but on the balcony of a motel in Memphis.

The Big Chill: Memphis, Martin Luther King, and the Killing of a Dream

Every now and then I think about my own death, and I think about my own funeral. . . . What is it that I would want said? Say I was a drum major for justice. Say that I was a drum major for peace.

— MARTIN LUTHER KING JR.

There was a chill that went through the studio when we heard of the death of Dr. King.

— ROGER HAWKINS

The murder of Martin Luther King on April 4, 1968, cast a profound shadow over the interracial exchange that took place in the recording studios of the South. Dr. King was in Memphis to support a strike by black sanitation workers. A few days earlier he had led a demonstration through downtown Memphis that had ended in violence. In the aftermath of the disturbances he vowed to return to Memphis to lead a nonviolent march. The day of his death he spent at the Lorraine Motel, also a place where local musicians and songwriters met and where Stax Records held business meetings. That evening, as he stood on the balcony outside his room, he was shot with a high-powered rifle. His jaw was shattered, and he died later that evening at the age of thirty-nine. The aftershock of the assassination was felt most profoundly in Memphis itself. Studios like Stax and American were located in the heart of black neighborhoods.

Reggie Young recalls that evening vividly and what happened when the news broke. At the time he was working for Chips Moman as house guitarist at Moman's American Studios. "Matter of fact we were in the studio and someone called and said, 'Man, turn on the radio or the TV.' Martin Luther King had just gotten shot, he wasn't pronounced dead yet," Reggie remembers.

> We were in a part of town that was predominantly black. [Chips] Moman and the owner of the studio, Donald Cruise, didn't know

what was going to happen, whether there was going to be riots.
They elected to stay in the studio that night . . . armed. When I
left they still hadn't said that he was dead yet. I had only gotten
a couple of blocks away and I had the radio on. It was on every
station and they said he'd just been pronounced dead. He'd died.
I am right in the middle of the ghetto area in Memphis—although
I didn't see anything. I thought 'Man, I am down here—Whitey.'
I had some fear. I got out and on home and by the time I'd got
home they'd started fire-bombing places, breaking windows, loot-
ing just, er, all that stuff. But nothing happened to the studio. It
was strange after that. Err . . . tension.[59]

While the physical structure of the studio was untouched, the emergent
structures of musical integration and trust were dealt a fatal blow.

The Stax house band, otherwise known as Booker T. and the MGs,
was a completely integrated group, including white guitarists and bass-
ists, Steve Cropper and Donald "Duck" Dunn, along with black musicians Booker T. Jones on organ and the legendary Memphis drummer Al
Jackson. The heartbeat of the band was Al Jackson. He was the one
whose instincts everybody followed in the studio. If James Jamerson's
bass-playing was the secret to Motown's success, Al Jackson's inventive
drumming was Stax's key ingredient. Tragically, he was murdered in
1975, shot in the back five times during a burglary at his Memphis
home. Booker, his closest friend in the band, remembers him with
mourning in his voice: "Al was so unique, so one of a kind. Although
he was in many ways sort of the epitome of a Memphis drummer."
Trained by his father, an upright bass player who also headed a well-
known swing orchestra, in the early 1960s Jackson became the most-
sought-after drummer in the clubs of Beale Street. Donald "Duck" Dunn
remembers: "Al Jackson was playing in a club called the Manhattan and
he'd play until three in the morning and I'd get off from my gig at one.
I'd always just stop by there and I'd be in awe, I had to hear Al. He was
the best in town and I know if ever I got to play with 'im he'd make me
a better bass player and my dream came true. His time was incredible
but he didn't just keep time he played the whole song. He was so creative
in his drum parts."[60]

Booker T. Jones was the most musically sophisticated of all the band
members. He played baritone sax, trombone, and guitar on Stax sessions
as well as keyboards. After recording the MGs' hit "Green Onions" at
Stax in 1962, he left for Indiana University to study classical music composition, conducting, and transposition. On weekends he would drive
four hundred miles back to Memphis to play on sessions, shuttling be-

Reggie Young (photograph by the author)

tween classical repertory and funky southern soul. "They complemented each other," he says, looking back. "I didn't want to get bored. It really kept me interested to do 'Born Under a Bad Sign' [which he wrote with William Bell for Albert King] and Beethoven's 5th. Beethoven is still around in a big way and so is 'Born Under a Bad Sign.' So I think I understood a little about the old masters' forms and I may have incorporated some of it. I learned a lot at that time. I learned Wagner, I learned Hindermiss and some Italian composers. I learned to conduct and to arrange and transpose. I think you can hear some of that influence in the melodies I wrote for 'Soul Dressing' or 'Time is Tight.'"[61]

"It was basically black music but some whites like Cropper, Stewart and Dunn helped perpetuate the music," reflects Booker.[62] "They were outcasts for that in a certain way. I think they were either ostracized or admired." Dunn, a self-taught young musician steeped in R&B sensibilities, had developed a new style of syncopated bass-playing. Similarly, Steve Cropper, while influenced by local black guitarist Clarence Nelson and by Lowman Pauling of the Five Royales, brought something new to soul guitar-playing. "Cropper is an innovator, Cropper was the first of his kind," continues Booker. "I had not heard a rhythm guitar player play what Steve Cropper played. It's quite a phenomenon to be the first. There was nobody like Steve in the South that I knew of—black or white." The contributions of players like Cropper and Dunn complicate the idea that white musicians were merely imitating their black counterparts, and in the context of the MGs they were a major creative force.

Before joining the MGs in 1965, Duck Dunn played in clubs with Ben Branch, the first white musician to play publicly with an all-black band. Dunn had worked for King Records and to this day can recite each recording on that label from its catalogue number. Up until that point white musicians who wanted to play with black bands in clubs had to sit behind a curtain.[63] The MGs had to be careful traveling around the South. "We weren't stupid enough to go out and try to flaunt that we were an integrated group because you could get hurt doing that," remembers Duck.[64] "When we rode in the car, Steve and I rode together in the front and Al and Booker road together in the back because we knew we'd get confronted with it sooner or later." With the murder of Martin Luther King, being together in public became problematic in itself.

> One day I was with Isaac Hayes and David Porter, I believe, and a guy named Benny Mabon, and we were all standing out front of Stax and I was the only white guy standing there and a police car passed. We were just standing out in front of Stax like we always do, on a break smoking a cigarette or talkin' in those days when we used to smoke. It was right after Dr. King had been shot. The car turned around and pulled up. This police officer asked me "You OK?" Well, man I just wanted to melt. I think he thought that they were a gang that was gonna beat me up—my friends—were gonna kill me or somethin' because I was the only white one there.[65]

Many mark the King assassination as a defining movement in a division among the players themselves. Others maintain that the solidarity among the musicians endured, but that the business started to divide along racial lines.[66]

"After Dr. King got killed up there I had a long vacation to think about it all," remembers Dan Penn.[67] Penn's adult life had been devoted to songwriting, which inextricably linked him to recording black music. After the King assassination he simply had nowhere to go.

> Suddenly, our music—when I say our music I mean black and white people cutting it, writing it and putting it down together, was gone. Until, that moment . . . as far as I knew that was the most fun being had on earth. It was them people in there, them white folks and them black folks making them records whether it was Stax or Muscle Shoals or New Orleans, wherever you had the whites and blacks working together, believe me, there was no more fun being had anywhere. I mean, there was so much respect going both ways. We respected the black singers and the black horns and pickers, I mean they were great, you respected them, you didn't have to dig it up—it was just there. They in turn respected us because we had the studios, we could write and believe it or not we could play. You put all that together and you've got sixties R&B. In a strange kinda way we were in the background and it was the black folks who were up front. Suddenly, after Dr. King's death, it was over.[68]

For Dan Penn there was simply no other life to lead. He was not a political person, but he had lived an integrated lifestyle. "It was all stopped that day because that was my mode of operation, I didn't have any other, I didn't have anything to fall back on, I didn't have well 'Oh I'll go country' or 'I'll do Beatles' or 'Oh, I guess I'll do jazz.' I couldn't do that, I couldn't do anything except what I did and so there was a big bunch of years of complete confusion for me." The result was seclusion, finding solace in drink and drugs.

Aretha Franklin identified herself closely with the Civil Rights movement and in particular with Martin Luther King's Southern Christian Leadership Conference. Dr. King was a friend of her father, and she sang for him many times. At his funeral she sang his favorite, "Precious Lord, Take My Hand." Jerry Wexler reflected later that hearing her sing this tribute was to witness "a terrible beauty, a holy blend of truth and unspeakable tragedy."[69] In June 1968 Aretha headlined a show called "Soul Together" in Madison Square Garden to raise money for the Martin Luther King Memorial Fund. The lineup included Joe Tex, Sam and Dave, and King Curtis as well as white artists Sonny and Cher and The Rascals. At the end of that month Aretha appeared on the cover of *Time* magazine.

The *Time* article referred to her as the "Queen of Soul," the voice of

Dan Penn with the author, Nashville, Tennessee (photograph by Ron Warshow)

black America, and an icon of black pride.[70] Documenting her career, it credited Jerry Wexler with the foresight to take her to record in the South; "Savvy Producer Jerry Wexler backed with a funky Memphis rhythm section (which she ably joined on piano), and cut loose to swing into soul groove. Her first disc, 'I Never Loved a Man,' sold a million copies."[71] Aretha was heralded as the embodiment of racial authenticity, the article continued: "the closer a Negro gets to a 'white' sound nowadays, the less soulful he is considered to be, and the more he is regarded as betraying his heritage . . . soul singers are so deeply embued with the enduring streams of blues and gospel, so consumed by those primal currents of racial experience and emotion, that they could never be anything but soulful. Aretha Franklin is one of them. No matter what she sings, Aretha will never go white, and that certainly is as gratifying to her white fans as to her Negro ones."[72]

Soul was defined as "the glorification of negritude in all its manifestations," and the question of white involvement in black music became a matter of question, if not derision. The article dedicated a whole section to this query: "Does this mean that white musicians by definition don't have soul?" The discussion continued: "A very few Negroes will concede that such white singers as Frank Sinatra and Peggy Lee have it, and Aretha also nominated Frenchman Charles Aznavour. A few more will accept such blues-orientated whites as the Righteous Brothers, Paul Butterfield, and England's Stevie Winwood—largely because their sound is almost indistinguishable from Negro performers. But for the most part, Negroes leave it up to whites to defend the idea of 'blue-eyed soul.'"[73] The etymology of the notion of blue-eyed soul is interesting in that it originates within black American speech. Ken Johnson pointed out in Chicago during the 1960s that whites were characterized through a range of positive and negative names.[74] The most negative names included "The Man," "blue-eyed devils," and "honky," and the most positive name was "blue-eyed soul brother" or "blue-eyed soul sister." Some white musicians saw these labels as pejorative, as Roger Hawkins commented: "it always seems to suggest that you can't quite get the feel of the music right."[75] The double irony of the *Time* article was that while it championed Aretha as soul sister par excellence, most of the musicians who played her music were white southerners.

The unfairness of the situation was not lost on the musicians themselves. In response to the *Time* cover story Memphis guitarist Charlie Freeman wrote a letter to the magazine. Freeman was a close friend of Steve Cropper and was later to go on to record with Aretha herself as a member of another Wexler-inspired rhythm section, The Dixie Flyers. His letter appeared alongside another that denied the capacity of white musicians to have "soul."[76] Freeman's letter quoted both the original article's mention of Aretha's band of "funky Memphis" musicians and the rhetorical question about blue-eyed soul; it read:

> Sir: To those Negroes who would leave it to us whites to "defend the idea of 'blue-eyed soul,'" I would like to point out that the "funky Memphis rhythm section" that became the vehicle which made it possible for Aretha to do her thing is composed of all white musicians.
>
> Charlie Freeman
> Memphis

The sentiment struck a chord in Memphis. At American Studios the letter was cut out and put up on the recording studio wall.[77] In the aftermath of the assassination of Dr. King several recording sessions with prominent black artists were canceled, including a session with The Sweet Inspirations, Aretha's backing singers. The Sweet Inspirations had recorded a number of their hits at American Studios, including the eponymously entitled "Sweet Inspiration," written for them by Dan Penn and Spooner Oldham. "I had this song written for the Sweet Inspirations called 'I met him in Church,'" explained Dan Penn from the stage of the Borderline to a packed audience in London in 1998. "Then they murdered Dr. King and no-one much came to Memphis after that. I turned the record around, made it 'I met *her* in Church' for Alex Chilton and the Boxtops. Sure would have liked to have heard those girls sing it though."[78] Many more hits were to emerge from American Studios by artists as diverse as Wilson Pickett, Joe Tex, King Curtis, Elvis Presley, Neil Diamond, and Dusty Springfield. As the years began to pass, the sonic traces of racial synergy and hope that characterized the records made during 1967 began to fade.

The studio enabled common terms of communication to be established in music that blurred the lines of racial segregation through coloring sound. This was black music practiced and innovated by both blacks and whites. Yet, at the same time, racially invidious sentiments could disrupt and intrude on these fragile, desegregated private places. In this sense I want to argue that the studio itself became a context in which a kind of innocent nonracialized world was lived and realized in sound. These utopian soundscapes lay beyond view, temporarily removed from the ravages of the destructive scopic regimes of race and racism. The tension between utopian transcendence and the realities of division and confinement is registered in the music itself, giving it a compelling urgency that defines southern soul as a form. I want to suggest that there is something significant about the way sound becomes the key medium for cultural dialogue and exchange—because it is in sound that a version of southern multiculture resonated that was beyond the crude classifications of race.

To characterize soul music as a "bi-racial" product, as Brian Ward has described it,[79] is to miss the nuances of transgression that it registers. It is not, as Ward suggests, some neat product of racial algebra, in which white musicians add their whiteness to the negritude of black musicians. This reduces the agency and creativity of the artists and pickers to some perverse form of racial alchemy. Rather, these musicians carried diversity of musical influences in themselves, be it the combination of Beethoven and the blues found in Booker T.'s organ virtuosity or Roger Hawkins's blending of the rhythms of the Pentecostal Church and the virtuosity of black drummers he saw play at local shows. In each case such heteroglot sound palettes provided the means to communicate across the line of color and produce a music that was culturally composite and also embodied an identifiably black cultural legacy. In the aftermath of the assassination there was a move back toward musical resegregation on all sides. As has been shown, this was most intensely felt in the Memphis recording community. But the sleepy, rural nature of Muscle Shoals meant that the consequences of the King assassination—at least initially—were not registered with such immediate devastation.

Same Culture, Different Color? Recognitions and Mistaken Identities

On April 5, 1968, the *Florence Times and Tri-Cities Daily* dedicated just a single column to the King assassination.[80] As James Brown prepared for his famous television broadcast from Boston Garden, credited by many with keeping the peace, life continued as normal in the Shoals. In the studio the impact of the murder was felt more profoundly. At Fame Studio, on hearing the news, Rick Hall decided to end a session with Wilson Pickett. He and the artist spent the night in Wilson's hotel room reflecting on what had happened. But this was relatively minor in comparison with Memphis, where the military were on the streets policing a curfew and producers like Chips Moman were armed and locked in their studios. It is perhaps not surprising then that, in the immediate aftermath of 1968, Muscle Shoals became a place where the integrated soul music recording culture endured at least initially.

When Hawkins, Hood, Johnson, and Beckett opened their new studio at 3614 Jackson Highway in 1969—financed by Jerry Wexler and Atlantic Records—they were immediately in demand. "We did the whole Atlantic roster at that time and the Studio was fully booked for the first ten months," commented Jimmy Johnson.[81] When relations soured with Atlantic, Al Bell, the most prominent black record executive of the era, brought virtually all the prominent Stax recording artists to Muscle Shoals to work with the rhythm section. Bell chose to come to the Shoals because he wanted to be able to produce artists with a band that would respond to his direction. He found working with Booker T. and the MGs difficult because they did not respect his musical instincts and his qualification to produce. Throughout the early 1970s Stax relocated not only its artists, but also its songwriters and producers to the Shoals. This corner of the South ironically became a place in which the dream of southern freedom embodied in the life of Martin Luther King found a new home, even though many thought it to be a bastion of racial intolerance.

Marvell Thomas,[82] a black musician who often made the trek along Highway 72 from Memphis, remembers that time:

> Muscle Shoals, Alabama, in the sixties and seventies was as racially repressive as any place on this planet. It was just a small town . . . it was a little bitty semi-rural community. But it was a fact that

Muscle Shoals Rhythm Section (left) with a group of Jamaican musicians
(photograph copyright Tommy Wright; all rights reserved)

here were creative people that were musicians and they were acknowledged rednecks. I mean Roger Hawkins and me used to tease
each other. It struck me as real strange sometimes after the fact—
we would throw little racial slurs at each other in fun. I think it was
a way of letting each other know that we were OK with each other
and nobody had any hang-ups about this stuff. As far as I could tell,
nobody did but that was like an oasis in a desert. The studio and the
guys in it were completely, radically different from the community
at large. Those guys they were great guys, I loved 'em—still do.[83]

In the late 1960s, before Barry Beckett established himself in the band,
Marvell was close to joining the Muscle Shoals Rhythm Section full-
time. Around this time black songwriter George Jackson was based at
Fame, where he co-wrote hits for Clarence Carter like "Too Weak to
Fight," "Snatch It Back" and "I Can't Leave Your Love Alone." Initially,
he lived in Memphis and commuted to Muscle Shoals to pitch songs.
Jackson supports Marvell's contention: "Surprisingly, the racial situation
in Muscle Shoals itself it was OK. But I'd be on the highway and you'd
see signs sometime on the side of the road like 'Dr. Martin Luther Coon
Training School' or 'Communist Training School.' They had them kind
of signs up so you knew that you had to be careful. Rick tried his best so

that the black musicians who came down there were shielded from that kind of thing."[84]

Guitarist Jimmy Johnson, whose humor and charm partially hide a thoughtful intelligence, reflects:

> We were untouched. The KKK[85] didn't bother us. I think back and I wonder why they didn't. I mean there was some pretty radical people around but we didn't pay any attention. We didn't give a shit, we didn't care, we were just into making music. We'd go out and eat with Wilson Pickett in a time when it wasn't popular to be seen eating at the same table as a black person and we'd carry him to the finest restaurants. But nobody would ever bother us. I'd feel more uncomfortable going out to eat with Duane Allman[86] because you see we didn't have any long haired people here and Duane would make us feel more uncomfortable than Wilson would because everybody would be looking and all the rednecks, man, they went crazy when he came to town—they'd never seen long hair on a man before.[87]

It is important to remember that these seemingly banal forms of everyday integration (where black and white musicians socialize and eat in the same restaurants) were in fact exceptional at this time, and elsewhere in the South the defenders of segregation were fighting to keep separate schools, restaurants, and restrooms.

Jimmy sums up the redemption he found in the studio. "I was brought up," he pauses and his voice takes on a more sonorous quality, "possibly, I am pretty sure, to be prejudiced. Whatever prejudiced bones I had in my body was dissolved by working with black artists and making this incredible music. I can't stand to see that happen now. I cannot stand to see discrimination and racialism against blacks. I can't stand to see that happen now and I won't have anything to do with anti-black jokes. They don't even tell me them jokes around me, anybody that knows me, they keep 'em to theirself."[88] It is not just that black and white musicians participated equally in the coloring of sound, but rather that involvement in this creative process engendered among the white musicians a deep sense of respect for black people that went beyond the studio. All the members of the rhythm section shared the view articulated here by Johnson.

There was a widespread assumption that all the Muscle Shoals players were black. "I always used to take that as a compliment," comments David Hood,[89] a sentiment shared by all the members of the band. There is something interesting at stake in these recognitions and mistaken

Jimmy Johnson (photograph by Dick Cooper)

identities. The music made by these musicians was manifestly "black" in sound, but equally it bore heteroglot sonic traces that defied any simple notion of racial authenticity. Aural culture in this sense has a potential to dislodge the easy elision of race and culture precisely because it cannot be circumscribed by the visual regimes of racism. As Hood comments, "Well, you know you never knew back before MTV [Music Television] and everything. You didn't know who was on what and what color they were. I mean, for years I thought Duck Dunn was black."[90] In sound there was the potential for expression in which the strictures of racial categories were partially transcended. This was not a matter of "passing as black," but rather of becoming more than white and, in so doing, creating music that could not be reduced to racial categories.

The misidentification of these musicians' race also took place in the community of session players. Roger Hawkins described the first time he met bass player Will Lee. "When I first met Will Lee, the famous bass player, I met him in New York. I was gonna play on a session with him, so the producer says 'Well, why don't you come over to my apartment tonight, I want you to meet Will Lee.' So he'd told Will Lee, 'I want you

The musician's choice: the Southland Restaurant, Sheffield,
Alabama (photograph by the author)

to come over to my apartment tonight, I want you to meet Roger
Hawkins.' So we go in there and we're both sitting on the couch, you
know. We hadn't been introduced. Then the producer comes in and says
'Will, this is Roger. Roger, this is Will.' We just looked at each other and
said, 'I thought you were black' [laughs]. We both said it at the same
time."[91] In the studio these players were artistically and literally out of
sight.

"I mean when the Staples Singers came to record with us they
couldn't believe that we were white," remembers Hood. Their interpreta-

Roger Hawkins at the drums (photograph by Dick Cooper)

tions of rhythm and blues brought something new to the music. Prior to the Staples Singers' sessions the group had recorded "Sitting in Limbo" with Jimmy Cliff. Hearing these tapes, the progressive rock group Traffic, also on Chris Blackwell's Island Records, decided to hire the services of the Muscle Shoals Rhythm Section. "We didn't even know who Traffic were," David Hood recalls, "but we played in places where there were more people in the auditorium than there was in this whole town."[92] For Hawkins, being out of the studio was a little disorienting precisely because he was in view: "I'm not comfortable unless I have my own little corner to play in and my own set of headphones. On stage I feel like an insurance salesman playing all those hot grooves."[93] Before the show, on the European leg of the tour, the music played over the house public address system before the concert was Bob Marley and the Wailers' first album, *Catch a Fire*. The imprint of reggae was left indelibly on the minds of these southern musicians.

Barry Beckett remembers: "I heard this reggae stuff and freaked. When they started doing three on the bass drum and one on the snare I said," accentuating his southern drawl, "what the hell is this?"[94] Arriving back fresh from the Traffic tour the band members put these new influences

David Hood (photograph by Dick Cooper)

to work. With Eddie Hinton on guitar they perfected a new style that reached its ultimate expression in the Staples Singers' hit "I'll Take You There." The acknowledgment to reggae in the opening sequence quotes directly from the Jamaican hit "The Liquidator" by Harry J. and the All Stars. Barry remembers: "It took us forever to get that feel. But we figured it out. Then Roger took the reggae thing and he played it straight and that made the line different."[95] The tracks would be cut live with the singer, and the band would pick up on the cues from both the producer and the singer. "The Muscle Shoals guys were just a *funk* band," enthuses Mavis Staples. "These guys were so cool. Man, we had some times. We would all do it together. The Muscle Shoals guys were a rhythm section that a singer would just die for. They were bad back then! That's what was happening up in there, magic."[96] These white southerners provided the missing link between the rhythms of downtown Kingston, Jamaica, and the sounds of the black church. According to Rob Bowman, the fusing of North American and Caribbean black musics fitted in with

Al Bell (right) and the Staples Singers at 3614 Jackson Highway (photograph copyright Tommy Wright; all rights reserved)

Al Bell's emerging commitment to pan-Africanism. Bell had marketed Stax's records in Jamaica, as had Atlantic Records, and he had similar plans to do so in Brazil.[97] These white southern musicians were also to play their part in making direct connections between reggae, rhythm and blues, and soul genres.

"The black people tried to conceal it too," recalls Hood. "They didn't want their fans to think that they were using white guys on their records."[98] In part, their identities were concealed precisely because of the forms of racial authenticity utilized within the record industry to market R&B. Black artists like Millie Jackson and Bobby Womack continued to come to Muscle Shoals throughout the 1970s and 1980s, but as time passed, the balance of their clients started to tip in the direction of white bands who came to Muscle Shoals in search of the rhythm section's "black sound." Paul Simon, Bob Seeger, Bob Dylan, Rod Stewart, and Dire Straits all made recording pilgrimages to Alabama. The rhythm section was recording a variety of genres, including country music. In 1974 Willie Nelson released his *Phases and Stages* album, recorded at Muscle Shoals Sound under the direction of Jerry Wexler.

David Hood continues: "Paul Simon heard 'I'll Take You There' and he thought 'Wow, I love that Jamaican band!' He calls Al Bell in Memphis and says, 'Man, you've got to give me the names of those Jamaican musicians that played on that record. I've got to record with them.' Al laughs and says 'I'll give you their names but they're not Jamaican, they live in Muscle Shoals, Alabama.'"[99] The session with Paul Simon produced hits like "Kodachrome," "Take Me to the Mardi Gras," "One Man's Ceiling Is Another Man's Floor," and "Love Me Like a Rock."[100]

More perniciously, white pop acts could be disappointed with what they saw as they walked through the studio door. Hood remembers:

> When Tom Dowd brought Rod Stewart to the studio, they came in, Rod looked around the studio and saw us all at our amps and instruments and things. He went back to Tom and said "Well, where's the band?" Tom says, "Well, they're out there." He says, "Well, I thought they were black. That's not the band is it?" He thought we were the roadies or somebody just setting the stuff up. He didn't really like that. It put him off a little bit because he was expecting to go in and see this black band. That's what he was wanting to work with. He didn't speak to us and wouldn't sing with us and we didn't find out until later but it was because he was disappointed by the fact that we were white.

This revealed Stewart's fetish for "real black musicians" that betrayed both ignorance and incomprehension.

It is important to be clear that these musicians did not "desire to be black." Neither did they cast themselves as "exceptional whites," to use Phil Rubio's phrase—that is, those whites "who prefer the culture of the oppressed to [their] own."[101] In order for whites to be "exceptional," they have to be visible. How can they be exceptional if their whiteness is not on display?[102] If all we had to go on was sound, if sound was the beginning and end of what defined a musician, then there would be no white musicians or black musicians, only the colors of sound. My point here, following Walter Benn Michaels, is that "race no more follows music than music follows race. What you become by playing [soul] music is a [soul] musician not a black person."[103] I want to argue that the discussion of the "black through white syndrome" has limited the critical imagination precisely because it has prioritized the visual over the aural. The session musicians I have been talking about here were identified solely in sound. They cannot be viewed as "exceptional whites" or some version of modern blackface freaks without the burnt cork because they never "crossed over"; they were never brought into focus. Put simply, no one knew what they looked like; they only knew what they sounded like. Jimmy Johnson summed up their point of view: "Musicians, you know, we don't connive. You don't have to, you just play."[104]

The situation for the session musicians was different from that of

Jerry Wexler (left) and Willie Nelson (right) trade hats outside 3614 Jackson Highway during the *Phases and Stages* sessions (photograph by Dick Cooper)

white record company owners within the business itself. The paradoxes in the position of the white record men were captured by Rick Hall in a interview he gave to *Cashbox* in 1977. During the 1970s he achieved mainstream success producing the saccharine teen group The Osmonds, along with a host of pop and country artists. He was asked how white southerners came to have the right sensitivity for cutting R&B hits for black audiences. He replied:

> I've thought about that a lot. And I'm still influenced a lot by black music. If you hear one of my records on the Osmonds[105] or

Marie Osmond, or one of my records even on Mac Davis, like, "Don't Get Hooked On Me," you'll hear a shade of the drums and some of the licks of R&B. I'll tell you what happened. I think that black people and white people in the South—and I consider myself poor white trash—the black people and the poor white trash have a lot in common that they don't even know that they have. Their skins are different color, but they had the same hardships. I picked cotton, hoed corn, went barefooted. My daddy cut my hair under the shade tree with a pair of scissors. I shared the same depressions, the same thoughts that the black boy did who was poor also and picked cotton and did all those things. The black person felt at ease with me. They felt I wasn't prejudiced. I think they felt I thought like they did.

At this point the interviewer suggested that this was because they were from the same culture. Hall immediately picked up on this: "The same culture, right. At the same time, a different color; but my color was an asset to them, because there are a lot of black people much more talented in the music business than I am, but these black people at that time in the early sixties couldn't work with the white president of a record company as quickly a white man could. So I was their token white boy that cut records and went in and did a number on the record company for them. That was fine with me because I felt at home with them."[106] Regardless of the feeling among the artists, musicians, and producers, the whiteness of producers like Hall mattered precisely because of the racism that was widespread in the industry itself. Hall played the role of the multicultural southerner in the studio and the white businessman in the boardroom. The tension here was that he was both an advocate of black interests and an instrument of a system that kept black people in the music industry out of positions of power and influence.

The racial divisions that occurred during the 1970s and 1980s impacted on the session musicians. However, their relationship to the music business was different from that of the record company owners. Roger Hawkins, looking back on that period, mourned the resegregation that occurred in the studio, but understood the forces that produced this situation:

I hated it but at the same time I really believe that it is a fact that black music has been ripped off by white people. Let's see, the classic example being "Tootie Fruitie" by Pat Boone and Little Richard writes and sings "Tootie Fruitie" and here comes ofay Pat Boone . . . I can see where that is a rip off. I think it just went on and on 'til where the feelings were so hurt, the feelings were so enraged. . . . They had a great desire not to be controlled by the white man in the ivory tower in the record company. They started asking themselves "Well, why is this? What's wrong with us? Why can't we do that?" 'Cause Al Bell knew that he could do that—a very strong influential man, a very intelligent man. I think it's a normal progression of thought and action taken on those thoughts. I don't look at it as anything really bad. I look at it as . . . a change and back then, a normal change. I don't think it was malicious on anybody's part. I don't think. I am not absolutely sure about that. I mean that made me very sad but what else could happen at that point.[107]

The Perversion of Sound

Some of the musicians who established themselves as session players in Muscle Shoals have turned to country music.[108] Barry Beckett left the studio band in 1986 and moved to Nashville. Beckett was always the member of the band who stayed closest to his country roots. His first musical idol was Floyd Cramer, and in order to fit in with the Muscle Shoals Rhythm Section he had to learn to play like Ray Charles. Before meeting him at his Nashville office in the summer of 1996, I drove into downtown Nashville to visit Ernest Tubbs's famous record shop and kill time before the interview. Thumbing through the racks I came across a record by Otis Williams and the Midnight Cowboys.[109] The cover is striking, for it shows former R&B singer Otis Williams[110] backed by an all-black band dressed in red cowboy outfits. The record was released on the Nashville-based independent Stop label, but its presence alongside the other country records was emblematic, a rare acknowledgment that black people sing country music. Williams himself had an interesting history in that his vocal group, The Charms, served as the house backing singers at Syd Nathan's King Records in Cincinnati, the label on which James Brown recorded. Williams, who was a longtime fan of country music, wanted to be a country artist, but had to satisfy himself with singing harmony vocals for the white singers who made country records for King. As I stood at the checkout, I saw Charley Pride's autobiography, and I added a copy to my pile of records.

Barry Beckett's office in Nashville is covered with gold and platinum records by Lorrie Morgan, Hank Williams Jr.,[111] and Neal McCoy. Beckett was, in many respects, the most musically literate of all the members of the Muscle Shoals Rhythm Section. He was the one who would write out the number charts—a system of notating music—for the rest of the band to follow. But when he joined the band in the late 1960s, he had trouble mastering the R&B feel. Now a thickset man with silver hair, he pulls his baseball cap with Mickey Mouse on the front down firmly on his head before saying, "It took me a year to figure out how to do R&B. They kept buggin' me." He starts to laugh. "Kept talking about Aretha Franklin, 'Hey, why don't you play like Aretha on this one?' I said, 'Look give me time.' Took me about a year and then one day it just clicked. I don't know whose session it was on but it just hit me—Oh, why hadn't I been doing this all the time? It was a feel thing. People who go through that and if they are smart enough to pick up on it, and if they feel it and then it gets you 'agh that's what it is.'"[112] In Nashville Beckett has achieved success through combining a rhythm and blues feel with country singers and steel guitars. He has replicated the approach to recording developed in Muscle Shoals and is applying the lessons that he learned working alongside Jerry Wexler.

With the image of those black cowboys on the cover of Otis Williams's record in my mind, I asked him about the influence of R&B on country music. Barry laughed and replied in a voice that is half whisper and half growl: "The biggest singing acts in country right now are all blues singers. People well versed in the blues. You get into Reba [McEntire] and what she does—she's a blues singer. You get into Randy Travis, listen to his turn offs—they're all blues, every single one of 'em. Even Clint Black on his last tour finished every set with twelve bar blues."[113] Later that night in the Wildhorse Saloon these words were ringing in my ears when the Brooks and Dunn hit "Redneck Rhythm and Blues" got a tumultuous response from the line-dancing fraternity, a small minority of whom were black dancers. "Black sounds" can be assimilated into country and coexist with the idea that country is above all a white form. Mr. Brown of MCA Records told Bruce Feiler: "Country basically is white music. Why would black people want to sing those straight notes? Why would a black person want to be in a format that gives any white singer who tries to do a little curlicue or deep groove so much grief? I work with artists, like Wynonna [Judd], who really draw on black music. But in the studio, when even a great hillbilly song doesn't feel good, my terminology is, 'It sounds too white.' That means it has no feeling to me. Black music is about feeling and white music is about no feeling."[114] This account reimposes a racial logic on sound even when it tries to make country music more culturally inclusive. More than that, it misrepresents the history of black artists in country music and the impact that country music has had on black communities in the South and elsewhere.[115]

While R&B and black music were broadcast into the homes of white young people in the 1950s, so, too, were black listeners tuning in country music on the radio. Bobby "Blue" Bland, an R&B legend, was a good example of this. While the black church was his chief influence, as a boy he learned to sing white country blues via Gene Steele's radio show and the Grand Ole Opry. On the street corners of his hometown he earned nickels and dimes singing hillbilly music. He moved to Memphis with his mother in 1947. It was the wrong time and wrong place for a black country artist to emerge, and the young singer took two steps for the blues. He told Margaret McKee and Fred Chrisenhall: "I like the soft touch. I don't like the harsh. I listened to a lot of Perry Como, Tony Bennett, Nat King Cole for diction, for delivery. And I still know more about hillbilly tunes than I do blues. Hank Snow, Hank Williams, Eddy Arnold,—so much feeling, so much sadness."[116] Dan Penn, a lifetime fan of Bobby Bland, commented:

> You know we're just beginning to find out that a lot of the black singers, and some of the better ones, had that influence. I don't know what that means except, put it this way that maybe he, and a lot of black singers of that period, had a pretty good insight into white people. They got a chance to check 'em out on Saturday night and it was interesting, I think, for them to hear that music. It was more interesting to them than it was to me, course I am cross listening the other way. Myself and a lot of other Southern whites, we were listening to the black stuff and we're interested in that. They're interested in hearing the Grand Ole Opry. Arthur Alexander was that way and I think Percy [Sledge] and all of those guys from Alabama and all of the Southern blacks listened into the Grand Ole Opry and a lot of 'em liked it.[117]

In his book *The Third Ear* Joachim-Ernst Berendt argues that modern Western societies place an excessive emphasis on the eye and the visual in virtually all aspects of social, philosophical, and cultural life.[118] Put crudely, he points out that we think too much with our eyes. He proposes a shift in which listening to the world is granted parity with observing it. Jazz musician Clark Terry made a similar point when he was criticized for using white musicians by a black member of an audience after a concert in Harlem. "Well, man," he replied to his interrogator, "Harlem is known as the home of good jazz, and I thought it was up to somebody to bring good jazz back here. In doing so, I picked the best cats I can get, and I don't *listen with my eyes*."[119] Similarly, I want to suggest that the history of black music in general, and of white involvement in it in particular, has been written as if we listen with our eyes.

Music and sound open up the possibility of combining new forms of human expression that prize open, however temporarily, the territorializing logic that reduces evident multiculture to racial essences. It is revealing that when people seek to describe equanimity and coexistence between people of different cultural backgrounds, they speak of multicultural or racial *harmony*. It is telling that there is no "seeing word" equivalent of this notion. Making sounds and listening to music are an invitation that privileges both mimesis and communion. Sound provides an opportunity to move beyond the visually governed time-space coordinates of racial segregation. This is a point that Berendt makes when he suggests that the ear shows us crossing places: "It shows them to us precisely where our other senses believe that there are insurmountable barriers."[120] In this chapter I have demonstrated how, in a time of segregation, crossing places were found through the radio and records and within the creative process of making music itself.

In the age of MTV music is no longer primarily a matter of sound. Today's music is crucially defined through vision and image where musical taste and genre are divided along stark racial lines. Here black music is R&B and hip-hop, and white music is country and western and rock. This perversion of sound has resegregated the airwaves in ways probably more destructive than even the most ardent supporter of segregation could have imagined. Bruce Feiler has written in the *New York Times* that the racial division in music echoes a widening social distance between blacks and whites.[121] He argues that country music in this context has become the de facto sound track of white flight. But, more than this, Country Music Television (CMTV) has provided the vehicle to set in motion a mythic representation of a white American past, present, and future. Nashville record executives may well want to import the feel of R&B, whether it be through white or black sessions players, but the visual landscape of CMTV is the "back porch" and a wholesome rural idyll into which white suburbanites can project themselves for solace and comfort. In the video age country and western has become the last oasis of white American values.

The patina of current music programming conceals a shared and heterogeneous musical history. I have drawn attention to some of the limitations in the way the relationship between race and popular music is understood. These can be condensed into four main points. First, there is a need to complicate the "black through white syndrome" beyond the current terms of reference in the whiteness literature. In the case of northern Alabama there were highly localized conditions in which musical forms crossed the airwaves. This was occurring in both directions across the color line, so that R&B, hillbilly, and blues became common reference points and a shared history out of which an integrated recording culture emerged. Second, I want to stress the importance of making these local circumstances a key starting point for the understanding of the forms of dialogue and segregation. Beyond this there is a need to specify the kinds of social spheres in which transcultural dialogue takes place and the particular nature of these arenas, be they recording studios, nightclubs, or schools. Third, I want to propose a position that rejects the prevailing logic of cultural geneticism and at the same time is attuned to the ambivalence in such cultural borderlands and alert to the dangers of marginalizing the contribution of black musicians. Fourth, I have demonstrated that white involvement in southern soul cannot be reduced to the notion of the "exceptional whites," whose relationship to black music is located somewhere between "rip-off and respect."[122] Rather, the white musicians discussed here earned their right to play soul and rhythm and blues by carrying the music forward, making a contribution, and adding their own voices within its mutable, living tradition.

Few of the studios in which rhythm and blues and soul music were recorded during the 1960s and 1970s have survived. Some, like the historic Stax Studio in Memphis, have been demolished. Others, left like ruins from another era, seem to act as metaphors for broader cultural and political dilemmas relating to how the past is remembered. Not long after I pulled into the courtyard of 3614 Jackson Highway in the summer of 1996, I found my way to W. C. Handy's birthplace and house in Florence. Handy had written "St. Louis Blues," the tune that French jazz fans renamed "La Tristesse de St. Louis" during World Was II so that the Nazi censors would not recognize a jazz standard from the set list.[123] Nancy Gonce, the organizer of the annual Handy Festival held in Florence to commemorate his birthplace, opened up this small wooden house so that I could see where the father of the blues had lived as a small child. Inside the house there was a book that George Gershwin had inscribed and dedicated to Handy, along with other family heirlooms and, of course, his trumpet. At the back of the room, on a small bookcase, was another book that caught my eye. It was entitled *The African American Heritage Guide to Alabama*. I flicked through the pages to find the entries for the Shoals area. To my surprise there was no mention of the area's recording studios where Aretha Franklin, Wilson Pickett, The Staples, and a host of others had made their historic recordings. There were just three entries: the first was W. C. Handy's birthplace; the second was the Greater St. Paul's African Methodist Episcopal, where his father preached; and the third site was a monument in St. Peters made of shells to commemorate a slave graveyard.

The home of W. C. Handy, Florence, Alabama (photograph by the author)

In Memphis both the Stax Studio and the American Studio have been demolished. The converted movie theater on McLemore Avenue in which the Stax Studio was housed was torn down in 1989. A sorely needed community center was planned to replace the unused building, but until recently the lot was rough ground intermittently used as a parking lot. In the 1980s the once-flourishing black communities around the historic McLemore Avenue site suffered the ravages of poverty and an epidemic of crime and violence. "In the politicians' minds you don't want to take people who are used to Disneyland through a black neighborhood and be faced with the America that nobody wants to think about," commented Sherman Willmott, who sells "Stax Bricks," claimed after the studio was destroyed, from his record shop on Madison Avenue. He continued: "But probably a hundred people a week still pass by the lot and shed a silent tear."[124] Dan Penn visited McLemore Avenue not long after Stax was demolished:

> I pulled up there and I just said to myself "There's where the control room was." I just had all kinda of flash backs, you know like within five minutes. I just said "I gotta get away from here. I wanna go." It turned me off so bad that they'd tear down a building that I personally had seen so much history go by. . . . I got to thinking that Stax was torn down because it was another effort to get rid of the fact that whites and blacks worked together. I think that's why both of 'em fell, both Stax and American. From both camps. That's what I think. There was just so much confusion following Martin Luther King's death that eh . . . nobody wanted to

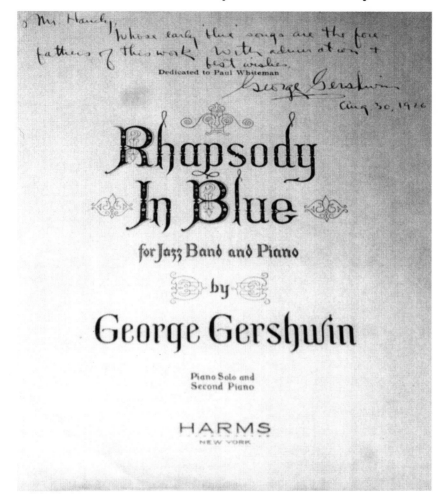

, Mr. Handy,
"Whose early 'blue' songs are the fore
fathers of this work" with admiration +
best wishes,
George Gershwin
Aug 30, 1926

Dedicated to Paul Whiteman

Rhapsody In Blue

for Jazz Band and Piano

by

George Gershwin

Piano Solo and
Second Piano

HARMS
NEW YORK

George Gershwin's gift to W. C. Handy, the Handy home, Florence, Alabama
(photograph by the author)

consider the fact that we were ever together. Musically, it is just now, we're just beginning to ask ourselves—"Can't we work together?"[125]

These studios occupy an ambivalent position in today's America, more than thirty years after the events of 1968. It may be that there is a wider dilemma in that Memphis cannot decide whether these historic sites represent havens of multicultural dialogue or sound plantations. What I have tried to suggest throughout this chapter is the inadequacy of each

The site of Stax Studio on McLemore Avenue, Memphis (photograph by the author)

of these ways of understanding the formation of rhythm and blues. I have pointed to the ways in which the color line was blurred in sound, while at the same time the white musicians and producers could be placed in a compromised position where their whiteness provided a privileged passport to success in the music industry and beyond. Recovering these stories invites new ways of understanding the complex combinations of dialogue, multiculture, and racism that are both the southern culture's lifeblood and its dowry. On April 20, 2001, construction began on the Stax Museum of American Soul Music and the Stax Music Academy. This is a much-needed neighborhood revitalization that will be built on the McLemore Avenue lot where the studio stood. Memphis musicians of the future will be trained here, providing an optimistic coda to the argument developed in this chapter. It is perhaps through a consciousness of sound that new possibilities beyond racialized culture will be opened. Wynton Marsalis, the jazz trumpeter, composer, and teacher, commented recently: "The consciousness of the world is changing. The end of the century has been about communication; now we're moving to integration. Music's going to be very important. The hardest thing to teach is the concept of harmony. There's no analogy. It's hard to describe, the art of the invisible, like a memory—and it's mobile, always changing. Harmony is not understood anything like as well as it will be in the twenty-first century. But maybe it will be a symbol for the twenty-first century." [126]

Vron Ware

9. ROOM WITH A VIEW

When I emerged, the lights were still there. I lay beneath the slab of glass, feeling deflated. All my limbs seemed amputated. It was very warm. A dim white ceiling stretched far above me. My eyes were swimming with tears. Why, I didn't know. . . . I seemed to have lost all sense of proportion. Where did my body end and the crystal and white world begin? Thoughts evaded me, hiding in the vast stretch of clinical whiteness to which I seemed connected only by a scale of receding greys.

—RALPH ELLISON

One of the most exciting and positive features of the new writing on whiteness has been the fresh impetus that it has given to all manner of contemporary debates about race. The various attempts to delineate and deconstruct whiteness are often able to animate new kinds of conversation that help to fill the awful silences that undoubtedly still persist. Leaving aside the fact that it has produced some theoretical and political arguments that are totally at odds with each other, the sheer proliferation of work is something that may be cautiously welcomed if it means that more and more people in different geographical locations are beginning to feel a personal investment in getting rid of white supremacism and to move away from the tyrannies of race-thinking that ensure their complicity.

As we have seen, one of the values of developing a critical analysis of whiteness is that it draws into dialogue groups of people who might have felt somehow unqualified or otherwise unable to talk about matters of "race" because their own social location means that they associate it with its victims and do not appreciate the racialized suffering of their own experience. But the task of exploring whiteness and making it visible loses any radical or subversive possibilities it might have had if it does not start from a recognition of the fundamental interrelation of all racialized categories. Even where that interrelation is acknowledged, there is still a danger that "whiteness studies" can promote a very conservative division of mental labor that reproduces the patterns of segregation embedded in race-thinking. To take just one example, we wonder whether Patricia Hill Collins's comparative review of *White Women, Race Matters,* by Ruth Frankenberg, and *Black Popular Culture,* edited by Gina Dent and Michele Wallace, suggests a rather too neat structure of political exchange. She writes: "Frankenberg's effort to create new conceptual space where White people can be White without being 'racist' parallels efforts by Black intellectuals to develop Black communities that reject an essential, exclusionary Blackness while maintaining a Black cultural integrity that gives dignity and purpose to Black political struggle."[1]

Collins looks forward to the prospect of a "White anti-racist culture," which would "provide a much-needed conceptual space for a White race-cognizant politic of resistance." Although she distances herself from those who adopt "quasi-nationalist, essentialist" views of black culture, she nonetheless offers a model of political solidarity in which blacks and antiracist whites retain their dignity and integrity by staying within their respective "communities." Within this simple framework the concept of race becomes something to be "owned" rather than discarded, in the interest of making whites aware of their privilege and responsible for resisting racism. But what are the differences that separate blackness from whiteness, and how and when can these differences be transcended, if at all?

If it sometimes appears a little too easy to speak about ways of dealing with whiteness, the alternatives can sometimes seem overwhelmingly difficult. The notion that there is an unbridgeable gap between those who are privileged as white and those who are on the receiving end of white supremacism rests on the conviction that any attempt at political solidarity must first recognize how little particular groups have in common. Ien Ang, for example, writes: "To claim otherwise would be tantamount to a form of incorporation of the (non-white) other within the (white) self without confronting the otherness of the other. In short, the overlap in our frameworks, discursive regimes, and repertoires of meaning may indeed be more or less considerable, but it is never complete, and it is at those instances when the overlap falls away that moments of incommensurability occur."[2]

Ang makes this claim in the course of a wider feminist debate about the manifestation of differences among women. She insists that "subjective knowledge" of what it is like to be "at the receiving end of racialized othering" is "simply not accessible to white people"—the same way as "the subjective knowledge of what it means to be a woman is ultimately inaccessible to men." In her view, however, those "moments of incommensurability" can be used as a starting point for common political pursuits if we acknowledge them and "accept that politics does not have to be premised on construction of a solid, unified 'we' . . . but on the very fragility, delicacy and uncertainty of any 'we' we forge."³

These extracts are indicative of wide-ranging, and often fiercely contentious, exchanges about the theoretical relationship among subjectivities, identities, and experience. To complete this section examining the momentum of political engagement produced by a critical analysis of whiteness, we now consider ways of talking about the role of the imagination and the significance of emotions in enabling political solidarity and active resistance. In our first chapter we applied a concept from anthropology to the problems of positionality that arise in relation to the investigation of whiteness, arguing that the application of what Charles Taylor called "a language of perspicuous contrast" offer one possible approach toward making sense of self and other in such a way that the investigator might understand across big cultural divisions. This path of connection, bordered by the marshes of incommensurability on one side and the swamps of relativism on the other, might then lead to a new awareness of complicity with, or at least incorporation in, the structures of white supremacism, and therefore provide a basis from which to act against it in politically engaged ways.

But this theoretical formula offers no guarantees that successful communication will take place between people who have very different experiences of racial hatred, violence, or less visible forms of routine exploitation and discrimination. Remembering Andre Gorz's advice that the project of transforming society requires "consciousness, action and will," we want to explore the idea that the "consciousness" of those who are preparing to act politically against whiteness entails first the recognition and then the translation of powerful human feelings that range from violent rage to utopian ecstasy. The political strategies that we are interested in need also to take into account the imaginative and emotional work required to make connections, to understand and interpret across those same cultural divisions. But race-thinking produces a particularly invidious form of segregation that sets up barriers to cross-cultural solidarity, emotional or otherwise. Added to this there are many people who, for whatever reason, have a stake in believing that their experience is closed to people outside their group: it's a black thing, you wouldn't understand; men are from Mars, women from Venus. But what possibilities emerge if those individuals who write about whiteness (assuming for the clarity of this argument that they can be defined as "white") feel personally involved in the suffering produced by white supremacism? Does the trauma of racial brutality and division have to be shared? Can one understand the damage that racism does if one has not experienced it? How do more seasoned activists communicate the importance of feeling to those with whom they have a pedagogical relationship without losing sight of the more rational, structural analysis of white supremacism?

Some writers have attempted to address these questions by investigating the toll that racism takes on whites. Mab Segrest, for example, in a powerful essay entitled "The Souls of White Folk," explores the ways in which whites have been psychologically damaged by racism:

> What then is the cost to white people of racism? Perhaps we can now more accurately make the assessment, recognizing that racism implicates systems of oppression based on gender and class, on patriarchy, capitalism and heterosexism:
>
> Racism costs us intimacy.
>
> Racism costs us our affective lives.
>
> Racism costs us authenticity.
>
> Racism costs us our sense of connection to other humans and the natural world.
>
> Racism costs us our spiritual selves: "a feeling of an indissoluble bond, of being one with the external world as a whole," as Freud's poet friend tried to explain.[4]

Segrest's essay draws partly on the autobiographical perspectives articulated in her earlier book, *Memoir of a Race Traitor.* Her disclosures about her own life experiences are carefully employed as a device to explore "the sources of pain in historical imbalances of power" and "close the gap between personal and political, between the intimate and the public, the emotional and the historical."[5] This work is all the more welcome for its synthesis of feminism with a political antiracism derived from her experiences in North Carolina in the 1980s.

Drawing attention to the toll that racial segregation takes on people privileged as white is clearly integral to this discussion of "white" accountability toward those positioned outside this category. What concerns us more specifically here, however, is the question of whether those who are involved in investigating whiteness as part of their intellectual work need to understand the depth of suffering endured by those on the receiving end of white supremacist systems, anywhere in the world. Here we have found it useful to evoke Renato Rosaldo's concept of the "cultural force of emotions" as a way of elaborating on the connections between feeling and experience.[6] In an essay entitled "Grief and the Headhunter's Rage" he describes how in his role as an anthropologist he was attempting to understand certain patterns of behavior among the Ilongot peoples in the Philippines. He was particularly challenged by their response to death, but through a devastating tragedy in his own life was finally able to grasp what the Ilongot had told him about their ways of dealing with grief, rage, and bereavement. This allows us to qualify Taylor's approach to ethnography with Rosaldo's awareness of the way in which life experiences can enable or inhibit particular kinds of insight. Rosaldo argues that without this appreciation of the force of human emotions it is possible to listen to someone's explanation of her or his behavior and not be able to traverse the cultural difference that appears to divide them. By being able to apply a particular kind of life experience of his own, he was able to bridge that gap; he did so not by carrying out Ilongot cultural practices himself, but by recognizing the way that the sheer force of emotion was a partial explanation of their rituals.

In trying to understand this profound sense of human connectedness that emerged out of unspeakable grief, Rosaldo made it plain that he was not invoking personal experience as a way of expressing "facile notions of universal human nature."[7] "One hopes to achieve a balance between recognizing wide-ranging human differences and the modest truism that any two human groups must have certain things in common." In an earlier chapter we discussed the testimony produced by John Howard Griffin and other antiracists who were driven by the need to experience something of racism in order to understand and to communicate what it might feel like to be a victim rather than an onlooker. An extended discussion of Griffin's work below allows us to address one possible way of talking about the relationship between experience, feeling, and understanding in the context of investigating whiteness, developing strategies to counter its effects, and ultimately destroying it.

The Enclosed Space of Suffering

Everything became clear: the smallness of those cheap rooms, the brightly flowered wallpaper, the living, breathing human beings whose lives no one would now be able to save. And I knew then that I could walk out into the streets and meet

people who considered themselves perfectly decent, who had no knowledge of
what was going on inside those rooms and who would go on rationalizing and justifying the very reason that led to the tragedy in those rooms.

Sometimes in discussing racism with people, I wish I could simply take them
into such rooms in this country. I think of rooms where I have sat with heartbro-
ken human beings who happen to be black and who have suffered great tragedy
for no other reason.

— JOHN HOWARD GRIFFIN

In a compressed version of his own mental and emotional discovery of
the impact of racism, written toward the end of his life, John Howard
Griffin recounts the moment when he first became aware of the gulf
between talking about the problems of racism and understanding the
"terrible human tragedy" that resulted from "the true evils of a racist
system." The realization came to him not in the segregated South, where
he was born, but in a dingy hotel room in France during the Nazi occupation of the 1940s. He had remained in the country when war broke
out, despite being ordered to leave, and had joined his student friends
working in the resistance. German-Jewish families were smuggled across
the French border and escorted to Tours, where Griffin helped to hide
them in cheap boarding houses until they could be taken to the port of
St. Nazaire and from there to England. This strategy was initially successful, but when the Nazi army began to invade France, it became increasingly difficult to obtain the right papers for the families to move on, and
their safety could not be ensured. One night Griffin was given the job
of going to the boarding house and telling the Jewish guests that it was
going to be impossible to move them any farther: the German army was
approaching, and the underground network was powerless to offer them
a safe passage.

When Griffin entered the hotel room that night, the adults knew
what he had come to tell them. They were perfectly aware that as soon
as the Nazis moved in they would be rounded up and shipped back to
Germany and the concentration camps. But Griffin was shocked by their
response. They asked him to take their children away from them because
children under the age of fifteen could be moved without any papers.

Suddenly all of our endless conversations about racism as university students seemed empty and meaningless. Racism, with the
rise of Hitler, had been an obsessive topic of conversation among
students, the great intellectual preoccupation. But sitting in those
rooms with men and women and children, innocent of any crime,
pursued only because they were Jewish, made me realize that we
had never understood anything about the true evils of a racist sys-

tem that solved problems by murdering those men, women and children.[8]

What was it about this experience that allowed Griffin to presume, first, that he had at last understood something of crucial importance and, second, that his friends and colleagues had not appreciated the full force of the evil that they were dealing with? Why was he so sure that he could "walk out into the streets and meet people who considered themselves perfectly decent, who had no knowledge of what was going on inside those rooms and who would go on rationalizing and justifying the very racism that led to the tragedy in those rooms"?[9] He was evidently describing his own traumatic realization that, for all his academic and political interest in the subject, he had not known what he was really talking about, but here he also seems to suggest that the impact of racism on human lives was not something that could be necessarily grasped by intellectual means. At the same time the "full force" of evil was directed not at him personally, but at the Jewish strangers who had been reliant on his support. Griffin does not elucidate on the range of emotions that he must surely have experienced as part of his altered awareness: overwhelming guilt, helplessness, a profound sense of failure at having been unable to help his charges to escape, and a strengthened resolve to fight that evil as if his own life depended on it. It is not clear from this passage what exactly did go through his mind that night and how the trauma affected his subsequent development as an activist against social injustice.

In *A Time to Be Human* Griffin uses the imagery of the room, the enclosed space of suffering, as a metaphor for "being with" the victims of racism in other places, at other times. He gives the impression that the empathy that he experienced in France readily enabled him to understand the connections between the anti-Semitism of the Nazis and the white supremacism of his native country. However, according to his biographer, Robert Bonazzi, this was not the case; Griffin was not immediately able to perceive the similarities between the brutally obvious evil of the Nazis and the more routine, everyday nature of southern racism with which he was more familiar, and in which his own parents acquiesced. Bonazzi, who knew Griffin personally and who has written extensively on the *Black Like Me* project, asserts that Griffin's horror was partly derived from the fact that the Jewish refugees were still "white" in his eyes, and therefore not intrinsically different from French Catholics or southern Protestants.[10] According to Bonazzi, the young Griffin was still under the impression that black people, whether Africans or Americans, were still "not like us," and it was not until after he had experienced "the full force of racism" while posing as a black man in 1959 that he was fully able to understand the connections that he expressed so coherently later on: "In Nazi Germany," he wrote in 1962, "this fear of destroying purity through mongrelization was based on the false premise that the Jew was inferior to the Gentile. In the South we segregate the Negro from the white to prevent mongrelization. The core of the matter is the same in both cases since both 'solutions' proceed from the same false premise of racial superiority. And yet, those who called Hitler's logic that of a madman, permit themselves to embrace a logical fallacy that is identical in essence."[11]

Griffin elaborated on this connection, warning his readers that "all the ingredients for genocidal racism such as we had in Nazi Germany are with us today."[12] "America is in an ugly mood," he wrote in 1977, "over matters that have little to do with minority people." The practice of blaming the victim for political and economic grievances takes a terrible toll on "the very climate of human civilization. It is leading us to genocide in ways that we do not want and do not really understand."

In *A Time to Be Human* Griffin makes a direct link between the Nazi holocaust and American racism by moving from this powerfully evoked scene in the French boardinghouse to a room in a farmhouse near Hattiesburg, Mississippi, where he sat with a woman whose son had been effectively murdered by the forces of white supremacy. Clyde Kennard was a young African American man who had served in the war and, upon his return, had attended the University of Chicago. Family matters required him to return to Mississippi, and he was obliged to interrupt his studies in order to look after his mother. In 1960 he applied to finish his schooling at Mississippi Southern University, which was a whites-only institution at that time. Kennard insisted on his right to attend and was subsequently jailed on trumped-up charges. Once in jail he was allowed to die of untreated cancer "in what amounted to a deliberate, slow lynching."[13]

Griffin describes this scene as one of many that he had encountered in his native country. Sitting with Clyde Kennard's mother, and seeing the heartbreak in her face, he wrote that he was intensely aware of the same kind of tragedy that he had first witnessed in Tours. Again, he felt acutely conscious of the fact that outside the room there were people who considered themselves decent human beings who had no idea what was really going on inside the room and "who went right on rationalizing and justifying the racism that led directly to the tragedy within the room." The list of rooms, he continued, could go on and on, and they are not confined to the South. He had sat in rooms in ghettoes of northern cities and had listened to the despair of parents whose children were being murdered "psychologically, spiritually, and intellectually" by the racist system that governed the whole country.

The stark description of the cheap room in the back streets of Tours with its brightly colored wallpaper helps to position the reader inside the same space as the writer. Griffin confides that he wishes he could take people into such rooms in the United States so that they might see for themselves the reality of racism closer to home. The imagery of the room, with all its associations of intimacy, confinement, privacy, and suffocation, supplies a vivid trope for expressing who has access to knowledge of racism and who remains ignorant. "Black people," he writes, "view the situation from the 'inside.' White people who never go inside those rooms always view it from the 'outside' and wonder why black people feel such deep rage. We whites have no idea what racism really does to people."

These three deceptively simple sentences demand scrutiny, since they try to express concerns that lie at the heart of this book. Griffin's assertion that racism confines blacks and whites to different compartments—one group held inside the space of confinement, the other permanently outside in a state of ignorance—returns us to the imagery of different worlds with which we began. Unlike Franz Fanon, however, Griffin does not propose that the walls of the room be torn down. Unlike Kipling, he does not advocate leaving the barriers safely intact. His solution comes nearer to Cornel West's proposition that what matters is perception, learning to see the world from each other's point of view, but he also acknowledges that by itself this is not enough to defeat racism. In these three sentences Griffin seems to offer a message both confused and confusing: he is bending over backward to invite his white readers to imagine that they will be different, that they can follow him with his privileged outlook into all the compartments of suffering that he has entered. The book will offer them the chance to become, in effect, temporarily black, like he did, so that they, too, can enter all those rooms with him; they will be able to cease being white people who have no idea of what racism really is and does, as Griffin himself once was. Reading other passages of this book, it becomes even more difficult to piece together these fragmentary statements, which also serve as a reminder of the "epistemological stickiness and ontological wiggling" that bedevil any attempt to pin down definitive statements about whiteness in relation to identity, authorship, and disavowal.

Griffin is inviting his readers not merely to peer into these rooms, but also to change themselves by learning to see how the world appears from the inside looking out. At this point the trope of the walls as a means of containment breaks down, since Griffin seems to be demanding that whites can enter the space of black suffering only by undergoing a traumatic episode of discovery not unlike the experiences that he suffered in France and later in Mississippi. Being emotionally open to "the terrible reality of racism" is likely to result not merely in changed perception, but also in a long process of gaining new awareness and understanding, which both demands and depends on an ability to shift one's point of view. His frank admission that "the deepest shock I experienced as a black man was the realization that everything is utterly different when one is a victim of racial prejudice"[14] underlines the continuous and accumulative nature of this process. The shock he endured in Tours as a young man was evidently not enough to imagine what it might be like to be on the receiving end of racism, as opposed to standing by as a helpless onlooker. Awareness and understanding are not sufficient on their own: what matters is to be able to interpret and connect each learning experience in order to "close the gap between personal and political, between the intimate and the public, the emotional and historical," as Mab Segrest set out to do in her exploration of "The Souls of White Folk."

The next point to consider is what the individual might expect to find once she or he has begun to make Griffin's leap of understanding, either by following him through his testimony or by finding her or his own way into that segregated enclosure. While he was writing and speaking on racism during the Civil Rights movement and after, Griffin was centrally concerned with communication, both between himself and his audiences and between black and white activists working to the same end. His collaboration and friendships with leading black campaigners, including Martin Luther King Jr., are further evidence of his sincerity, commitment, and ability to communicate.[15] But what kind of subjectivity permitted him to form these alliances and demonstrate this remarkable level of solidarity? Did he see blacks as equal but still different in some way, or did he aspire to a more radical humanism that junked the very notion of race as a meaningful category? And if the latter, how did he regard himself in relation to the white identity that had governed his thinking and behavior since the day he was born? It was a long time before he understood how deeply he had internalized racial prejudice despite his determination to stop "thinking white," and it is worth reconsidering that moment of revelation. We have already discussed the passage in *Black Like Me*, in which Griffin turns on the light and catches the first sight of his blackened face in the mirror. It is useful to compare that famous description of his visceral response to seeing his reflection with an amended account written a few years later in an essay entitled "The Intrinsic Other" (1966). It was this second version that was repeated a decade later in *A Time to Be Human*. In these later texts Griffin shifts this moment of perception from the bathroom of his friend's flat to the tiny room in the Sunset Hotel where he sought refuge only hours after he had left the flat in his new disguise. Bonazzi has compared the two descriptions, observing that the second was not "a conscious distortion of the first but a result of their deep association."[16] In his narrative of Griffin's spiritual journey he provides an insightful commentary on this scene, which is entirely relevant here.

> "My room was scarcely larger than a double bed. An open transom above the door into the hall provided the only ventilation." There are no windows and he does not mention a mirror. The things themselves are personalized—it becomes *my* room, *my* linoleum floor, *my* light; the room is cramped, the floor is too flimsy to keep out the noises from below, the light is "so feeble" he can barely see and, even the air, which circulates only within the building, is as stale as his gloom. The broken ceiling fan catches the faint light, "casting distorted shadows of the four motionless blades against the wall." The shadowy distortions are the reflections of a metaphorical mirror of his internal despair—useless and without substance. Griffin becomes the room in all its aspects—"boxed in, suffocating"—unconsciously "mingled with that of other rooms," and specifically the room of the *Other Griffin*. This scene at the Sunset Hotel correlates to the earlier scene, but the crisis remains unspoken, unspeakable. His earlier attempt to deny it and thus attempt to displace the reality choke him "with an almost desperate sadness."[17]

In *A Time to Be Human* Griffin describes how he was at once overwhelmed by hopelessness and despair because he realized that although he had liberated himself intellectually from all of his prejudices, "those prejudices had been so deeply ingrained that at the emotional level they were still very strong. I wondered how I could have committed myself so deeply to the cause of racial justice, only to discover now that at the level of emotional response I still carried those old racist poisons within me. I had to face this and recognize it for what it was."[18]

Griffin carried this burden of "emotional garbage" until he found a way to allow it to dissolve. This, he wrote, was achieved by sitting with "black parents and seeing that they responded to human frustration exactly as all other people do." The fact was "that the 'other' was not other at all. The other was my own self."[19] The process of understanding that might allow whites to communicate with blacks and other victims of racism was ineffective unless it worked on two levels, the intellectual and the emotional. Griffin does not speculate on the merits of having an emotional understanding on its own, but clearly, as was the case with his student comrades in the resistance, talking and intellectualizing about racism were not enough to disrupt deeply ingrained prejudice. Quoting philosopher Jean Lacroix, he argued that "before we can authentically communicate with one another we must first 'open ourselves to the other.' I believe that before we can truly dialogue we must perceive intellectually and then at the profoundest emotional level that there is no 'other'—that the other is simply oneself in all the important essentials."[20]

Bringing together these different elements of Griffin's philosophical discourse, which, though associated with unorthodox and exceptional methodologies, had also been strongly influenced by his commitment to a particular branch of Christian theology, we are left with a stubborn conundrum.[21] The dialogue that needs to take place between human beings across the segregation imposed by racism requires an intellectual and emotional openness before those barriers can be transcended or removed. In Griffin's own life that openness was nearly always precipitated by a traumatic encounter with the victims of racism, with whom he was already in some kind of dialogue, but this trauma was not sufficient to dissolve his "emotional garbage."

So what should come first: the attempt at preliminary dialogue in order to acquire understanding or the quest for openness (and freedom from prejudice) that precedes more profound exchanges? This leads to our final question in this section: must an individual who is raised within a racialized order that defines her as white, experience emotional trauma, and in particular the trauma of racism, before being able to understand and open herself to authentic communication with those positioned differently within that hierarchical order? Rosaldo's theory of "the cultural force of emotions" is clearly very helpful to this discussion because it validates the way in which significant life experiences can be used to enable (or inhibit) insights across cultural divides. But this is not a simple prescription for the "who feels it knows it" model of politics. Within the context of anthropology the ethnographer may prepare for fieldwork by diligently reading the appropriate literature and developing a sense of self-awareness in an attempt to avoid "ignorance and insensitivity," but this systematic scrupulousness may bring only "false comfort."[22] Emotional experience is invariably mediated by social relations and cultural expectations, which may mean that it is not necessarily enough for the ethnographer to have had life experiences similar to those of the members of the culture she or he is studying. It depends on, first, how the personal emotional experience is interpreted and, second, how it is allowed to connect with the very different cultural responses encountered in fieldwork. Moving away from the methodologies of ethnography into the more chaotic arena of nonracial politics, a recognition of the "cultural forces of emotion" might help the critic or analyst of whiteness to think imaginatively about the range and depth of feelings that might be produced by being both a victim of and a witness to racism.

Griffin was not an anthropologist seeking to make sense of African American cultural practices, but a man who eventually abandoned the social sciences as a means of measuring racism precisely because the discipline's demand for objectivity did not require him to understand the brutality of the segregationist system. For him, the recognition of the congruency of parental concerns across the southern color line was one more revelatory factor in the shedding of his "emotional garbage" of prejudice. One of the most emotive episodes in *Black Like Me* is his attempt to reconcile a painful awareness of the privileged life of his own children with the impoverishment of the joyful black family who offered him hospitality for the night. Here he could be said to be bringing particular insights derived from his life experience as a parent to bear on the specific occasion of a child's birthday celebration. He had enough information before him to imagine what it would be like if his own children's rights and freedom were denied just because their skin was dark, and it was this fresh awareness of what it might be like to be a permanently black parent that terrified him. "One can scarcely conceive the full horror of it unless one is a parent who takes a close look at his children and then asks himself how he would feel if a group of men should come to his door and tell him they had decided—for reasons of convenience to them—that his children's lives would henceforth be restricted, their world smaller, their educational opportunities less, their future mutilated."[23]

Griffin reiterated his own disbelief and sense of horror as a means to shock his targeted audience of well-meaning but uncomprehending Americans, raised white not to know any better. Although we would certainly question whether you need to be a parent in order to appreciate the systemic injustice that he described, this quotation helps to illustrate how the power of the imagination can produce strong emotions, which in turn can help to raise the greater level of awareness (or consciousness) required to interpret, communicate, and act.

Although we will now leave Griffin behind, there is one aspect of his political philosophy that leaks into the next section of this inquiry into the momentum of political engagement. Griffin based his final diagnosis of racial politics on his experience while living as a black/white man in the South. He clearly felt that this enabled him to see things from more than one perspective and to speak either "as a white man" or "as a black man" to suit his argument. But is it possible to step outside of the chambers of racial identification, not by Griffin's means, but by the acts of calculated betrayal involved in becoming a self-confessed "race traitor"? As we have seen, the members of the *Race Traitor* group who have been the most consistent advocates of this strategy depict whiteness as a club. Those who are deemed fit to belong are compelled to become members whether they like it or not. In fact, it requires concerted and conscious effort—and willpower, too—to opt out of the club and stay out of it. This is achieved only through repeated acts of treason and is accomplished only by those who are truly prepared to risk their lives, or at least their livelihoods. The easiest stance, in the face of manifest injustice, is to do nothing, and it is this silence and passivity that allow whiteness to persist unchecked. Treasonable acts can range from challenging the structures and institutions of power and authority to identifying consciously, both outwardly and inwardly, with those who are not privileged as white.

As we have observed throughout this book, it is important to recognize that the demand for disaffiliation from the structures of white privilege requires an acknowledgment of the way that other complex factors—notably gender, sexuality, class, and geography—compound social identity and hence produce a complex configuration of whitenesses. This has caused many critics of the New Abolitionism to parody the idea that individuals are being asked to opt out of one aspect of their identity that they consider to be problematic. But if the utopian rhetoric of abolishing the ideological tentacles of whiteness masks the rather more complex practical issues involved in the political work that makes the project meaningful, is that enough reason to turn away from the principle that lies behind it? The strategy of identifying whiteness, renouncing the privilege it can confer, and counterattacking the structures and institutions that perpetuate it demands, even depends on, an ability to imagine the consequences of those actions. Frederic Jameson has pointed out that in the age in which we live it is easier to imagine the end of the world than to imagine the end of capitalism. Antirace activists must be able to envisage an end of whiteness in its dominant forms in order to be able to work for the principle of nonracialism. Joel Kovel expressed the enormity of this task with clarity and precision: the cure for white racism is "quite simple, really. Only get rid of imperialism, and, what comes to the same thing, see to it that people freely determine their own history."[24]

The power of the imagination must be linked to any program of action against white supremacism. To accede to the idea that whiteness can be accommodated within freshly laundered democratic fabrics is to surrender to the basic precept of fixed racial difference that underlies the fatal demands for purity and segregation. The fact that it is often difficult to comprehend the ways in which whiteness is manifest in everyday life is evidence of the need to go beyond rational argument in order to work toward the eradication of whiteness. The ability to feel connected to the suffering that white supremacism brings, the will to try to transform society for the better, and the imagination to envisage a world without injustice and exploitation are all vital components of the abolitionist consciousness required to act decisively in the name of politics.

From Rooms to Buildings

Lillian Smith is a valuable figure in this discussion for several reasons. First, she realized that antiracist political consciousness was not a static quality, but something that must be encouraged and allowed to grow. Individuals might test their resolve only once they had begun to challenge the unfairness and inequalities happening outside their front door—or even in their own home. We have discussed her instructions to white southerners in a previous chapter. A second reason for her importance here is that she gave credit to thinking as a precursor for acting; in particular, she encouraged those who were less inclined to draw attention to themselves by their deeds to start to imagine what it might feel like to be black and to suffer the routine discrimination and harassment produced by segregation. Her insistence that individuals could make a difference by breaking "the twin taboos of silence and action" acknowledged that it was necessary for people to understand what they were doing before they took part in coherent collective action. Third, by explicitly grouping her instructions into different categories aimed at those with different levels of commitment, she reinforced the idea that the most effective tactics against the system were likely to be organized on a collective basis rather than by individual acts of bravery.

Smith's awareness of gender and class as determining aspects of every-day experience, identity, and oppression that perpetuate the structures of white supremacy has provided an invaluable legacy for feminists during and after the Civil Rights movement. There *are* lists of "Things to Do," wrote Minnie Bruce Pratt in her now-classic feminist essay "Identity: Skin Blood Heart," published in 1984.[25] Citing Smith's "Address to Intelligent White Southerners," compiled over forty years earlier, Pratt added:

> We can learn something from such an agenda, but most of it is commonsense: we already know that work against anti-Semitism and racism can range from stopping offensive jokes, to letters to the editor, to educational workshops, to changing the law, to writing poetry, to demonstrations in the street, to a restructuring of the economy. But because knowing what to do in a situation that you suspect may be racist or anti-Semitic, even knowing that the situation *is*, involves judgment and ethics and feeling in the heart of a new kind than we were raised with, then we will only be able to act effectively if we gather up, not just information, but the threads of life that connect us to others.

A further value of Smith's writing is that her insights into ways that these "threads of life" might be made visible and given new meaning were not confined to the South or to the United States. As we have seen, she was acutely conscious of the war against fascism in Europe and the struggles for decolonization in India and Africa, seeing them as part of a global battle against white supremacy. Unlike Griffin, Smith was not a witness to atrocities carried out in Europe in the name of Aryan purity, nor had she been enlisted to fight in the U.S. Army. Her powerful account of the psychology of southern racism offered insights gained from her own life as a girl growing up in close proximity to blacks in a segregated town. Her subsequent travels in China and encounters with psychoanalysis helped her to develop and refine her understanding of human development. Although she defiantly rejected the claim that she was a "nice woman" dedicated to helping blacks, she evidently knew that as long as racism stunted the psychological and emotional growth of southern culture, there could be no freedom for young people of all backgrounds to achieve their potential.

There is no evidence that Lillian Smith read *The Diary of Anne Frank*, started in 1942, at the same time when her "Address" appeared, but it is highly likely that if she had known about it, she would have brought it to the attention of the young American girls attending her summer camps. *The Diary* was first published in 1947 in Dutch, under the name of *Het Achterhuis* (The Attic), and was subsequently translated into more than fifty languages. Today an estimated twenty-five million copies of *The Diary* have been sold worldwide. In 1957 the Anne Frank Foundation was founded to ensure the preservation of the attic in Amsterdam where Anne and her family were incarcerated and to promote the ideals that she expressed in her writing. Three years later the Anne Frank House, at 263 Prinsengracht, was opened, and visitors were able to visit the Secret Annex, which was kept in its original state, in accordance with the wishes of Anne's father, Otto Frank. The lower part of the building housed a small museum that provided information about Anne Frank's life, World War II, and the rise and fall of Nazism. In 1993 the building was further restored in order to accommodate the 600,000 visitors who make the journey to the house each year. The refurbishment has allowed the narrative of *The Diary* to be further brought to life by providing information about the other occupants of the house and their helpers. The Secret Annex occupied by the Frank family, Fritz Pfeffer, and the Van Pels family has been retained with minimal changes so that it is possible for visitors to imagine the stark conditions under which the group lived for two years.

The tour of the house begins by following a narrow staircase up to the first floor, which was used for offices. Although this floor was not part of the Secret Annex, Otto Frank kept a private room here, and the group would often creep downstairs after the staff had gone home to listen to radio broadcasts from England. On the second floor the route leads past the bookcase that concealed the entrance to the Secret Annex. Here was the bedroom of Otto and Edith Frank and their elder daughter, Margot, and next to this was the tiny room that Anne shared with Fritz Pfeffer. On the third floor were the kitchen and the Van Pels's bedroom; their son Peter stayed in the attic above them. The museum's route leads past these rooms into the attic space of 265 Prinsengracht, which is used as an exhibition space. Adjacent to this an entirely new building is under construction; when completed, it will house a media library, an auditorium, and rooms for temporary exhibitions.

Those who have read *The Diary* will have formed their own impression of the building and will already have a mental picture of the small, cramped space occupied by these five adults and three teenagers. Even this cannot be adequate preparation for the shock of standing in the same room and experiencing that sense of "being with" the young woman who spent two years of her short life incarcerated within its brown walls. Although the shutters would have been drawn for most of the time, Anne was still able to glimpse the same tall chestnut tree stand-ing in the garden outside that now, fifty years later, rises up almost as high as the house itself and reaches out with an enormous span over the narrow garden below. The postcards and clippings on the walls belong to any young teenager—films stars, celebrities, royalty—collected se-cretly at their home by Otto Frank before his daughter even knew that they would have to go into hiding at the place of his work.

Because of the sheer number of visitors, it is hard to be alone in the room unless one knows to go late in the day when the crowds have gone. Unlike any other famous dwelling place that is open to the public, this exhibit bears very little tangible trace of the personalities of its for-mer occupants. It is uncanny in the sense that it invites the visitor to inspect the dimensions of the rooms, knowing full well that the apart-ment was both a refuge and a prison; its stark emptiness is all the more shocking because of the liveliness and hope and optimism expressed in Anne's writing. The visitor knows full well what fate awaited her when she was taken from that building and separated from her parents. The testimony of her friend describing their last meeting in Bergen-Belsen is offered toward the end of the tour by means of a video. The effect of hearing an eyewitness talk about her last conversation with Anne helps to provide a link with her life in the present, as if all those who were born long after 1945 might still feel connected to the person that they already know from her writing and from her pictures on the walls.

The final room contains copies of the earliest editions of *The Diary,* and a glass case displays fifty first editions and reprints published in fifty-five different languages. The spirit of Anne Frank may be felt most in-tensely while standing in that place of memory, but her legacy has been allowed to extend far beyond its walls. Apart from the expansion of the museum site, the Anne Frank Foundation has continued to develop an extensive range of publications and materials for use in schools. This educational work is intended to make connections between the anti-Semitism of the German Nazis and other forms of racism, discrimina-tion, and prejudice with which young people might be more familiar today, whether this is the persecution of gypsies in the Czech Republic or Slovenia, or the intimidation and violence aimed at refugees and mi-grant workers in Germany, for example. Recent exhibitions organized in England by the foundation and its local contacts have included panels on the racist murder of Stephen Lawrence and his family's continuing campaign for justice. Above all, the museum is intended to promote the ideals of antiracism that Anne expressed in her writing.

In an earlier chapter we discussed the ways in which racism produces a politics of memory, looking specifically at the heritage and genealogies of social movements against white supremacy as well as the commemoration of special events and people. The work of the Anne Frank Foundation provides a concrete illustration of the immense value of making connections between different kinds of oppression and refusing to close ranks around one particular strand of history. Young people are invited to imagine what it might be like to be a victim of persecution on the basis of designated "race," color, or religion. The historical facts and details of Anne Frank's short life are made to work in and through the present; they are directed as much to a young Turkish girl in Brussels as they are to a middle-class child in an affluent part of Chicago or a mixed group of teenagers in Johannesburg. Her story may not be claimed by any one group as speaking directly to them, though at the same time it will resonate very differently among its diverse audience. For Anne's voice does not just summon up the experience of hiding from persecution, but also speaks about wider forms of resistance and solidarity that made their refuge possible. Remembering her story of suffering must always entail a complex account of the courage, as well as the cowardice, that is integral to the history of breaking the "twin taboos of silence and action."

Notes

Introduction

1. Herman Melville, *Moby-Dick* (1853; reprint, Harmondsworth, England: Penguin, 1991), p. 559.

2. Ibid.

3. Ibid., p. 288.

4. For a full account of the Lawrence family's campaign for justice, see Brian Cathcart, *The Case of Stephen Lawrence* (London: Viking Books, 1999).

5. Joe L. Kincheloe, Shirley R. Steinberg, Nelson M. Rodriguez, and Ronald E. Chennault, eds., *White Reign: Deploying Whiteness in America* (New York: St. Martin's Press, 1998), p. 12.

6. George Orwell, "Inside the Whale," in *Inside the Whale and Other Essays* (London: Penguin, 1957), p. 42.

7. W. T. Lhamon Jr., "Core Is Less," *Reviews in American History* 27, no. 4 (December 1999): 566–71. *Raising Cain: Blackface Performance from Jim Crow to Hip Hop* is published by Harvard University Press (Cambridge, 1998).

8. See David Macey's useful discussion of this phrase in an article about his recent translation of Fanon's work in "Fanon, Phenomenology, Race," *Radical Philosophy* no. 95 (May/June 1999): 8–14. Macey explains here why the previous translation of the the title of chapter 5 of *Peau Noire, Masques Blancs* as "The Fact of Blackness" ought to have been, in his view, "The Lived Experience of the Black Man."

9. Joachim-Ernst Berendt, *The Third Ear: On Listening to the World* (New York: Henry Holt, 1985), p. 32.

10. Henry Louis Gates, *Loose Canons* (New York: Oxford University Press, 1993).

11. Anthony Jackson, "The New Dark Age," *Bass Player* 9 (1991): 78.

12. Tim Malyon, "Tossed in the Fire and They Never Got Burned: The Exodus Collective," in *DIY Culture: Party and Protest in Nineties Britain,* edited by George Mackay (London: Verso, 1998).

13. This book was written before the mass mobilizations against globalization from Seattle (1999) onward. While this is easily the most exciting and hopeful political movement since the 1960s, it is clear that being against globalization is not necessarily the same as being against racism and the racial hierarchies that sustain it. We need to work hard to make the connections.

14. Tim Jordan and Adam Lent, eds., *Storming the Millennium: The New Politics of Change* (London: Lawrence and Wishart, 1999), p. 1.

15. Mackay, *DIY Culture.*

Chapter 1

1. Rudyard Kipling, "Beyond the Pale," in *Plain Tales from the Hills* (London: Wordsworth, 1993), pp. 173–80.

2. Franz Fanon, *The Wretched of the Earth* (Harmondsworth, England: Penguin Books, 1973), pp. 29–30.

3. W. E. B. Du Bois, "The White World," in *Du Bois Writings* (New York: Library of America, 1986), p. 653.

4. Cornel West, *Tikkun* 10, no. 6 (1996): 12.

5. David R. Roediger, *Towards the Abolition of Whiteness* (London: Verso, 1994), p. 75.

6. Homi Bhabha, "Anish Kapoor: Making Emptiness," in *Anish Kapoor* (Berkeley: University of California Press, 1998), p. 12.

7. Richard Dyer, "White," *Screen* 29, no. 4 (1988): 44–65, and *White* (London: Routledge, 1997).

8. David R. Roediger, *Black on White: Black Writers on What It Means to Be White* (New York: Schocken, 1998), p. 23.

9. David R. Roediger, *The Wages of Whiteness* (London: Verso, 1991); see also Part 1: "The New Labor History and Race," in *Towards the Abolition of Whiteness* (London: Verso, 1994).

10. Toni Morrison, *Playing in the Dark: Whiteness and the Literary Imagination* (Cambridge: Harvard University Press, 1996).

11. Shelley Fisher Fishkin, "Interrogating 'Whiteness,' Complicating 'Blackness': Remapping American Culture," in *American Quarterly* 47, no. 3 (1995): 428–66; Ralph Ellison, *Shadow and Act* (New York: Random House, 1964).

12. Lillian Smith, *Killers of the Dream* (London: Cresset Press, 1950); Lillian Smith, *Strange Fruit* (1944; reprint, New York: Harcourt, Brace, 1992); John Howard Griffin, *Black Like Me* (1960; reprint, Boston: Houghton Mifflin, 1961); John Howard Griffin, *A Time to Be Human* (New York: Macmillan, 1977); Joel Kovel, *White Racism: A Psychohistory* (New York: Pantheon Books, 1970); Winthrop D. Jordan, *White over Black: American Attitudes towards the Negro 1550–1812* (1968; reprint, New York: Norton, 1977); David Wellman, *Portraits of White Racism* (Cambridge: Cambridge University Press, 1977). The work of Dorothy Sterling also requires an assessment in this context. Her first book to be published in Britain, a antiracist novel for children written during the Civil Rights movement, evoked an extraordinarily powerful world of callous, routine white supremacy and courageous resistance through the eyes of black and white school friends: *Mary Jane* (London: Constable, 1960).

13. Roediger, *Black on White.*

14. Kovel, *White Racism,* p. 4.

15. Matthew Frye Jacobson, *Whiteness of a Different Color: European Immigrants and the Alchemy of Race* (Cambridge: Harvard University Press, 1998).

16. Ibid., pp. 280, 12 (emphasis in original).

17. Ibid., p. 21.

18. Ibid., p. 273.

19. Ruth Frankenberg, *White Women, Race Matters: The Social Construction of Whiteness* (New York: Routledge, 1993), and *Displacing Whiteness: Essays in Social and Cultural Criticism* (Durham, N.C.: Duke University Press, 1997).

20. Frankenberg, *Displacing Whiteness,* p. 2.

21. Ibid., p. 3.

22. John Hartigan Jr., *Racial Situations: Class Predicaments of Whiteness in Detroit* (Princeton, N.J.: Princeton University Press, 1999). See also Hartigan's essay entitled "Locating White Detroit" in Frankenberg's collection, *Displacing Whiteness,* pp. 180–213.

23. Michael Omi and Howard Winant, *Racial Formations in the United States: From the 1960s to the 1980s* (New York: Routledge, 1986).

24. Hartigan, *Racial Situations*, p. 282.

25. Margaret Talbot, "Getting Credit for Being White," *New York Times Magazine*, 30 November 1997, 116–19.

26. W. E. B. Du Bois, "The Souls of White Folk," in *Darkwater: Voices from within the Veil* (1920; reprint, Millwood, N.Y.: Kraus-Thomson, 1990), p. 29.

27. Robert T. Carter, "Is White a Race? Expressions of White Racial Identity," in *Off White: Readings on Race, Power and Society*, edited by Michelle Fine, Lois Weis, Linda C. Powell, and L. Mun Wong (New York: Routledge, 1997), p. 207.

28. Matt Wray and Annalee Newitz, eds., *White Trash* (New York & London: Routledge, 1997), p. 6.

29. Andre Gorz, *Farewell to the Working Class* (London: Pluto Press, 1982), p. 12.

30. Noel Ignatiev and John Garvey, eds., *Race Traitor* (New York: Routledge, 1996), p. 10.

31. Ibid., p. 288.

32. Carter, "Is White a Race?" pp. 206–7.

33. Roediger, *Black on White*, p. 22.

34. Grace Elizabeth Hale, *Making Whiteness: The Culture of Segregation in the South 1890–1940* (New York: Pantheon Books, 1998); Jane Lazarre, *Beyond the Whiteness of Whiteness: Memoir of a White Mother of Black Sons* (Durham, N.C.: Duke University Press, 1996); see also France Winddance Twine, "The White Mother: Blackness, Whiteness, and Interracial Families," *Transition* 73 (1998): The White Issue, 144–54.

35. George Lipsitz, "The Possessive Investment in Whiteness: Racialized Social Democracy and the 'White' Problem in American Studies," *American Quarterly* 47, no. 3 (1995): 369–87. Lipsitz's thesis is expanded at length in his book of essays: *The Possessive Investment in Whiteness: How White People Profit from Identity Politics* (Philadelphia: Temple University Press, 1998).

36. Writers who are actively interested in questions of pedagogy are often among those who express more hesitancy in the face of political demands to dismantle whiteness. This position is thoughtfully articulated by Kincheloe and Steinberg: "A central feature of any pedagogy of whiteness, of course, involves the unlearning of racism. . . . Now we are taking our first baby steps in the study and teaching of whiteness; accordingly, we are not sure either of which path to take or of what the effects of our efforts will be." Joe L. Kincheloe, Shirley R. Steinberg, Nelson M. Rodriguez, and Ronald E. Chennault, eds., *White Reign: Deploying Whiteness in America* (New York: St Martin's Press, 1998), p. 19.

37. Mike Hill, ed., *Whiteness: A Critical Reader* (New York: New York University Press, 1997), p. 2.

38. Ibid., p. 3.

39. Ibid., p. 5.

40. Ibid., p. 7.

41. Adrienne Rich, "Notes towards the Politics of Location," in *Blood, Bread and Poetry* (London: Virago, 1986).

42. Charles Taylor, *Philosophy in the Human Sciences* (Cambridge: Cambridge University Press, 1990).

43. Ibid., pp. 124–25.

Chapter 2

1. Nick Griffin was elected leader of the British National Party through a postal ballot on September 15, 1999.

2. The research involved colleagues John Solomos and Michael Keith, is entitled

"The Cultural Mechanisms of Racist Expression Project," and was funded by the Harry Frank Guggenheim Foundation. I would like to thank the foundation for its support and John and Mike.

3. "Ungoodthink: Race Busy Bodies in Big Flap," in *Spearhead* 347 (January 1998): 17.

4. The hate mail was a response to a story about research I had been doing on racism in the institutions of English soccer. The article, entitled "Racism 'Still Rife' among Football's Leading Figures," appeared in a traditionally conservative newspaper, the *Sunday Telegraph,* 7 December 1997, 17. In part, I agreed to do the story because I felt this newspaper was the one mostly likely to be read by people in the higher echelons of the football industry. It became clear that it is also the piece of mainstream media taken by people on the extreme right of the political spectrum, an audience I had neither counted on nor anticipated. George Orwell wrote in 1940 that so much left-wing thought was "a kind of playing with fire by people who don't even know that fire is hot." "Inside the Whale," in *Inside the Whale and Other Essays* (Harmondsworth, England: Penguin, 1957), p. 37. It might also be said that much of the scholarship and academic work on racism suffers from the same syndrome. The experience of being the object of hate altered my comprehension of the exact nature of the white heat of racism and its experiential consequences.

5. Had this incident happened prior to my having children, I think it would not have resonated in quite the same way in terms of the deep sense of vulnerability and risk that it engendered. It made me reflect on how the issue of personal safety intersected not only with issues of gender and class, but also with life cycle. Previously, I had not felt vulnerable, no doubt related to the embodiment of particular codes of masculinity. Being a parent with young children changed all this, and my biggest fear was that my three-year-old daughter would pick up the phone and be subjected to a tirade of abuse. Fortunately, such calls were never made to my private telephone number at home, although they were common at my workplace for a time.

6. Emmanuel Levinas, *Totality and Infinity: An Essay on Exteriority* (Pittsburgh, Pa.: Duquesne University Press, 1969), p. 194.

7. These are the towns where black servicemen were stationed during the World War II, discussed in chapter 7.

8. See Joyce Ladner, ed., *The Death of White Sociology* (New York: Vintage Books, 1973), and Robert Staples, *Introduction to Black Sociology* (New York: McGraw-Hill, 1976), for the U.S. debate; see Centre for Contemporary Cultural Studies, ed., *Empire Strikes Back* (London: Hutchinson, 1982), and Clive Harris and Winston James, eds., *Inside Babylon: The Caribbean Diaspora in Britain* (London: Verso, 1993), and Michael Keith, "Angry Writing: (Re)Presenting the Unethical World of the Ethnographer," *Society and Space* 10 (1992): 551–68, for the debate in the United Kingdom.

9. D. Hymes, ed., *Reinventing Anthropology* (New York: Random House, 1969).

10. Eric Wolf "They Divide and Subdivide and Call It Anthropology," *New York Times,* 14 December 1980, sec. IV.

11. Robin Fox, *Encounter with Anthropology* (New York: Harcourt Brace Jovanovich, 1973).

12. Roland Littlewood, "In Search of the White Tribe," *Mindfield* 1 (1998): 25–26.

13. Renato Rosaldo, *Culture and Truth: The Remaking of Social Analysis* (London: Routledge, 1989).

14. Littlewood, "In Search of the White Tribe," p. 26.

15. Ibid.

16. Ibid., p. 27.

17. Erving Goffman, *The Presentation of Self in Everyday Life* (New York: Anchor, 1959).

18. Gregory Bateson, "A Theory of Play and Fantasy," in *Steps to an Ecology of Mind* (London: Paladin Books, 1978).

19. I have discussed this in full elsewhere. See Les Back, "Gendered Participation: Masculinity and Fieldwork in a South London Adolescent Community," in *Gendered Field: Women, Men and Ethnography,* edited by D. Bell, P. Caplan, and W. Jahan Karim (London: Routledge, 1993), pp. 215–33.

20. James Clifford and George E. Marcus, eds., *Writing Culture: The Poetics and Politics of Ethnography* (Berkeley: University of California Press, 1986).

21. Vincent Crapanzano, "Hermes' Dilemma: The Masking of Subversion in Ethnographic Description," in ibid., pp. 51–76.

22. James Clifford, "Introduction: Part Truths," in ibid., p. 10.

23. George E. Marcus, "After the Critique of Ethnography: Faith, Hope and Charity, but the Greatest of These Is Charity," in *Assessing Cultural Anthropology,* edited by Robert Borofsky (New York: McGraw-Hill, 1994), p. 41.

24. Charles Taylor, *Philosophy and the Human Sciences: Philosophical Papers 2* (Cambridge: Cambridge University Press, 1985), p. 125.

25. Levinas, *Totality and Infinity,* p. 191.

26. Hans-Georg Gadamer, *Truth and Method* (London: Sheed and Ward, 1975), p. 358.

27. Clifford Geertz, "The Uses of Diversity," in Borofsky, *Assessing Cultural Anthropology,* p. 465.

28. Richard Rorty, "On Ethnocentrism: A Reply to Clifford Geertz," in *Objectivity, Relativism, and Truth: Philosophical Papers,* vol. 1 (Cambridge: Cambridge University Press, 1991), p. 203.

29. Vincent Crapanzano's acclaimed study of white South Africans, *Waiting: The Whites of South Africa* (New York: Vintage Books, 1986), provides a good example of the tensions this approach can engender around issues of authority, representation, and critique. Inspired by Russian literary critic Mikhail Bakhtin, Crapanzano presents his book as a cacophony of voices in an attempt to foster a plurivocal approach to ethnography (pp. xv–xvi). However, some white South African academics were scathing in their criticism of the sleight of hand involved in this mode of representation. June Goodwin and Ben Schiff report a conversation about *Waiting* they had with Louwrens Pretorius—a sociologist—and Pierre Hugo—a political scientist—in their study *Heart of Whiteness: Afrikaners Face Black Rule in the New South Africa* (New York: Scribner, 1995): "Hugo and Pretorius had a complaint about . . . Crapanzano's methodology, claiming that the study was unrepresentative of whites and that Crapanzano had betrayed the confidences of the interview subjects. In the course of the evening 'Crapanzano' became a verb: 'Please, don't Crapanzano us in your book.' The evening grew more relaxed, but their fears were clear and their warning explicit. We promised to do our best to let the Afrikaners do the talking in our book" (pp. 15–16). Yet the appeal to merely "let people speak" runs the peril of relegating or abandoning social critique, while at the same time Crapanzano's *Waiting* gives only the effect of multivocality. The tension between "giving a voice" to whites and criticizing whiteness is central to the problem that I am concerned with here, and neither of the texts resolves this dilemma adequately.

30. Geertz, "The Uses of Diversity," p. 458.

31. At the time a policeman told me that the "victim was no angel." This expectation itself seemed to be informed by the stereotypical images of black masculinity held by the white policemen.

32. The names of the people involved in this case have been changed.

33. Field notes, 17 October 1996.

34. This point is supported by the examples of insightful interpretations of whiteness from African American intellectuals from W. E. B. Du Bois to bell hooks and Patricia Hill Collins. See W. E. B. Du Bois, "The Souls of White Folk" (1910), in *W.E.B. Du Bois: A Reader,* edited by Meyer Weinberg (New York: Harper Torchbooks, 1970), pp. 298–308; bell hooks, *Black Looks* (London: Turnaround, 1996); Patricia

Hill Collins, "Learning from the Outsider Within: The Sociological Significance of Black Feminist Thought," in *Beyond Methodology: Feminist Scholarship as Lived Research*, edited by Mary Margaret Fonow and Judith A. Cook (Bloomington: Indiana University Press, 1991).

35. See Diane Bell, "Yes Virginia, There Is a Feminist Ethnography: Reflections on Three Australian Fields," in Bell, Caplan, and Jahan Karim, *Gendered Field;* see also Jennifer Hunt, "The Development of Rapport through the Negotiation of Gender in Field Work among Police," *Human Organization* 43, no. 4 (1984): 283–94.

36. In David T. Wellman's classic study *Portraits of White Racism* (Cambridge: Cambridge University Press, 1977), black on white dialogue produced some of the most insightful interviews. Wellman's research team included a number of black interviewers and in one case—Alex Papillion—a founder member of the Black Panthers: "Who would think that a white person could open up to a black and honestly express his or her fears, emotions—or talk about deeply troubling racial controversies? And so when Alex Papillion, a black man on our research team, asked me if he should interview white people, I was hesitant. . . . How many white people would be willing to talk with a known Black Panther?" (p. 74). Wellman's fears were unfounded: "Some of the interviews Alex conducted with white people were the finest in our sample. He tended to interview people who were strong, sure of themselves, and not easily put off by his demanding style. . . . Alex's opinionated nature did not inhibit interviews; it stimulated them (p. 75).

37. Raphael S. Ezekiel, *The Racist Mind: Portraits of American Neo-Nazis and Klansmen* (New York: Penguin Books, 1995), pp. xix–xx.

38. For a fuller discussion of this research, see L. Back and A. Nayak, "Signs of the Times: Violence, Graffiti and Racism in the English Suburbs," in *Divided Europeans: Understanding Ethnicities in Conflict,* edited by Tim Allen and John Eade (London: Kluwer Law International, 1999), pp. 243–84.

39. Field notes, 10 April 1994.

40. I was struck in the aftermath of this incident by the folly of trying to bring groups of white and minority youth together in this setting for face-to-face forms of "cultural exchange." The danger of such encounters is that they are more likely to entrench racial divisions rather than deconstruct them.

41. Ruth Frankenberg, *White Women, Race Matters: The Social Construction of Whiteness* (London: Routledge, 1993), p. 23.

42. Ibid., p. 40.

43. Ibid., p. 35.

44. Following Ann Oakley, "Interviewing Women: A Contradiction in Terms," in *Doing Feminist Research,* edited by Helen Roberts (London: Routledge & Kegan Paul, 1981).

45. Judith Stacey, "Can There Be a Feminist Ethnography," *Women's Studies International Forum* 11, no. 1 (1988): 25.

46. Interview by author, London, 2 April 1998.

47. The National Front magazine, *Nationalism Today,* ran a feature interview with Akkebala in the mid-1980s.

48. Court transcription, Harrow Crown Court, Thursday, 30 April 1998; transcription from tape by Newgate Reporters Ltd.

49. Ibid.

50. Paul George, "Black Leaders Fly in to Help Racist Activist," *Daily Telegraph,* 10 May 1998; Ross Slater, "Revealed: BNP's Black Buddies," *New Nation,* 4 May 1998; Darcus Howe, "Two Black Separatists Came All the Way from Florida to Harrow to Defend a White Supremacist in Court: Hatred United in a Cause," *New Statesman,* 15 May 1998.

51. Interview by author, London, 2 April 1998.

52. Stacey, "Can There Be a Feminist Ethnography," p. 26.

53. Daniel Jonah Goldhagen, *Hitler's Willing Executioners: Ordinary German and the Holocaust* (London: Abacus, 1996), p. 471.

54. Ibid., p. 472.

55. Christopher R. Browning, *Ordinary Men: Reserve Police Battalion 101 and the Final Solution in Poland* (New York: Harper Collins, 1992).

56. Goldhagen, *Hitler's Willing Executioners*, p. 563; see also Jeremiah M. Reimer, "Burden of Proof," in *Unwilling Germans: The Goldhagen Debate*, edited by Robert R. Shandley (Minneapolis: University of Minnesota Press, 1998), pp. 175–83.

57. Christopher R. Browning, "Ordinary Men or Ordinary Germans," in Shandley, *Unwilling Germans*, p. 64.

58. There are possible parallels here in the literature on the linguistic and rhetorical aspects of racist discourse. See Michael Billig, Susan Condor, Derek Edwards, Mike Gane, David Middleton, and Alan Radley, *Ideological Dilemmas: A Social Psychology of Everyday Thinking* (London: Sage, 1988).

59. For his memoir of his incarceration and liberation, see Primo Levi, *Is This a Man & The Truce* (London: Abacus, 1979).

60. Primo Levi, *The Periodic Table* (London: Abacus, 1985) and *The Drowned and the Saved* (London: Abacus, 1989).

61. Murray Baumgarten, "Primo Levi's Periodic Art: Survival in Auschwitz and the Meaningfulness of Everyday Life," in *Resisting the Holocaust,* edited by R. Rohrlich (Oxford: Berg, 1998), p. 115 (emphasis added).

62. I am thinking of the point made by Levi regarding stereotypes and false equivalents in the comparison between the Lager and other moments of hunger or incarceration. See Levi, *The Drowned and the Saved*, p. 128.

63. Ibid., p. 25.

64. Ibid., p. 27.

65. Levi names Herman Langbein in Auschwitz, Eugen Kogan in Buchenwald, and Hans Marsalek in Mauthausen in this regard. Ibid., p. 30.

66. Ibid., p. 35.

67. Jean Améry, *At the Mind's Limit: Contemplations by a Survivor on Auschwitz and Its Realities* (Bloomington: Indiana University Press, 1980), p. 19.

68. Ibid.

69. Ibid., p. 20.

70. Levi, *The Drowned and the Saved*, p. 102.

71. Ibid., p. 114.

72. Ibid.

73. Ibid., p. 141.

74. For a discussion of these tensions, see also Tzvetan Todorov, *Facing the Extreme: Moral Life in the Concentration Camps* (London: Weidenfeld & Nicolson, 1999), pp. 260–71.

75. Paul Gilroy, personal communication, 11 March 1999.

76. See Deborah Lipstadt, *Denying the Holocaust: The Growing Assault on Truth and Memory* (Harmondsworth, England: Plume, 1993), pp. 160–61. Lipstadt characterizes Faurisson as "one of the world's leading deniers" (p. 160).

77. Field notes, Harrow Crown Court, 29 April 1998.

78. Primo Levi, *Moments of Reprieve* (London: Abacus, 1987), p. 171.

79. Ezekiel, *The Racist Mind*, p. xxxv.

80. Pat Caplan's extraordinary book *African Voices, African Lives: Personal Narratives from the Swahili Village* (London: Routledge, 1997), is a good example of how such an analysis can be achieved.

81. Kathleen M. Blee, *Women of the Klan: Racism and Gender in the 1920s* (Berkeley: University of California Press, 1991), p. 6.

82. Levi, *The Periodic Table*, pp. 222–23.

83. At the end of Griffin's trial some weeks later he was found guilty of incitement to racial hatred; he did not go to prison, and he received a suspended sentence and a fine. He was sentenced to nine months suspended for two years and ordered to pay a fine of £2,300. The British National Party paid the fine.

84. At his trial a policewoman reported a telephone conversation she overhead in which Griffin said to an unknown caller: "It's alright at least there are no Pakis or Jews," referring to the officers searching his house.

Chapter 3

1. John Howard Griffin, *Black Like Me* (1960; reprint, Boston: Houghton Mifflin, 1961), p. 128 (hereafter referred to as *BLM*).

2. Although these stories take place in different parts of the world, I use the paradigm of black and white to connect the territory of racial and cultural oppression that each writer is investigating. This is not to suggest, however, that Israeli Jews who consider themselves superior to Arabs automatically think of themselves as "white" or that Turks in Germany are invariably referred to as "black" rather than "foreign" (or *auslander*). It is not particularly useful to see whiteness as a blanket term that can uniformly cover all forms of racist, nationalist, or neo-fascist regimes indiscriminately, but whiteness can provide a powerful metaphor for connecting forms of oppression based on characteristics such as skin color, religion, and language.

3. John Howard Griffin, *A Time to Be Human* (New York: Macmillan, 1977), p. 21 (hereafter referred to as *TTBH*).

4. Ibid., p. 24.

5. Ray Sprigle, *In the Land of Jim Crow* (New York: Simon and Schuster, 1949), p. 9.

6. *BLM*, Preface.

7. Sprigle, *In the Land of Jim Crow*, p. 18.

8. Ibid., p. 210.

9. Ibid., pp. 77–78.

10. Quoted in Robert Bonazzi, *The Man in the Mirror: John Howard Griffin and the Story of Black Like Me* (New York: Orbis Books, 1997), p. 17.

11. Ibid., p. 22.

12. Grace Halsell, *Prophecy and Politics: The Secret Alliance between Israel and the U.S. Christian Right* (Chicago: Lawrence Hill Books, 1986), p. 6.

13. Grace Halsell, *Soul Sister* (New York: World, 1969), p. 13.

14. Ibid., p. 209.

15. Grace Halsell, *Black/White Sex* (Greenwich, Conn.: Fawcett, 1972); *Bessie Yellowhair* (New York: William Morrow, 1973); and *Prophecy and Politics*.

16. Gunter Walraff, *The Lowest of the Low* (London: Pluto Press, 1988), p. 2.

17. Ibid., p. 208.

18. Yoram Binur, *My Enemy, My Self* (New York: Doubleday, 1989), pp. 209–10.

19. Amy Robinson, "It Takes One to Know One: Passing and Communities of Common Interest," *Critical Inquiry* 20 (Summer 1994): 715–36.

20. Ralph Ellison, "Change the Joke and Slip the Yoke," in *Shadow and Act* (New York: Random House, 1964), p. 53.

21. Eric Lott, "White Like Me: Racial Cross-Dressing and the Construction of American Whiteness," in *Cultures of U.S. Imperialism*, edited by Amy Kaplan and Donald Pease (Durham, N.C.: Duke University Press, 1993).

22. Eric Lott, *Of Love and Theft: Blackface Minstrelsy and the American Working Class* (New York: Oxford University Press, 1993).

23. *BLM*, pp. 1–2.

24. *TTBH*, p. 24.

25. Binur, *My Enemy, My Self,* pp. 211–12.

26. Ibid., p. 74.

27. Halsell, *Soul Sister,* p. 38.

28. Ibid., p. 3.

29. Ibid., pp. 208–9.

30. Halsell, *Black/White Sex,* p. 25.

31. In *Black/White Sex,* Halsell describes visiting places that she last went to in her pose as a "black" woman, marveling at the difference in the ways she is treated. It does not seem to occur to her that she still has a choice as to whether or not she accepts the automatic privilege that comes with looking like a well-off white woman.

32. *BLM,* p. 4.

33. Ibid., p. 156.

34. Bonazzi, *Man in the Mirror,* p. 30.

35. Ibid.

36. *BLM,* p. 12.

37. Ibid., p. 2.

38. *Black Like Me* (New York: Signet, 1972), p. 161.

39. Zygmunt Bauman, *Life in Fragments* (Oxford, England: Blackwells, 1995), p. 208.

40. *BLM,* p. 95.

41. Ibid., p. 97.

42. Ibid., p. 104.

43. Halsell, *Soul Sister,* p. 149.

44. Ibid., p. 195.

45. Walraff, *Lowest of the Low,* pp. 81–83.

46. Binur, *My Enemy, My Self,* p. 91.

47. Ibid., pp. 69–70.

48. Ibid., p. 74.

Chapter 4

1. The joke is taken from Trad skinhead Doug Herbert's "FAQ alt.skinheads." It is attributed to Dominic Green and was posted on alt.skinheads, 1 August 1998.

2. Giles Deleuze and Felix Guattari, *A Thousand Plateaus: Capitalism and Schizophrenia* (London: Athlone, 1986).

3. Judith Butler, *Gender Trouble: Feminism and the Subversion of Identity* (New York: Routledge, 1990).

4. Sherry Turkle, *Life on Screen: Identity in the Age of the Internet* (New York: Simon and Schuster, 1995), p. 15.

5. Sadie Plant, *Zeros and Ones* (London: Fourth Estate & Doubleday, 1998); Donna Haraway, *Simians, Cyborgs, and Women: The Reinvention of Nature* (New York: Routledge, 1991); see also Mike Featherstone and Roger Burrows, *Cyberspace/Cyberbodies/Cyberpunk: Cultures of Technological Embodiment* (London: Sage, 1995).

6. Deleuze and Guattari, *A Thousand Plateaus,* p. 214.

7. Ibid., pp. 214–15.

8. See David Capitanchik and Michael Whine, *The Governance of Cyberspace: The Far-Right on the Internet* (London: Institute for Jewish Policy Research, 1996); Anti-defamation League of B'nai B'rith, *Hate Group Recruitment on the Internet* (New York: Anti-defamation League, 1995); Simon Wiesenthal Center, *Lexicon of Hate: The Changing Tactic, Language and Symbols of American Extremists* (Los Angeles: Simon Wiesenthal Center, 1998).

9. Turkle, *Life on Screen.*

10. Umberto Eco, "Ur-Fascism," *New York Review of Books,* 22 June 1995, 14.

11. This was particularly apparent at the Harry Frank Guggenheim–sponsored conference "Brotherhoods of Race and Nation," New Orleans, December 1995.

12. Thanks to Keith Harris for this observation.

13. Walter Benjamin, "The Work of Art in the Age of Mechanical Reproduction," in *Illuminations* (London: Harcourt, Brace and World, 1968), p. 244.

14. Les Back, Michael Keith, and John Solomos, "The New Modalities of Racist Culture: Technology, Race and Neo-fascism in a Digital Age," *Patterns of Prejudice* 30, no. 2 (1996): 3–28.

15. After Arturo Escobar, "Welcome to Cyberia: Notes on the Anthropology of Cyber-culture," *Current Anthropology* 35, no. 3 (1994): 211–31.

16. John Solomos and Les Back, *Racism and Society* (Basingstoke, England: Macmillan, 1996).

17. See Phil Cohen, "Subcultural Conflict and Working-Class Community," in *Working Papers in Cultural Studies,* vol. 2 (Birmingham, England: University of Birmingham, 1972); Dick Hebdige, "Skinheads and the Search for a White Working-Class Identity," *New Socialist,* September 1981, 38.

18. Hebdige, "Skinheads and the Search for a White Working-Class Identity," p. 28.

19. Anoop Nayak "'Pale Warriors': Skinhead Culture and the Embodiment of White Masculinities," in *Thinking Identities: Ethnicity, Racism and Culture,* edited by A. Brah, M. Hickman, and M. Mac an Ghaill (Basingstoke, England: Macmillan Press, 1999), pp. 71–99.

20. This history has been recovered in Murray Healy's excellent study *Gay Skins: Class, Masculinity and Queer Appropriation* (London: Cassell, 1996), p. 72.

21. Following Hebdige, "Skinheads and the Search for a White Working-Class Identity."

22. Roger Hewitt, "Us and Them in the Late Space Age," *Young* 3, no. 2 (1995): 24 (emphasis added).

23. Ibid.

24. Marc Griffiths, *Boss Sounds: Classic Skinhead Reggae* (Dunoon, Scotland: S. T. Publishing, 1995).

25. Quoted in George Marshall, *Spirit of 69: A Skinhead Bible* (Dunoon, Scotland: S. T. Publishing, 1991), p. 122.

26. There is an account of this culture in Roger Hewitt, *White Talk, Black Talk: Inter-racial Friendship and Communication amongst Adolescents* (Cambridge: Cambridge University Press, 1986), p. 30.

27. See Joanne Hollows and Katie Milestone, "Welcome to Dreamsville: A History and Geography of Northern Soul," in *The Place of Music,* edited by A. Leyshon, D. Matless, and G. Revill (New York: Guilford Press, 1998).

28. Russ Winstanley and David Nowell, *Soul Survivors: The Wigan Casino Story* (London: Robson Books, 1996).

29. Keb Darge, interview by author, London, 30 September 1997.

30. Ibid.

31. Elaine Constantine, interview by author, London, 28 September 1997.

32. Ibid.

33. Sue Henderson, interview by author, London, 11 November 1997.

34. Tim Ashibende, interview by author, Stoke on Trent, England, 20 October 1997.

35. Dean Anderson, interview by author, Newark, England, 6 October 1997.

36. Ibid.

37. Paul Gilroy and Errol Lawrence, "Two Tone Britain: White and Black Youth and the Politics of Anti-racism," in *Multi-racist Britain,* edited by P. Cohen and H. Bains (London: Macmillan Education, 1988), pp. 121–55.

38. Marshall, *Spirit of 69.*

39. Heléne Lööw, "White Power Rock 'n' Roll: A Growing Industry," in *Nation and Race: The Developing Euro-American Racist Subculture,* edited by J. Kaplan and T. Bjorgo (Boston: Northeastern University Press, 1998), pp. 126–47.

40. Lynyrd Skynyrd recorded "Sweet Home Alabama" in 1973, and it fast became a quintessential southern rock anthem. The song was largely a response to Neil Young's 1970 song "Southern Man," which appeared on his *After the Gold Rush* album (Reprise 7599–27243-2), and "Alabama," which appeared on his *Harvest* album (Reprise 7599–27239-2), released in 1972, both of which included pronouncements against southern racism. The members of Lynyrd Skynyrd were from Jacksonville, Florida, but spent their early recording careers in Muscle Shoals, Alabama. The area was renowned for its studios and became a recording center for rhythm and blues and soul music. Many of these musicians were white and helped to facilitate black artists and producers; see chapter 8. In 1970 their manager, Alan Walden, who mostly managed soul groups and was the brother of Otis Redding's manager, Phil Walden, arranged for the band to record at Quinvy Studios in neighboring Sheffield, Alabama. The band went on to forge a relationship with Jimmy Johnson and cut tracks at Muscle Shoals Sound, including the first version of their epic "Freebird." What is interesting about "Sweet Home Alabama" is the way it acknowledges the involvement of white southern musicians in black music as a response to the image of the redneck, which is very much central to Neil Young's portrayal of the South. Leon Russell had dubbed the all-white Muscle Shoals Rhythm Section "The Swampers" after he had recorded with them. Lynyrd Skynyrd honored the band with a verse of "Sweet Home Alabama" dedicated to them:

> Now Muscle Shoals has got the Swampers
> They've been know to pick a song or two (Yes, they do)
> Lord they get me off so much
> They pick me up when I am feeling blue
> Now how about you?

The song is interpreted as a redneck *cri du coeur,* but in fact it combines a subtle rejection of George Wallace's segregationist politics and a celebration of Muscle Shoals's integrated recording culture. Ronnie Van Zant himself had an interesting interracial past because he grew up in a racially mixed working-class neighborhood and as a young person he sang with a choir of black women gospel singers. All this complicated the "rebel image" that in large part was encouraged as a marketing tool by the band's record company. When Skrewdriver covered the song, they replaced the verse commemorating the Muscle Shoals Swampers with a eulogy to the Klan. Skrewdriver's version appears on their album *After the Fire* (SK001). The last verse is rewritten in the following way:

> Them carpetbaggers tried to swamp her
> But to the Klan we all came through
> Lord the Klan they give me so much
> They pick me up when I am feeling blue
> How about you?

The best postmodern antidote to Skrewdriver's bile is the Leningrad Cowboys' version of "Sweet Home Alabama." This live recording includes a faithful reproduction of the Lynyrd Skynyrd version, complete with the tribute verse about Muscle Shoals and the addition of a Russian orchestra leitmotif provided by the Alexandrov Red Army Ensemble. The result is an extraordinary cocktail of southern rock, Finnish surrealism, and the meter of the Soviet parade ground. See Leningrad Cowboys and the Alexandrov Red Army Ensemble, *Total Balalaika Show—Helsinki Concert* (PlutoCD 7004).

41. Mark Hamm, *American Skinheads: The Criminology and Control of Hate Crime* (Westport, Conn.: Praeger, 1993).

42. Lööw, "White Power Rock 'n' Roll."

43. "Pride in Our Nation," in *Blood and Honour* 1 (1993): 7, quoted in Lööw, "White Power Rock 'n' Roll," p. 140.

44. See Mark Hamm, *American Skinheads*.

45. Hilary Pilkington, "Farewell to the Tusovka: Masculinities and Femininities on the Moscow Youth Scene" in *Gender, Generation and Identity in Contemporary Russia* (London: Routledge, 1996), p. 257.

46. Ibid., p. 278.

47. Healy, *Gay Skins*, p. 208.

48. Field notes, 15 December 1993.

49. Alt.skinheads newsgroup, August 1998.

50. Rick Eaton, telephone interview by author, 20 August 1998.

51. An offshoot of racist skinheads, Hammerskins take their name from the marching hammers that represented skinheads in the Pink Floyd rock movie *The Wall*. The branches in America include Confederate, Northern, Western, and Eastern Hammerskins; international branches have also emerged, including Britain Hammerskins, Charlemagne Hammerskins in France, and the Southern Cross Hammerskins in Australia.

52. Eaton, telephone interview.

53. Mark Potok, telephone interview by author, 24 August 1998.

54. Ibid.

55. "Music of the White Resistance: An Interview with George Eric Hawthorne conducted with Kevin Alfred Strom," at http:/www.natvan.com/free-speech/fs954b.html, p. 3.

56. Michael H. Kater, *The Twisted Muse: Musicians and Their Music in the Third Reich* (Oxford, England: Oxford University Press, 1997).

57. Stephan Talty, "The Method of a Neo-Nazi Mogul," *New York Times Magazine*, 25 February 1996, 40–43.

58. "Music of the White Resistance," p. 7.

59. Ibid., pp. 7–8.

60. Ibid., p. 8.

61. Ibid.

62. An example of this form is RAHOWA's anti-Communist ballad "The Snow Fell" on the *Cult of the Holy War* album (Resistance Records CRA-201 A), released in 1995.

63. See Johnny Rebel, *For Segregationists Only* (Sunwheel Records), reissued in 1994. These recordings are disconcerting, well-played renditions in the style of country or hillbilly music of the period.

64. Cindy MacDonald, "White Women in Music," at http://www.adp.tptoday.com/musicfem.htm, 1997, p. 1 (emphasis in original).

65. This is rendered explicit in an essay entitled "White Women Awake," posted on the Women for Aryan Unity page, at http://www. adp.tptoday.com/musicfem.htm, p. 1:

> The Women's Liberation Movement is a sham, all these feminists with their pro-abortion stance have done nothing more than cause conflict between the sexes, they say we are equal, yet we are not. Each sex is gifted with its own special talents and attributes. Why do they insist on defying Nature's Laws? . . . The women of W.A.U. are proud to stand by their men and we definitely want to secure the existence of our people and a future for white children. We hope to see more healthy Aryan families working together as strong men and strong women. With support, love and mutual respect, both can live and prosper together.

66. Macdonald, "White Women in Music."

67. Ibid.

68. Ibid., p. 4.

69. Simon Frith and Angela McRobbie, "Rock and Sexuality," *Screen Education* 29 (Winter 1978): 3–19.

70. Stuart Hall and Tony Jefferson, *Resistance through Rituals: Youth Subcultures in Post-war Britain* (Birmingham, England: Centre for Contemporary Cultural Studies, 1976).

71. Stieg Larson, "Racism Incorporated—White Power Music in Sweden," in *White Noise: Inside the International Nazi Skinhead Scene,* edited by Nick Lowles and Steve Silver (London: Searchlight Publishing, 1999), pp. 57–64.

72. See Enzio Di Matteo, "Rightist Buys Record Label," *NOW Magazine,* 13 August 1998.

73. Back, Keith, and Solomos, "Technology, Race and Neo-fascism in a Digital Age," pp. 3–28.

74. Todd Copilevitz, "Dallas Man Runs Skinhead Site," *Dallas Morning News,* 20 April 1996, 1A, 19A.

75. Michael Shapiro, "Skinhead Is 'Out to Lunch,'" *Web Review,* at http://webreview.com/96/04/26/news/nazi2.html.

76. See Emmanuel Levinas, "Reflections on the Philosophy of Hitlerism," *Critical Inquiry* 17 (1990): 63–71.

77. Anne Miller, "Racialist Tattoos," at http://www.adp.fptoday.com/tattoo.htm.

78. Quoted from Anti-defamation League 2000, "Alex Curtis: Lone Wolf of Hate Prowls the Internet," at http:/www.adl.org/curtis/default.htm.

79. From personal ads, at http://www.adp.fptoday.com/f0090.htm.

80. From personal ads, at http://www.adp.fptoday.com/f0085.htm.

81. Ibid.

82. From personal ads, at http://www.adp.fptoday.com/m0267.htm.

83. "Letters from the Front," at http://www.stormfront.org.

84. This is taken from a sample of 107 pieces of e-mail sent to *Stormfront* between 26 May and 2 August 1995. These letters also included examples from antifascist activists.

85. Quoted in Jon Casimir, "Hate on the Net," at www.mh.com.au/archive/news/950905/news6–950905.html, 1995.

86. L. R. Beam, "The Conspiracy to Erect an Electronic Iron Curtain," at www.stormfront.org/stormfront/iron-cur.htm, 1996.

87. After Susan Zickmund, "Approaching the Radical Other: The Discursive Culture of Cyberhate," in *Virtual Culture: Identity and Communication in Cybersociety,* edited by Steven G. Jones (London: Sage, 1997), pp. 185–205.

88. Ibid., p. 195.

89. Quoted in ibid., p. 198.

90. Cindy Patton, "Tremble, Hetero Swine!" in *Fear of a Queer Planet: Queer Politics and Social Theory,* edited by Michael Warner (Minneapolis: University of Minnesota Press, 1993), pp. 143–77. See also Cindy Patton, "Refiguring Social Space," *Social Postmodernism: Beyond Identity Politics,* edited by Linda Nicholson and Steve Seidman (Cambridge: Cambridge University Press, 1995), pp. 216–49.

91. Harold A. Covington, "The Future of the White Internet," 19 March 1998, e-mail posting to alt.politics.white-power, alt.nswpp, alt.skinheads, and alt.revisionism newgroups.

Chapter 5

1. David R. Roediger, *Towards the Abolition of Whiteness* (New York: Verso, 1994), p. 3.

2. *The Observer,* 27 September 1998, 26; *The Independent,* 3 October 1998, 15.

3. John W. Cell, *The Highest Stage of White Supremacy: The Origins of Segregation in*

South Africa and the American South (Cambridge: Cambridge University Press, 1982), p. ix.

4. George Fredrickson, *White Supremacy: A Comparative Study of American and South African History* (New York: Oxford University Press, 1981). See also John Higginson, "Upending the Century of Wrong: Agrarian Elites, Collective Violence, and the Transformation of State Power in the American South and South Africa, 1895–1914," *Social Identities* 4, no. 3 (October 1998): 399–416.

5. Nelson Mandela, quoted in Julie Frederikse, *The Unbreakable Thread* (London: Zed Books, 1990), p. 3.

6. Albie Sachs, quoted in ibid., p. 268.

7. Extracts from the Freedom Charter given in the first epigraph to this section are reprinted in ibid., pp. 65–66.

8. Ibid., p. 109.

9. Ibid., p. 108.

10. Ibid., p. 133.

11. Ibid., p. 135.

12. Ibid., p. 161.

13. After the book was published, First was murdered when a bomb sent by the apartheid regime exploded.

14. Frederikse, *Unbreakable Thread*, p. 96.

15. Ibid., pp. 143–44.

16. Ibid., p. 212.

17. Ibid., p. 218.

18. Spike Lee, with Ralph Wiley, *By Any Means Necessary—The Trials and Tribulations of the Making of Malcolm X* (London: Vintage, 1993), p. 278.

19. *The Autobiography of Malcolm X* (Harmondsworth, England: Penguin, 1965), pp. 393–94.

20. Ibid., pp. 494–96.

21. Lee, *By Any Means Necessary*, p. 300.

22. bell hooks, *Reel to Reel: Race, Sex, and Class at the Movies* (New York: Routledge, 1996), p. 174.

23. Barbara J. Flagg, "'Was Blind, But Now I See': White Race Consciousness and the Requirement of Discriminatory Intent," in *Critical White Studies: Looking behind the Mirror*, edited by Richard Delgado and Jean Stefancic (Philadelphia: Temple University Press, 1997), p. 629.

24. Ibid., p. 605.

25. Ibid., p. 664.

26. Kathleen Neal Cleaver, "The Antidemocratic Power of Whiteness," in Delgado and Stefancic, *Critical White Studies*, pp. 157–63.

27. Ibid., p. 157.

28. Margaret Rose Gladney, ed., *How Am I to Be Heard? Letters of Lillian Smith* (Chapel Hill: University of North Carolina Press, 1993).

29. See Grace Elizabeth Hale, *Making Whiteness: The Culture of Segregation in the South, 1890–1940* (New York: Pantheon Books, 1998), chap. 6, "Stone Mountains."

30. Lillian Smith, "Address to Intelligent White Southerners," in *From the Mountain*, edited by Helen White and Redding S. Sugg Jr. (Memphis, Tenn.: Memphis State University Press, 1972), pp. 116–30. Unless otherwise stated, all quotes in this section of the chapter are from this document.

31. Gladney, *How Am I to Be Heard?* pp. 84–85.

32. Jacquelyn Dowd Hall, *Revolt against Chivalry: Jesse Daniel Ames and the Women's Campaign against Lynching* (New York: Columbia University Press, 1979), pp. 195–96.

33. Lillian Smith, *Killers of the Dream* (London: Cresset Press, 1950), p. 129.

34. Ibid., pp. 127–28.

35. Ibid., p. 130.

36. Gladney, *How Am I to Be Heard?* p. 333.

37. A reprint of "How to Be a Race Traitor" can be found in Delgado and Stefancic, *Critical White Studies,* p. 613.

38. Adrienne Rich, "Disloyal to Civilization: Feminism, Racism, Gynephobia" (1978), in *On Lies, Secrets, and Silence* (New York: Norton, 1979), pp. 275–310.

39. Noel Ignatiev and John Garvey, eds., *Race Traitor* (New York: Routledge, 1996), p. 36.

40. Ibid., p. 37.

41. Ibid.

42. Ibid., p. 288.

43. Ibid., p. 289.

44. Roediger, *Towards the Abolition of Whiteness,* p. 6.

45. Ignatiev and Garvey, *Race Traitor,* p. 37.

46. Frederikse, *Unbreakable Thread,* p. 90.

47. Howard Winant, "Behind Blue Eyes: Whiteness and Contemporary U.S. Racial Politics," in *Off White: Readings in Race, Power and Society,* edited by Michelle Fine, Lois Weis, Linda C. Powell, and L. Mun Wong (New York: Routledge, 1997), p. 49.

48. Ibid., p. 289.

49. David Stowe, "Uncolored People," *Lingua Franca,* September/October 1996, 68–77.

50. Ibid., p. 75.

51. Ibid., p. 76.

52. Ignatiev and Garvey, *Race Traitor,* p. 281.

53. Ibid., p. 288.

Chapter 6

This chapter was originally published as "Nazism and the Call of the Jitterbug," in *Dance in the City,* edited by Helen Thomas (London: Macmillan, 1997), pp. 175–97. It appears here in slightly altered form by permission of Macmillan Press, Ltd.

Special thanks to Graham Smith for his help and generosity with source materials for this chapter and to Valerie Preston-Dunlop, who shared her insights into the life and career of Rudolph Laban; Andy Simons of the National Sound Archive; and Cynthia Korlov of the Ford Motor Company Archives.

1. Duke Ellington, "The Duke Steps Out," *Rhythm,* March 1931, 22.

2. Ibid., p. 21.

3. Chris Goddard, *Jazz Away from Home* (London: Paddington Press, 1979).

4. L. F. Emery, *Black Dance from 1619 to Today,* 2nd ed. (London: Dance Books, 1988).

5. The first national jitterbug contests were held in Britain in 1939 and 1940. See Terry Monaghan, "'Jitterbugs,' 'The Lindy Hop' and 'The Jitter-bug,'" *Jazz, Jump and Jive* 6 (1997): 10.

6. This view of the politics and youth subculture owes its origin to Dick Hebdige's famous assertion that it is possible to find a "phantom history of race relations" in the style movements and musical cultures. See Dick Hebdige, *Subculture: The Meaning of Style* (London: Methuen, 1979), p. 44.

7. Marshall Sterns and Jean Stearns, *Jazz Dance: The Story of American Vernacular Dance* (New York: Macmillan, 1968).

8. Katrina Hazard-Gordon, *Jookin': The Rise of Social Dance Formations in African-American Culture* (Philadelphia: Temple University Press, 1990).

9. David W. Stowe, *Swing Changes: Big Band Jazz in New Deal America* (Cambridge: Harvard University Press, 1994).

10. Ibid., p. 33.

11. Monaghan, "'Jitterbugs,' 'The Lindy Hop' and 'The Jitter-bug,'" pp. 6–10.

12. Ibid., p. 9.

13. For American moralists during the 1920s the emergence of jazz was a symbol of the excesses of urban modernity. It caused concern precisely because of the music's popularity with the young. Henry Ford Senior denounced jazz in his newspaper, the *Dearborn Independent,* as a product of Jewish manipulation:

> Many people have wondered whence come the waves upon waves of musical slush that invade decent homes and that have the young people of this generation imitating the drivel of morons. Popular music is a Jewish monopoly. Jazz is a Jewish creation. The mush, slush, the sly suggestion, the abandoned sensuousness of sliding notes, are of Jewish origin. Monkey talk, jungle squeals, grunts and squeaks and gasps suggestive of calf love are camouflaged by a few feverish notes and admitted in homes. . . . The fluttering music sheet discloses expressions taken directly from the cesspools of modern capitals, to be made the daily slang, the thoughtlessly hummed remarks of school boys and girls.

Henry Ford Sr., *The International Jew: Abridged Articles from the Dearborn Independent 1920–22* (London: G. F. Green, 1948), p. 163.

In 1925 Ford, himself an accomplished dancer, began a campaign to revive—or more accurately to reinvent—rural folk dancing. He brought two hundred Michigan and Ohio dance instructors to his plant to learn old-time steps that they in turn could pass on. See Richard A. Peterson, *Creating Country Music: Fabricating Authenticity* (Chicago: University of Chicago Press, 1997), pp. 59–62. In 1926 the *Dearborn Independent* published a series of articles entitled "A Dance a Week" that outlined particular steps with accompanying sheet music and set forth Ford's philosophy:

> The word "dance," when seen in print, conveys different notions to different people. Some think of it as a jazzy rout from which they would themselves shrink and from which they would protect their children if possible. Others think of it as a monotonous round of steps, endlessly the same. But those who know the old American dances, the dances which were part of the life of the pioneers from the Atlantic to the Pacific, have an entirely different conception of the dance . . . people who are not acquainted cannot dance the quadrille or the circle two-step or the Virginia reel without quickly becoming acquainted. People on unfriendly terms cannot dance these at all and remain so. These dances are social in the sense that they inevitably make for sociability among all who dance them. Thus they are pre-eminently the home, neighborhood and community dances, in the sense that other dances cannot be.

Dearborn Independent, 16 January 1926. Ford's failed attempt to invent and popularize a nascent version of white American folk culture in many respects anticipated what the Nazis implemented in Germany ten years later. It is no surprise, then, that Henry Ford Senior was the only American to be mentioned in Adolf Hitler's *Mein Kampf.*

14. See Malcolm X, *The Autobiography of Malcolm X* (London: Penguin, 1968); Langston Hughes, *The Langston Hughes Reader* (New York: George Braziller, 1958).

15. Stowe, *Swing Changes,* p. 30.

16. Hans Peter Bleuel, *Sex and Society in Nazi Germany* (Philadelphia: J. J. Lippincott, 1973), p. 50.

17. Susan A. Manning, "From Modernism to Fascism: The Evolution of Wigman's Choreography," *Ballet Review* 14, no. 4 (1987): 87–98.

18. Richard D. Mandell, *The Nazi Olympics* (Chicago: University of Illinois Press, 1987).

19. Brandon Taylor and Wildred van der Will, eds., *The Nazification of Art: Art,*

Design, Music, Architecture and Film in the Third Reich (Winchester, England: Winchester Press, 1990).

20. Valerie Preston-Dunlop, "Laban and the Nazis: Towards an Understanding of Rudolf Laban and the Third Reich," *Dance Theatre Journal* 6, no. 2 (1989): 4–7.

21. Susan Manning, "Modern Dance in the Third Reich: Six Positions and a Coda," in *Choreographing History,* edited by Susan Leigh Foster (Bloomington: Indiana University Press, 1995), pp. 165–76.

22. Preston-Dunlop, "Laban and the Nazis," p. 5.

23. Valerie Preston-Dunlop, interview by author, 10 June 1996.

24. Preston-Dunlop, "Laban and the Nazis," p. 5.

25. Hedwig Müller, "Wigman and National Socialism," *Ballet Review* 15, no. 1 (1987): 65–73.

26. Quoted in ibid., p. 66.

27. Manning, "From Modernism to Fascism," p. 94.

28. Walter Benjamin, *Illuminations* (London: Harcourt, Brace and World, 1968).

29. Norbert Servos, "Pathos and Propaganda? On the Mass Choreography of Fascism," *Ballet International* 13, no. 13 (1990): 64.

30. Bleuel, *Sex and Society in Nazi Germany,* p. 92.

31. J. Haskins, *Black Dance in America: A History through Its People* (New York: Thomas Y. Cromwell, 1990).

32. Quoted in Manning, "From Modernism to Fascism," pp. 89–90.

33. Rudolf Laban, *A Life for Dance* (London: Macdonald and Evans, 1975).

34. Michael H. Kater, *Different Drummers: Jazz in the Culture of Nazi Germany* (Oxford, England: Oxford University Press, 1992), p. 31.

35. Quoted in John Jeremy's film *Swing under the Swastika* (Leeds, England: Yorkshire Television, 1988).

36. Quoted in Robert Crease, "Divine Frivolity: Hollywood Representations of the Lindy Hop, 1937–1942," in *Representing Jazz,* edited by Kim Gabbard (Durham, N.C.: Duke University Press, 1995), p. 211.

37. Kater, *Different Drummers,* p. 102.

38. Ibid., p. 104.

39. Quoted in Detlev Peukert, *Inside Nazi Germany: Conformity, Opposition and Racism in Everyday Life* (London: Penguin Books, 1989), p. 166.

40. Bleuel, *Sex and Society in Nazi Germany,* p. 245.

41. Ibid., p. 243.

42. Peukert, *Inside Nazi Germany,* pp. 202–3.

43. See Kater, *Different Drummers.*

44. Joseph Skvorecky, "Red Music," in *Talkin' Moscow Blues* (London: Faber and Faber, 1983), pp. 83–97.

45. Bleuel, *Sex and Society in Nazi Germany,* p. 238.

46. Norman Longmate, *The G.I.s: The Americans in Britain 1942–45* (London: Hutchinson, 1975), p. 262.

47. Brian Rust, *The Dance Bands* (London: Ian Allen, 1972).

48. Ibid., p. 269.

49. Graham Smith, *When Jim Crow Met John Bull: Black American Soldiers in World War II Britain* (London: I. B. Tauris, 1987).

50. Ibid., p. 108.

51. Graham Smith, interview by author, 12 December 1995.

52. Peter Powell, interview by author, Hemel Hempstead, England, 28 January 1999. Leslie Hutchinson continued to play the American GI bases up until the late fifties. He was killed in a car crash in 1959 on his way back to London after a concert at a base in Suffolk. See also Andrew Simons, "The First to Swing: Early Black British Jazz," *Playback,* Summer 1999, 4–5.

53. David Reynolds, *Rich Relations: The American Occupation of Britain 1942–45* (London: Harper Collins, 1995).

54. Gunther Schuller, *The Swing Era: The Development of Jazz 1930–1945* (Oxford, England: Oxford University Press, 1989).

55. Juliet Gardiner, *"Over Here": The G.I.s in Wartime Britain* (London: Collins and Brown, 1992), p. 114.

56. Steven Seidenberg, Maurice Sellar, and Lou Jones, *"You Must Remember This . . ." : Songs at the Heart of the War* (London: Boxtree, 1987), p. 100.

57. There were also a small but significant number of West Indian musicians and artists who had settled in London. Most notably British Guyanian Ken "Snakehips" Johnson was performing with a band of black musicians from early 1936 and played luxurious restaurants like the Old Florida in South Bruton Mews (*Melody Maker,* 29 May 1937). Tragically, Johnson was killed in 1941 while playing at the Café de Paris during an air raid. The members of his band re-formed in the latter stages of the war under the leadership of Leslie "Jiver" Hutchinson. The district of Soho in particular was known for being a meeting place for black musicians and for having a cosmopolitan feel. Black GIs journeying to the capital would invariably head for Soho. Graham Smith, interview by author, 12 December 1995.

58. Walter White, *A Rising Wind* (New York: Doubleday, Doran, 1945), p. 15.

59. Reynolds, *Rich Relations.*

60. Smith, *When John Bull Met Jim Crow.*

61. White, *A Rising Wind,* p. 11.

62. Bolero Combined Committee, Minutes of Meeting Held at Norfolk House, St. James Square SW1, Problem of American Coloured Troops, B.C.(L)(42) Misc. 3, 1st meeting, 12 August 1942, 11:00 A.M.

63. Ibid., p. 2.

64. Ibid.

65. Ibid.

66. "The Lindy Hop," *Life,* 23 August 1943, 95–103.

67. George H. Roeder, *The Censored War: An American Visual Experience during World War Two* (New Haven, Conn.: Yale University Press, 1993), p. 57.

68. Eric Vogel, "Jazz in a Nazi Concentration Camp," parts 1–3, *Down Beat,* 7 December 1961, 20–22; 21 December 1961, 16–17; 4 January 1962, 20–21.

69. Mike Zwerin, *La Tristesse de Saint Louis: Jazz under the Nazis* (New York: Beech Tree Books, 1985).

70. Stowe, *Swing Changes.*

71. Taken from Jeremy's *Swing under the Swastika.*

72. Paul Connerton, *How Societies Remember* (Cambridge: Cambridge University Press, 1989).

73. Emery, *Black Dance from 1619 to Today.*

74. See Smith, *When John Bull Met Jim Crow,* pp. 1–4, 184–86. Paul Seed's film *The Affair* (London: British Broadcasting Company Worldwide, 1996) is an interesting and informed portrayal of a black GI who is falsely accused of rape during this period.

75. Taken from Jeremy's *Swing under the Swastika.*

76. Peukert, *Inside Nazi Germany.*

77. Mark Abrahams, *The Teenage Consumer* (London: Routledge & Kegan Paul, 1959).

78. Quoted in Marek Kohn, *Dope Girls: The Birth of the British Drug Underworld* (London: Lawrence and Wishart, 1997), p. 179. Kohn also shows how these types of drug narratives are continuous with the way drugs were connected with Chinese settlement in London during the 1920s.

Chapter 7

1. Roger Hewitt, *Routes of Racism: The Social Basis of Racist Action* (Greenwich, England: Trentham Books, 1996), p. 33.

2. I. MacDonald, *Murder in the Playground: The Burnage Report* (London: Longsight Press, 1989), p. 348, quoted in Hewitt, *Routes of Racism*, pp. 42–43.

3. Ann Leslie, "Pride, the Cure for Prejudice," in *Mindfield: The Race Issue*, edited by Susan Greenberg (London: Camden Press, 1998), p. 79.

4. Hewitt, *Routes of Racism*, p. 16.

5. This point is made more effectively in K. Anthony Appiah and Amy Gutmann, *Color Conscious: The Political Morality of Race* (Princeton, N.J.: Princeton University Press, 1996), p. 90.

6. Stuart Hall, "Race and 'Moral Panics' in Post War Britain" (lecture to British Sociological Association), 1978.

7. The guide to the Black Heritage Trail was originally researched by Byron Rushing and edited by staff at the Museum of Afro-American History Inc. The Boston African American National Histories Site offers guided tours of the trail. This brief account of the memorial's history inevitably conflates a much longer and more tortuous process, during the course of which the African American community was totally marginalized. As Kirk Savage points out in *Standing Soldiers, Kneeling Slaves: Race, War and Monument in Nineteenth-Century America* (Princeton, N.J.: Princeton University Press, 1997), "The irony is that the traditional hero monument contemplated by [Joshua] Smith was transformed . . . into a monument commemorating black soldiery as well" (pp. 196–97).

8. See ibid., pp. 199–207, for a brilliant, detailed description of this sculpture and its significance in terms of representing racial difference.

9. Clare Taylor, *British and American Abolitionists: An Episode in Transatlantic Understanding* (Edinburgh: Edinburgh University Press, 1974), p. 183.

10. According to the guide to the Black Heritage Trail.

11. Dolores Hayden, *The Power of Place: Urban Landscapes as Public History* (Cambridge: MIT, 1995), pp. 54–57.

12. Ibid., pp. 56–57.

13. Nell Irvin Painter, *Sojourner Truth: A Life, a Symbol* (New York: W. W. Norton, 1996), pp. 116–17.

14. Matthew Frye Jacobson, *Whiteness of a Different Color: European Immigrants and the Alchemy of Race* (Cambridge: Harvard University Press, 1998), p. 12.

15. Ibid., p. 31.

16. Ibid., pp. 32–33.

17. Ibid., p. 275.

18. Patrick Wright, *On Living in an Old Country* (London: Verso, 1984), p. 26.

19. Ibid.

20. This has become something of a preoccupation in the late 1990s: Jeremy Paxman, *The English: A Portrait of a People* (London: M. Joseph, 1998); Kevin Davey, *English Imaginaries: Six Studies in Anglo-British Modernity* (London: Lawrence and Wishart, 1999). A BBC television program broadcast in April 1999 was entitled "Counterblast: The Race That Dare Not Speak Its Name: One Proud Englishman Speaks Up for Englishness" (*The Guardian G2*, 20 April 1999, 24).

21. Geoffrey Cubitt, ed., *Imagining Nations* (Manchester, England: Manchester University Press, 1998), p. 1.

22. Ibid., p. 5.

23. John Taylor, *A Dream of England: Landscape, Photography and the Tourist's Imagination* (Manchester, England: University of Manchester Press, 1994), p. 22.

24. Stuart Hall, "New Cultures for Old," in *A Place in the World? Place, Cultures*

and Globalization, edited by Doreen Massey and Pat Jess (London: Oxford University Press, 1995), p. 184.

25. Scotland and Ireland also share a common history of slave-trading from their ports. See Nigel Tattersfield, *The Forgotten Trade* (London: Jonathan Cape, 1991), p. 349.

26. Taylor, *A Dream of England,* p. 20. See also David Matless, *Landscape and Englishness* (London: Reaktion Books, 1998).

27. Stephen Daniels, *Fields of Vision: Landscape Imagery and National Identity in England and the United States* (Princeton, N.J.: Princeton University Press, 1993), p. 7.

28. Ibid., p. 5.

29. Wright, *On Living in an Old Country,* p. 74.

30. Pat Barrow, *Slaves of Rapparee: The Wreck of The London* (Devon, England: Lazarus Press, 1998).

31. *Old Times in the West Country: Stories, Legends, and Highwaymen; Traditions, and Rhymes of Old North Devon* (c. 1873), Ilfracombe Museum, cited in Barrow, *Slaves of Rapparee,* pp. 34–35.

32. Geoffrey Gibbs, "Grant Wants Memorial to Slaves," *Guardian* (Manchester, England), 3 March 1997, 5.

33. Barrow, *Slaves of Rapparee,* p. 10.

34. Wright, *On Living in an Old Country,* pp. 175–76.

35. Ibid., p. 26.

36. Tattersfield, *Forgotten Trade.*

37. Nick Merriman and Rozina Vizram, "The World in a City," in *The Peopling of London: Fifteen Thousand Years of Settlement from Overseas,* edited by Nick Merriman (London: Museum of London, 1993), p. 3.

38. William Wordsworth, *The Prelude,* bk. VII, 158 & 228–44 (1805; reprint, Harmondsworth, England: Penguin, 1995), pp. 258–62.

39. James Walvin, *An African's Life: The Life and Times of Olaudah Equiano 1745–1797* (London: Cassell, 1998).

40. Norma Myers, *Reconstructing the Black Past: Blacks in Britain 1780–1830* (London: Frank Cass, 1996), p. 1.

41. Michel-Rolph Trouillot, *Silencing the Past: Power and the Production of History* (Boston: Beacon Press, 1995), p. 16.

42. Ibid., p. 148.

43. Clare Midgley, *Women against Slavery: The British Campaigns 1780–1870* (London: Routledge, 1992), pp. 206–7.

44. Vron Ware, *Beyond the Pale: White Women, Racism and History* (London: Verso, 1992), pp. 173–75.

45. William Wells Brown, *The Travels of William Wells Brown,* edited by Paul Jefferson (New York: Marcus Wiener, 1991).

46. Geoffrey Gibbs, "MP Joins Row over 'Darkie Day' Revel," *Guardian* (Manchester, England), 20 January 1998, 6.

47. Conversation with John Buckingham, December 1998. He pointed out that Padstow has "traditions coming out of its ears."

48. Edward Said, *Culture and Imperialism* (London: Chatto and Windus, 1993), p. 73.

49. Ibid., p. 72.

Chapter 8

1. See Dick Hebdige, *Subculture: The Meaning of Style* (London: Methuen, 1979), pp. 52–54. The development of the U.K. soul scene is referred to in chapter 4 in relation to what came to be known as "northern soul."

2. See Roger Hewitt, "Black through White: Hoagy Carmichael and the Cultural Reproduction of Racism," in *Popular Music 3, Producers and Markets,* edited by Richard Middleton and David Horn (Cambridge: Cambridge University Press, 1983), pp. 33–54.

3. Brian Ward, *Just My Soul Responding: Rhythm and Blues, Black Consciousness and Race Relations* (London: UCL Press, 1998), p. 240.

4. Ibid., p. 243.

5. Walter T. Lhamon Jr., *Raising Cain: Blackface Performance from Jim Crow to Hip Hop* (Boston: Harvard University Press, 1998). See also Eric Lott, *Love and Theft: Blackface Minstrelsy and the American Working-Class* (Oxford: Oxford University Press, 1993).

6. Made famous by Norman Mailer's essay "The White Negro" in *Advertisements for Myself* (New York: Putnam, 1959), pp. 337–58.

7. See David Roediger, "Guineas, Wiggers, and the Dramas of Racialized Culture," *American Literary History* 7 (1995): 652–68.

8. Nelson George, *The Death of Rhythm and Blues* (London: Omnibus, 1988).

9. Phil Rubio, "Crossover Dreams: The 'Exceptional White' in Popular Culture," in *Race Traitor,* edited by Noel Ignatiev and John Garvey (New York: Routledge, 1996).

10. David Stowe, "Uncolored People: The Rise of Whiteness Studies," *Lingua Franca* 6 (September/October 1996): 76.

11. Walter Benn Michaels, "Autobiography of an Ex-white Man: Why Race Is Not a Social Construction," *Transition: An International Review* 7, no. 1 (1998): 122.

12. Henry Louis Gates, *Loose Canons* (New York: Oxford University Press, 1993).

13. K. Anthony Appiah, "Race, Culture, Identity," in K. Anthony Appiah and Amy Gutmann, *Color Conscious: The Political Morality of Race* (Princeton, N.J.: Princeton University Press, 1996), p. 90.

14. Jerry Wexler, telephone interview by author, 10 September 1996.

15. E. Culpepper Clark, *The School House Door: Segregation's Last Stand at the University of Alabama* (Oxford: Oxford University Press, 1993).

16. Some of the most interesting discussions of transculturalism have looked at different aspects of sound culture, be they language or music. See Roger Hewitt, *White Talk Black Talk: Inter-racial Friendship and Communication amongst Adolescents* (London: Cambridge University Press, 1986).

17. Idrissa Dia, telephone interview by author, 3 September 1996.

18. Jimmy Johnson, interview by author, Sheffield, Ala., 18 June 1996.

19. Idrissa Dia, telephone interview.

20. I am particularly thinking of Paul Garon's position in this regard. Since the mid-1970s he has argued that the "effect of white participants on black artists usually results in some form of *dilution* of the blues" (emphasis in original). Paul Garon, "White Blues," in Ignatiev and Garvey, *Race Traitor,* p. 168. While Garon makes a sometimes compelling case about the way in which white blues players reap the rewards of being more palatable for white audiences, he preempts the possibility that white musicians may have contributed innovations to the form. One interesting recent phenomenon has been the growth of a legion of both black and white imitators of Texas blues guitarist Stevie Ray Vaughn. In the case of southern soul and rhythm and blues Garon's charge that white musicians are no more than pale imitators is at odds with the innovations that these musicians contributed to the genre. See also Paul Garon, *Blues and the Poetic Spirit* (New York: Da Capo, 1979).

21. Shoals Chamber of Commerce, *Shoals Chamber of Commerce Guide and Member Directory* (Florence, Ala.: Florence Times Daily, 1996), p. 26.

22. Jerry Landrum, "Memories of Early Radio Broadcasts in Muscle Shoals," *Journal of Muscle Shoals History* 14 (1995): 147.

23. Roger Hawkins, interview by author, Sheffield, Ala., 19 June 1996. This experience was not uniform for all of the white southern musicians. Jimmy Johnson, for example, had a white southern Baptist background that he described as "pretty stiff. I was influenced by the black church through the artists like Benny Spellman" (Johnson, interview).

24. This is a position that Jerry Wexler himself veers close to. See J. Wexler (with David Ritz), *Rhythm and the Blues: A Life in American Music* (New York: Alfred Knopf, 1993), pp. 191–94.

25. This is particularly apparent in Nelson George's *The Death of Rhythm and Blues* (London: Omnibus Press, 1988), in which he states boldly: "Blacks create then move on. Whites document and then recycle. In the history of popular music, these truths are self-evident" (p. 108). Such bold generalizations misrepresent the contributions made to black music by white studio musicians, many of whom developed unique and innovative styles in their own right and augmented the creative process. Mentions of the contributions made by whites are made only in passing and are sometimes inaccurate (p. 105). Rather, George is intent on understating white involvement in rhythm and blues as, at best, gifted retronuevo or, at worst, opportunistic pastiche. Equally, it is telling that Rickey Vincent, author of *Funk: The Music, the People and the Rhythm on the One* (New York: St. Martin's Griffin, 1996), omits any reference to the Muscle Shoals Rhythm Section in relation to the Staples Singers and their recordings with James Brown, particularly "It's Too Funky in Here" (PD14557), released in 1979.

26. There are traces of this in the accounts of popular historians, particularly in Barney Hoskins's *Say It One More Time for the Broken Hearted* (London: Fontana, 1987) and to a lesser extent in Peter Guralnick's epic *Sweet Soul Music: Rhythm and Blues and the Southern Dream of Freedom* (London: Penguin, 1986).

27. "A lot of people talk about how we came to play the way we did but our style evolved from listening to the people we played with. The first thing we did when a session was booked, we'd go down to the record store and buy that particular artist's records and learn their music." David Hood, interview by author, Sheffield, Ala., 28 June 1996.

28. G. Hirshey, *Nowhere to Run: The Story of Soul Music* (New York: Da Capo, 1984), p. 83.

29. Ibid.

30. Roger Hawkins, interview by author, Sheffield, Ala., 28 June 1996.

31. See Guralnick, *Sweet Soul Music,* pp. 205–12.

32. Ralph Ellison, "Harlem Is Nowhere," in *The Shadow and Act* (New York: Vintage Books, 1963), p. 296.

33. Ibid.

34. Donna Thatcher-Godchaux, interview by author, Sheffield, Ala., 18 June 1996.

35. Wexler, *Rhythm and the Blues* (New York: Alfred Knopf, 1993), p. 210.

36. Spooner Oldham, interview by author, Rogersville, Ala., 19 June 1996.

37. Wexler, *Rhythm and the Blues,* p. 210.

38. Oldham, interview.

39. Ibid.

40. Dan Penn, interview by author, Nashville, Tenn., 26 June 1996.

41. Rick Hall told Peter Guralnick that Penn "knew more about black music than all of us put together." Guralnick, *Sweet Soul Music,* p. 187.

42. On his mother's side of the family these include Creek Indian relatives, while on his father's side, Cherokee.

43. Reggie Young, interview by author, Nashville, Tenn., 20 June 1996.

44. His vocal style was a product of his two main influences, Ray Charles and

Bobby "Blue" Bland. Penn had played the college circuit with the Mark V's and then the Pallbearers (the group took its name from the hearse it used to travel to gigs). Penn also put his own records out on Rick Hall's Fame label, initially under his own name, and then the pseudonym of Lonnie Ray was chosen because "it sounded blacker." He had written a song entitled "Is a Bluebird Blue," based on a catchphrase that he had picked up from one of the older youths in Vernon. The song had all the touches of Ray Charles's composition, but it was in fact picked up in Nashville by Conway Twitty, who had a country hit with the song in 1960. Dan Penn was a singer and songwriter and spent practically all his time hanging around recording studios. Initially, he worked with Rick Hall at Fame, co-writing many of his songs with Spooner Oldham, including hits for Percy Sledge like "Out of Left Field" and "It Tears Me Up" and James and Bobby Purify's "I Am Your Puppet." He went on to develop a close relationship with Chips Moman, and by the time of the Aretha sessions he had moved to Memphis and was based at Moman's American Studios.

45. The relationship between Jews and black music has been discussed most sophisticatedly by Mark Lisheron, "Rhythm and Jews: The Story of the Blacks and Jews Who Worked Together to Create the Magic of R&B," *Common Quest* 3 (Summer 1997): 20–33.

46. Wexler, telephone interview.

47. Penn, interview.

48. Wexler, *Rhythm and the Blues*, p. 210.

49. Penn, interview.

50. See Guralnick, *Sweet Soul Music*, p. 342.

51. Johnson, interview.

52. Wexler, telephone interview.

53. Hawkins, interview, 19 June 1996.

54. Paul D. Zimmermann, "Over the Rainbow," *Newsweek*, 21 August 1967, 21.

55. Quoted in Guralnick, *Sweet Soul Music*, p. 345.

56. Hawkins, interview, 28 June 1996.

57. Aretha Franklin, *Aretha's Gold* (1969) (SD8227).

58. Etta James came to Muscle Shoals to record following the success of the Aretha Franklin sessions. She writes in her autobiography that she was attracted to the "southern-fried soul style. The backup musicians were a bunch of bad white boys who could play sure-enough R&B with as much authenticity as Little Richard or James Brown . . . Leonard Chess [the label owner] was no dummy. He figured what was right for 'Re was good for me." Etta James (with David Ritz), *Rage to Survive* (New York: Da Capo, 1998), pp. 171–72.

59. Interview by author, Nashville, Tenn., 20 June 1996.

60. Duck Dunn, telephone interview by author, 30 September 1998.

61. Booker T. Jones, telephone interview by author, 6 October 1998.

62. Ibid.

63. Young, interview.

64. Dunn, telephone interview.

65. Ibid.

66. This unfolded dramatically at the National Association of Television and Radio Announcers (NATRA) convention in 1969 in Miami. White record executives were severely criticized and even physically intimidated. Jerry Wexler was to receive an award, but was hung in effigy. Marshall Sehorn was pistol-whipped. Phil Walden, manager of Otis Redding, remembered: "I saw all the things I worked for destroyed, Dr. King killed, and someone like me being hit with more racist stuff than George Wallace ever was. It made me SICK." Quoted in Guralnick, *Sweet Soul Music*, p. 384.

67. Penn, interview.

68. Ibid.

69. Wexler, *Rhythm and the Blues,* p. 215.

70. Hilton Als has recently suggested that the image of Aretha as an icon of black authenticity was in many respects a product of a certain kind of whiteness. He argues: "Her big black sound appealed to whites because it was easy to grasp; she sounded just the way white people imagined a black woman would sound—plaintive but feisty, indomitable but sad. Franklin never really had to cross over, because whites were willing to follow her into her manufactured impersonal form of blackness—a safe place where no one got cut up after a rowdy fish fry. And, of course, she looked the part. Whether she was sporting marabou feathers and a beehive or, later, a dashiki dress and turban, she remained a backwoods mama tarted up for big-city doings." Hilton Als, "'No Respect': Is the Future of Black Soul in the Hands of a White British Woman?" *New Yorker,* 26 October and 2 November 1998, 234. The fairness and veracity of these claims are, at best, debatable. It is surely too much to try to fix Aretha Franklin's creativity in cultural inheritance in such a reductive way. However, Als's thesis, read alongside the *Time* magazine cover story, raises important questions about how Aretha's music was refigured and assimilated within white America.

71. "Lady Soul: Singing It Like It Is," *Time,* 28 June 1968, 62–66. In truth, only half of the rhythm section was from Memphis.

72. Ibid., p. 66.

73. Ibid.

74. Ken Johnson, "The Vocabulary of Race," in *Rappin' and Stylin' Out: Communication in Black America,* edited by T. Kochman (Urbana: University of Illinois Press, 1972).

75. Hawkins, interview, 28 June 1996.

76. Lloyd W. Raikes wrote from Los Angeles: "Sir: Soul is black and beautiful and like any black cat will tell you, baby—it's ours. Blue-eyed soul? The answer to your question—'Does this mean that white musicians by definition don't have soul?' is simply and unequivocally yes." *Time,* 12 July 1968, 6.

77. Reggie Young and Bobby Emmons confirm this; both were members of the house band at American Studios at this time.

78. Notes taken at a concert at the Borderline, 1 December 1998.

79. Ward, *Just My Soul Responding.*

80. "Single White Man Assassinated King," *Florence Times and Tri-Cities Daily,* 5 April 1968, 1.

81. Johnson, interview.

82. Marvell was part of perhaps the most famous family in Memphis R&B. His father, Rufus Thomas, was both a DJ and an artist, and the hits he recorded for Stax included "Walking the Dog" and "Do the Funky Chicken." His sister Carla Thomas also had a long and established career as a Stax artist.

83. Marvell Thomas, interview by author, Memphis, Tenn., 3 July 1996.

84. George Jackson, telephone interview by author, 14 February 1997.

85. Outposts of segregationist politics could be found within a few miles of the integrated studios. Up until the late 1970s one of the warring factions of the Ku Klux Klan had its national headquarters in a hamlet of the Shoals area called Tuscumbia. The Tennessee Valley had a history of Klan organization going back to the period of the Reconstruction. One of the earliest Alabama Klan organizations was set up in Tuscumbia in April 1868. Later that year 150 Klansmen lynched three black men in Tuscumbia; the black men had been imprisoned for suspected arson. See Allen W. Trelease, *White Terror: The Ku Klux Klan Conspiracy and Southern Reconstruction* (Baton Rouge: Louisiana State University Press, 1971), p. 122. In 1922 the Klan held a public meeting in Florence; 125 people attended and the Klan claimed "[t]hat there were a number of members of the Klan in Florence and others were being

added to the 'Invisible Empire' in this city." *Florence Times,* 28 July 1922. In the summer of 1979 Klansmen were responsible for a series of acts of intimidation and violence against black people in Florence. *Shoals News-Leader,* 1 August 1979, 2:17. Paradoxically, segregationist politics coexisted in these small rural communities with an integrated music scene. A generation of blue-eyed soul musicians with a deep love of and feel for rhythm and blues often unwittingly walked the same streets as the Klansmen.

86. Duane Allman had played sessions at Fame and attracted Jerry Wexler's attention through the guitar fade on Wilson Pickett's "Hey Jude." Throughout 1969 Allman was the regular lead guitarist at 3614 Jackson Highway.

87. Johnson, interview.

88. Ibid.

89. Hood, interview.

90. Ibid.

91. Hawkins, interview, 28 June 1996.

92. Hood, interview.

93. Quoted in *The Congressional Record,* 17 May 1979, 125:63—"Ten Years of the Muscle Shoals Sound," presented by Hon. Ronnie G. Flippo of Alabama.

94. Barry Beckett, interview by author, Nashville, Tenn., 21 June 1996.

95. Ibid.

96. Quoted in Rob Bowman, *Soulsville U.S.A.: The Story of Stax Records* (New York: Schirmer Books, 1997), p. 211.

97. Ibid., p. 260.

98. Hood, interview.

99. Ibid.

100. Simon's 1973 album *There Goes Rhymin' Simon* (KC 32280) featured full credits and a picture of the 3614 Jackson Highway Studio.

101. Rubio, "Crossover Dreams," p. 151.

102. It is telling that Rubio draws repeatedly from film for his examples of crossover: for example, *The Jerk, The Blues Brothers, The History of White People in America Parts I and II, The Commitments, Dances with Wolves, Sommersby, The Long Walk Home, Mississippi Burning, Do the Right Thing,* and *White Men Can't Jump.*

103. Walter Benn Michaels, "Autobiography of an Ex-white Man," p. 134. For Benn Michaels's discussion of the racial essentialism that underscores the current debate about cultural identity, see Walter Benn Michaels, "Race into Culture: A Critical Genealogy of Cultural Identity," *Critical Inquiry* 18 (Summer 1992): 38–62.

104. Johnson, interview.

105. There is a deeper irony here, for Muscle Shoals came to prominence nationally during the 1970s, not because of its paradoxical combination of segregation and multiculture, but as the birthplace of perhaps the quintessential "white bread" pop group. In 1970 the president of MGM Records approached Rick Hall at Fame to produce a teenage group called The Osmonds. Hall accepted the offer and produced two consecutive number one pop singles. The first, entitled "One Bad Apple," sold over five million copies in the United States alone; it was followed by a tune entitled "Yo Yo." "One Bad Apple" was written by Hall's resident black songwriter, George Jackson. The group cut two albums at Fame, *The Osmonds* and *Homemade,* both of which earned gold status. During 1971 Hall's productions sold eleven million records, and at the end of the year he was honored as Billboard's Producer of the Year.

106. Quoted in "Rick Hall Explains the Method behind His Magical Ways," *The Sounds from Muscle Shoals: Cashbox,* 7 August 1977, 10.

107. Hawkins, interview, 28 June 1996.

108. This is also true of many of the white session players who recorded soul music in the 1960s and 1970s. Those players who have subsequently made careers

in country include Reggie Young, Bobby Wood, Bobby Emmons, and Gene Chrisman. In addition, black players like Willie Weeks and Richard Tee have played sessions. Reggie Young has recorded with Dolly Parton, Willie Nelson, and Charley Pride, and recently he played on Steve Wariner's hit "Holes in the Floor of Heaven."

109. *Otis Williams and the Midnight Cowboys* (STLP 1002). The engineer on these sessions was Elvis Presley's former guitarist Scotty Moore.

110. These hits included "Hearts of Stone," "Ling, Ting, Tong," and "Ivory Tower," all recorded on Deluxe Records.

111. Hank Williams Jr. is himself the embodiment of a complex legacy. In 1988 he sang a rebel anthem, "If the South Woulda Won," on national television, causing controversy.

112. Beckett, interview.

113. Ibid.

114. Quoted in Bruce Feiler, "Has Country Music Become a Soundtrack for White Flight," *New York Times,* 20 October 1996, 40.

115. Pamela E. Foster, *My Country: The African Diaspora's Country Music Heritage* (Nashville, Tenn.: My Country Press, 1998).

116. Margaret McKee and Fred Chrisenhall, *Beale, Black and Blue* (Baton Rouge: Louisiana State University Press, 1981), p. 249.

117. Dan Penn, telephone interview by author, 30 April 1999.

118. Joachim-Ernst Berendt, *The Third Ear: On Listening to the World* (New York: Henry Holt, 1985).

119. Quoted in Gene Lees, *Cats of Any Color: Jazz Black and White* (Oxford: Oxford University Press, 1994), p. 190 (emphasis added).

120. Berendt, *The Third Ear,* p. 47.

121. Feiler, "Has Country Music Become a Soundtrack for White Flight," pp. 38, 40.

122. Phil Rubio, "Crossover Dreams," p. 151.

123. Zwerin, *La Tristesse de Saint Louis.*

124. Sherman Willmott, interview by author, Memphis, Tenn., 5 July 1996.

125. Penn, interview.

126. Quoted in John Fordham, "This Man Is Killing Jazz or Is He?" *Guardian* (Manchester, England), 23 June 1999, 14.

Chapter 9

1. *Signs* 22 (Spring 1995): 731.

2. Ien Ang, "Comment on Rita Felski's 'The Doxa of Difference': The Uses of Incommensurability," *Signs* 24 (Autumn 1997): 60.

3. Ibid., p. 61.

4. Mab Segrest, "The Souls of White Folk," in *The Making and Unmaking of Whiteness,* edited by Birgit Brander Rasmussen, Eric Klinenberg, Irene Nexica, and Matt Wray (Durham, N.C.: Duke University Press, 2001).

5. Ibid., p. 65.

6. Renato Rosaldo, *Culture and Truth: The Remaking of Social Analysis* (Boston: Beacon Press, 1989), p. 2.

7. Ibid., p. 10.

8. John Howard Griffin, *A Time to Be Human* (New York: Macmillan, 1977), pp. 16–17 (hereafter referred to as *TTBH*).

9. Ibid.

10. Robert Bonazzi, *Man in the Mirror: John Howard Griffin and the Story of Black Like Me* (New York: Orbis Books, 1997), pp. 10–11.

11. Ibid., p. 11.

12. *TTBH,* p. 91.

13. Ibid., p. 17.

14. Ibid., p. 2.

15. Bonazzi, *Man in the Mirror,* p. 146.

16. Ibid., pp. 46–47.

17. Ibid., p. 46.

18. *TTBH,* p. 31.

19. Ibid., p. 33.

20. Ibid., p. 34.

21. Griffin converted to Catholicism in 1951. He was especially influenced by French philosopher Jacques Maritain, and when he died, he was compiling a biography of Thomas Merton.

22. Rosaldo, *Culture and Truth,* p. 8.

23. John Howard Griffin, *Black Like Me* (1960; reprint, Boston: Houghton Mifflin, 1961), p. 120.

24. Joel Kovel, *White Racism: A Psychohistory* (New York: Columbia University Press, 1984), pp. lv–lvi.

25. Minnie Bruce Pratt, "Identity: Skin Blood Heart," in *Yours in Struggle,* edited by Elly Bulkin, Minnie Bruce Pratt, and Barbara Smith (New York: Long Haul Press, 1984), pp. 46–47.

Index

Lightning Source UK Ltd.
Milton Keynes UK
UKOW02f1519101116

287278UK00002B/248/P

9 780226 873428